Prisoners of the Home Front

Studies in Canadian Military History

The Canadian War Museum, Canada's national museum of military history, has a threefold mandate: to remember, to preserve, and to educate. It does so through an interlocking and mutually supporting combination of exhibitions, public programs, and electronic outreach. Military history, military historical scholarship, and the ways in which Canadians see and understand themselves have always been closely intertwined. Studies in Canadian Military History builds on a record of success in forging those links by regular and innovative contributions based on the best modern scholarship. Published by UBC Press in association with the Museum, the series especially encourages the work of new generations of scholars and the investigation of important gaps in the existing historiography, pursuits not always well served by traditional sources of academic support. The results produced feed immediately into future exhibitions, programs, and outreach efforts by the Canadian War Museum. It is a modest goal that they feed into a deeper understanding of our nation's common past as well.

1 John Griffith Armstrong, *The Halifax Explosion and the Royal Canadian Navy: Inquiry and Intrigue*

2 Andrew Richter, *Avoiding Armageddon: Canadian Military Strategy and Nuclear Weapons, 1950-63*

3 William Johnston, *A War of Patrols: Canadian Army Operations in Korea*

4 Julian Gwyn, *Frigates and Foremasts: The North American Squadron in Nova Scotia Waters, 1745-1815*

5 Jeffrey A. Keshen, *Saints, Sinners, and Soldiers: Canada's Second World War*

6 Desmond Morton, *Fight or Pay: Soldiers' Families in the Great War*

7 Douglas E. Delaney, *The Soldiers' General: Bert Hoffmeister at War*

8 Michael Whitby, ed., *Commanding Canadians: The Second World War Diaries of A.F.C. Layard*

9 Martin Auger, *Prisoners of the Home Front: German POWs and "Enemy Aliens" in Southern Quebec, 1940-46*

Prisoners of the Home Front

German POWs and "Enemy Aliens" in Southern Quebec, 1940-46

Martin F. Auger

UBCPress · Vancouver · Toronto

15 14 13 12 11 10 09 08 07 06 05   5 4 3 2 1

Printed in Canada on ancient-forest-free paper (100% post-consumer recycled) that is processed chlorine- and acid-free, with vegetable-based inks.

Library and Archives Canada Cataloguing in Publication

Auger, Martin F., 1974-

Prisoners of the home front : German POWs and "enemy aliens" in Southern Québec, 1940-46 / Martin F. Auger.

(Studies in Canadian military history, ISSN 1499-6251)
Includes bibliographical references and index.
ISBN-13: 978-0-7748-1223-8 (bound); 978-0-7748-1224-5(pbk.)
ISBN-10: 0-7748-1223-0 (bound); 0-7748-1224-9 (pbk.)

1. German Canadians – Evacuation and relocation, 1940-1945. 2. World War, 1939-1945 – Prisoners and prisons, Canadian. 3. Prisoners of war – Germany. 4. Prisoners of war – Canada. 5. Concentration camps – Québec (Province) – History – 20th century. I. Title. II. Series.

D805.C3A94 2005   940.54'7271   C2005-905689-4

Canada

UBC Press gratefully acknowledges the financial support for our publishing program of the Government of Canada through the Book Publishing Industry Development Program (BPIDP), and of the Canada Council for the Arts, and the British Columbia Arts Council.

This book has been published with the help of a grant from the Canadian Federation for the Humanities and Social Sciences, through the Aid to Scholarly Publications Programme, using funds provided by the Social Sciences and Humanities Research Council of Canada.

Publication of this book has been financially supported by the Canadian War Museum.

UBC Press
The University of British Columbia
2029 West Mall
Vancouver, BC V6T 1Z2
604-822-5959 / Fax: 604-822-6083
www.ubcpress.ca

Contents

Tables

Foreword

In so many ways, Canada's story in the Second World War was one of success. Its navy kept the sea lanes open in the North Atlantic; its air force played an indispensable role in Britain's Bomber Command; and its army assumed a seminal part in securing victory in the Italian and Northwest European campaigns. At home, Canada transformed itself into an industrial giant through the massive production of armaments. Public demand for services for soldiers and their families encouraged an increasingly prominent federal government to usher in the modern welfare state. Despite the tremendous suffering of those years, the Second World War became known as the "Good War," a characterization born of the conviction that if there ever were a war that had to be fought, it was this one. How could it be otherwise? Did the Nazis not epitomize evil, as revealed by the concentration camps and the Holocaust? Had the Japanese not brutalized Allied prisoners of war through starvation, torture, and slave labour? But what of the Canadian record in this domain? Did we, too, succumb to hatred of the enemy and commit violations of international law in our treatment of prisoners?

Few Canadians today realize that nearly 40,000 Germans were interned or imprisoned in Canada. Yet not one was killed or tortured. Although the internment system was initially unprepared for such numbers, and although significant tensions were experienced by the imprisoned, improvements took place steadily over time. By 1945, five camps were established in southern Quebec, and these are the focus of Martin Auger's study. Each camp was designed to house prisoners according to their service branch or according to the intensity of their Nazi beliefs.

Martin Auger's work provides a comprehensive account of the administrative development of the Quebec camps and furnishes a significant contribution to social history by describing day-to-day life behind barbed wire. Although conditions in the camps conformed to the requirements of the Geneva Convention, Auger shows that psychological strain – among other difficulties – remained an integral part of POW life, and that outbreaks of violence and attempted escapes occurred. We also learn about the substantive efforts by Canadian authorities to make camp life more tolerable. One example is the off-site farm labour programs that relieved monotony for the inmates, enabled them to earn a little money to purchase extra provisions, and helped the local economy by providing desperately needed workers. Canadian authorities also implemented educational programs, including ones designed to impart the principles of democracy – an initiative that apparently altered the thinking of many former Nazis and led to several applications to stay in Canada. Overall, Martin Auger has provided an exceptionally valuable addition to local, military, and social history, and revealed yet another dimension of Canada's participation in the Second World War in which Canadians can justly take pride.

Jeffrey A. Keshen
Professor, Department of History
University of Ottawa
July 2005

Preface

Several years ago, my grandfather told us stories about a German prisoner of war who had worked on his brother-in-law's farm near Granby, Quebec, during the Second World War. He explained to us that this man was one of several inmates from a local internment camp to have volunteered for employment on local farms. The prisoner worked the fields by day and stayed in the farmhouse at night. He ate all of his meals with his employer's family. No armed guard supervised him. According to my grandfather, communication was the major problem, as the German understood very little English or French. I remember him laughing when he told me that many people in the area feared that the prisoner might kill his brother-in-law and his whole family. Influenced by wartime propaganda that often portrayed the enemy as savage beasts, local inhabitants assumed that because he was German this internee was a dangerous Nazi. They firmly believed that it was only a matter of time before he attempted to escape or committed acts of barbarity. Fortunately, no such thing happened, and the man was repatriated to Germany when war was over.

This story is one of many about the German prisoners and the internment camps of southern Quebec during the Second World War. From that rainy July evening when the first trainload of internees rolled into the region in 1940 to the repatriation of the last inmate in June 1946, the five permanent internment camps located on the south shore of the St. Lawrence River at Farnham, Grande Ligne, Île-aux-Noix, Sherbrooke, and Sorel held thousands of German internees.

Fascinated by my grandfather's story, I began research on this topic in 1998 as part of my history MA thesis project at the University of Ottawa. I was surprised to find out that no historian, journalist, or other researcher in the humanities or social sciences had written an in-depth analysis of any of the internment camps of this region. Aside from first-hand accounts such as Eric Koch's *Deemed Suspect* (1980) and inclusion in broader studies dealing with the entire Canadian internment operation like Yves Bernard and Caroline Bergeron's *Trop loin de Berlin* (1995), David J. Carter's *POW behind Canadian Barbed Wire* (1998), Chris M.V. Madsen and R.J. Henderson's *German Prisoners of War in Canada* (1993), and John Melady's *Escape from Canada* (1981), little has been written about the camps of southern Quebec. In fact, no thorough study of southern Quebec's internment facilities exists. Until recently many of the official government documents relating to Canadian internment camps remained closed to public consultation. Only in the late

1980s and early 1990s, when these sources were opened at Library and Archives Canada (then known as the National Archives of Canada), did researchers become aware of these documents and begin venturing into the uncharted waters of the Canadian internment operation. By focusing on the internment camps of southern Quebec, this book fills an important gap in the existing literature on Canada's Second World War internment operation. Not only do I hope to shed light on a still obscure topic in Canadian history, I also hope to please both readers and researchers alike.

Acknowledgments

Researching and writing the history of the internment camps of southern Quebec has been a wonderful and fascinating journey, and there are many people I would like to thank for helping to bring this project to fruition. First, I wish to extend special thanks to my MA and PhD supervisor, Professor Jeffrey Keshen of the University of Ottawa. A great mentor and military historian, his guidance and valuable commentary proved indispensable in transforming the first draft of my manuscript into the book that is today. I also wish to thank Professors Peter Bischoff, Serge Durflinger, Jan Grabowski, and Mark Stolarik of the University of Ottawa for their insightful comments, all of which strengthened this work.

I would like to thank Dr. Dean Oliver, Director, Historical Research and Exhibit Development, at the Canadian War Museum, for his encouragement and for agreeing to include this book in the Studies in Canadian Military History series. My appreciation also goes to my former colleagues and friends at the Canadian War Museum; I am especially indebted to the museum's outstanding and highly professional team of historians for their support, particularly Dr. Laura Brandon, Dr. Tim Cook, Dr. Peter MacLeod, Glenn Ogden, and Dr. Cameron Pulsifer.

Many people at UBC Press devoted time and energy to improving this book and making it more readable. I wish to express my sincere gratitude to Emily Andrew, for showing an interest in this project and overseeing it until the end, and to Camilla Blakeley, for guiding this work through the editing and production process. I was most impressed by their professionalism, thoroughness, and dedication. I am also particularly grateful for financial support from the Canadian Federation for the Humanities and Social Sciences' Aid to Scholarly Publications Programme, which uses funds provided by the Social Sciences and Humanities Research Council of Canada.

The completion of this project required countless hours of research at several archival centres. I particularly wish to thank the staff of the Eastern Townships Research Centre, the Department of National Defence's Directorate of History and Heritage, and Library and Archives Canada for their assistance in facilitating access to their vast archival collections.

I would not have been able to accomplish this undertaking without the support of family and friends. I am profoundly indebted to my parents, Robert and Yvette Auger, as well as my brother, Yannick, for their years of support and encouragement. Merci beaucoup. I would also like to thank my Acadian in-laws, Ronald,

Edmonde, Leesa, and Carole Richard, for always having shown interest in my work. Finally, I wish to thank my friends Ludovic Béliveau, Mélanie Brunet, Andrew Burtch, Gaétan Guilbert, Dominic Jasmin, Yves Pelletier, Jean-Sébastien Plante, and Ryan Touhey for making university life, as well as the writing of this book most enjoyable.

Last but certainly not least, I must thank my wife, Sacha, for her continuous and seemingly unending support, patience, inspiration, and love over the years. Je ne serais pas où je suis aujourd'hui sans ta présence dans ma vie. Je t'aime de tout mon coeur.

Prisoners of the Home Front

1
A History of Internment

When Canada declared war on Nazi Germany on 10 September 1939, the federal government immediately took measures toward incarcerating "enemy subjects," believing internment to be an effective method for preventing the threat of subversive activities on Canadian soil. Initiated by the federal government as part of the War Measures Act, the Canadian internment operation was run entirely by the Department of National Defence. During the war, approximately 38,000 Germans were detained in twenty-five permanent internment camps and in dozens of smaller work camps located throughout Canada. Among the internees were some 34,000 prisoners of war who came from all branches of the German armed forces. The rest consisted of German civilians and refugees, and of enemy merchant seamen, to whom British and Canadian military authorities had granted prisoner of war status in 1942.[1] As part of these precautionary measures, Canadian authorities authorized the construction of five internment camps in southern Quebec: Farnham, Grande Ligne, Île-aux-Noix, Sherbrooke, and Sorel.

The internment operation in southern Quebec can be divided into two phases. The first, from 1940 to 1943, witnessed the incarceration of civilians. The goal was to neutralize any potential threat to the defence of the Canadian nation. Any person suspected of sympathizing with the enemy was perceived to be a potential spy and saboteur and was placed in an internment camp. Individuals of German origin were first among these. During this phase, the camps in southern Quebec were used to detain men of German descent, most of whom were civilians who had been initially interned in the United Kingdom and transferred to Canada for security reasons.[2] As the war progressed, it became evident that these civilian internees were no threat to the nation. Consequently, most were either transferred to other camps or liberated between 1941 and 1943. However, when more and more German prisoners of war came to be captured by British and Commonwealth soldiers overseas, the Canadian government agreed to ship many of them to Canada for confinement. The Department of National Defence decided to use the camps of southern Quebec to incarcerate this new class of captives. The new inmates (all of them were men) began to arrive in southern Quebec's internment camps in early 1942. The incarceration of German prisoners of war constituted the second phase of the Canadian internment operation in southern Quebec, lasting from 1942 to 1946. Canadian soil became the home of thousands of such prisoners.

The purpose of this book is to evaluate the importance of the internment camp operation and examine how it developed on the south shore of the St. Lawrence River. The choice of this area is significant: half of the internment camps in Quebec were located in this small region. This study analyzes how these camps functioned and how the region's internment operation evolved. It also takes a look at life behind barbed wire and at the physical and psychological strains that inmates suffered. Most of these camps operated work programs, and this study observes how the internment enterprise contributed to the local economy. Educational programs for inmates are analyzed as well. This study of the camps of southern Quebec demonstrates that the internment operation in Canada, although occasionally lacking proper organization, was a positive experience overall. Canada's treatment of internees was humane, in contrast to what took place in the internment operations of other countries, namely Germany and Japan.

Before an analysis of Canada's internment camps can be properly undertaken, a definition of what is meant by the term "internment operations" and some historical background are necessary. Internment operations consist of a complex network of prisoner of war camps and concentration camps. Each type of facility serves a specific purpose. Prisoner of war camps can be defined as centres for the detention of enemy combatants (normally members of regularly organized armed forces) captured on the field of battle or elsewhere by a belligerent power.[3] They are usually set up in times of war. Concentration camps, on the other hand, are designed specifically to incarcerate civilians. They have been used during times of war and peace to confine political prisoners and minority groups for reasons of state security, exploitation, or punishment.[4] During the Second World War, all belligerents used both types of establishments.

Prisoner of War Camps

Although prisoners of war have been a reality of warfare for thousands of years, their treatment has rarely been humane. For many centuries, war prisoners were brutalized, beaten, tortured, mutilated, exchanged for ransoms, enslaved, and executed by their captors. On every continent and in every culture, such practices were customary at some point in history.[5] It was not until the eighteenth-century Enlightenment that modern rules relating to the treatment of captives in war appeared. The writings of philosophers like Montesquieu, Jean-Jacques Rousseau, and Emmerich de Vattel led to an awareness in most European countries that prisoners of war should be humanely treated. Captives were no longer to be disposed of at the whim of their captors, but were to be removed from the fight and protected until the end of hostilities.[6]

With the advent of large, conscripted national armies during the Napoleonic Wars, it became clear to most European nations that they needed to establish special facilities to detain prisoners of war. Old prisons and dungeons were no longer adequate to house the masses of surrendered enemy troops captured in battle. The result was the creation of large camps suited for the incarceration of large populations of prisoners. The use of such facilities became widespread throughout the nineteenth century, when they became officially known as prisoner of war camps. Although better than their predecessors, these camps were still often inadequate to handle and sustain large numbers of prisoners.[7] No armed conflict highlights this shortcoming better than the American Civil War. During that struggle, the men captured by both sides were forced to endure terrible hardships. Overcrowding, unsanitary conditions, lack of heat, disease, starvation, thirst, and death were all realities of life in the prisoner of war camps of the American Civil War. The most notorious of these was the Confederacy's Andersonville camp in Georgia, where it is estimated that as many as 13,000 Union inmates died between 1864 and 1865.[8]

It soon became apparent that the treatment of captives in war had to improve. A first attempt occurred in 1863 when American jurist Francis Lieber formulated a document entitled *Instructions of the Government of Armies of the United States in the Field,* whose provisions dealt almost exclusively with the protection of war prisoners. Later known as the Lieber Code, this innovative set of regulations stipulated that "a prisoner of war is subject to no punishment for being a public enemy, nor is any revenge wreaked upon him by the intentional infliction of any suffering, or disgrace, by cruel imprisonment, want of food, by mutilation, death, or any other barbarity." The Lieber Code was significant because it was the first government-issued comprehensive codification of laws relating to prisoners of war. The document became the base on which subsequent international lawmakers wrote about the subject of prisoners of war.[9]

It was only a matter of time before an international set of rules protecting war prisoners appeared. The first step was the creation of the Geneva Convention in 1864, which provided for the relief of wounded combatants. Although none of the clauses addressed the issue of prisoners of war, the convention, which was signed by most European countries, proved that it was possible to reach an international consensus on certain regulations regarding warfare.[10] At the 1874 Brussels Conference, an attempt was made to establish an international standard for the treatment of war prisoners. Known as the Brussels Declaration, this set of rules reiterated most of the provisions of the Lieber Code. Unfortunately, it was never ratified by the European delegates attending the conference. It was not until the Hague International Peace Conferences in 1899 and 1907 that prisoners of war became protected by international law.[11]

Widespread concern about the development of new weaponry and the possibility of world war led to the Hague conferences. The Industrial Revolution had provided the perfect breeding ground for the progress of military technology and the creation of new and more lethal weapons. The wars of the second half of the nineteenth century were testimonies to the increased levels of destruction and casualties caused by the industrialization of warfare. The aim of the conferences was to limit armament development and to find ways to "humanize" war through law. Although both conferences achieved nothing in the field of disarmament, they did produce regulations on the laws and customs of war. Regarding the status of prisoners of war, the Hague Rules expressly forbade the killing of enemy soldiers who had surrendered. They stipulated that captors had to protect their captives "from violence, insults, and public curiosity." A captive who was being interrogated was obliged to reveal only his name and rank and "no pressure may be brought to bear to force him to give any other information." All forms of corporal punishment were prohibited. The rules also emphasized that prisoners should "be detained in safe conditions." All inmates were to be fed, clothed, and accommodated on the same footing as the troops of the government that captured them.[12] During the First World War most belligerents complied with the Hague Rules.

Concentration Camps

Civilians have been victims of war since the dawn of warfare. Throughout the centuries, non-combatants have suffered the worst atrocities at the hands of soldiers: destruction of property, pillage, mistreatment, rape, torture, imprisonment, deportation, enslavement, and death. It was not until the seventeenth and eighteenth centuries that modern rules of conduct regarding the treatment of civilians in wartime were developed in Europe. This change was partly prompted by the humanist writings of several intellectuals, namely Hugo Grotius and Emmerich de Vattel. These thinkers believed that war was the domain of regular armies and that civilians should be spared. Although by the nineteenth century most western armies adhered to the principle of non-combatant immunity, the absence of international laws governing the treatment of civilians in wartime made it difficult to control the actions of soldiers.[13] Irregular or guerrilla warfare eroded the barrier that distinguished combatants from non-combatants. Because armed civilians formed the bulk of guerrilla movements, it was difficult for legitimate authorities and regular armed forces to differentiate between innocent civilians and guerrilla fighters. Complicating matters was the fact that guerrilla forces often relied on the support of local populations to survive. Consequently, regular soldiers committed ruthless acts of reprisal against innocent civilians.[14]

The concentration camp system was created in the late nineteenth century as an instrument for the suppression of guerrilla activities. The original purpose of the camps was to incarcerate civilian populations suspected of providing aid to guerrilla forces. It was during the 1895-98 Cuban War of Independence that concentration camps were used for the first time. Upon his arrival in Cuba in 1896, Spanish General Valeriano Weyler y Nicolau immediately instituted what became known as the *reconcentrado* or "reconcentration policy." The program called for the concentration of civilians in fortified towns placed under Spanish military jurisdiction and the destruction of the Cuban countryside through a scorched earth policy, to contain the rebels and deprive them of support. General Weyler believed that implementing the reconcentration program would prevent Cuban civilians from joining the insurgents and make it impossible for them to furnish the rebels with food, shelter, other material support, or intelligence on Spanish military movements. He also believed that the policy would undermine the rebels' morale by dooming their families and relatives. Reconcentration was forced upon the entire population of the island. Anyone failing to obey the evacuation orders was considered a rebel and killed.[15] In practice, however, the program, was ill conceived and badly implemented. There were numerous problems with housing, sanitation, food, and supplies. Estimates suggest that as many as 200,000 Cubans died of famine and disease in reconcentration camps before the policy was rescinded in 1898.[16] Condemnation of the reconcentration program by the United States was one of many factors that led to the 1898 Spanish-American War.

Ironically, American troops resorted to similar procedures during the 1899-1902 Philippines insurrection. In order to neutralize Filipino guerrilla movements, American commanders adopted a "pacification" policy intended to isolate the insurgents from the population. The aims were similar to those in Cuba: demoralizing the guerrilla forces and preventing them from relying on the support of the local populace. In several zones of operations, American soldiers placed civilians into controlled areas where food and shelter were provided. The brutal 1901-2 campaign launched by General J. Franklin Bell in the province of Batangas became a testimony to the ruthlessness of this policy. The entire population of Batangas was herded into purposely designed concentration camps, and everything outside of these enclosures was systematically destroyed under a scorched earth policy. It is estimated that more than 11,000 Filipinos perished from malnutrition and disease in these camps, which one author of the period labelled "models of health and sanitation."[17]

Concentration camps were also used by the British during the 1899-1902 South African War. When the Boer *Kommandos* turned to guerrilla warfare in 1900, Lord Kitchener and the British authorities in South Africa implemented a scorched earth and population clearance policy designed to break the Boers' will to fight. The goal was to systematically destroy the two Boer republics of the Transvaal and Orange Free State and to punish their inhabitants for their continued resistance to British occupation. As British troops burned villages, confiscated livestock, and ravaged the countryside, the Boers who were captured during these operations – mostly women, children, and old men – were deported to so-called refugee camps. The intention was to deprive the guerrillas of the support of the civilian population. These concentration camps were set up in haste and were poorly regulated, unsanitary, overcrowded, and badly managed.[18] Indifferent care eventually led to some 28,000 deaths from disease and hunger. These deaths amounted to about 10 percent of the Boer population of the two republics. Also, it is estimated that up to 20,000 Africans died in similar camps during the war. The high death rate among camp inmates shocked the public in many parts of the world.[19] Interestingly, it was during the South African War that the term "concentration camp" was officially used for the first time. It was borrowed in 1901 by British politicians C.P. Scott and John Ellis from the notorious Spanish *reconcentrado* camps in Cuba.[20]

As demonstrated by the American, British, and Spanish experiments, colonialism played an important role in the origins of concentration camps between 1898 and 1902. The camps not only permitted these three western nations to isolate guerrillas, they also allowed these countries to subjugate hostile populations in their overseas colonies. Although these early concentration camps were often inadequate and much criticized on humanitarian grounds, the experience created a precedent that was imitated by other western states. An example is the incarceration by German soldiers of Africans in labour camps during the 1904-7 Herero and Nama Revolt in German South West Africa. It is estimated that more than half of the 17,000 Herero and Nama prisoners died in these facilities from exhaustion, hunger, and disease. Overall, the Germans exterminated more than 75,000 Hereros and Namas during the rebellion.[21] It was the coming of the First World War that transformed the concentration camp system from a repressive measure designed to crush colonial insurrections to one that modern states could use in times of warfare to neutralize potential internal enemies. During that war, most belligerents resorted to concentration camps to intern political prisoners and civilians of "enemy nationality."

Internment Operations and the First World War

It was during the First World War that internment operations combining both prisoner of war camps and concentration camps came into being. Belligerents organized complex networks of internment facilities purposely designed to incarcerate civilians and war prisoners. In many countries, special departments were created to manage these camps under the auspices of internment operations. Though their status was different, both types of internees often saw their fate administered by the same authorities. This phenomenon was to repeat itself throughout the twentieth century.

Canada was among the first to adopt such measures, and its policies, therefore, arguably represent the best example of how internment operations were organized during the war by all belligerents. The United Kingdom declared war on Germany and its allies on behalf of the British Empire on 4 August 1914. Internment facilities were created in all British colonies to detain civilians of "enemy descent" and to incarcerate prisoners of war. The belief was that "enemy subjects" could become threats to the security of the British Empire. It was assumed that a man who owed his first allegiance to the land of his birth could endanger the British war effort. The result was that the United Kingdom, the dominions of Australia, New Zealand, South Africa, and Canada, along with India and other regions of the British Empire, detained thousands of civilians and prisoners of war of Austro-Hungarian, Bulgarian, German, and Turkish descent.[22]

In Canada, the introduction of the War Measures Act on 22 August 1914 played an important role in establishing the Canadian internment operation. This emergency legislation enabled "the Governor-in-Council to do whatever was deemed necessary or advisable for the security, defence, peace, order, and welfare of Canada ... during war, invasion or insurrection." It gave the Canadian government "extraordinary powers with which to meet the emergency" created by the war. Among those extraordinary powers was the right to "arrest, detain, exclude, and deport" all individuals believed to be "enemy aliens."[23] These were foreign-born residents of enemy nationality who were not Canadian citizens by virtue of parentage or naturalization. Though the government initially maintained a policy of tolerance towards civilians of "enemy descent," this situation soon changed. Keeping in step with British policy as well as with wartime hysteria and xenophobic sentiments in Canada, Ottawa authorized the appointment of civilian registrars in major urban centres on 28 October 1914. All enemy aliens who had not yet been naturalized as Canadian citizens were obliged to report to the nearest registrar and were forbidden to leave the country. If a registrar so decided, a suspected enemy alien could be interned.[24] Individuals ordered for internment were kept in temporary detention centres until their transfer to permanent internment camps. Overall, some 85,000 enemy aliens were registered by the Canadian authorities during the war.[25]

Coordinating and administrating internment operations was the Department of Militia and Defence (1914-15) and the Department of Justice (1915-20), with Major-General Sir William Dillon Otter placed in charge.[26] Throughout the war, some 8,579 men of enemy alien origin were detained in twenty-four internment camps in Canada. These were located in Nova Scotia, Quebec, Ontario, Manitoba, Alberta, and British Columbia.[27] The inmates included persons of Austro-Hungarian, Bulgarian, German, and Turkish origins. Only 3,138 of these internees, according to Major-General Otter's calculations, could be regarded as prisoners of war; the remainder were civilians. Families were permitted to accompany the men into internment, and a total of 81 women and 156 children were also detained in the Canadian camps. The total number of Germans incarcerated during the war was estimated to be around 2,000.[28] The bulk of the internees were Austro-Hungarian subjects, mostly Ukrainians who had been born in the provinces of Galicia and Bukovyna.[29]

All of these so-called enemy aliens were interned because they were considered to be either dangerous or potential burdens to the local welfare system (many were unemployed). The greatest fear was that they might resort to espionage, sabotage, or other means to undermine Canada's war effort. Those incarcerated as prisoners of war were mostly young men suspected of belonging to enemy military reserves. Internment prevented these individuals from leaving Canada and rejoining enemy armies. The reliance of most First World War armies on universal conscription was a major factor leading to the detention of these potential enemy reservists.[30] Moreover, at the United Kingdom's request, some 817 prisoners of war, mostly sailors caught in various ports under British jurisdiction, were transferred to Canada in 1915 from Barbados, Bermuda, British Guiana, Jamaica, Newfoundland, and St. Lucia. These were the only prisoners interned in Canada to be categorized by Otter as "captured in arms."[31] As for enemy soldiers captured by Canadian troops on the European battlefields, most were interned in the United Kingdom. This was done for logistical reasons, namely the United Kingdom's proximity to the European front lines. In fact, Great Britain absorbed most of the prisoners of war caught by British Imperial forces. By 1918, some 250,000 prisoners of war were detained in close to 500 camps throughout the British Isles.[32]

Canadian authorities treated both civilian internees and prisoners of war in accordance with the 1907 Hague Convention. In all Canadian internment camps, inmates were given the same standard of clothing, food, and quarters as Canadian soldiers and were free to entertain themselves. They held concerts, played sports, viewed weekly movies, wrote letters, attended educational classes, practised hobbies, and participated in numerous other recreational activities. In addition, prisoners had access to camp libraries where they could read censored books, magazines, and newspapers. Medical facilities and religious services were also provided.[33] Moreover, the internees benefited from the services of relief societies such as the International Red Cross and the Young Men's Christian Association (YMCA). The International Red Cross was the most important of these associations. It had been founded at Geneva in 1864 by Henri Dunant to prevent and alleviate human suffering. During the war, it kept track of all prisoners of war and enemy aliens detained by all belligerents, provided medical assistance, and coordinated a huge traffic of parcels usually filled with clothes, food, and medicine intended for war prisoners.[34] The YMCA, a benevolent organization founded in 1844 by Sir George Williams, contributed greatly to the welfare of prisoners during the war, providing recreational and sports equipment, games, and books to internees.[35] Camps were constantly inspected by delegations from neutral powers, namely Switzerland and Sweden, to ensure the humane treatment of inmates.

Work projects were also integrated into camp life. According to the 1907 Hague Convention, prisoners could work on various tasks "as long as the projects had no connection to the war effort, the labour was not excessive, and the men were paid a rate equivalent to that of soldiers."[36] When the labour shortage became critical in Canada during 1915, the federal government believed that it could compensate by employing both civilian internees and prisoners of war on work projects. Not only was this strategy advantageous for the government, it also afforded a way of distracting the prisoners from the monotony and constraint of internment. Numerous duties awaited inmates. They were used to clear land, work on farms, build roads and railways, cut wood, and work in mines and mills. The federal government was not the only benefactor of internee labour. Prisoners were also employed by municipal and provincial governments and by many private companies and businesses that were short of manpower owing to the war. At all times, armed guards followed the prisoners in their tasks.[37] As of 1916, selected prisoners were released into the custody of farmers who agreed to pay internees the prevailing rate for farm labour and to report on their behaviour.[38] Prisoners were paid 25 cents a day for their work, which was the same as the working pay of a Canadian soldier. They could use this money to buy tobacco and other goods from camp canteens.[39]

Despite the protection of the Hague Rules, life behind barbed wire was a strenuous experience. The pressures imposed by years of captivity as well as by the difficult living and working conditions in the camps took their physical and psychological toll. Consequently, insubordination and other acts of dissension on the part of prisoners became quite frequent, as did escape attempts. Passive resistance was also common in the camps, with the prisoners simply refusing to work. On rare occasions, there were more serious demonstrations of discontent. Such was the case in 1916 when a full-scale riot involving several hundred internees took place in the Kapuskasing Camp in northern Ontario.[40]

The majority of the internees proved to be no threat to the security of Canada, and most were released between 1916 and 1917 after signing a parole agreement that demanded "loyalty and obedience to the laws of Canada and a periodical report to the nearest police authority."[41] Many internment facilities were closed as a result of this decision. When the Armistice agreement of 11 November 1918 ended hostilities, there were approximately 2,200 prisoners still confined in Canadian internment camps. The majority were prisoners of war.[42] The release of these inmates would be somewhat slower. With Canada's military commitment to fight Bolshevism in Siberia in the winter of 1918-19, Ottawa threatened to expand the Canadian internment operation by adding Russians and Finns to the category of enemy aliens.[43] The repatriation of the prisoners began only after the Treaty of Versailles, which officially ended the First World War, was signed in June 1919. Although most remaining enemy aliens were released at that time, the repatriation of prisoners of war lasted until May 1920, owing to logistical problems.[44] Altogether 107 internees died in Canadian internment camps during the war. A high percentage of these deaths resulted from tuberculosis and the influenza epidemic of 1918.[45] The Canadian example illustrates how intensified internment operations had become a reality of modern war by 1914-18.[46] It also showed how nations at war possessed the ability to detain large populations. During the First World War, similar internment experiences also took place in Austria-Hungary, France, Germany, Italy, Russia, the United States, the Ottoman Empire, and most other belligerent nations.[47] Overall, some 3,847 Canadian soldiers were captured by the enemy on the field of battle during the First World War.[48]

Internment Operations in the Interwar Years

The First World War internment experience proved its worth, and in the interwar years numerous nations resorted, once again, to such measures. During those years, the treatment of prisoners of war continued to be a topic of interest. The First World War experience had demonstrated the deficiencies of certain clauses of the Hague Rules, namely those dealing with the labour, punishment, relief, and repatriation of prisoners of war.[49] Finding ways to overcome these problems became the order of the day. It was in 1929 that delegates of thirty-eight nations, including Canada, met in Geneva to frame a new treaty that would supersede the Hague Convention. The result was the Geneva Convention Relating to the Treatment of Prisoners of War. This set of international rules elaborated and corrected many of the provisions that had proven troublesome. Unlike the Hague Convention, which was effective only if ratified by all of the belligerents in a war, the 1929 Geneva Convention's importance lay in the fact that it was effective between any two states that had ratified it.[50] Consequently, it was the Geneva Convention of 1929 that regulated the treatment of prisoners of war during the Second World War.

The problem, however, was that no international set of rules regulating the treatment of civilians existed. Although it was universally recognized that hostilities were restricted to the armed forces of belligerents and that the ordinary citizens of the contending states had to be treated leniently, this understanding excluded those who took up arms against enemy forces. It was this exclusion that had led to the creation of concentration camps in the late nineteenth century and that had given carte blanche to some First World War belligerents to act with great ferocity against civilian populations. For example, when the invading Germans came into conflict with insurgents in Belgium in 1914, they responded by shooting several hundred innocent Belgian civilians.[51] It was in the Ottoman Empire, however, that the handling of non-combatants was at its worst. The genocidal massacre of more than 1.5 million Armenians by the Ottoman Turks between 1915 and 1923, of whom more than 600,000 died in concentration camps, was by far the most inhumane treatment of civilian populations by military forces during the First World War.[52] But the lessons of such events were not taken into account when the Geneva Convention was ratified in 1929. This neglect would have grave consequences for civilian populations worldwide in later years.[53]

It was during the interwar years that totalitarian regimes began to use concentration camps to neutralize and annihilate so-called enemies of the state. In the Soviet Union, Fascist Italy, Imperial Japan, Nazi Germany, Antonio Salazar's Portugal, and

Francisco Franco's Spain, concentration camps were intensively used throughout the interwar period and subsequent years.[54] The first serious case occurred in Russia during the 1918-21 civil war. During those years, the newly established Bolshevik, or "Red," government that took power in the middle of the 1917 Revolution was forced to fight a brutal civil war against "White" counter-revolutionaries and the foreign armies that supported them. Desperately struggling to remain in power, the Bolsheviks instituted a complex system of internment camps designed to detain both prisoners of war and civilians. The Bolsheviks used such camps, commonly known as gulags, as "instruments of terror" for the repression and eradication of counter-revolutionaries, political opponents, and other dissidents. The goal was to isolate all potential adversaries of the newly formed Bolshevik regime. Numerous gulags were established in northern Russia, Siberia, and Central Asia.[55]

Although deportations to these regions had been common in Russia under the czars, it was Bolshevik revolutionary Leon Trotsky who, as commissar of war, decided in 1918 to integrate this tradition into the concentration system. Trotsky used his experience as an internee in a Canadian internment camp in 1917 to lay the foundation of his internment policy, which by 1919 included hundreds of corrective labour camps and penal colonies. In such facilities, thousands of political prisoners were used as forced labour to clear land; to build railways, roads, airports, and waterways; and to work in factories, oil fields, and mines. Gulags became known as "institutions of slavery."[56] In the aftermath of the civil war, the gulag system expanded; the number of internees rose from approximately 150,000 in late 1921 to an estimated nine million in 1939.[57] This radical increase coincided with the rise to power of Joseph Stalin and the purges he implemented in the 1930s, which resulted in the death of millions of people throughout the Soviet Union. It is estimated that thirty million people, perhaps even more, were sent to the gulags between 1917 and the early 1990s, when the system was abolished with the fall of the Soviet Union and the end of the Cold War. It is believed that approximately half of these prisoners died of hunger, disease, exhaustion, overwork, cold, torture, and execution.[58]

It was in Germany, however, that the harsh nature of concentration camps was exploited to its maximum. When Adolf Hitler and the Nazis came into power in 1933 and established the foundations of the Third Reich, concentration camps, otherwise known as *Konzentrationslager*, were used for the containment, suppression, and exploitation of political enemies of the state. Any individual suspected of conspiring against or opposing Hitler's regime was sent to such facilities, where many were tortured and killed. Nazi racial policies ultimately led to the radicalization and expansion of the German internment system. Concentration camps became used as tools in the persecution of minority groups, especially the Jews.[59] The advent of the Second World War marked the expansion or "internationalization" of the Third Reich's concentration system. As German armies overran and conquered most of continental Europe between 1939 and 1941, the number of civilian prisoners increased dramatically in the occupied territories. The Nazis responded to this problem by building an enormous and highly complex concentration system that consisted of hundreds of concentration and labour camps, as well as subsidiary facilities. Most of these were spread throughout Central and Eastern Europe.[60] In these camps, living conditions were minimal and prisoners were kept barely alive. The bulk of the inmates were used as slave labour on farms and in factories and mines, thus contributing to Germany's war effort. Many died of overwork, beatings, torture, sickness, disease, cold, hunger, and murder.[61]

The Nazis also added a new dimension to concentration camps by introducing death camps. These were facilities designed and deliberately used with one single aim in mind: the complete and systematic extermination of all people considered to be "undesirable," "subhuman," or "inferior" by the Nazis, notably Jews, Gypsies, Jehovah's Witnesses, Slavs, homosexuals, and several other groups. Mass extermination became general policy following the German conquest of Poland in 1939, and killing centres and extermination camps were the backbone of the Nazi concentration system by 1941. The efficiency of the killing process was borrowed from industry. Trainloads of prisoners entered these camps and were exterminated in gas chambers, their bodies disposed of in mass graves, in the ovens of crematoria, and in bone-crushing machines.[62] Hair, teeth, skin, skulls, bones, and ashes were sometimes used for various commercial purposes, such as in pillows and fertilizers.[63] Millions of prisoners died in extermination camps like Auschwitz, Belzec, and Chelmno in Poland.[64] Many prisoners also died from deadly medical experiments. Nazi doctors and scientists used prisoners as human guinea pigs. Medical experiments in the camps included evaluations of human reaction to freezing temperatures, low air pressure, high altitudes, and to various seawater experiments; the testing of drugs on people in whom diseases such as malaria and typhus had been artificially induced; the removal and transplantation of bones and muscles to examine regeneration; the ingestion of poisons and toxins to find antidotes; the infliction of phosphorus burns to analyze their effects; the testing of new surgical techniques; and sterilization and castration.[65] It is estimated that between 1933 and 1945, more than eighteen million people were interned in Nazi concentration camps, eleven million of whom died including more than six million Jews.[66] The Holocaust became a testimony of the inhumanity and evil of the Nazi regime.

Internment Operations and the Second World War

During the course of the Second World War, internment operations expanded. This expansion was in large part due to the intensity and global nature of that conflict. The war affected a great number of countries around the world, and internment operations were initiated on every continent. All belligerents, including

Canada, France, Germany, Italy, Japan, the Soviet Union, the United Kingdom, and the United States, used internment camps to contain civilian populations and prisoners of war.[67] Even neutral states such as Sweden, Switzerland, Spain, and Ireland resorted to such facilities to detain civilian refugees and belligerent soldiers caught inside their territories, and to hold exchanged prisoners of war. Switzerland alone housed almost 300,000 military and civilian internees during the Second World War.[68] It is estimated that around 80 million people served in the armed forces of the belligerent powers between 1939 and 1945 and, while exact figures will probably never be known, it is estimated that as many as 35 million of them spent some time in enemy hands. These numbers deal solely with prisoners of war and do not include the millions of interned civilians.[69]

Throughout the war, nearly 10,000 Canadian soldiers, sailors, and airmen fell into enemy hands while serving with the Canadian forces.[70] This number was quite small when you consider that more than one million people served in the Royal Canadian Navy (RCN), the Royal Canadian Air Force (RCAF), and the Canadian Army during the Second World War.[71] Compared with other Allied countries, Canada had very few prisoners of war held by the enemy. More than 190,000 members of the British armed forces and over 110,000 American servicemen were held captive during the war. The armed forces of these two powers were, of course, much bigger than Canada's. Some British Commonwealth nations also had more war prisoners than Canada. For example, close to 30,000 Australians and over 12,000 South Africans were captured in battle.[72] Clearly, all of these countries had a much bigger stake in prisoners of war matters than Canada had.

Not all countries treated civilians humanely or abided by the provisions of the Geneva Convention when dealing with prisoners of war. The Nazi concentration system is a perfect example of the barbaric ways in which some belligerents treated civilian internees. But prisoners of war also suffered abuses. For instance, because the Soviet Union had refused to ratify the Geneva Convention in 1929, the Soviet army felt no obligation to live up to the terms of the treaty when it invaded Polish territory in September 1939. Thousands of Polish officers and servicemen were executed by the Soviets and buried in mass graves in a forested area known as Katyn, near Smolensk, Russia.[73] Likewise, the German army felt no obligation to abide by the provisions of the Geneva Convention when it invaded the Soviet Union in 1941. It is estimated that more than three million Soviet prisoners of war died in German captivity during the war.[74]

Similarly, the handling of prisoners of war by Japan, which had also refused to ratify the Geneva Convention, also fell short of any sense of humanity. The Japanese Army committed some of the worst atrocities against prisoners of war. According to bushido, the centuries-old samurai code of conduct espoused by the Japanese military, a soldier's greatest calling was to die on the battlefield. Surrender was unthinkable; Japanese soldiers were required to commit hara-kiri, or ritual suicide, in the advent of capture rather than face disgrace. Prisoners of war were viewed with utter disdain, which may explain why Japanese troops behaved so cruelly against captured enemy soldiers.[75] Tens of thousands of Allied troops caught on the field of battle, among them 1,689 Canadian soldiers captured during the fall of the British Colony of Hong Kong in December 1941, experienced the horrors of Japanese captivity.[76] Prisoners of war were relentlessly humiliated, mistreated, beaten, and tortured, and many were cold-bloodedly killed by ruthless Japanese captors.[77] It is estimated, for example, that some 10,000 American and Filipino prisoners of war died during the infamous Bataan Death March that followed the American surrender of the Bataan peninsula in the Philippines in April 1942.[78]

Prisoners of war were also exploited as slave labour. Many were forced to work on farms and in mines, munitions factories, and shipyards. Others were assigned to heavy manual labour projects that included constructing airfields, roads, and railways. The most notorious project was the infamous Burma-Thailand Railway, which involved approximately 64,000 prisoners of war, many of whom died in the ordeal.[79] Like the Nazis, the Japanese also conducted medical and biological warfare experiments on humans, many of whom were prisoners of war. These included the testing of poisons, gases, and flame throwers; electrocutions; transfusions using horse blood; the explosion of bombs containing gangrene, anthrax, and cyanide; exposure to high doses of X-rays; transplantations; the injection of diseases such as syphilis, cholera, and tetanus to test new drugs; vivisections; and experiments analyzing the time it took to die from fatigue, malnutrition, cold, lack of sleep, and dehydration.[80] These acts were in complete defiance of the fundamental principles of the laws of war and clearly exemplify the dreadful treatment prisoners of war received in Japanese hands. It is estimated that approximately one in four of the 140,000 Allied personnel captured by the Japanese died in captivity.[81]

The barbarous ways in which Japanese troops treated prisoners of war also was reflected in their handling of non-combatants. Captured civilians were systematically beaten, tortured, and often executed.[82] Estimates claim that 5 percent of the British, 11 percent of the American, and 17 percent of the Dutch civilians captured by the Japanese died in captivity. But it was against the civilian populations of Asia and the Pacific region that the Japanese committed the worst atrocities and, as a result, millions were killed.[83] In some instances, Asian civilians, were used by Japanese soldiers as human guinea pigs for martial arts and bayonet practices.[84] Many died as slave workers on Japanese labour projects. Of the more than 250,000 civilians who worked on the construction of the Burma-Thailand Railway, half of them perished.[85] Others were used as human guinea pigs in medical and biological warfare experiments. It is estimated that as many as 30,000 people were killed in these experiments between 1933 and 1945.[86] The experience of captured women was particularly harsh. At least 200,000 women were forcibly abducted by invading

Japanese armies and placed in "comfort stations" where they became sexual slaves. In these special camps, women were made to serve up to ninety soldiers per day and were repeatedly beaten and raped. Between 70 and 90 percent of these women died in captivity.[87]

The German and Japanese examples show how great extremes existed in the treatment of war prisoners and civilian internees during the Second World War. At one end of the spectrum were the western Allies, who largely complied with the provisions of the Geneva Convention when dealing with interned enemy subjects, civilians, and prisoners of war alike. At the other end were those, like Germany and Japan, who ignored humanitarian ideals and deliberately chose to act with brutality against enemy prisoners and civilian populations. However, despite the differences, it would be wrong to believe that all prisoners were badly treated by the Axis powers. Germany, for example, generally respected the provisions of the Geneva Convention when dealing with western Allied prisoners of war, including Canadians.[88] Nor would it be right to maintain that the Allied powers were always fair in their treatment of prisoners. The forced relocation and internment of civilians of Japanese origin in Canada and the United States, for instance, serves as a reminder of the drastic policies and decisions that were taken against ethnic and racial minorities in the name of national security by some democracies.[89] But in the end, when all the evidence is weighed, nothing that the Allies did can compare with the loss of millions of lives at the hands of brutal and sadistic German and Japanese captors during this war that caused more than 55 million deaths worldwide.

As a result of the outrageous war crimes committed by countries such as Germany and Japan during the war, the Geneva Convention Relative to the Treatment of Prisoners of War was revised in 1949 and, for the first time, a Convention Relative to the Protection of Civilian Persons in Time of War was set up. Both conventions were ratified by sixty-one nations. The convention covering prisoners of war reiterated most of the provisions of the 1929 Geneva Convention, but redefined the term "prisoners of war" to include not only members of regular armed forces but also members of resistance movements and persons who accompanied armed forces without being a member thereof, such as war correspondents and civilian supply contractors. It also re-emphasized the humane treatment of prisoners of war and broadened clauses dealing with the delivery of relief supplies, food rations, prisoner of war work, and punishments.[90] The second convention, which dealt exclusively with the treatment of civilians in wartime, guaranteed certain immunities for non-combatants. It strictly forbade the deportation of individuals or groups; the taking of hostages; outrages upon personal dignity; torture; collective punishment and reprisals; the unjustified destruction of property; and discrimination in treatment on the basis of race, religion, nationality, or on political grounds.[91]

The Second World War showed the extent to which internment operations integrating prisoners of war and concentration camps had become generally accepted by most world powers. The fact that all belligerents used internment camps as a means of incarcerating enemy combatants and potentially hostile civilian populations demonstrates that establishing internment operations had become standard procedure in times of war. When compared with the internment operations of major powers like the United States, the Soviet Union, the United Kingdom, Germany, and Japan, the Canadian internment experience was fairly limited. The internment camps built by the Canadian government in southern Quebec never housed more than a thousand prisoners each at a time. Nevertheless, the Canadian example provides a fascinating account of how well one Allied power treated its enemy prisoners. Until now, no thorough study of the camps of southern Quebec has been made. This book provides a view of how the Canadian internment operation worked in one region and how strictly it abided by the provisions of the Geneva Convention.[92]

2
Organizing and Developing Southern Quebec's Internment Operation

The Canadian government began planning Canada's Second World War internment operation in 1936. At the time, the totalitarian states of Europe, namely Nazi Germany and Fascist Italy, were pursuing aggressive foreign and military policies that undermined the balance of power on the European continent. As the United Kingdom prepared for war, so did Canada and other parts of the British Commonwealth. Among the measures adopted by Ottawa were contingency plans for the incarceration of "enemy subjects" in the advent of hostilities. When war was declared on Germany in September 1939, Canada immediately initiated its internment policies. Several hundred Canadian civilians of German descent were arrested and detained for security reasons. For many, this was a revival of Canada's First World War internment experience. It was not until the early summer of 1940, when Canada agreed to accommodate internees detained by the United Kingdom, that southern Quebec's internment operation began.

The region's internment operation can be divided in two phases. During the first phase (1940-43), civilians of German descent formed the bulk of the inmate population, while during the second phase (1942-46) German prisoners of war made up the majority. The civilian internment phase was of great importance. It was during this period that the region's camps went from being small ghettos to being highly sophisticated internment centres. The knowledge gained in dealing with the civilian internees enabled camp authorities to improve early deficiencies, correct mistakes, and upgrade installations. As a consequence, when it was decided in 1942 to use the region's internment camps to incarcerate German prisoners of war, the authorities were prepared to meet the new challenge.

The Origins of Canada's Second World War Internment Operation

Canada's internment operation during the Second World War was the result of several years of planning. The process began on 20 August 1936, when Order-in-Council PC 2097 was passed, forming a Canadian Defence Committee whose purpose, among others, was to handle the issue of "enemy aliens" in the advent of war. The architect of this was Minister of National Defence Ian Mackenzie.[1] In March 1938, this committee was divided into a number of subcommittees, including a Committee on the Treatment of Enemy Aliens on the Outbreak of Hostilities, later renamed the Interdepartmental Committee on the Treatment of Enemy Aliens and Enemy Property. Chaired by the undersecretary of state and taking in members from the departments of the Secretary of State, External Affairs, Justice, Mines and Resources, National Defence, and Finance, this subcommittee was to "inquire into and report upon the treatment of aliens and alien property in time of war or emergency, real or apprehended." Working in conjunction with the Royal Canadian Mounted Police (RCMP), it compiled a list of all enemy aliens believed to be involved in subversive activities.[2]

When the United Kingdom declared war on Germany on 3 September 1939, Canada, though not yet officially a belligerent, responded by issuing the Defence of Canada Regulations, which, among other measures, provided in Section 21 for the internment of "all individuals acting in any matter prejudicial to the public safety or the safety of the state."[3] The establishment of this regulation had been possible because a state of "apprehended war" had been proclaimed since 23 August 1939 and because civil rights had been suspended with the introduction of the War Measures Act on 1 September 1939. When the regulation became law, suspected German sympathizers (whose names were taken from the list compiled by the Committee on the Treatment of Enemy Aliens on the Outbreak of Hostilities) were rounded up by the RCMP.[4] This was said to be a precaution against espionage, sabotage, and the rise of a Canadian "fifth column." Canada's Second World War internment operation had begun.

When Canada declared war on Germany on 10 September, the anti-German manhunt intensified. All German immigrants who had arrived in Canada after 1922 were forced to register with the authorities. Of the 16,000 German Canadians who did so, only a few hundred were arrested.[5] As explained in the Defence of Canada Regulations, "all enemy aliens legally admitted to Canada and ordinarily resident in Canada, so long as they peacefully pursue their ordinary avocations, shall be allowed to continue to enjoy the protection of the law and shall be accorded the respect and consideration due to peaceful and law-abiding citizens, and they shall not be arrested, detained or interfered with, provided they comply with the requirements in respect of registration."[6] The reason for this leniency was the indifference that most German Canadians displayed regarding German politics. The overwhelming majority of persons of German origin in Canada had either been born in Canada or had immigrated to the country in order to escape Germany and its problems. The Canadian government understood this, which explains why only 850 German Canadians were interned during the war out of a population of some 600,000.[7] Because the Canadian authorities expected to handle only the Canadian civilian internees imprisoned under the Defence of Canada Regulations, no measures were taken in 1939 to expand the country's internment operation. In fact, Canada operated only two internment camps at the time, located at Kananaskis, Alberta, and Petawawa, Ontario. Both facilities had been used as unemployment relief camps during the Great Depression.[8]

The limited nature of Canada's internment operation changed in the spring of 1940 when the British government began negotiating with Ottawa for the transfer of thousands of German internees to Canada. At the time, the United Kingdom detained both enemy aliens and prisoners of war. The internment operation on the British Isles was initiated when the United Kingdom declared war on Germany on 3 September 1939. At the time, there were some 75,000 enemy aliens of German origin in the country, 55,000 of whom were refugees.[9] Since 1933, Nazi policy had been to expel all "undesirables" from Germany, especially the Jews. Thousands of Jewish refugees, many of whom had been interned in German concentration camps, found their way to the United Kingdom and several other countries.[10] According to one Jewish emigrant, "The purpose was to rob us ... force us to leave and ... blackmail other countries into taking us. And it worked."[11] The problem, however, was that British authorities continued to classify these refugees as enemy aliens. Because civilians of German descent were perceived as potential threats, special tribunals were set up later that month to examine all enemy aliens over the age of sixteen with the object of "sifting out anyone who might not be friendly to the country." Overall, some 120 tribunals were established, each dealing with more than 500 cases.[12] Enemy aliens were graded into three categories: Class A were aliens whose loyalty and reliability were doubted by the tribunals and who might constitute a potential security risk; Class B were aliens whose loyalty and reliability the tribunals found to be uncertain and who for one reason or the other should be kept under a form of supervision; and Class C were all those whom the tribunals found to be not suspect.[13]

When German armies overran Western Europe in May 1940, xenophobia and war hysteria increased in the British Isles and London responded with the order to "intern the lot": in other words, the mass internment of most enemy aliens classed under the "ABC" system.[14] For the German refugees who had fled Nazi Germany, the United Kingdom's general internment policy came as a shock. "I was surprised in England that they had interned us in the first place because we came as their friends," recalled one internee. "There is an Arab proverb ... 'The enemy of my enemy is my friend' ... we were the enemies of Hitler. The British were the enemies of Hitler so we assumed that they must be our friends."[15] The civilian internees were added to the few German war prisoners already detained in the United Kingdom. Most of these prisoners of war were enemy merchant seamen whose ships had been caught in British ports. There was also Kriegsmarine sailors captured at sea by the Royal Navy and Luftwaffe pilots whose aircraft had been shot down over the British Isles or during the Norwegian campaign of April 1940. Finally, some 1,200 German paratroopers were captured by the Dutch and transferred to the United Kingdom before the Netherlands fell in May 1940.[16] Suddenly, the United Kingdom was forced to detain large populations of civilians of German descent and prisoners of war.

The goal of the British government's transfer of all of its prisoners overseas in the spring of 1940 was to alleviate the pressures that internment operations imposed on the home front. At the time, the United Kingdom was facing the prospect of a German invasion. Because the British government felt that "internment on the British Isles was no longer sufficiently secure," the chiefs of staff recommended that most German internees be transferred overseas.[17] As Eric Koch wrote in *Deemed Suspect*, three reasons guided this decision. First, in the advent of a German invasion, the danger of fifth columnists would be lessened; second, there would be fewer mouths to feed in Britain; and third, fewer military personnel would be required to guard British internment camps.[18]

In late May 1940, the British government began sending requests to its dominions asking them if they would be prepared to accept large numbers of enemy aliens and prisoners of war who had been interned in the United Kingdom. As British Secretary of State Viscount Caldecote told Canadian High Commissioner Vincent Massey on 7 June 1940, "The United Kingdom government sincerely hopes that the Canadian government may be pressed to come to the assistance of the United Kingdom by agreeing to receive, at the earliest possible moment, at least the internees whose removal from this country it is desired to secure on the ground that their continued presence in this country is bound to be a source of the most serious risk."[19] The Canadian government debated the issue. While it was suggested that the British government might give consideration to transporting these internees to Newfoundland or the West Indies rather than to Canada, "it was observed that Canada possessed locations where internment camps might safely be set up, such as Sable Island, the Magdalene Islands, Grosse Isle (where the immigration quarters would be available) and possible locations in Northern Canada."[20] The British suggested that Canada should agree to accept up to 4,000 civilian internees and 3,000 prisoners of war.[21] On 19 June 1940, Prime Minister William Lyon Mackenzie King announced in the House of Commons that Canada had "agreed to accept German prisoners of war and internees from the United Kingdom."[22]

The first batch of prisoners sent to Canada left Liverpool on 20 June 1940, aboard the *Duchess of York*, a 20,000-ton vessel belonging to the Canadian Pacific Steamship Company. The ship's cargo of 2,100 Class A internees and 500 German prisoners of war reached Quebec City on 29 June. Although the *Duchess of York*'s trip across the Atlantic Ocean went according to schedule, the same cannot be said of the ill-fated *Arandora Star*. Having left Liverpool on 1 July 1940 with a contingent of some 480 Class A internees and more than 730 Italian inmates, the *Arandora Star*, once a Blue Star luxury liner, was torpedoed by a German U-boat off the Irish coast on 2 July. Approximately 150 Germans and 450 Italian internees died. Those who survived the *Arandora Star* disaster were later packed aboard other ships, also bound for Canada. Then, on 3 July 1940, the *Ettrick* left Liverpool with more than 1,300 Class B and Class C internees as well as 900 German prisoners of war and 400 Italians. The last vessel to leave the United Kingdom for Canada with a cargo of internees was the *Sobieski*, a Polish luxury liner. Having left Greenock, Scotland, on 4 July 1940, with 980 Class B and Class C internees, 450 German prisoners of war and 400 Italians, the *Sobieski* reached Quebec City on 15 July, two days after the *Ettrick*.[23] It is also important to note that 244 Class A internees, 2,290 Class B and Class C internees and 200 Italians were sent to Australia aboard the *Dunera* on 10 June.[24]

What this transfer demonstrated was that there were fewer prisoners of war than civilian internees being sent to Canada. Furthermore, the bulk of the internees were Class B and Class C captives, "most of whom should never have been sent from England," according to historian John Joseph Kelly.[25] As author François Lafitte indicated in 1940, "This showed clearly – out of the mouths of the Ministers themselves – that the War Office, the Home Office and Mr. [British prime minister Arthur Neville] Chamberlain between them made a complete mess of the job of selecting people for deportation in a sensible and democratic way and of organizing the overseas transport of less than 8,000 men."[26] Lafitte further stated, "The plain fact is that thousands of innocent refugees have been treated like cattle in the name of national security."[27] Because the internees were being kept for the British government, the Canadian authorities had no choice but to detain them. Only the British home secretary had the "overriding power here of ordering release in any case where he is convinced that release will be in the national interest, or in the interest of our [British] war effort."[28]

Canada was unprepared to accommodate this influx of prisoners and lacked enough proper detention facilities. Ottawa was forced to create new internment camps to accommodate the internees. The immediate result was the creation of temporary internment centres in the province of Quebec, where the internees disembarked. The construction of two such facilities began in June 1940: Camp "L" built at Cove Fields on Quebec City's Plains of Abraham, and Camp "T" located on the Trois-Rivières exhibition ground property.[29] A third temporary internment facility was to be Camp "V" in Valcartier, but it was turned down as being too close to the Dominion Arsenal ammunition factory.[30] It was in these facilities that the arriving prisoners were first held. At the same time, the Canadian authorities started planning the construction of permanent detention facilities. These were to be built in New Brunswick, Ontario, and Quebec. They chose these provinces because they believed it was unwise to send the internees to western Canada, where there were significant German populations.[31]

Because there was not enough time allocated to construct new internment camps, the task was to retrofit existing buildings, such as empty factories, mills, and forts, with proper heating, sewage, and lighting facilities. Moreover, all of these camps were to be located near railway lines to facilitate transfers of prisoners. Several sites were eventually chosen.[32] In New Brunswick, the Acadian Forest Experiment Station near Fredericton became Camp "B". In Ontario, the Calydor Sanatorium at Gravenhurst was chosen as the site for Camp "C"; Camp "E" was constructed on the property of the Abitibi Pulp and Paper Company in Espanola; Fort Henry in Kingston was selected as Camp "F"; the industrial farm at Mimico became Camp "M"; the buildings of the Monteith Industrial Farm in Monteith were used for Camp "Q"; and Camp "R" was built on the property of the Lake Sulphite Company at Red Rock. In Quebec, Camp "A" was constructed on the site of the Dominion Experimental Farm at Farnham; Fort Lennox on the Île-aux-Noix was chosen for Camp "I"; the Quebec Central Railroad (QCR) property at Newington outside Sherbrooke became Camp "N"; and the fort on the Île Ste-Hélène in Montreal became Camp "S". All of these detention centres supplemented the two internment camps that already existed in Canada, namely Camp "K" at Kananaskis and Camp "P" in Petawawa.[33] In the end, most of the civilian internees from the United Kingdom were accommodated in the four permanent internment camps built in the province of Quebec in 1940. Except for Camp "S", which was located in Montreal and whose purpose was to incarcerate Italian inmates, all of the other camps were situated in southern Quebec and detained civilians of German descent.

Responsibility pertaining to the "administration, treatment and security of prisoners of war and internees" belonged to the Department of National Defence's Directorate of Internment Operations – later re-named the Directorate of Prisoners of War. Military District 4 headquarters in Montreal was in charge of all internment camps located in Quebec. In each camp, the Veterans Guard of Canada (VGC) had complete jurisdiction over camp personnel. The VGC had been established on 24 May 1940, as a special corps of First World War veterans to be used for guard duties wherever needed. The aim was to exploit the veterans' military experience for the benefit of the home front. The unit's task was to guard internment camps, cable stations, oil refineries, bridges, canals, ammunition depots, factories, and many other such sites. Although the age limit for enlistment was fixed at forty-nine, a number of older men were accepted, including some veterans of the South African War, which freed up the younger military personnel for overseas service. The VGC replaced the Canadian Provost Corps as the predominant guards at internment camps. By 1945, the VGC numbered 15,000 men who served in Canada, British Guiana, Newfoundland, the West Indies, and the United Kingdom. In southern Quebec, most of the VGC personnel were unemployed French-Canadian veterans.[34]

Southern Quebec's First Phase of Internment Operations: Civilian Internees

Because it was urgent to find proper quarters for the internees from the United Kingdom, the three camps in southern Quebec were set up in haste in 1940. The first camp built in the region was Camp "I" at Île-aux-Noix. It was constructed within the walls of old Fort Lennox, an early-nineteenth-century fortress situated on the Île-aux-Noix, an island in the Richelieu River near St. Jean.[35] The history of Camp Île-aux-Noix began on 1 July 1940, when Major Eric D.B. Kippen was asked by the officer commanding Military District 4 to find a suitable location for an internment camp. Following a thorough investigation of the Île-aux-Noix's existing facilities, Kippen reported favourably to his superiors about the site and work on the camp began on 4 July.[36]

Converting old Fort Lennox into an internment camp was no easy task. Kippen wrote in the camp's war diary on 5 July that "there is a lot to do. The old barracks and other buildings have not been inhabited since 1880. Water and light must be installed; wire fences put up and a great many other things attended to."[37] He went on to write, "I'd taken about three weeks [to build the camp]. I had some engineers working on it night and day. They had to install ... proper lighting and had to do a lot about the water and the drainage and all that sort of thing, because it [Fort Lennox] hasn't been lived in about 60 or 70 years. It was full of bats ... and all sorts of animals ... it was a rotten place, really, but it was the only thing I could find in a hurry."[38] When Major Kippen received the order to prepare for the arrival of the first internees on 15 July 1940, the camp was still in the midst of construction. "This news causes considerable excitement in view of the fact that the camp was far from complete, at the time."[39] In fact, civilian workers were still being employed by the camp three weeks after the arrival of the prisoners.[40]

The inexperience of the camp staff was another problem, as was revealed in the lack of coordination that characterized the arrival of the first trainload of prisoners on 15 July. Upon reaching St-Paul, a small town facing the Île-aux-Noix, at 7 p.m., the 273 prisoners were divided into groups of 35 and shipped to the island on a large barge escorted by a fleet of motor boats. Because only one barge could be used, the transfer to the Île-aux-Noix was a slow process. By midnight, some 76 prisoners were still waiting on the St. Paul shore to be transferred to the island. Complicating matters was the fact that the entire operation was done at night and in the midst of pouring rain. As they arrived in the camp, prisoners were thoroughly searched, given a hot shower, and examined by medical officers before being sent to their quarters. So slow was this process that the prisoners were not completely settled until 4 a.m. The internees' transfer from St. Paul to the camp took nearly ten hours. Major Kippen summarized why the transfer was so slow: "The whole thing was quite a job, considering the camp was partly finished and the staff were quite inexperienced of this kind of work."[41]

Inexperience led to further logistical problems. The camp staff's handling of the inmates' luggage is one example. Prisoners were allowed a maximum of 40 pounds of baggage. Most disobeyed orders and brought with them between 75 pounds and 250 pounds. Moreover, nothing was done to protect the prisoners' belongings as they were transferred from St. Paul to the camp. Transported amid pouring rain, most of the poor-quality luggage sustained serious damage; wet cases often ripped due to the sheer weight of their contents. While the internees were blamed for this problem, the camp staff also held its share of responsibility. Despite the bad weather, no soldier made any attempts to preserve the prisoners' luggage. Instead, the already broken possessions were piled up, covered with small canvas sheets, and left outside for a couple of days.[42] Many soldiers also resorted to pillage. Stolen items included gold and silver wristwatches, lighters, kitchen utensils, silverware, wallets, knives, and even boots, shirts and pants.[43] Major Kippen seemed unaware of the looting. He explained to the internees that their baggage had been handled some ten times since it left the United Kingdom, "thereby running all the hazards of loss, damage and theft." He added, however, that "under war time ... the prisoners are regarded with some considerable hostility by civilians and in some cases soldiers are inclined to look upon prisoners of war property as fair game."[44] A court of inquiry was assembled in September 1940 to investigate the matter.[45] The court came to the conclusion in February 1941 that it was "unable to arrive at a definite conclusion and to hold anyone in particular accountable for the unfortunate mishap." There was not enough evidence, it claimed, "to show exactly how and where the alleged loss or pilfering had taken place." Too many opportunities to tamper with the luggage existed during the long journey from the United Kingdom to Canada. Furthermore, because most of the luggage was made of poor-quality fabrics that "could hardly stand the wear and tear incidental to traveling by land and sea," the court wondered how anyone could know whether some of the baggage had not already been broken before it arrived at Camp Île-aux-Noix. Because no receipts had been issued, no one could be found directly responsible for the safety of the luggage. The court of inquiry mentioned that it might be "worthwhile to have the Provincial Police pursue inquiries, not only in Montreal but also St. Jean and the vicinity of St. Paul."[46]

The Quebec Provincial Police's investigation of the matter was more conclusive. After interrogating several witnesses, the police concluded in July 1941 that "it is therefore proven that the articles lost by the prisoners had been stolen at Île-aux-Noix by the soldiers, the members of the Veterans Home Guard and the employees of National Defence and the officers in charge are to be blamed for what occurred."[47] According to the civilian workers employed by National Defence Headquarters (NDHQ) for the construction of Camp Île-aux-Noix, the luggage was looted on the island. One worker admitted that "the suit cases were opened and several broken and torn. Lots of stuff was stolen. The guards who were there were kicking the suit cases open with their heels, saying that all these things were to be burned and that the prisoners were never to see their belongings any more."[48] Once this happened, civilian workers began searching the luggage for valuables. One recalled, "There was about 50 soldiers and these men went through and pilfered the luggage of the internees."[49] Undoubtedly, the beginning of the internment operation at Camp Île-aux-Noix was chaotic.

Meanwhile, hoping to alleviate crowding in the temporary camps already established in Quebec, the government considered new sites in August 1940. In southern Quebec, the result was the creation of Camp "A" on the Dominion Experimental Farm at Farnham and Camp "N" on the property of the QCR at Sherbrooke. These camps were situated in Quebec's Eastern Townships. Another location was offered by the Quebec government on the Brompton Farm near Sherbrooke. This site, which would have been known as Camp "O," never materialized because federal authorities did not deem necessary the construction of a fourth camp in the region.[50]

The story of Camp "A" began on 1 August 1940, when the Dominion Experimental Farm in Farnham became the property of the Department of National Defence.[51] Immediately, a thorough investigation of the site was made by members of the Directorate of Internment Operations for the construction of a new camp. As they stated in their report on 8 August, "It is important that this camp be completed ... so as to move the internees now in temporary camp "L" Cove Fields, Quebec City, a very unsatisfactory place."[52] Despite the urgent need, construction did not begin until mid-September. As a result, work was still in progress when order was given to open the facility in early October 1940. Camp Farnham became operational on 9 October 1940, when Major Eric D.B. Kippen, who was then in command of Camp Île-aux-Noix, was transferred to Farnham. When he arrived, the camp was in a primitive state. At the time, some 120 civilians were still working on the camp facilities. There was still a lot to be done, for only one line of barbed wire had been erected. Although nearing completion, most of the buildings still remained uninhabitable. Further, no towers were yet installed at the four corners of the compound, which was strewn with debris. Still, orders had been given to Kippen and his men to settle the camp. This was no easy task since no huts existed to house the camp's staff. Kippen tried to correct this deficiency by immediately ordering the conversion of two old tobacco-drying buildings – remnants of the Dominion Experimental Farm – into huts for his men. In the meantime, large tents had to serve as living quarters for the troops; Kippen and his officers stayed at the Montcalm Hotel in Farnham.[53]

Major Kippen's job was to accelerate the construction process and supervise "the last stages of the building."[54] To increase production, Kippen began using night shifts. This enabled work to go on twenty-four hours a day. In the span of five days, the entire barbed wire fence system was built, most of the buildings and huts were completed, and the four towers were erected.[55] The camp was able to welcome its first internees on 15 October 1940. Kippen wrote in the camp's war diary that "it will probably take another week to complete the work going on in the camp."[56] Clearly, camp authorities were not ready to welcome a huge influx of inmates. Nevertheless, in the course of a few days, Camp Farnham was forced to accommodate 520 internees. The initial batch, which consisted of 140 men who arrived by train on 15 October, was followed by a second shipment of 180 men on 16 October,[57] and a third group of 200 inmates on 18 October.[58] Work was still in progress, and the camp also lacked beds, forcing many internees to sleep on the floor.[59] This problem was solved three days later when long awaited double-decker iron beds were sent to Camp Farnham.[60]

To accelerate the construction of the camp, the civilian workmen were replaced by internees. An entry in the camp's war diary reads, "A lot of work inside the compound can now be done by the internees and there seems to be many skilled men among them."[61] Despite the prisoners' belief that the camp should have been completed prior to their arrival, most complied with the authorities' request and began working on the facility.[62] This decision carried a risk; if internees became injured, no facilities existed within the camp to treat them. The internees' hospital was still in the midst of construction, and camp authorities possessed no trucks or cars. Wounded prisoners could not be evacuated rapidly to a nearby hospital.[63] Fortunately, no inmates sustained serious injury.

Camp "N" Newington in Sherbrooke was also still being constructed when prisoners arrived. The site originally belonged to the QCR and was transferred to the Department of National Defence in September 1940. It consisted of two large hangars that originally served as repair sheds for locomotives and railway cars; an old machine shop and boiler house; an oil house; and an administration building. Railway tracks and oiling pits extended throughout the yard. The camp's war diary reported: "The facilities are so inadequate that when the Sherbrooke Fusiliers made an inspection in September 1940, exploring the possibilities of using the site as their headquarters, the officer commanding flatly rejected the project." Nevertheless, Brigadier-General Edouard de Bellefeuille Panet, Director of Internment Operations, requested Major D.J. O'Donahoe, engineer officer at Military District 4, to inspect the site in late September with a view to using it as a camp. According to O'Donahoe's report, dated 24 September 1940, "The camp could be made ready for occupation by 4 October 1940."[64]

The decision of the Directorate of Internment Operations to authorize the construction of an internment camp on the QCR site completely contradicted the Sherbrooke Fusiliers' report. Transforming this property into an internment facility proved a slow process. There was an enormous amount of work to be done, and none of Major O'Donahoe's deadlines were fulfilled. When the camp opened on 5 October 1940, the site was far from being completed. Major S.H. Griffin, camp commandant, reported that "there are virtually no sanitary arrangements other than 6 out of date toilets in the boiler house. The lighting system is extremely limited, and the uncleanliness of the main buildings is beyond description."[65] Despite the harsh conditions, Griffin's men tried to "give the place a semblance of habitability" while preparing for the arrival of the internees.[66] Still, the site remained unready to welcome internees. When 618 prisoners arrived on 15 October, the "appalling conditions at the camp" generated a considerable amount of discontent.[67] "The railway tracks and oiling pits that ran through the sheds were filled with black water," Eric Koch recalled. "The place had six-old fashioned lavatories without ventilation, two urinals and seven low-pressure water taps which also had to serve the kitchen. The windows were broken and the roofs were leaky; so were the noisily hissing heating pipes."[68]

Internees soon came to the conclusion that this camp was "not fit for human habitation."[69] The camp lacked bedding equipment. "When we arrived at these sheds," one internee remembered, "we started to laugh and say, 'This is a camp? Where are the beds, where are the mattresses, where are the blankets?' ... it was completely ridiculous."[70] This had resulted from the faulty routing of the camp's bedding equipment; mattresses destined for Camp Farnham were sent to Camp Sherbrooke while bed frames were sent to Montreal.[71] Furthermore, prisoners had to wash "by means of a small bowl, after having queued up for about half an hour's time to get a spot of hot water, if any, in a coal pit under the boilers. And if one wanted to make use of one of six lavatories, another hour had to be spent."[72]

Obviously, camp conditions were inadequate. This shocked most of the prisoners who had been told by the authorities of Camp "L" Cove Fields that living conditions in southern Quebec camps would be much better. One internee even recalled a guard telling him "that there will be no barbed wires [in Camp Sherbrooke] ... you're on the honour system. We know you're not Nazis."[73] It was such promises that led to the "deep-rooted belief that they [internees] had been ousted from their comfortable quarters at Camp Cove Fields to make way for Nazi prisoners." Feeling betrayed, the internees immediately resorted to passive resistance by refusing to prepare meals, eat, or do work of any nature.[74] The camp staff quickly negotiated with the internees to quell this small mutiny. J.A. Edmison, assistant adjutant, addressed the internees on the morning of 16 October. Because most of them were Jews, Edmison pointed out "that their present conduct was highly damaging to their own cause, that it would arouse resentment rather than sympathy, would aid the spread of anti-Semitism in Canada and severely handicap the efforts of Canadian Jewry to work out plans for post-war Jewish immigration."[75] According to Eric Koch, Edmison made a great impression on the internees and persuaded most of them to cooperate with the authorities. "His main point was that, if we were more flexible, we could make the camp more livable," remembered Koch. "He said, even the [Canadian] officers had to put up with sub-standard accommodation."[76]

The prisoners finally agreed to cooperate, but on the basis of a three-day trial. Although this ended the hunger strike, it did not erase the inmates' discontent. Helping to cool down the already heated climate was the camp commandant's speech of 18 October, in which he pleaded for cooperation. The camp commandant told the internees that Sherbrooke was not going to be a temporary camp. "Both you and I are going to be here for a long time," he added. "There are among you many clever and qualified men; to them, I throw out the challenge to assist in the planning and erection of this new camp ... The winter is fast approaching and every day's delay is serious ... I speak to you now not only as commandant but as man to man, and I hope a lot of things will be different from now on."[77] To further entice the inmates into cooperating, Major D.J. O'Donahoe and the camp authorities agreed to pay each internee 25 cents per day for any work done to improve the camp. A work committee of internee technicians was formed to "draw up plans for immediate requirements."[78] Internee labour was used to construct outside latrines, patch leaks in the roofs and holes in the floors, prepare the kitchen and mess hall, install iceboxes and cookstoves, and to improve lighting.[79] From this moment on, the situation began improving, though there still remained a lot of work to be done. Working on the camp's infrastructure helped the morale of the internees. When a brief snowstorm struck the camp on the night of October 18-19, for instance, the internees expressed satisfaction at the warmth of the buildings.[80]

Change of Status: From Internee to Refugee

In all three southern Quebec internment camps, the treatment of the internees was in accordance with the 1929 Geneva Convention. Although the convention was to apply solely to enemy combatants, the Canadian government had decided in 1939 that it should also pertain to civilian internees. This was done by integrating prisoners of war and civilians into the same category. Prisoners of war were referred to as "prisoners of war Class 1," and civilian internees were termed "prisoners of war Class 2." This system of classification enabled civilian internees to benefit from the same rights as prisoners of war. As stated by the Canadian authorities, "Enemy aliens interned as prisoners of war under the Defence of Canada Regulations are not entitled to the special rights and privileges accorded to those prisoners of war defined in ... the International Convention Relative to the Treatment of Prisoners of War. It is intended that the provisions of that convention shall be made applicable to them as regards their general treatment, but saving and excepting certain articles of said Convention which are considered applicable to prisoners of war."[81] This interpretation was reinforced on 31 May 1940, with the introduction of Order-in-Council PC 2322, which mentioned that all interned individuals in Canada were to be classed as prisoners of war.[82] The problem, according to historian John Stanton, was that there was now "no legal distinction between the British internees and prisoners of war sent to Canada; the prisoners of war captured in combat by Canadian soldiers; the Canadian citizens who were political dissenters; and the enemy aliens." As he concluded, "It was a neat way of disguising the fact that these people [civilian internees] were in fact political prisoners."[83] Because the guards at southern Quebec camps had been told that they were guarding dangerous "enemies of the state" and prisoners of war, the arrival of the civilian inmates created much confusion. Major Eric D.B. Kippen, commandant of Camp Île-aux-Noix, recalled how he was shocked at the sight of the internees, especially the Orthodox Jews. "First of all, an old fellow comes out [of the train] ... I guess he must have been at least 80 ... he could hardly walk ... then there was a young boy, he was 16 or 17 ... these were all ... refugees, that had been brought over in this ship [*Sobieski*]. Well, the information I had got was entirely wrong, and I got quite a shock when I saw them, because I said, 'Hell, these aren't prisoners of war' ... a lot of them were Orthodox Jews."[84] This amalgamation of civilian internees and prisoners of war into the same category demonstrated that the Canadian government did not fully understand who their inmates were. Although it created a climate of uniformity and enabled civilian internees to be protected by the Geneva Convention, the situation made it difficult for camp guards to distinguish the needs of one type of prisoner from those of another. This confusion also affected the prisoners. Captured military personnel understood the concept of internment and knew what treatment they could expect to receive if caught in battle. Most had completed courses pertaining to the subject while they were serving with their respective military units, and all understood the provisions of the Geneva Convention. They knew that if captured they would remain incarcerated until the end of the war. On the other hand, civilian internees had not been prepared psychologically for internment. In most cases, they did not understand the reasons for their internment, and few knew about the provisions of the Geneva Convention. They did not comprehend why the Canadian government treated them as prisoners of war, for most of them wished no harm to the British Commonwealth. This situation meant that camp authorities had to deal with very different psychological profiles among the internees. The imposed uniformity of the prisoners' status created discomfort and discontent among the civilian prisoners.

The issue was solved in early 1941 when the British government, which remained responsible for southern Quebec's internees, acknowledged the fact that most of the civilian inmates were "friendly aliens" or refugees and that they constituted no threat to the security of the realm.[85] It was finally recognized that the mass internment policy of the previous year was an injustice.[86] When the Canadian government was made aware of this change in attitude, measures were immediately taken to modify the civilian prisoners' status. On 25 June 1941, Ottawa issued Order-in-Council PC 4568, which finally granted these inmates refugee status.[87] This meant that civilians of German descent were no longer to be treated as prisoners of war

Class 2 and that they were no longer covered under the provisions of the Geneva Convention. Suddenly, the camps of southern Quebec became refugee camps. Because the administration of such camps was to be distinct from that of prisoner of war camps, a Central Committee for Interned Refugees was created by the Department of the Secretary of State. Though the Department of National Defence remained responsible for the camps' staff, it was the Department of the Secretary of State that coordinated all refugee camps.[88]

As refugees, the civilian inmates of southern Quebec benefited from new privileges that were introduced on 15 July 1941 with Order-in-Council PC 5246.[89] Internees were given complete freedom in the performance of their religious duties, were allowed to obtain liquor and receive visitors, and were given special privileges regarding mail quotas; they also saw their prison uniforms discarded and surveillance by guards reduced.[90] At Île-aux-Noix, inmates could almost walk out of camp undisturbed and "take a stroll on the island or take a swim in the Richelieu River."[91] Dissatisfaction lingered, however, among those internees who had mistakenly believed that their new status would ensure drastic changes in camp life. An example occurred in late July 1941 at Camp Sherbrooke, where some inmates who expected more liberties and even the complete removal of the barbed wire openly expressed their dissatisfaction to camp authorities.[92]

Because the British government had been releasing refugees in the United Kingdom since April 1941, Canada did the same as of October 1941. Refugees could either return to the United Kingdom, where their manpower could be used for the war effort, or remain in the Canadian internment camps until they could qualify for admission to Canada under the prevailing immigrant regulations.[93] Most of the refugees chose to return to the United Kingdom. The first refugees to be released were the very old , the sick, and the very young – all those who should never have been interned at all. They were followed by what might be termed "special cases," individuals who through ignorance or neglect were classed as Germans, but could speak no German and who had been in the United Kingdom uninterruptedly since early childhood. Then there were those whose work was considered vital for the British war effort such as engineers, scientists, technicians, and factory owners.[94] Prisoners could also accelerate their release by enlisting in the Auxiliary Military Pioneer Corps, a non-combat unit of the British Army made up of refugees and engaged in such projects as building roads, camps, and airfields; shovelling coal; loading and unloading military stores from aircraft, trucks, and railway cars; clearing bomb debris; and other manual work.[95] For refugees between eighteen and fifty years old, enlistment in the Pioneer Corps was an opportunity to demonstrate their friendliness to the Allied cause. For most of southern Quebec's inmates, the Pioneer Corps was one of the fastest ways to return to the United Kingdom. Many refugees interned in Canada joined the Pioneer Corps during the war.[96]

As for the refugees who chose to remain in Canada, their release was a very slow and meticulous operation. Before being released, inmates were interviewed by immigration officers working for the Canadian Central Committee for Interned Refugees. In most cases, they cooperated with the United Jewish Refugee and War Relief Agencies of Canada (later known as the United Jewish Relief Agencies). To be released, refugees also had to be sponsored by Canadian civilians or recognized institutions. The sponsoring of refugees led many visitors into the camps of southern Quebec.[97] Although numerous businessmen, families, farmers, private companies, and universities sponsored inmates, the Canadian Jewish Congress was the most active institution in this field. The sponsorship operation not only helped the prisoners but also went some way to enlighten Canadian civilians that the vast majority of refugees were no threat to the security of Canada.[98] The release of individual refugees occasionally created humorous situations. Such was the case for Kurt Swinton, one of the first to be released from Camp Farnham. Once freed, he joined the Royal Canadian Corps of Signals as an officer. Swinton recalled the visit he made to Camp Farnham in his new military uniform, "It was a traumatic experience both for me and for the others. And the guards, they thought they were dreaming ... The guards saluted! It killed them but they did it."[99] Overall, 966 refugees were allowed to remain in Canada for the duration of the war. Most were released to study or work in the country. When the war came to an end in 1945, many of them applied for Canadian citizenship.[100]

By 1942, the strength reductions in southern Quebec camps had become so drastic that the Canadian government began to consider new applications for the region's internment operation. In early 1942 Ottawa decided to use the camps of southern Quebec for the incarceration of prisoners of war Class 1. It was during that same year that all of Camps Farnham's and Sherbrooke's refugees were transferred to Camp Île-aux-Noix. As a result, Île-aux-Noix remained the only facility in southern Quebec to detain refugees. Because more and more refugees were being released by October 1943, it was finally decided to close that camp altogether.[101] In fact, only forty-two inmates resided in the camp by November 1943. All of the camp's captives were transferred to the internment camp in Hull, Quebec, on 4 November 1943. Camp Hull had been created in 1941.[102] Unlike the other camps situated in southern Quebec, Île-aux-Noix was not converted to accommodate war prisoners. Instead, the site was handed over to the Department of Mines and Resources in June 1944.[103] This marked the end of a chapter in the history of southern Quebec's internment operation, for civilian internees would no longer be incarcerated in this region. Southern Quebec's first phase of internment had thus come to an end with the closure of Camp Île-aux-Noix in 1943.

Southern Quebec's Second Phase of Internment: Prisoners of War

Southern Quebec's second phase of internment, which was marked by the incarceration of German prisoners of war, was initiated in early 1942. This phase resulted from intense negotiations between the British and Canadian governments. The process began in February 1941, when representatives of the British War Office suggested that "all prisoners taken by United Kingdom and dominions' forces, whether acting separately or in combination, should be placed in an Empire pool in respect of which the United Kingdom would be the detaining power and the dominions would have the status of agents."[104] In other words, German prisoners of war were to be shipped overseas for incarceration in the dominions. The main reason was that prisoners of war had to be removed from the battlefields and kept away from danger. This was in keeping with the Geneva Convention. Article 7 stipulated that as soon as possible after their capture, prisoners of war were to be evacuated to depots sufficiently removed from the fighting zone for them to be out of danger.[105] Because the United Kingdom constantly faced the prospect of German aerial bombardments, it was deemed logical to send the prisoners to camps in the British Commonwealth. The Canadian government initially refused this measure. But when the British authorities persisted, it finally agreed to "serve as one of the official gaolers for the Allied war effort."[106] Arrangements were immediately formalized whereby the Canadian government accepted to incarcerate German prisoners of war in North America as long as the British authorities agreed to cover the costs of transporting and maintaining them: "The Canadian government would prefer to maintain the view that the U.K. remain the detaining power, the Canadian government being the agent of the United Kingdom government in respect of prisoners of war transferred to Canada."[107] This decision meant that Canada accepted some degree of British leadership on prisoners of war matters.

German prisoners of war originated from all branches of the German Wehrmacht (armed forces), which included the Luftwaffe (air force), the Kriegsmarine (navy), and the Heer (army), as well as the Waffen-SS and even the Gestapo (secret police). These prisoners were caught on a variety of battlefields. While many were captured at sea or during the air war over the United Kingdom and on other aerial fronts, most of the prisoners surrendered to British and Commonwealth forces during military campaigns in North Africa, the Middle East, Italy, and Northwest Europe between 1940 and 1945. Also included in the prisoner of war category were enemy merchant seamen, to whom British and Canadian authorities had granted prisoner of war status in 1942, for administrative convenience.[108]

This decision to incarcerate prisoners of war in Canada led Ottawa to reorganize its internment operation. New internment camps had to be created to detain incoming prisoners, which led to facilities being established at Neys, Angler, and Bowmanville in Ontario. By October 1941, to facilitate bureaucratic efficiency, Canadian internment camps were classed numerically in accordance with the military district in which they were located. For instance, the camps registered by Military District 4 headquarters in Montreal were assigned codes in the forties. The first digit indicated the camp's district and the second its number. The camps of southern Quebec were registered as followed: Camp No. 40 Farnham; Camp No. 41 Île-aux-Noix; and Camp No. 42 Sherbrooke. The old classification system whereby camps were designated by letters of the alphabet, used since 1939, was abandoned.[109]

Camp Farnham was southern Quebec's first internment centre to accommodate prisoners of war. The process began in September 1941 when Military District 4 headquarters advised camp authorities that Farnham was to be converted for the detention of prisoners of war.[110] All of the camp's 445 refugees were transferred to Camp Sherbrooke on 23 January 1942. Camp Farnham was then closed for three months to prepare for the arrival of the enemy combatants.[111] A report dated 27 January 1942 stated, "It is anticipated that this camp will be re-opened about the middle of April and will contain POW[s] ... from the U.K."[112] The camp became operational on 18 April 1942, when 597 enemy merchant seamen arrived at Farnham.[113] In the autumn of 1942, Canadian authorities decided to convert Camp Sherbrooke into a facility for enemy merchant seamen and to transfer all of its 299 refugees to Camp Île-aux-Noix on 25 November 1942.[114]

Camp Sherbrooke was used to contain enemy merchant seamen until its closure in June 1946.[115] Its refugee population was replaced on 2 December 1942 by 594 enemy merchant seamen from Camp Farnham. At the time, Farnham was chosen for the temporary incarceration of prisoner of war officers. In accordance with the Geneva Convention, enemy officers were to be segregated from other prisoners of war. Also, they were to be treated differently.[116] Article 21 stipulated that belligerents were required to inform each other of the titles and ranks in use in their respective armed forces, with a view to ensuring equality of treatment between the corresponding ranks of officers and other persons of equivalent status. Officers and persons of equivalent status who were prisoners of war were to be treated with due regard to their rank and age.[117] This regulation meant that the incoming officers could not be detained in the same facilities as enemy merchant seamen. In the end, some 177 German officers and 50 other ranks were sent to Farnham on 6 December 1942.[118] The reason why a limited number of other ranks were sent to Farnham was because officers were, according to Article 22 of the Geneva Convention, not allowed to perform manual labour.[119]

Camp Farnham had not been originally created for prisoner of war officers, and the newcomers were appalled by camp conditions. As they indicated to the consul general of Switzerland in Canada – who represented German interests in Canada – on 6 December 1942:

> As you perhaps know already, it concerns a camp of wooden barracks made for soldiers only, which is in every respect completely unsatisfactory for officers even for only temporary lodging for the following reasons: (1) Mass lodging in wooden huts

> without considering the various grades. Thus for older senior officers the same quarters only is available as for lieutenants and as for the youngest soldiers; (2) One washroom, shower and toilet for 89 men; (3) Huts are dilapidated. They represent the most primitive lodging that can be imagined. It is in contradiction to numerous rulings of the Geneva Convention and forms an immense contrast to the lodging which is given to the British officers in German camps – even in temporary camps.[120]

The prisoners' conclusion was that "this camp here was absolutely unfit in every respect for officers even for temporary accommodation."[121] As camp authorities recorded in the Farnham war diary, "They were pretty arrogant and considered the camp absolutely unfit for German officers, lighting inadequate and no cubicles or small rooms for senior officers and staff officers and many other complaints ... It would appear that they complained about being overcrowded at Bowmanville and Gravenhurst [Ontario] early in the summer but cannot understand why they were moved to this temporary camp just before Christmas. They say it must be considered as a punishment."[122]

Camp authorities tried to rectify some of the inmates' complaints. For instance, the prisoners were given permission to "divide their huts into cubicles with spare sheets belonging to them" and to improve lighting.[123] In the meantime, measures were being taken to find a suitable camp for the prisoner of war officers. Since the autumn of 1942, the Department of National Defence advised Military District 4 of its intention to create a prisoner of war officer camp in Quebec. At the time, the aim was to find a better location for the German officers who were temporarily incarcerated at Camp Farnham. Several properties were considered.[124] One such site was a golf club in Beaconsfield, near Montreal, which, according to Military District 4 officials, would be available as of mid-September 1942.[125] A different site was located seventy-five miles north of Montreal at St-Donat in the Laurentians. The complex consisted of a hotel and several large cottages. The advantage of this site was its isolation in hilly, sparsely populated countryside covered with heavy bush. But this advantage also created a problem of logistics, as only a single gravel road led to the site. This meant that in winter the camp would have to be supplied by snowmobiles.[126]

Another potential site, known as the Domaine de l'Esterel, was located at Ste-Marguerite in the Laurentians, some sixty-five miles north of Montreal. The property, like the one at St-Donat, had the advantage of being located in a hilly area with heavy bush. However, unlike the previous site, its location was a popular one for summer vacations and winter sports. Situated on a small plateau, the property was surrounded by three precipitous cliffs. Furthermore, the ground was very rocky and irregular, rendering tunnelling difficult if not impossible.[127] The site's hotel was then occupied by the Canadian School of Army Administration. Because this property could not be occupied until alternative accommodations could be provided for the school, the project was rejected.[128]

Military District 4 officials also tried to find a suitable location in southern Quebec. On 12 September 1942, they began investigating the possibility of using the Grande Ligne Mission's Feller Institute premises situated near Napierville in the village known as Grande Ligne.[129] Located on a 240-acre farm, the property originally served as a residential school for young men and consisted of a four-storey stone building, a brick gymnasium, eight frame houses, a large barn, and numerous smaller buildings.[130] Finding it suitable in every way to serve as an internment camp for prisoner of war officers, the Privy Council began negotiating with the Grande Ligne Mission. An agreement ensued on 24 November 1942 whereby the mission agreed to lease its property to the Crown for the sum of $15,000 per annum.[131] On 15 January 1943, Military District 4 headquarters authorized the creation of internment Camp No. 44 Grande Ligne.[132] Work began immediately to convert the Feller Institute into an internment facility.[133]

Meanwhile, the situation in Farnham remained problematic. When prisoners learned that a new camp was being built at Grande Ligne, they pressured authorities to accelerate their transfer to this new facility.[134] Conditions at Camp Farnham had not improved. Large groups of prisoners were still being housed in the same wooden barracks. As the prisoners indicated to Swiss representatives in April 1943, "The quarters are not different at all from those provided for corporals and men. The oldest staff officers have the same quarters as Lieutenants and the youngest privates. During the winter months, it was not possible to heat the barracks adequately. And with the spring thaw, water is running from the ceiling in various places. Taking everything into consideration, the quarters here can only be called unworthy of an officer."[135] This issue led to much debate when the consul general of Switzerland in Canada was requested by the German legation in Berne to inquire into the situation at Camp Farnham. As the Swiss consul indicated to the Canadian Department of External Affairs, "The German authorities have gained the impression from reports that camp Farnham is not suitable for officers and request an early removal to the new quarters. In case the transfer should not take place in the immediate future, I am asked to request the Canadian authorities to alleviate the principal deficiencies such as insufficient electric light, housing of officers in large dormitories, and lack of cupboards through which personal effects are damaged from exposure to dust."[136]

By contrast, Swiss representatives were much impressed by the facilities at Camp Grande Ligne. As one diplomat indicated following his inspection of the camp on 18 June 1943, "I was deeply impressed by the work undertaken in order to adapt perfectly the existing buildings and annexes to the new purpose. I think that, in spite of the natural difficulties due to the very hard winter and conditions prevailing in wartime, the Canadian authorities have done splendid work on this place and I have no doubt but that the new camp will be on the same level, in the way of comfort and facilities, as the Bowmanville officer's camp, which is universally regarded as being an outstanding place of internment."[137] Nevertheless, it was not until 28 June 1943, that all of Camp Farnham's inmates were transferred to Camp Grande Ligne. With Farnham now empty, Military District 4 authorities decided to use this camp as a regional headquarters for the Veterans Guard of Canada.[138]

In October 1943, a "scout school" was established within the camp to train VGC personnel. Its purpose was to familiarize guardsmen with the administration of internment camps and the detention of prisoners of war. Training sessions normally lasted four weeks.[139] Within this short time span, guardsmen were given classes on the Geneva Convention, chemical warfare, internal security, camp discipline, and first aid. They learned how to guard prisoners of war, conduct camp searches, read maps, uncover escape plans and detect tunnels; they also learned how to recapture escapees and operate the latest types of rifles, pistols, and machine guns.[140] The Camp Farnham scout school was a complete success. As camp authorities indicated in the Farnham war diary in February 1944, "This course has improved their [VGC guardsmen's] outlook on scout duties and they all agree that the knowledge they have gained in this course will be of great benefit to them in their future work."[141] The camp school was so successful that guardsmen from all over Canada came to Farnham to be educated. By April 1944, some 498 guardsmen were staying in the camp.[142] The operation came to an end when an order was received from the Department of National Defence on 13 May 1944, to close the camp altogether. No reason was given and the order came as a shock for camp authorities. As indicated in the camp's war diary, "This [closure] is an impossibility unless we just walk out and leave it on that short notice. No provisions were made of where staff and 160 attached men could go for rations and quarters."[143] Nevertheless, the camp was officially closed on 15 May 1944.[144]

Camp Farnham reopened on 18 September 1944 with the arrival of some 547 German officers and 49 other ranks from the United States.[145] Originally, these German prisoners had been shipped from the European theatres of war to the United States for internment. It was only upon their arrival in New York City that authorization was granted to send them north to Camp Farnham.[146] This step was taken to relieve the pressure on American internment camps, as the US government had agreed since the summer of 1942 to incarcerate in the United States many of the German prisoners of war captured by British and Commonwealth forces. This process was known as the 50/50 Sharing Agreement. Throughout the war, the American government detained some 380,000 German prisoners of war[147] in the United States as well as thousands of German "enemy aliens."[148] The agreement with the Americans was intended to alleviate the shortage of facilities in the Commonwealth, so it was only fair that Canada help the United States when it faced internment-related difficulties of its own. Camp Farnham was chosen for this purpose. Because it had been modified and improved between June 1943 and May 1944 for the Canadian troops, the internment camp in Farnham, like Camp Grande Ligne, was deemed acceptable for the detention of prisoners of war officers. The camp held German officers until it was closed in 1946.

Following the successful Allied landings in Normandy on D-Day, 6 June 1944, both British and Canadian forces began capturing German soldiers by the tens of thousands. The First Canadian Army had captured more than 25,000 German prisoners in Northwestern Europe alone by September 1944.[149] This number rose to about 66,000 by January 1945, creating serious problems in terms of accommodation. Although the bulk of these prisoners were being interned in camps located in France, Belgium, the Netherlands, and eventually Germany, the British government pressured the Canadian government in December 1944 to accept 50,000 additional inmates. At the time, some 34,000 German prisoners of war were already being held in Canada.[150] Compared with the efforts being made by the United Kingdom and the United States, each of which detained more than 300,000 German prisoners of war on their home soil, it appeared that Canada was not bearing its full share of the burden. Even British Commonwealth countries such as India and South Africa were taking a much bigger role, providing, as early as 1943, permanent accommodation to over 50,000 German prisoners.[151] London, therefore, hoped that Ottawa could help alleviate the prisoner of war accommodation problem in Northwestern Europe.[152] The Canadian war cabinet, however, refused the British request on 11 December 1944. Although the manpower crisis that prevailed in Canada with the introduction of conscription for overseas service in November 1944 served as excuse, the aggressive nature of some of the German prisoners of war in Canada had a much greater role. At the time, Canadian authorities were deeply concerned by the extremely tense situation that had developed at Camp Grande Ligne, where some of the most ardent Nazis had set up a secret organization known as the HARIKARI Club, whose sole purpose was to prepare suicide squads and saboteurs for an eventual mass escape that promised to bring death and destruction to the surrounding region, particularly Montreal (see Chapter 3). There were justifiable fears in Canadian military and government circles that similar plots might exist in other Canadian internment camps.[153] As Prime Minister William Lyon Mackenzie King wrote in his diary that same day, "Cabinet decided not to increase the number [of German prisoners of war in Canada] ... because those we have are a real menace. We have not sufficient adequate protection for them and there is reason to believe they are forming suicide squads which may cause great trouble later on."[154] General A.G.L. McNaughton, the minister of national defence, added that "reception of more than 7,000 [German prisoners of war] could not be recommended because of the additional strain on the already tight manpower situation and because of the potential risk involved."[155]

When the British authorities attempted on 16 January 1945 to "re-open the question of the acceptance of further German POW by Canada," King left the matter in the hands of the minister of national defence. Meeting with the British high commissioner to Canada on two occasions, McNaughton explained "that there are insurmountable practical difficulties here" and that "for the time being at any rate, no further commitments in this matter should be assumed by the Canadian government."[156] Norman A. Robertson, Canada's undersecretary of state for external affairs, reiterated McNaughton's reasons in his official report to the British High Commission on 22 January:

> No further commitments in this matter should be assumed by the Canadian government ... General McNaughton said that he had to reckon on the possibility of serious trouble with the prisoners of war now in Canada. There is a good deal of evidence of plans amongst the prisoners to make demonstrations and to attempt mass escapes. Many of the prisoners are desperate and fanatical Nazis ready to cause trouble even though this in effect means their committing mass suicide. He is taking steps to reduce this danger ... But in the meantime he cannot afford either to reduce the numbers of the guards or to lower the quality of the men employed as guards.[157]

It was also noted that because Canadian internment camps were widely spread across different parts of the country and guard forces were too far apart to provide mutual support in case of trouble, the number of guards assigned to each internment camp had to be much higher than in the United Kingdom or in Northwestern Europe. While close to 5,400 VGC guards were assigned to the 34,000 German prisoners of war already on Canadian soil, it was expected that 8,000 extra guardsmen would be required to guard 50,000 additional inmates. Such a figure was said to be "completely out of the question under present circumstances in Canada."[158] The British government was deeply disappointed by the Canadian decision and, ultimately, few additional German prisoners of war were sent to Canada.[159]

Canada's refusal to accept the United Kingdom's 50,000 German prisoners of war demonstrated how internment had caused severe strains on the Canadian home front. There is no doubt that should Ottawa have accepted this huge influx of internees, the internment camps of southern Quebec would have been affected. It would have meant a huge increase in the number of prisoners in the region and necessitated much larger and more complex internment camps. So far, the internment camps of southern Quebec had been fairly small. Never were there more than a thousand prisoners per camp. Compared with the large Alberta camps like Medicine Hat and Lethbridge, which both housed more than 10,000 inmates, the internment operation in southern Quebec was very limited in size.[160] Few German prisoners of war were sent to Canada after this dispute with the British government. Instead, the Canadian authorities decided to concentrate their efforts on the political re-education and de-Nazification of those prisoners of war already being held on Canadian soil, a topic that is covered in Chapter 5.

The Canadian government decided in February 1945 to create a reassessment camp for the purpose of re-educating German prisoners of war along democratic lines. At the time, the United Kingdom was developing its own re-education camps and was hoping that Canada could do the same. As a special British report indicated, "Sociologists and psychologists are of the opinion that the future peace depends first and foremost on a change in the German national character and the patterns of inter-personal relations." The document further stipulated the main purposes for operating such experimental facilities. First, such camps were to offer inmates training in social responsibility. This included valuable training and experience in spontaneous democratic leadership and social responsibility. The aim was to use the graduates for "practical employment under military government, control commission or elsewhere to form focus points of healthy influence within the German community." Second, these experimental camps were to study the effects of Allied propaganda, including re-education literature, films, and broadcasts. Also, re-education lectures, debates, and study groups were to be given in such facilities so that authorities could study the degree of social change among inmates. The main purpose of such facilities was to "help medical authorities to know how to coordinate and control German POWs."[161]

In March 1945, the Canadian government proposed two sites for the purpose of re-education. These were situated at Sorel and Montmagny in southern Quebec. After much discussion, only the Sorel option was retained.[162] It was this site, which was situated on the property of the military's Sorel Basic Training Centre, that became Internment Camp No. 45 Sorel.[163] The camp became operational on 9 May 1945, with the arrival of the camp's staff and the start of work on the site's facilities. Barbed wire fences were laid and the huts were repaired and improved.[164] The first prisoners arrived at the camp on 22 and 29 June 1945.[165] Unlike in other internment camps, prisoners were selected on a voluntary basis and came from all Canadian prisoner of war camps. The aim was to gather internees who were willing to cooperate with the Allies.[166] Furthermore, because military ranks and hierarchy had been abolished at Camp Sorel, the camp housed nearly as many German officers as other ranks, an anomaly in southern Quebec and elsewhere in Canada.[167]

Although hostilities with Germany officially came to an end on VE Day, 8 May 1945, German prisoners of war held in Canada were not immediately released despite the fact that the Geneva Convention stipulated that "the repatriation of prisoners shall be effected as soon as possible after the conclusion of peace."[168] Because the war still raged in the Pacific, Allied authorities decided to wait before sending the German prisoners of war back to Germany. However, the end of hostilities in the Pacific in mid-August 1945 and the unconditional surrender of Japan on 2 September 1945 did not alter the prisoners' status. Largely because of logistical problems involved in repatriating thousands of German prisoners back to Germany, the Canadian government decided to wait until early 1946 before starting to transfer the internees. Bringing home the tens of thousands of Canadian troops overseas was more of a priority. Authorities also wanted to continue to observe the effects of the re-education program on German prisoners. A third, less evident reason for the delays was the fact that Canadian officials were searching among prisoner of war populations for war criminals and witnesses to war crimes. In June 1945, for instance, three soldiers of the 12th SS Panzer Division who had been captured during the Normandy Campaign in 1944 were interrogated at Camp Farnham regarding the vicious and brutal murder by members of their unit of more than 150 Canadian soldiers.[169]

Because the United Kingdom was responsible for most of the prisoners of war detained in Canada, the Canadian government agreed to send all of its inmates to the British Isles. From there the prisoners would return to their "fatherland."[170] Camp Sorel was the first internment centre in southern Quebec to repatriate its prisoners. This camp's success at re-education played a role in the decision to release its prisoners quickly. Sorel inmates were to be repatriated to Germany as fast as possible in order to work for the Allied Control Commissions in the American and British zones of occupation.[171] All of Camp Sorel's prisoners were initially transferred to the United Kingdom on 4 March 1946.[172] The camp was not closed until 17 April 1946. The main reason for this delay was that camp staff were cleaning up the facilities.[173] The next camp to be closed in the region was Camp Grande Ligne. The process began on 16 April 1946, when the bulk of the camp's inmates were transferred to Camp Farnham and Camp Gravenhurst to await repatriation.[174] The camp was finally closed on 30 April 1946, following the disbanding of the camp staff.[175] For the Grande Ligne Mission's Feller Institute, the legal owner of the site, the closure of Camp Grande Ligne was more than welcome. Ever since the hostilities in the Pacific had come to an end on 14 August 1945, the Grande Ligne Mission board had applied pressure upon the Department of National Defence for the return of its property, "since our board plans to re-open the school at the earliest possible date." Because the lease stipulated that "the lessees shall have the right to so renew the present lease for only one period of one year subsequent to the termination of the present world war," the camp remained operational well into 1946.[176] When the camp closed, the site was immediately returned to the Grande Ligne Mission.[177] As for Camp Farnham, the bulk of its prisoners were transferred to the United Kingdom on 22 May 1946.[178] The Department of Labour took over most of the camp's huts on 6 June 1946.[179] The camp was officially closed on 17 June 1946.[180] Finally, all of Camp Sherbrooke's prisoners were repatriated on 11 June 1946, and the camp closed its doors on 14 June 1946.[181] The closure of Camp Sherbrooke marked the end of internment in southern Quebec.

By July 1946, only 4,000 German prisoners of war out of a total population of 34,000 remained in Canada. All of them were evacuated by November 1946, except for sixty inmates who had been hospitalized. The Canadian internment operation came to an end in January 1947, when these last internees were transferred to the United Kingdom.[182] It is interesting to note that more than 6,000 German prisoners of war had made applications to stay in Canada. Because the Geneva Convention stipulated that all prisoners had to be repatriated and because Canadian immigration policies were very strict about allowing in Germans, none of these internees were allowed to stay. Nevertheless, a great many immigrated to Canada in later years.[183]

Summary

The internment operation that evolved in southern Quebec was set up in haste. Although Canada began interning civilians of German descent as early as September 1939, the country's internment operation was still limited by the spring of 1940. Ottawa's decision to accept Britain's request to intern some 7,000 British enemy aliens and prisoners of war on Canadian soil in June 1940 led to the urgent creation of internment camps. With this in mind, three sites were chosen in southern Quebec: Camp Farnham, Camp Île-aux-Noix, and Camp Sherbrooke. The conditions at these internment centres showed how the Canadian authorities were unprepared to accept the huge influx of internees from the United Kingdom. The main problem was that not enough time had been allotted for the construction of these sites. As a result, none were properly ready to welcome internees. This situation created much discontent among the internees, especially at Camp Sherbrooke, where a hunger strike ensued. In short, the early days of internment in southern Quebec were not a success; however, over time, the region's internment operation improved and flourished.

When the bulk of the civilian refugees were released between 1942 and 1943, authority was granted to use the region's facilities to incarcerate German prisoners of war. The region's prominence as an internment centre was further enhanced by the construction of two new internment camps: Camp Grande Ligne in 1943 and Camp Sorel in 1945. The prisoner of war phase of southern Quebec's internment operation proved how flexible it had become. Each camp specialized in a certain type of operation: Sherbrooke focused on enemy merchant seamen; Farnham and Grande Ligne concentrated on German officers; and Sorel served as a re-educational facility. When the bulk of the region's inmates were repatriated in 1946 southern Quebec's internment operation came to an end.

3
Life behind Barbed Wire

Although most internees in the camps of southern Quebec were protected by the provisions of the 1929 Geneva Convention and enjoyed numerous privileges, the reality of being held captive generated physical and psychological strain. Camp authorities did their best to improve the prisoners' standard of living. They permitted inmates to benefit from the generosity and humanitarianism of international relief organizations and to create their own entertainments. But such attempts could never completely eradicate the pressures imposed by years of internment. Restricted mobility, sexual deprivation, social alienation, and the lack of material comforts all influenced the morale of captives. As a consequence, prisoners occasionally became restless and uncooperative. Moreover, dissension often led to a rise in escape attempts. Such behaviour forced camp authorities to consolidate their powers and increase the degree of camp discipline, a situation that only worsened conditions behind barbed wire. The divergent political and ideological orientations of prisoners were another factor that affected their behaviour. The presence of Nazis, anti-Nazis, and Communists inside the camps of southern Quebec often created a stressful and divisive environment with which camp authorities had to deal.

Camp Representatives

Captives were given the opportunity to appoint delegates to represent their interests, as stipulated by Article 43 of the Geneva Convention.[1] This provision permitted prisoners to administer their own affairs and enabled them to have some influence in the day-to-day running of the camp. A camp spokesman elected by the internees represented the communal interests of the entire inmate population and served as the official intermediary between the prisoners and camp authorities.[2] Only the most competent individuals were to be chosen for this administrative position. "For internal government, a lot depends on the camp leader and assistant camp leader and they are positions that have to be filled with considerable care," it was pointed out in the Camp Île-aux-Noix war diary.[3] Being a camp spokesman was no easy task. These individuals had to bear huge pressures and endure all sorts of demands from their brethren. They were often blamed by their peers for collaborating with camp authorities, a situation that forced one Camp Sherbrooke spokesman to resign in June 1941.[4]

Camp spokesmen were supported by the hut leaders. Inside each internment camp, internees were divided into small hut groups. Each barracks appointed a representative commonly known as a hut leader, who was responsible for the administration of and discipline in the living quarters. Canadian regulations described the duties of these individuals:

> The members of each group will select a representative who will assist the camp staff in maintaining order in his group and will bring to the notice of the staff any matter bearing upon the comfort or well being of the prisoners which requires attention. The appointment of such representatives shall be subject to the approval of the commandant. Prisoners of war are not permitted to set up any other form of administrative organization among themselves unless and until such form of organization has been submitted to the Director of Internment Operations and been duly approved.[5]

Camp spokesmen and hut leaders worked together. In *La ville sans femmes*, Mario Duliani maintained that the camps' internal administration resembled in many ways the municipal council of a small city. He explained how it functioned:

> Each barrack selects a representative, or hut leader. The twelve hut leaders are responsible for the activities taking place in their respective barracks. They exercise their functions in concert with the camp spokesman, who is elected by the internees themselves at a general assembly. The camp spokesman is the official intermediary between the internees and the camp commandant. The camp commandant passes his orders of what's allowed and what's prohibited on to him. The spokesman then transmits these orders at the biweekly assemblies, composed of the twelve hut leaders and some others, such as the hospital director and the administrator of the canteen, and together they discuss the camp problems that have arisen.[6]

Aside from this system, prisoners were not permitted to set up any other form of administrative organization among themselves unless it had been approved by the Department of National Defence.[7]

Protecting Powers

The proper treatment of internees was supervised by delegates from neutral nations. According to the Geneva Convention, each belligerent nation could choose a neutral country to act as its protecting power. According to Article 86 of the convention, "The representatives of the protecting power or their recognized delegates shall be authorized to proceed to any place, without exception, where prisoners of war are interned. They shall have access to all premises occupied by prisoners and may hold conversation with prisoners, as a general rule without witness, either personally or through the intermediary of interpreters. Belligerents shall facilitate as much as possible the task of the representative or recognized delegates of the protecting power."[8] Protecting powers were important assets in times of war. They enabled belligerents to know exactly how their captured military personnel were being treated by the enemy. They also forced belligerents to comply with the Geneva Convention. The protecting power reported back to the nation it represented. If this country was not happy with the treatment experienced by its prisoners, it could always retaliate on the enemy subjects it detained. Although the laws of war forbade such actions, retaliatory measures prevailed and remained one of the most important elements guiding the treatment of prisoners of war.

In the case of Germany, the protecting power was Switzerland. The Consulate General of Switzerland in Canada had as its main responsibility the requirement for personnel to visit internment camps; they were given complete freedom to inspect all buildings and to interview internees without a third party being present. At no time were the Swiss delegates to deliver to or receive from prisoners of war or internees any papers, documents, letters, or parcels.[9] Swiss representatives acted as mere inspectors. They also supervised exchanges of prisoners of war between Canada and Germany.[10] Civilian internees in southern Quebec refused contact with their Swiss protectors. Because most of these internees were German refugees, they objected to being represented by a country that was acting in the interests of Nazi Germany. These prisoners became in effect stateless, their interests represented by no one, because no power other than Switzerland was permitted to fill that role. Many civilian internees also resented being treated like prisoners of war. It was not until the arrival of the first prisoners of war in early 1942 that the Swiss consul general began taking care of inmates in the camps of southern Quebec.[11]

Relief Societies

Internees also depended upon the generosity of relief societies. According to Article 78 of the Geneva Convention, such organizations were authorized to visit internment camps and permitted to provide relief to prisoners."[12] Thousands of neutral relief organizations were created around the world during the Second World War, to help with the educational, spiritual, and recreational needs of prisoners of war. German internees benefited from the work of international organizations such as the Red Cross and the YMCA, as well as from the efforts of relief societies from Germany and neutral nations. Few Canadian relief agencies helped German prisoners, for their mission was to support Canadian soldiers, sailors, and airmen in captivity overseas.[13]

The International Committee of the Red Cross and the War Prisoners' Aid of the YMCA were the two main international relief organizations that addressed the needs of German internees. Both organizations were neutral, based in Switzerland, and offered their services to all belligerents. While the International Red Cross concentrated on the material, physical, and sanitary conditions in internment camps, the YMCA concerned itself with the intellectual, recreational, and religious needs of prisoners. This division ensured that the organizations complemented rather than duplicated each other's efforts.[14] On 28 August 1940, the International Red Cross received the honour of being the first relief organization to be permitted into Canadian internment camps, followed by the YMCA on 9 September 1940.[15] Representatives from these associations visited the camps of southern Quebec on numerous occasions.[16] During such visits, delegates talked with camp commandants and camp spokesmen. On such occasions, internees often requested special services from relief organizations, most often asking to purchase items, usually recreational equipment, that would alleviate the pressures of internment.[17]

In principle, internment camps provided the inmates with the basic necessities of shelter, food, clothing, and personal hygiene, in accordance with the Geneva Convention. Article 10 of the convention stipulated that prisoners of war were to be lodged in buildings or huts that were clean and safe. The premises had to be entirely free from damp and adequately heated and lighted. All precautions were to be taken against the danger of fire. The size of the dormitories was to be the same as for the troops of the detaining power, and they were to be provisioned with adequate fittings and bedding material.[18] Article 11 stated that the food ration of prisoners of war was to be equivalent in quantity and quality to that of the detaining power's troops. Article 12, which dealt with the inmates' dress, stated that clothing, including underwear and footwear, was to be supplied by the detaining power and be regularly replaced and repaired.[19] Finally, hygiene matters were described in Article 13, which said that belligerents were required to take all necessary measures to ensure the cleanliness and salubrity of the camps, and to prevent epidemics.[20] In essence, the Geneva Convention provided a working framework of obligations and set a minimum standard that all detaining powers had to meet.

Despite the fact that such responsibilities were mandated by international law, some Canadian citizens became envious of the internees' standard of living. Throughout the Second World War, goods were rationed in Canada. A reporter for the Toronto *Globe and Mail* noted in 1943 that "some Canadians obviously felt that rations for German POWs were better than they should be; 'we are giving our German prisoners of war better food than the average Canadian taxpayer can afford to buy.'"[21] Major Eric D.B. Kippen recalled that during his command at Camp Farnham "in some cases, people were jealous of the prisoners." While civil society faced rationing of some food items, prisoners were being fed Canadian Army rations, in accordance with the Geneva Convention. Kippen further recalled what some local ladies told him: "We're having an awful time getting certain articles of food and we understand that these refugees are getting, at no trouble at all, army rations."[22] Despite such complaints, Canadian authorities continued to provide inmates with basic necessities. Anything beyond this had to be acquired by the prisoners themselves, through relief organizations.[23]

Sending parcels to inmates was one of the prime activities conducted by aid societies. Parcels delivered to internment camps were divided into five types: (I) FOOD: canned goods, cheese, chocolates, etc.; (II) CLOTHING: uniforms, shoes, gloves, underwear, socks, etc.; (III) CIGARETTES AND TOBACCO; (IV) WELFARE: billiard tables, books, games, gramophones, musical instruments, sport articles, moving picture projectors, etc.; and (V) MIXED PARCELS.[24] However, there were certain restrictions. Relief organizations were prohibited from including such items as field glasses, photographic apparatuses, sextants, compasses, electric flashlights, maps, money, fountain pens, telegraphic and telephonic materials, radios, inflammable materials, spirits, liquors, wines, drugs, weapons, foreign literature, and civilian clothing.[25] In other words, they were banned from sending any items that might help or entice prisoners to escape or act in a rebellious fashion. All parcels had to be carefully examined by Canadian censors. To make certain that prisoners received their parcels, the German government requested, in the summer of 1941, that the Canadian government issue proper reports of all packages received in internment camps.[26] Canada's undersecretary of state for external affairs acquiesced to this request on 23 August 1941 by ordering the Directorate of Internment Operations to begin compiling summaries of parcels received in all Canadian camps and to send these reports to Germany.[27] Each form had to be completed and signed by the camp spokesman. It was then examined by the camp's commandant before being sent to Internment Operations headquarters in Ottawa for transmission to the Swiss consulate.[28]

Packages were sent by relief organizations from such countries as Argentina, Chile, Germany, Paraguay, Switzerland, and the United States.[29] Table 2.1 shows the large number of parcels received by southern Quebec camps between 1944 and 1946 and clearly demonstrates that the bulk of the packages came from Germany. (No sources exist concerning packages received by these camps in other years.) Such parcels enabled southern Quebec internees to enjoy numerous arts, sports, and educational activities. Recreational equipment sent by relief organizations contributed greatly to the welfare of the prisoners. While some internees turned to physical activities, others played music, made handicrafts, read books, and played games like poker, bridge, and bingo. Such activities, especially concerts, plays, and athletic competitions, helped raise morale.[30]

Recreational Activities

Provided with recreational equipment through relief organizations, prisoners could

Table 2.1

Number of parcels received in the camps, 1944-46

Relief organization	Type of parcel	Camp: Farnham	Sherbrooke	Grande Ligne	Sorel
German Red Cross	I	779	578	51	0
	II	245	1	657	88
	III	0	488	260	0
	IV	130	437	5,658	12
	V	1	51	39	0
Private individuals in Germany	I	368	27	3,146	1
	II	12	0	443	0
	III	1	25	23	0
	IV	8	3	98	0
	V	27	418	2,936	1
International Committee of the Red Cross	I	28	88	2	0
	II	1	3	8	17
	III	8	78	1	1
	IV	11	136	26	32
	V	13	54	41	6
Other aid societies and private sources outside Germany	I	296	79	126	4
	II	3	8	17	14
	III	3	147	8	2
	IV	127	490	121	225
	V	12	941	460	13

Note: The types of parcels were (I) Food; (II) Clothing; (III) Cigarettes and Tobacco; (IV) Welfare; and (V) Mixed.

Sources: Library and Archives Canada (LAC), RG-24, Reel: C-5375, File HQS 7236-1-11-40, "Statement of Parcels Received at Camp Farnham," 1944-46; LAC, RG-24, Reel: C-5375, File HQS 7236-1-11-42, "Statement of Parcels Received at Camp Sherbrooke," 1944-46; LAC, RG-24, Reel: C-5376, File HQS 7236-1-11-44, "Statement of Parcels Received at Camp Grande Ligne," 1944-46; LAC, RG-24, Reel: C-5376, File HQS 7236-1-11-45, "Statement of Parcels Received at Camp Sorel," 1944-46.

undertake numerous activities in the arts, education, and sports. Prisoners read books, played games, wrote letters and poems, painted, and made handicrafts. Music and sports were among the most important sources of communal entertainment. Both helped prisoners bond with one another and fostered a sense of community. Sherbrooke civilian internee Helmut Blame recalled that music "was of great importance, not only to us musicians but to the camp as a whole ... I think that in this environment of uncertainty and fear, which any type of prisoner behind barbed wire would feel, music helped a great deal to re-establish a kind of a balance and a kind of hope."[31] With musical instruments – which included accordions, basses, cellos, clarinets, flutes, guitars, harmonicas, saxophones, violins, and even pianos – lent by relief organizations, camp musicians formed orchestras and bands to entertain fellow prisoners.[32] During the civilian phase, internees benefited from the presence of numerous professional musicians of European renown. Many had been educated in the great musical academies of Vienna and Berlin, and they brought to the camps a taste of European operas and concert halls.[33] Some internees had a richer musical life behind barbed wire than they ever had before or after internment. "I cannot ever hear the *Wandererfantasie* by Schubert or the F-Minor *Ballade* by Chopin without thinking of Helmut Blume practicing these pieces ... in shed 'A' in Sherbrooke," recalled Eric Koch. Musicians were so engrossed with the "sound of music" that they often did not want to be disturbed when playing their instruments or listening to others. Such was the case at Camp Sherbrooke on 7 December 1941, when pianist John Newmark and his friends were listening to the radio broadcast of a concert held at Carnegie Hall by Arthur Rubinstein. When a fellow internee burst into the hut to announce Japan's aerial bombing of the American Pacific fleet anchored at Pearl Harbor in the Hawaiian islands, Newmark hushed him and whispered, "Quiet please. The war will go on for a long time, but Rubinstein is an old man. Who knows how long we'll still be able to listen to him!"[34] So good were the musicians at Camp Sherbrooke during the civilian phase that when concerts were given at the camp, locals would gather on the other side of the St. François River to hear the music.[35]

String quartets, jazz bands, brass bands, and choirs were formed in all southern Quebec camps, and there were also larger orchestras that played classical music, military marches, and even operatic music.[36] A forty-man orchestra specializing in classical music existed at Camp Grande Ligne during the prisoner of war phase, along with two dance bands and a smaller ensemble that played lighter hymns.[37] These bands usually gave weekly concerts.[38] Musicians also coordinated theatrical productions. During the phase of civilian internment, Camp Sherbrooke internee John Newmark directed numerous plays and often chose stories with which the prisoners could identify. For instance, the camp's first play was George Bernard Shaw's *Androcles and the Lion*, about the Roman persecution of Christians. Newmark chose this story because a parallel could be made with the persecution of the Jews in Germany. After all, many of Camp Sherbrooke's inmates at the time were German Jews. As Newmark recalled, the story was switched. The characters "were not called victims of Roman persecution but ... victims of Nazi persecution."[39]

Sports were very popular inside the camps of southern Quebec. Physical activity was considered vital for the well-being of inmates because it helped keep their bodies and souls in shape. Sport equipment was usually furnished through relief organizations. Prisoners were given the opportunity to practise a great variety of activities. These included badminton, baseball, basketball, boxing, fencing, gymnastics, handball, ice hockey, jiu-jitsu, table tennis, soccer, tennis, volleyball, and weightlifting.[40] At Camp Sherbrooke, starting in 1945, weekly skiing parties were organized.[41] Special courts and facilities were constructed in most camps by the prisoners themselves.[42] In each camp, inmates appointed sport supervisors whose task was to make arrangements for the necessary equipment, organize sporting events, teach various classes, and take part in competitions.[43] Prisoner of war officers would often encourage esprit de corps through team sports. Physical activities became so important during the prisoner of war phase that Camp Grande Ligne inmates even went as far as building their own sports ground in May and June 1944. It consisted of a five-hundred-yard oval running track, a hundred-yard track, jumping pits, tennis courts, and soccer fields. Camp authorities justified these facilities by saying, "These improvements will be of immense benefit to the generation of young Canadians who will come to the Feller Institute after the War."[44] So vital were sports to the well-being of prisoners that Camp Sorel authorities decided that Tuesday and Thursday afternoons would be used for physical activities: "These sport days are not holidays and no soldiers will leave the camp area."[45]

Numerous athletic competitions were held in the camps of southern Quebec. During such events, prisoners organized teams representing various regions of Germany and units of the German armed forces.[46] During such contests, the most successful prisoners won special prizes. During one such tournament held at Camp Sherbrooke in November 1944, the winners were awarded a variety of German sausages.[47] In the summer, soccer was the prisoners' favoured sport. It was played every evening in all of the camps.[48] As Camp Farnham authorities noted, "They [soccer players] are getting in shape, and also selecting members for future teams. Owing to the lack of football shoes, momentarily, the dress for these soccer practices is a bit unorthodox, but surely catches the eye. Namely, shorts and jackboots!"[49] In winter, ice skating and hockey were most popular. Ice rinks were created in all of the camps and were maintained by the prisoners. Although skating was a novel activity for most Germans, the inmates' interest in this form of outdoor recreation never seemed to fade.[50] In March 1945 at Camp Farnham, for instance, a hockey tournament was organized by the internees following the viewing of a short film on ice hockey. Camp authorities recalled that "the rink is just crowded, POW trying to master some of the play pictured in the film. One can see these officers rushing up and down the ice with fervour, their lack of hockey-technique being made up by enthusiasm, and even hard spills not curbing their affection for the game."[51]

Physical and Psychological Strains

Recreational activities enabled inmates to ease the conditions behind barbed wire, but they could not prevent them from experiencing physical and psychological strain. The pressures imposed by years of internment could not be eased overnight. In his book entitled *Essai sur la psychologie du prisonnier de guerre*, Jean Cazeneuve described the pressures imposed by years of internment. Captured by the Germans in 1940 while defending his native France from invasion, Cazeneuve lived the remainder of the war in a prisoner of war camp.[52]

The privation of material comfort was the most important strain that internees had to endure. Cazeneuve wrote, "The food, the sleep, the lodging arrangements, the furniture, the clothing, and the means to protect oneself against changes in temperatures constitute a noticeable regression in standard of living from that previously experienced in civil society. These factors are among the most elementary causes of suffering for captives."[53] For the German prisoners incarcerated in southern Quebec, exposure to the cold Canadian weather was one source of physical discomfort, and adaptation was the only remedy. Psychological discomfort, on the other hand, was at its most acute when prisoners recalled the vanished luxuries of their former lives. A sufficient and healthy portion of camp food could be seen as inadequate when compared with fine cuisine. As Cazeneuve noted, "an individual who did not possess any elements of comparison would not suffer and would not even talk of privation ... We are unhappy when an electrical failure or blackout ruins an evening, but is it fair to assume that our ancestors who illuminated their nights with oil lamps felt deprived of a luxury that they did not even know existed?"[54] Acceptance of one's fate was the only solution to combat psychological suffering.

But adaptation and acceptance did not always eliminate physical and psychological strains. While prisoners became more accustomed to life behind barbed wire over time, they could never totally forget lost pleasures.[55] According to one Sherbrooke civilian internee, prisoners there became so demoralized by the camp's environment that some attempted suicide while others suffered nervous breakdowns.[56]

Restricted mobility was another stress on prisoners. Limited to camp enclosures, prisoners were often struck by "barbed wire psychosis," also known as "barbed-wireitis" or "stalag syndrome." This term was coined in 1919 by A.L. Vischer to describe a psychological condition that afflicted prisoners of war and civilian internees.[57] Vischer identified a number of symptoms of the so-called disease, including intense irritability, difficulty concentrating, restlessness, memory failure, moodiness, extreme lethargy or listlessness, suspicion or paranoia, depression, feelings of intense hatred, and even violent impulses. Historian Jonathan Vance has outlined some of the factors identified by Vischer that produced this state of mind:

> The first is simply the loss of freedom, the prisoners' inability to do as they please, when they please ... Monotony, the realization that every day was the same as the last, is also a factor. This lack of variety is complicated by the fact that it is indefinite ... The

> POW has no way of knowing if his captivity will last weeks or months or years; there is no release date to look forward to, and this accentuates the prisoners' feeling of helplessness. The lack of privacy is also important. In the cramped confines of a prison camp, it is virtually impossible to get a moment to oneself ... Finally, Vischer identified sexual deprivation as a factor in barbed-wire disease.[58]

As Cazeneuve indicated, "barbed wire psychosis rests on the simple conscience of an impossibility. Even if nothing incited the prisoners to cross the wire fence, the simple knowledge that such an interdiction existed around the camp would be enough to generate intense feelings of discontent among prisoners. The barbed wire represents for the mind an interdiction."[59] This restriction of personal freedom created both monotony and boredom. As Cazeneuve explained, "even if we could give the prisoners all the material goods and delicacies in the world, the simple fact of being imprisoned would continue to make life behind barbed wire extremely difficult."[60]

"Barbed wire psychosis," known to most southern Quebec prisoners as "internitis," contributed greatly to the inmates' mental suffering. In *Deemed Suspect*, Eric Koch described the symptoms as "a combination of despondency, touchiness, and worst of all, self-absorption and self-pity."[61] A southern Quebec internee later explained that "it is hell on earth mentally to wake up in the middle of the night ... and to say to yourself, 'I'll never get out of here,' 'This war is not going to end in my lifetime,' and 'They'll keep me here for life.' That feeling was the worst of internment."[62] This sense of isolation led some prisoners to consider suicide. As one Sherbrooke prisoner of war explained, "One slowly declines here morally. One has days that one would like to take one's own life. Nobody can imagine what it means to be five years behind barbed wires."[63] On 26 February 1943, one Farnham prisoner of war attempted to commit suicide. Camp authorities reported, "One POW officer missing off the evening count was found in an unconscious condition in a bath with a cut on wrist in the officers' recreation room with the door locked. He apparently tried to commit suicide."[64] Overall, camp authorities acknowledged that some prisoners suffered from captivity-induced psychosis. As noted in the Camp Île-aux-Noix war diary in September 1940,

> The trouble is of course that men behind barbed wire develop various complexes and one very definite one is to magnify molehills into mountains and there are "many tempests in the compound teacup." A vague disease known as "barbed wireitis" seems to develop in some prisoners. It is a combination of languidness, fatalism and despair and in some cases expresses itself violently and in a devil-be-care way, and in others by passive resistance. During the last two days, there have been symptoms of this malady and it has been necessary for the commandant to address the camp and section leaders using a mixture of sternness, philosophy, tact and salesmanship.[65]

The absence of women was another factor that influenced the prisoners' psyche. The lack of females created a suitable climate for sexual obsession. Unable to fulfill their sexual instincts, prisoners would often talk or dream about women. Jean Cazeneuve remarked, "The lost pleasures constantly invade the minds, the dreams, and conversations of prisoners. No longer able to be physically expressed, sexual instincts take the form of intellectual reflection instead in order to survive."[66] Mario Duliani described the phenomenon in *La ville sans femmes*. Interned briefly at Camp Farnham, Duliani recalled that women dominated the collective thoughts of prisoners.[67] "This is the city without women ... Among men we speak of women. We speak of them in the morning, in the afternoon, in the evening. At times, at night, in the barracks there is agitation, unrest, uproar. We go on talking of women. Of those we have loved, of those we still love, of those we hope to love. And this irritates, fatigues, riles us. It gets on our nerves ... In each barrack coloured pictures form shrilling blotches on walls, on windows, on the boxes that separate the bunks, even on the back of chairs. They are scraps of newspapers and magazines that show naked, or almost-naked women, in lascivious, provocative poses. The photos have been cut out from *Esquire*, and other periodicals, by comrades bursting with sexual urges. Through this ingenuous iconography the absent woman remains ever present."[68] This nostalgia for past pleasures was often expressed in art. In their paintings, poems, and sculptures, prisoners would idealize the female body. Ann Cowan of the Canadian Jewish Congress observed this phenomenon when she visited Camp Île-aux-Noix in 1941. When Cowan arrived to interview civilian inmates regarding their future liberation, the camp commandant informed her that the prisoners had not seen a woman in two years. For her personal security, she was escorted into the camp's compound by armed guards with fixed bayonets. As she recalled, the prisoners were eager to be interviewed. They gave her presents that included poems, watercolours, and a wooden ashtray.[69] A Grande Ligne prisoner of war recalled an episode involving a note from a woman outside the wire: "One day, we found an envelope in the middle of our gardens. Inside was a white sheet of paper with a message: 'My name is Mimi, I am not an enemy.' Just imagine the popularity that this letter had among us inmates ... During the following weeks, everybody went to the gardens hoping to find other messages from Mimi. Although no letters were ever found, it gave us much hope."[70]

Idealization created distorted views about women. As Cazeneuve explained, "The portrait that prisoners remember of women is not a photographic cliché. It is a moving image that becomes more and more distorted from reality as time passes." Without any physical contact with women, prisoners relied on their imagination to fill the void. As a result, what they remembered of mothers, sisters, wives, and sweethearts over years of internment became increasingly different from reality. Prisoners often expressed feelings of "extreme susceptibility" whenever they resumed contact with reality and measured for themselves the differences, explained

Cazeneuve. This was particularly the case when a prisoner received a letter from home and realized first hand that the "real" woman he loved would not express herself in the same manner as the "ideal" woman he had created in his imagination.[71] This reality often generated feelings of abandonment: "Those who had a wife or a lover back home, and have lived here for a long time, find that the Wall of Distance has turned into the Wall of Forgetfulness. And it takes considerable strength of character not to be crushed by discouragement."[72] The absence of women made some prisoners aggressive. Unable to satisfy their sexual needs, they would become restless and violent. Sherbrooke civilian internee John Newmark remarked that "when you're in prison as we were, with no sex, food takes place instead ... to the extent that I've seen grown men with knives going at each other for a bigger steak."[73]

Only on rare occasions did prisoners came into contact with women. Eric Koch claimed that "if you were a favorite of the Sergeant Major, you were sometimes allowed to go along on the garbage truck to the city dump [and] see downtown Sherbrooke. The truck driver was a nice man, and on at least one occasion he took the favorite to the entrance of the local whorehouse, put three dollars in his hand and said, 'Go in, have a good time. I'll pick you up in half an hour.'"[74] Needless to say, this charitable act was done in complete defiance of camp regulations. Another incident occurred at Camp Sherbrooke in January 1941, when one of the guards proved to be involved in illicit activities with three internees. Fraternization between camp personnel and internees was strictly forbidden. Guards were to refrain from communicating with any prisoners unless it was in the execution of their duties. The situation began when a guard gave an internee artist a photograph of his daughter so that the man could draw a sketch of her. In exchange, the guard agreed to give the artist a bottle of rum, food from the camp staff's kitchen, and a few bottles of beer. Furthermore, the prisoner was given the opportunity to write to the guard's daughter. The situation deteriorated when other internees began writing to the young girl, begging her to send letters to friends and relatives in the United States and to other Canadian internment camps. When higher authorities learned of the situation, the offending internees were sentenced to twenty-eight days' detention and the guard was tried by court martial.[75]

When circumstances permitted and internees were able to meet women, they often did not know how to react. Years of seclusion and inexperience took their toll. When a small group of young Farnham refugees was taken to Montreal for matriculation examinations in the fall of 1941, the Canadian Jewish Congress organized a party that was attended by Jewish girls. According to one internee,

> It's the strangest experience ... you think you sort of immediately go and grab them ... but most of us really didn't know how to handle the situation at all ... The girls were very nice looking and we had sort of bragged among ourselves what we would do

> with those girls ... Some of them were going to go right to bed with them ... I doubt that I as much as said ten words to a girl and I found that experience really traumatic ... suddenly to be with the opposite sex after all this time. And actually, I had a sleepless night after that. I was so mad at myself for not taking more advantage of the opportunity.[76]

Separation from women also contributed to homosexuality. Not much is known about such sexual behaviour in the camps of southern Quebec, but a few inmates claimed that homosexual activities were an everyday occurrence.[77] According to Eric Koch, who was interned at Camp Sherbrooke during the civilian phase, the absence of women had a predictable influence on the lives of many inmates. Koch claimed that most of the men who engaged in homosexual behaviour were straight before and after their internment, although "a small number of men ... had been gay before their internment, and some of them may have had to leave Germany or Austria for that very reason."[78]

In one or two camps, special areas were entirely "reserved" for gay activities. Couples lived together, and some older men found it prestigious to be seen with young boys. There were apparently some jealous fights, and some young boys who sold themselves. Others, Koch explained, found such activities deeply repugnant and made every effort to protect the young from being exploited. "In the end there was only one therapy which worked," wrote Koch. "Girls."[79] Homosexual activity remained strictly circumscribed, especially during the prisoner of war phase. Under Nazi law and belief, homosexuality was a serious infraction punishable by death; in the opinion of the German armed forces, homosexuals posed a serious threat to discipline. According to historian Chris Madsen, "Many German POWs felt a strong moral dislike and fear of homosexuals ... Active gays often faced the full wrath of an enraged prisoner population."[80]

Social alienation was another cause of psychological strain. Isolated from their families, friends, and colleagues, and cut off from their customs, prisoners often became "homesick." According to Jean Cazeneuve, "the breakage of all links with home causes important internal turmoil in all prisoners, which translates into sentiments of regret, sadness, social alienation, and results in the complete abandonment of long-held personal habits."[81] This feeling of alienation was accentuated by the prisoners' realization that life went on at home without him. Although the internment camps were "micro-societies" that replicated many features of "home," inmates remained nostalgic for their native countries and for their past lives: "Intense suffering is encountered whenever the prisoner realizes that life in his home country continues without him, when he finds out reading newspapers or letters that society easily prevails without his presence, that the void filled by his absence has been filled by other people, and that someone else is doing his job. For many prisoners, this sense of social abandonment results in a sort of internal death."[82] The only remedy was adaptation to life behind barbed wire. Alienation was also intensified by the prisoners' recognition that Canadian society flourished outside the camps. Prisoners were often reminded that life continued in the "outside world" through Canadian newspapers and magazines. Rare contact with Canadian civilians also confirmed this awareness. Knowing that communities prospered beyond the barbed wire was a source of frustration and envy, sometimes enticing prisoners to escape. Authorities were always alert to the threat of illicit correspondence between prisoners and civilians, and contact between them was kept to a strict minimum.[83] In this respect, authorities could cite Article 2 of the Geneva Convention, which stipulated that prisoners were to be protected from public curiosity at all times.[84]

Public curiosity was a major problem. Although Canadian propaganda pictured the Germans as "bloodthirsty Huns and savages," Canadian civilians still wanted to see for themselves who was behind the barbed wire. According to a Sherbrooke resident, "My mother would worry ... about us going out at night when there was an escape that was sounded ... The thing that my mother did not know was that these prisoners of war used to go skiing. They would walk with guards to the Bowen Hill, and they would go down and ski down there. Us girls would ski down the hill ... and we'd kind of talk to these prisoners ... They weren't allowed to say much to us because of the guards. We never got near the fence."[85] Some civilians even approached the camps' enclosures. One Sherbrooke woman admitted, "We used to walk up there ... where the prisoner of war camp was and look at those fellows through the fence. We had no business there at all, but I remember tracking up there on a nice fall day and seeing those German prisoners through the fence ... I never got any closer to them than that, but that was off limits, and we didn't go often."[86] The problem became so frequent at Camp Farnham in 1942 that warning signs had to be posted around the camp because curious motorists and pedestrians often approached the camp's periphery.[87] Such incidents enabled the prisoners to see, if only for a slight moment, faces from the "outside world." The sight of Canadian civilians was a constant reminder that while they were incarcerated, others were free.

Dissension

One result of physical and psychological strain was dissension among the prisoners, which they expressed through numerous forms of protest. In their acts of rebellion, internees exploited the Canadian government's fear of German reprisals against Canadian POWs. Retaliatory measures were common between belligerents and the Canadian government remained committed to the principle of reciprocity. "The treatment of prisoners in Canada," wrote historian Jonathan Vance, "was seen to be inextricably linked to the treatment of Canadians in enemy hands, and the government generally lodged a protest when conditions affecting

Canadians in Axis hands were markedly worse than those experienced by POWs in Canada."[88] It is important to note that the German government adhered to similar policies. Understanding this situation, German internees in Canada often pressured camp authorities to cave in to their demands.

The power of retaliatory means was well demonstrated during the shackling controversy of 1942-43. The crisis began in the immediate aftermath of the ill-fated Dieppe raid of 19 August 1942 when some 1,000 British and 5,000 Canadian troops crossed the English Channel and landed on the French coast. Angered by the discovery of operational orders that directed British and Canadian troops to bind the hands of prisoners to prevent them from destroying documents, the German government threatened to handcuff all Allied soldiers captured at Dieppe. The British sent a mollifying reply, but the crisis escalated when German soldiers captured during a British commando raid on the occupied English Channel island of Sark in early October 1942 had their hands tied. German authorities responded by shackling some 1,376 Canadian and British prisoners of war on 8 October. Immediately, Britain threatened to shackle an equivalent number of German prisoners in the United Kingdom and in Canada. When Germany raised the stakes by chaining additional prisoners, raising the numbers to more than 4,100, the United Kingdom requested the Canadian government to approve the handcuffing of more than 3,800 German prisoners of war on 10 October. Four Canadian internment camps were chosen to implement this request: No. 20 Gravenhurst, No. 21 Espanola, No. 23 Monteith, and No. 30 Bowmanville.[89]

Canadian officials encountered resistance in all four camps. At both Espanola and Monteith, the prisoners resorted to passive resistance, while those at Gravenhurst "threw their shackles into the stoves, rendering them useless and making it necessary to locate additional supplies." Resistance was even stiffer at Bowmanville, where a full-scale riot occurred. Refusing to be handcuffed, German officers barricaded themselves in the mess hall and their barracks on 10 October. Armed with hockey sticks, baseball bats, broom handles, and other homemade weapons, the inmates were able to repulse the camp staffs' attempt to dislodge them. The guards fired several warning rifle shots during the action, and one prisoner was wounded. On 11 October, several hundred Canadian soldiers arrived in the camp as reinforcements. At around noon on 12 October, the Canadians charged the buildings, using unloaded rifles with fixed bayonets, hardwood clubs, and high-pressure fire hoses. As they moved into the compound, the storming squads were met by a hail of stones, bottles, and bricks. The battle raged for more than six hours. When it was all over, approximately eighty Germans and twenty Canadians suffered injuries. In the end, the riot was suppressed and the prescribed shackling was carried out. To ensure that no trouble re-emerged, some of the prisoners were eventually moved to the other officer camp at Gravenhurst.[90] When the British and Canadian governments decided to unshackle the German prisoners in early December 1942, many of the ringleaders of the three-day "Battle of Bowmanville" were immediately transferred to Camp Farnham, and then to Grande Ligne a few months later.[91] It seems that Canadian authorities were anxious to isolate these troublemakers from the rest of the officer populations at Bowmanville and Gravenhurst.[92] The shackling controversy ended in November 1943 when Germany finally agreed to unchain the Canadian and British inmates.[93]

The Canadian government's fear of German reprisals encouraged the internees to adopt rebellious behaviour. One form of pressure used by prisoners was to complain to the Swiss consul general. Acting as the German prisoners' protecting power, Swiss delegates to the camps had to report all incidents to the German government. To avoid this situation, camp authorities would agree to improve treatment of the prisoners. One such incident occurred at Camp Farnham in October 1942 when the crew of the German merchant ship *Gonzenheim* complained to the Swiss delegation that they were not being treated properly as prisoners of war. According to these enemy merchant seamen, they possessed identification papers that integrated them into the German Navy. The fact of the matter was that the German government wrongfully assumed that all captured merchant seamen were to be treated as prisoners of war. Their logic was that, under German law, merchant mariners were employed by the state and, therefore, served as an arm of the military in times of war. But Article 81 of the Geneva Convention stipulated that "persons who follow the armed forces without directly belonging thereto ... who fall into the hands of the enemy, and whom the latter think fit to detain, shall be entitled to be treated as prisoners of war, provided they are in possession of an authorization from the military authorities of the armed forces which they were following."[94] Although the Swiss were skeptical of the prisoners' statement, they conducted a proper investigation and wrote a report that said:

> Captain Krieger, of the M/S *Gonzenheim*, complains that he and his crew are entitled, under Article 81 of the Geneva Convention, to be treated as prisoners of war since they were at the time of capture furnished with the papers necessary to establish such a right. While it is not thought likely that such papers could have been issued to the crew of a merchant ship or, if issued, would substantiate such a claim, ... inquiry is being made in the United Kingdom to determine what papers, if any of this sort were taken from the prisoners at the time of capture ... The problem is that Article 81 was not applicable to merchant seamen or members of the reserve forces when employed in auxiliary capacity to army forces.[95]

Passive resistance was another method inmates used to express their discontent, and their chief tool was the hunger strike. By refusing to prepare meals or to eat, prisoners threatened the Canadian authorities with the possibility that their health might be affected, which could result in German reprisals. Belligerent nations often did not care to find out whether it was the prisoners or the camp administrators who were responsible for the health problems, and chose simply to blame enemy authorities.[96] To limit the chances of retaliation on Canadian prisoners of war, camp authorities usually nodded to the prisoners' demands. Such was the case at Camp Farnham during the civilian internment phase when a hunger strike was initiated to oppose the punishment of an internee who had not made his bed right. As a result of the strike, the internee was immediately released, with camp authorities telling the inmates, "We cannot deny you food because if we do that, in one camp in Germany, our soldiers will also be denied food."[97]

Another popular form of protest was the postal strike. Inmates stopped sending letters home, hoping to cause their worried families and friends to put pressure upon the German government to make formal inquiries.[98] Prisoners also resorted to labour strikes on the special work projects conducted by the camps. Such a strike occurred at Camp Sherbrooke on 3 September 1943, when the prisoners noticed that the camp censor had thrown away all of their incoming mail without even having opened it. The prisoners' spokesman told the camp authorities, "I am sorry to have to inform you that we have evidence and witnesses that the camp censor has destroyed and thrown away incoming mail from Germany as well as England dated June and July, 1943 destined for prisoners of war ... This matter has aroused considerable excitement and protest from the community of this camp and I would herewith inform you that I am not responsible for the consequences resulting out of this and I shall have to report this matter to the Protecting Power and the Director Prisoners of War."[99] The internees started a labour strike that forced camp authorities to initiate an investigation that resulted in the censor's arrest. Realizing that suitable action was being taken, the prisoners returned to work.[100]

Sometimes, inmates adopted riotous behaviour, including camp mutinies. Such incidents were rare, but one such case occurred at Camp Farnham during the civilian internment phase in late September 1941. At the time, a strong Communist movement had grown inside the camp. As camp authorities indicated earlier that month, "A Communistic element among the refugees is becoming most assertive and vocal ... An effort is being made to discover who the ring-leaders of the Communists are."[101] They further stated that "there are about ten to twelve professional politicians and Communist leaders who work with indirect and undercover methods. Someday their efforts will probably blossom forth in some kind of riot or trouble."[102] The camp Communists became a nuisance, especially as they classified non-Communists as Nazis and began harassing them.[103] It is important to note that the internees of this camp were divided over the issue of Communism. Camp authorities noted that "it is quite apparent that the refugees in this camp are a mixed group as previously reported and differences consists not only of race and religion but there are differences of a violent political and social nature. Communists as previously reported are very strong."[104] Rioting emerged when camp authorities decided to transfer seven of the most politically active Communists to Camp Île Ste-Hélène on 26 September.[105] The process began in the early morning when the camp spokesman, who was a Communist, requested that "the movement be immediately cancelled, [and] if it was not a hunger strike would immediately commence." In order to place more pressure, he further added that "heads would fall over this move." Camp authorities recorded that "there was great commotion, excitement and high feeling in the compound over the whole matter."[106] The riot that ensued was described by Major Eric D.B. Kippen who was then camp commandant:

> At approximately 1200 hours on Friday, September 26th the hunger strike started and the refugees removed the rations from the kitchen and brought them down to the main gate of the camp although much was strewn over the compound ... The refugee canteen was closed by the compound hut leaders at 1400 hours when the [seven] refugees were embussed and left for Camp "S" [Île Ste-Hélène]. This was the cause of tremendous excitement in the compound and semi-rioting and general confusion. Just before the bus was about to start three rifle shots were discharged into the air outside the guard room and this had the effect of calming down the compound for awhile ... After the bus had left, the various factions in the compound were involved in disturbances and some of the refugees were injured although none very seriously, which was more by good luck than by anything else. During the rest of the afternoon the sentries were doubled and the police force inside the compound was increased so as to give full protection and furthermore to protect groups of refugees from each other. Attacks were made on individuals and on groups. During the balance of the day the agitation continued ...
>
> The hunger strike continued all day during the 27th and there was outbreaks of rioting and attempted attacks on groups and individuals. Approximately 100 to 125 refugees broke away from the strike and managed to get some breakfast and lunch although their fires were put out on several occasions by raids made on the kitchen. The compound police were able to control the situation very well but at times groups were able to break through their cordon. It was necessary to move about 51 refugees out of the various huts and they were segregated in the quiet room. This was done for their protection ...
>
> The next day, September 28th camp representatives were interviewed and given instructions to stop the hunger strike. They were given until 1430 hours ... and at that time they reported that the hunger strike was over. During the balance of the day there were a number of disturbances but they were small incidents. On September 29th the situation improved considerably and by noon of September 30th it was considered normal.[107]

This riot, which was caused by the tense political atmosphere that reigned among Camp Farnham inmates, made it necessary to segregate the prisoner compound. While such violent incidents were rare, they clearly showed the intensity of communal actions inside the camps.

Dissension was also expressed through illicit activities. Hoping to escape the hardships of life behind barbed wire, prisoners often consumed alcohol to the point of drunkenness. Inebriation, although vigorously prohibited by Canadian officials, was a serious problem inside the camps. To control this phenomenon, beer was made available to the internees on a limited scale. Canadian regulations stipulated that internees were permitted to purchase beer daily, during a period not exceeding one hour. No limits were to be placed upon the amount purchased during the hours of sale, but strict control was to be maintained to prevent drunkenness. The permission to purchase beer was considered a privilege and could be withdrawn at any time by the camp commandant and disciplinary action taken against offenders should the privilege be abused in any way.[108] Camp authorities did their best to prevent drunkenness and to restrict prisoners from having access to other alcoholic beverages, but they could not prevent the clandestine making of such drinks. Prisoners did their best to concoct their own hard liquor, known as "moonshine." Eckehart Priebe, who was a Camp Grande Ligne prisoner of war, described the process: "First, one needs an electrical hot-plate. The base was fashioned from some clay we found in the compound, the bedsprings provided the wire to make the coil. The big pot to go on the plate originally contained two pounds of tobacco, the copper piping for the cooling and drip-off process was 'requisitioned' from the overflow tubes of the toilets. The fruit used as basic ingredients came from the canteen with which we had a 'contact' for all the rotten apples or peaches they could not sell. The biggest difficulty was to hide the equipment."[109]

Drinks could be made from all sorts of ingredients, including peaches, apples, and cacao, but certain precautions were necessary, according to Priebe: "Came the 'historic' moment when the first drop was about to appear at the lower end of the piping. We crowded around the originator of the project, spoon at the ready. He was eager to exercise his privilege of first tasting. Full of anticipation he lifted the first teaspoonful of self-made booze, brand name 'Grande Ligne special,' to his tongue, immediately dropped it and blew the precious booze all over the place. We learned the hard way, that the first drops of such a distillation were 100% pure alcohol which, like acid, can burn a hole in your tongue."[110]

Canadian authorities often conducted searches to find stills and moonshine ingredients. On 13 September 1941, for instance, the Camp Farnham authorities reported, "Four large demi-jars of wine confiscated in the compound today. The wine is really fermented potato juice, raisins, etc. It is a very strong wine and from time to time jars of it are spotted by the compound police and confiscated."[111] The same situation applied at Camp Sherbrooke between January and March 1944 when camp authorities confiscated at least four homemade stills.[112]

Illicit activities also included using illicit radio receivers. As Eckehart Priebe recalled, "The POW is always hungry for news; news from home, news from the war theatres, news of things to come, news, news, news. He is a notorious optimist, always expecting good news as bad news from the war fronts would prolong his confinement."[113] Radio sets were improvised by the prisoners themselves. As Camp Farnham authorities noted in March 1941, "It has been brought to our attention that parts of sound projectors for films can be used in the manufacture of improvised wireless sets by experts in wireless. No doubt there are many such experts among the prisoners of war and internees. Therefore, those camps, to which sound projectors have been donated or loaned, must take the necessary precautions to prevent any prisoner from having the opportunity of taking any parts from or in any way tampering with the apparatus."[114] Eckehart Priebe explained how a radio was created by Grande Ligne inmates during the prisoner of war phase:

> We had a particularly gifted Air Force Reserve officer ... one of those ingenious types who can make anything from nothing. Together with some Navy engineers he started building a shortwave receiver from tin cans, pieces of wire, aluminum foil, even toothbrushes. The result was a most amazing contraption lacking only the most important ingredients, the tubes ...The Canadians were the only possible source ... A request was submitted and returned with the condition that we could have an amplifier, but only on our word of honour that it would only be used for concerts with the record player ... A few weeks later we had our record player and amplifier ... Our experts went to work and a few days later the "voice of Germany" came through loud and clear behind Canadian barbed wire.[115]

Only a handful of POWs knew of the existence and whereabouts of this new source of information, recalled Priebe. It was used under the most elaborate of precautions twice a day. While stenographers worked feverishly, watchful eyes protected the listening post from the inquisitive guard patrols. Searches were often initiated by the Camp Grande Ligne authorities to find this primitive shortwave receiver, which was known as the *Staubsauge*. As Priebe explained, "It was concealed in window sills, double-bottom self made easy chairs, even double bottoms of record containers or in gymnastic equipment, such as medicine-balls when the receiver had to be moved."[116] In the end, this homemade radio was found in February 1945.[117]

Secret correspondence was another form of illicit activity. Although Article 36 of the Geneva Convention stipulated that all detaining powers were to allow prisoners of war to send a specific number of letters and postcards each month, inmates often tried to transmit valuable information to individuals in Germany and other Canadian internment camps in their correspondence. It was largely for this reason that Canadian censors read all prisoners' mail and scratched out any information that was considered of sensitive importance to the Allied cause or the enemy.[118] Daniel Costelle described this situation in *Les prisonniers:*

> The letters were read by censors, who scratched out any words or sentences incorporating military information of any sort. The bags of letters were then shipped overseas aboard neutral ships – Swedish, South American, or Swiss – and were then brought to Marseilles, where they were placed in armoured railway cars and sent to Geneva. They were then transported to the German border and handed over to the Germans. The letters were then re-opened and read by German censors, who struck out any information that might resemble praise of life in North America. It was between entire paragraphs scratched out with black ink by censors that the parents, women, and children of prisoners could try to guess the conditions in which their loved ones lived overseas ... The same procedure occurred when next of kin sent letters to prisoners. In some cases, censors scratched out entire pages.[119]

Letters could not contain controversial subjects such as references to "armed forces, political situation, numbers interned, passages from documents or books, cipher code, secret writing, shorthand, marking signs, underlinings, criticisms of, or reference to the business of the camp or conduct of any other prisoner of war ... Letters must not contain political propaganda or abusive, insolent, derogatory, or threatening language with respect to the government or military authorities of the Allied nations."[120] These restrictions led prisoners to adopt several methods to convey important information in their letters. The most ingenious were "invisible ink" and secret codes.[121]

Secret writing materials were usually received inside the camps in parcels sent by German relief organizations and by pro-German associations in Europe, Latin America, and even the United States.[122] The most commonly used materials "for developing by heat are writings in milk; orange juice; orange juice, sugar and water; starch and water; cabbage juice; potato juice; urine; equal parts of sulphate of copper and salamoniac dissolved in water; sulphuric acid and water, also the common styptic pencil ... Another form of secret writing is by the use of linseed oil, ammonia and water."[123] Although "new sensitized paper which prevented the use of any liquid secret writing ink, or other commonly known secret writing techniques in prisoner of war correspondence" was introduced by Allied chemists, the use of "invisible ink" prevailed inside the camps of southern Quebec.[124] As for secret codes, numerous techniques could be adopted. Canadian authorities warned censors to examine letters for the following coding methods: "Underlining of phrases, words or letters or use of question marks; veiled and obscure language in music, spelling of words backwards, and by chess problems or mathematical formulae; the use of drawings to conceal messages in shorthand, Morse, or other codes."[125] Prisoners sometimes even tried to send secret letters by concealing them in outgoing packages. Such was the case on 29 April 1943, when one Camp Farnham prisoner attempted to slip out a letter among parcels destined for a prisoner of war camp in Alberta. Camp authorities reported that the message was found when the truck driver pilfered some cigarette papers from one of the parcels and gave them to a friend who discovered a letter written in German.[126] In most cases, secret letters were used to transmit valuable military information, to report cases of ill-treatment on the part of the Canadian authorities, and to send to Germany the names of prisoners of war who were unfaithful to Nazism.[127] As the Camp Sherbrooke censor indicated in March 1945, "Attempts have been made, or are being made, by officer camps to contact this camp. This was overheard in a conversation in the Works Program office of this camp by two POW. Several weeks ago, a POW of this camp was asked by a German officer of another camp to furnish the names of the anti-Nazis of this camp. The answer was to be given to the next POW who was going to Ste-Anne-de-Bellevue Military Hospital."[128]

Escapes

Although Canadian regulations warned that "any prisoner of war attempting to pass the boundary fence, wall, or to go out through any gate, exit or other opening without a permit signed by the commandant after being only duly warned and disregarding that warning, will be fired on," internees continued to attempt escapes.[129] During southern Quebec's civilian internment phase, there were very few escape attempts. Most internees were refugees; they understood that good behaviour might accelerate their chances of eventually being released and that escaping could prolong their internment. Also, unlike prisoners of war who escaped to return to Germany, refugees had nowhere to go. Still, the idea of escaping was always on the mind of some internees. As one Sherbrooke inmate recalled,

> We had no idea how long we would be there, how long the war would last, or if we would be released before the war was over ... so I made plans for building a tunnel ... I managed to steal maps of the area out of one of the military automobiles and ... I thought seriously that I would start digging if it [the war] went on for too long ... what I had done was to arrange the floor of one of the huts ... so to have some boards easily removable so I could get into the sub-floor. And I reckoned that the sub-floor would have sufficed to accept all the earth I would have to dig out. And the fence was not very far from that hut.[130]

Although this prisoner did not try to escape, others did. Most of these attempts took place in the latter part of the civilian phase at a time when the pressures imposed by years of internment were at their highest. The most ambitious attempt occurred at Camp Île-aux-Noix in the early morning of 24 May 1943 when one inmate tried to leave the island by stealing the camp's motor boat. Unable to start the engine, the escapee paddled the vessel down the river until the current took hold of it. He then jumped into the river and swam for the mainland. It was at this point that the escapee was spotted by a local innkeeper who immediately contacted the Camp Île-aux-Noix authorities. The internee was recaptured that same day.[131]

Successful escape attempts intensified in southern Quebec with the arrival of the prisoners of war (Table 2.2). German prisoners of war saw it as their military duty to try to break free and return to Germany. They knew that preventing getaways was a tiresome enterprise for camp guards, who constantly had to be vigilant, and that it forced detaining powers to deploy more men and resources for the protection of internment camps.

Cutting through a camp's barbed wire system was one of the most common means of escape. The prisoners usually did this at night, using stolen tools or improvised equipment, including stolen kitchen knives converted into saws, saws made from old gramophone springs, and wire cutters made from the crosspieces and springs of the prisoners' iron beds. This was a very delicate operation because the internee had to work in the open in the compound, without any means of concealment.[132] Snowstorms sometimes facilitated escapes. When deep snowdrifts formed against the wire fences, inmates might dig through them and use the tunnels as means of concealment while they cut the wire. Camp authorities worked constantly to keep the fences clear.[133] Such escape endeavours took time, for usually three lines of barbed wire fences had to be cut. Inmates used this method on numerous occasions and succeeded.[134] On 24 March 1946, for instance, a Camp Sherbrooke inmate was able to cut a hole in the camp's barbed wire using a pair of pliers he had stolen from the camp's workshop.[135]

Prisoners also escaped by climbing over the wire fences. Camp Farnham authorities warned that "if a man cannot go through the wire, that is to say by using wire cutters, he might go over it with the aid of ladders. Cases have been known where a ladder in three or four sections has been carried towards the wire in a creeping position and then the movement of the sentry timed so as to bring it into action at a favourable time."[136]

Building tunnels was a complex and time-consuming procedure that needed special tools. These usually were fashioned by the prisoners' themselves from scrap wood and iron and from kitchen utensils.[137] Digging operations needed to be properly coordinated. The men had to know where to dig, how to hide the tunnel's entrance, how to organize the work, and where to dispose of the excavated earth. Constructing a tunnel could take several months. Camp Farnham authorities indicated that "it is practically impossible to tunnel faster than say a yard a day and even that is difficult; therefore, to build a tunnel 30 or 40 yards long it would take

Table 2.2

Number of successful escapes from southern Quebec camps, 1940-46

Year	Date of escape	Date of recapture	Internment camp	Number of escapees
1942	16 July	17 July	Farnham	1
	8 November	28 November	Sherbrooke	2
	6 December	11 December	Sherbrooke	2
1943	8 April	9 April	Sherbrooke	2
	14 April	17 April	Sherbrooke	2
	22 April	22 April	Farnham	1
	24 May	24 May	Île-aux-Noix	1
	28 June	29 June	Farnham	1
	5 August	6 August	Sherbrooke	1
	13 August	13 August	Grande Ligne	6
	19 August	22 August	Farnham	1
	27 August	27 August	Grande Ligne	1
1944	16 March	16 March	Grande Ligne	2
	17 April	17 April	Sherbrooke	1
	3 May	3 May	Sherbrooke	4
	6 May	6 May	Sherbrooke	1
	7 May	7 May	Sherbrooke	3
	29 July	30 July	Sherbrooke	1
	13 September	14 September	Grande Ligne	1
	26 September	26 September	Grande Ligne	1
	18 December	18 December	Farnham	3
1945	29 March	1 April	Farnham	1
	14 May	15 May	Sherbrooke	1
	17 November	17 November	Sorel	1
1946	24 March	27 March	Sherbrooke	1

Sources: Library and Archives Canada (LAC), RG-24, Vol. 15,397 to 15,398, vols. 22 to 51, War Diary of Internment Camp Farnham, 1942-45; LAC, RG-24, Vol. 15,399, vol. 35 (May 1943), War Diary of Internment Camp Île-aux-Noix, 24 May 1943; LAC, RG-24, Vol. 15,400 to 15,401, vols. 26 to 66, War Diary of Internment Camp Sherbrooke, 1942-46; LAC, RG-24, Vol. 15,403, vols. 8 to 21, War Diary of Internment Camp Grande Ligne, 1943-44; LAC, RG-24, Reel: C-5389, File HQS 7236-44-42, "Escape Plans and Correspondence, Camp Sherbrooke," 1943-45; LAC, RG-24, Reel: C-5389, File HQS 7236-44-40, "Escape Plans and Correspondence, Camp Farnham," 1941-45; LAC, RG-24, Reel: C-5416, File HQS 7236-94-6-42, "Intelligence Reports, Camp Sherbrooke," 1943-46; LAC, RG-24, Reel: C-5421, File HQS 7236-99, "Organization and Administration, Camp Sorel," 1945.

at least 30 or 40 days for the tunnelling alone." Numerous internees had to be involved in such projects, and secrecy had to be preserved.[138]

Tunnelling operations were rare, but there were incidents in southern Quebec camps. A tunnel was found at Camp Farnham on 25 January 1943. While working under one of the camp's huts, a Canadian electrician discovered an air vent sticking out of the ground. He mentioned to camp authorities that he could hear two prisoners working underground. Not knowing where the entrance was, VGC personnel found their way into the tunnel by digging around the air vent using spades. The trapdoor to the eighteen-foot-long tunnel was found behind a hut stove, concealed behind a cord of wood.[139] Another tunnel was found at Camp Grande Ligne in 1948, long after the prisoners of war had been repatriated, when "a truck driver backed up a loaded gravel truck and the wheels of the vehicle sank into the earth. Evidently, the truck had crossed over the incomplete escape tunnel built by the Germans."[140]

Other approaches to escape were employed. Inmates sometimes went out through the main gate, "the prisoner hiding himself in the garbage and ash boxes or by concealing himself in a truck, car, or under it."[141] On 14 April 1943, two Sherbrooke prisoners attempted to escape by hiding themselves in large freight bags to be loaded aboard a train. Both were caught on 17 April.[142] Another case occurred at Camp Grande Ligne on 13 September 1944, when a captive hid himself inside a truck and avoided detection when the vehicle was searched at the gate.[143] Camp authorities were greatly annoyed by this incident, indicating that "this is old routine stuff and should not have happened."[144] All motor vehicles and horse-drawn carriages were supposed to be thoroughly searched with a sharp-ended iron prodding stick.[145] Walking along the shore of the Richelieu River, the escapee reached the United States, where he was caught on 14 September near Rouses Point, New York.[146] When he was handcuffed by members of the Canadian Provost Corps (in violation of the Geneva Convention), his fellow prisoners protested. "I herewith most pointedly protest against this action," wrote the camp spokesman. "We as German officers consider such an action an attack on our honour. Simultaneously I refer to the German note of protest of fall 1943 concerning the shackling of German POWs."[147] Although the situation did not deteriorate, it reminded Canadian officials of the 1942-43 shackling controversy.

Other internees attempted escapes by impersonating camp guards. Camp Farnham authorities warned,

> It would be possible for a prisoner to get hold of a uniform, although it might be difficult. At the same time, many prisoners are ingenious, intelligent, imaginative and courageous and difficulties are not insuperable to such people. This stunt is also worked on the lone wolf basis, that is to say, prisoners dressing up as officers, NCOs or sol-

> diers and coming boldly up to the gate and asking for exit. This is generally done late in the afternoon, just before dusk, when the light would not show up any imperfections in his uniform ... There have been actual cases of impersonation. It generally takes a good actor to do this and it is a very daring operation.[148]

To conceal their escapes, some prisoners placed dummies in their beds "to look as if they were sleeping in them."[149]

Before the entry of the United States into the war in December 1941, the goal for German escapees was to reach that country. With most Canadian internment camps located close to the American border, the United States was a natural asylum. Stimulating the prisoners' intentions was the legend of prisoner of war Franz Von Werra, a German Luftwaffe officer who managed to escape Canada and return to Germany by fleeing through the United States (at that time a neutral country) in January 1941. As the story goes, Von Werra jumped out of a train as it neared the American border near Prescott, Ontario, in the midst of a snowstorm. Reaching the German embassy in Washington, D.C., a few days later, Von Werra was told that the best way to return to Germany was through South America. Issued with false identification papers, Von Werra was sent to Brazil, where he boarded an Italian aircraft bound for Rome. Arriving in the Italian capital in April 1941, he was then taken to Germany aboard a Luftwaffe aircraft. The success of Von Werra's adventure gave hope to all German prisoners of war held in Canada.[150]

Even after the United States joined the Allied cause in December 1941, the German prisoners' zest for escape continued. Their new aim was to traverse the United States undetected with the help of sympathetic German-Americans and reach Mexico.[151] As the Federal Bureau of Investigation (FBI) reported to the RCMP in November 1942 while searching for two Camp Sherbrooke escapees, "These two men will attempt to enter the United States by all means possible and will then probably try to return to Germany via South America."[152] When another escape occurred at Camp Sherbrooke in December 1942, the FBI and the American immigration authorities "began an investigation into the possible existence of an underground system to aid prisoners in escaping from Canada to the United States."[153] The most elaborate escape attempts occurred in May and September 1943 when the Kriegsmarine attempted two rescue operations, code-named "Elster" and "Kiebitz," with German submarines on the Canadian Atlantic Coast. Both forays ultimately failed as no prisoners ever appeared at the rendezvous points; *U-262* waited in vain off Prince Edward Island while *U-536* entered Chaleur Bay but found no escapees.[154]

In all of southern Quebec's internment camps, measures were taken to prevent escapes. A document entitled *Notes on Prevention of Escapes* was issued by the Department of National Defence on 24 December 1940:

> The whole question of safe custody of prisoners must depend on the constant alertness of each and every member of the staff and guard. No amount of mechanical equipment, no matter how efficient, will prevent escapes, if the individual guard is not constantly and at all times on alert. If one gets in the habit of assuming that the fence is unclimbable, that the rocky nature of the ground or the frost will prevent tunnelling or that illumination by flood and pistol-grip searchlights makes escape practically impossible, then escapes will occur ... The troops employed in connection with prisoners ... should be made to realize that the prisoners are always studying their habits and trying to discover their weaknesses, and any person connected with an internment camp who becomes apathetic in his duties is a menace to the security of the camp.[155]

Because "plots and preparations for escape [were] constantly going on among the prisoners, especially among combatant prisoners of war," camp guards were thoroughly trained in prevention. The main problem with the VGC was that most of its members had not seen active service since the First World War. The necessity for training was well demonstrated in the early days of southern Quebec's internment operations. For instance, a false alarm was initiated in Camp Île-aux-Noix on 19 July 1940 when a sentry accidentally fell against the siren button. Although the alarm was a good practice for the camp staff, it demonstrated how unfamiliar VGC personnel were with the facilities.[156] The result was extensive training for the guards not on duty. The entry in the camp's war diary on 15 August states that, "All troops not on duty received considerable training and drill in squad and rifle drill. From now on this will be a daily occurrence and it is planned to give lectures on various military subjects."[157] A notation in the Camp Farnham war diary on 24 October 1940 also emphasized the training of guards:

> The guards have to be instructed in internment camp work as guarding an internment camp is very different from guarding say a bridge or a munition plant or something of that nature. The guards have received several lectures from the commandant and other officers on their work, and it is pointed to them that everlasting vigilance is their first duty and that they must not rely too much on the mechanical equipment of the camp, such as the wire, flood lights, etc. Sentries, provost police and escorts for working parties must be made to realize that prisoners are continually studying their habits and customs and endeavour to pick the weak points of each one personally or the organization as a whole.[158]

Every week, the guards in southern Quebec's internment camps trained to perfect their skills. The guards had to understand the rules pertaining to the treatment of the prisoners and the methods they could use to enforce regulations.[159] They also needed to know what to look for in the event of escapes:

> When an escape is being planned, there is an atmosphere about the camp that is unmistakable. When you sense tension in the air do not ignore it as a figment of your imagination, but see that everybody is on their toes. Prisoners who intend to escape usually accumulate chocolate, cake or food. Special attention should be paid to prisoners who are noticed taking exceptionally vigorous walking exercise; also to any group who appear to be somewhat pale and who sleep continuously in the daytime, which may indicate night tunnelling operations. Periodical searches should be made for contraband, that is, civilian clothes, money, maps, compasses, etc ... Watch for signs of fresh earth, etc., sprinkled over the exercise ground or filling up holes, etc. If prisoners are noticed leaving the huts or going out on working parties with bulging pockets, examine same in case they are carrying out earth from excavations. Wood is essential in building tunnels. Keep a close watch for planks removed from walls, floors, etc. Avoid leaving boxes and boards in places that are accessible to the prisoners.[160]

They were also told that "a prisoner planning an escape generally arranges with accomplices for a diversion so as to attract attention to something else rather than his own particular activities. There are many possible diversions ranging all the way from a commotion to a fire. When anything out of the ordinary happens ... it is a good rule ... not to concentrate too much attention on the particular incident."[161] The inmates' practice of substitution during roll calls, "that is to say, one prisoner attempting to give the name and number of another so as to cover up a comrade who may have escaped or is attempting to do so," was also noted.[162]

To prevent escapes, prisoners were issued with special uniforms. Aside from the prisoner of war officers, who were authorized to wear their military uniforms, and the refugees, who were granted permission to wear civilian clothing, all internees were issued dark blue upper garments marked on the back by a fourteen-inch red circular patch and grey trousers with a three-inch red stripe down one leg. The circle on the shirt was to serve as a target if a guard was aiming his rifle at an escapee and was big enough to ensure that it could not be removed without wrecking the garment. Every civilian internee and prisoner of war in Canada was photographed and fingerprinted by the RCMP. These pictures were distributed to local police forces and the media whenever escapes occurred. Prisoners were not allowed to have long hair or beards.[163]

Daily camp inspections, known as roll calls, were crucial in preventing escapes. On such occasions, prisoners would fall into two ranks in their numerical order and be counted and inspected by the camp commandant. Such inspections helped ensure that the "discipline of the prisoners is maintained." Moreover, they permitted camp authorities to know if prisoners had escaped.[164] As a rule, each camp was to have two roll calls per day: one in the morning and one in the evening. Occasionally, a third inspection was made as an extra precaution.

Preventing escapes was a tiresome enterprise for camp authorities. In many ways, it was a game of cat and mouse that constantly forced camp guards to remain on alert. Camp authorities knew that prisoners were always preparing escapes, but they had no way of knowing when such events might occur. At Grande Ligne, inmates began attempting escapes as soon as they arrived: camp guards discovered the entrance of a tunnel as early as 6 July 1943.[165] When six prisoners attempted to escape by cutting their way through the wire fences on 13 August 1943, camp authorities became anxious. What worried them was that the prisoners had in their possession documents that included detailed maps of eastern North America, which meant that they had access to restricted information.[166]

When a second escape attempt occurred on 27 August 1943, Military District 4 headquarters immediately responded by ordering a surprise search of the prisoners' compound. More than a hundred VGC personnel and fifty RCMP constables took part.[167] The operation was a complete success. Confiscated were numerous forged documents of Argentine, British, Canadian, Dutch, Latvian, and other origins, as well as a variety of identification certificates, including US Army draft certificates. Also found were detailed maps of eastern Canada (New Brunswick, Nova Scotia, Ontario, and Quebec) and the United States (Maine, Massachusetts, Michigan, New Hampshire, New York, and Vermont) along with homemade daggers, code books, escape diaries, wire cutters, compasses, saws, and other handmade tools. Furthermore, it was discovered that the prisoners of war had kept detailed records of the movements of camp sentries and of trains arriving at the local railway station.[168] When homemade VGC shoulder badges were found on 2 September 1943, and a metal tunnel framework the next day, camp authorities began to panic.[169] To meet the threat of prisoners impersonating camp personnel, on 6 September staff were issued special identity discs to be worn around the neck like "dog-tags."[170] The issue also led to an intensification of the camp's security system. Large searchlights were put on each of the camp's towers and extra lines of barbed wire were built in October 1943.[171]

These measures did not prevent prisoners from attempting escapes. In fact, between January and February 1944, Camp Grande Ligne authorities became convinced that the prisoners were building another tunnel when large stones belonging to the foundation wall of one of the buildings were discovered.[172] One, which weighed 225 pounds, was even found concealed under the piano in the prisoner officers' mess. Night after night, camp authorities began searching for the tunnel's entrance. It was finally found on 27 February 1944, under a window in the prisoner of war library room. When the tunnel was inspected, an electrician's rock drill and two pieces of galvanized pipe were found in the hole. It was estimated that the prisoners had removed some 1,500 pounds of rocks from the foundations.[173]

To keep a closer watch on the prisoners in March 1944, camp authorities formed a special intelligence group known as the Ferrets. Their duties were to make nightly searches in the prisoners of war compound to find out if the inmates were preparing escapes.[174] In the summer of 1944, digging operations resumed at Camp Grande Ligne. As a result, experiments were carried out at night by camp authorities using listening apparatuses borrowed from the RCMP, but sounds from the water pipes and other underground noises rendered these instruments ineffectual.[175] In the meantime, some prisoners tried to cut through the wire on 30 July 1944, while some 350 inmates were in the camp's yard watching a soccer match. As a result, the camp guards intensified their supervision of the enclosure.[176] Camp authorities stated, "It will be extraordinary if some well planned scheme of escape is not tried this month – between now and the middle of September. The gardens are now full of vegetables, fruits, etc. and it is possible for a man to exit for days without much in the way of provisions ... next attempt might be a slick wire job. It's a great game and the zest of it is the unknown."[177]

Eventually, the Ferrets discovered the internees' tunnel on 26 August 1944.[178] Several extensive surprise searches of the camp compound were initiated in September, and many contraband items were found. These included complete VGC uniforms with handmade wedge caps, shoulder insignias, and badges; camouflage suits and civilian clothing made of blankets; sandbags; escape tools; tunnelling equipment, particularly wires, escape rigs and ventilators; false documents, maps, and escape diaries; and a tremendous amount of scrap iron. Camp authorities even found charts of American and Canadian airports and the detailed plan of a Douglas DC-3 transport aircraft.[179] In late September 1944, camp authorities reported that VGC guardsmen were becoming exasperated by the escape attempts: "VGC personnel feel they should get $10 to $11 gratuity, in view of duties guarding POW, being similar to battlefield duty."[180]

Whenever prisoners escaped, camp authorities requested local support. In 1940, for instance, Camp Farnham authorities formed an "emergency car brigade" manned by fifteen civilian volunteer motorists.[181] This unit was used to provide transportation for search parties in the event of escapes. Each car carried up to five VGC personnel. The brigade was also used for other tasks. When severe thunderstorms created power failures at Camp Farnham in November 1940 and June 1941,[182] the unit's cars were "placed around the outside wire with the lights shining in; in this way the approaches to the wire were fairly well lighted up."

Because "it is to be expected that a prisoner will endeavour to reach the United States border and will make use of any available means of transportation, such as motor vehicles, trains, bicycles, etc.," camp personnel had to react rapidly. After having notified Military District 4 headquarters, local security forces would immediately be contacted. These included the RCMP, the Quebec Provincial Police, the New York State Police, the Vermont State Police, the Canadian Provost Corps, the Canadian National Railway and Canadian Pacific Railway security forces, the Royal Canadian Air Force service police, the United States Immigration Border

Patrol, the American immigration department authorities, municipal police corps, local military units, and Canadian Army training centres. Search parties would then be formed and sent around the region. RCMP special agents and dog handlers would usually coordinate such teams which, more than often, consisted solely of policemen. Roadblocks and observation posts would also be established in the local countryside, to warn civilians about the escape and to interrogate and search pedestrians and motorists.[183]

Local newspapers and radio stations would be advised of the escapes and asked to communicate this information to the public. Newspapers usually printed a photo of the escapee along with a short text describing the individual's physical characteristics. Radio stations broadcasted the prisoner's description in English and French every fifteen minutes. Warning Canadian civilians about escapes was the only time the media were authorized to discuss camp-related matters. Canadian censorship regulations forbade newspapers and radio stations to communicate to the public any information concerning Canadian internment camps. Local journalists and reporters were almost never allowed to visit southern Quebec internment camps. This strict control of information meant that Canadian civilians were often unaware of the existence of internment camps in their regions.[184] This situation was well reflected by the type of articles written about Camp Sherbrooke by *La Tribune*. Of the twenty-four articles published about the camp during the war, sixteen dealt exclusively with the issue of escapes. As for the other articles, they dealt with such vague topics as a change of camp commandant and campfires.[185]

The civilian population responded well to the media warnings about escapes, contributing on occasion to the recapture of escapees. One such case occurred on 28 November 1942, when two Camp Sherbrooke escapees who had been hiding in the region's forest for nearly three weeks were found. The two had recently begun working on a local farm, and a neighbouring farmer saw their pictures in a newspaper and contacted the RCMP. Ever since they had left the camp on 8 November 1942, the two escapees had stayed in a small bivouac that they had built out of bedcovers and had lived on charity and theft. The two prisoners explained why they had sought work: "We were tired of living in the bivouac. It was starting to get cold and our money was diminishing, so we decided last Friday to find jobs. We were forced to move the location of our bivouac earlier this week as Canadian army patrols were extremely active on nearby roads."[186] Another case occurred in December 1942 when two Camp Sherbrooke internees were caught in Newport, Vermont, after a local grocer recognized them from pictures in a Canadian newspaper. Both prisoners had reached the United States by walking along Lake Memphremagog.[187] Although most escapees were usually recaptured within a day, some were able to dodge searching parties for several days. A few, such as a Sherbrooke prisoner who escaped on 24 March 1946 and was recaptured in Montreal on 27 March 1946, were able to reach metropolitan areas.[188] Another prisoner escaped from Camp Farnham on 28 June 1943, several hours before the transfer of the camp's population to Grande Ligne, and was recaptured the next day by the Quebec Provincial Police near Dorval airport in Montreal.[189]

Discipline and Punishment

When they did not conform to camp rules, prisoners could be legitimately punished by the detaining power. According to Article 45 of the Geneva Convention, "Prisoners of war were to be subjected to the laws, regulations, and orders in force in the armed forces of the detaining power.[190] In accordance with Articles 46 to 53, all punishments were to be humane. The most severe disciplinary punishment was solitary confinement.[191] As Article 54 stipulated, the duration of any single punishment was not to exceed thirty days. It was also noted that if a prisoner was sentenced to a fresh disciplinary penalty during the course or after the termination of a period of imprisonment, a period of at least three days was to intervene between each of the periods of imprisonment if any of these periods was of ten days or more.[192] The condition of prisoners inside detention cells was governed by Articles 55 to 59, which stated that facilities were always to be kept clean and that prisoners were to be given at least two hours per day for outdoor activities and provided with reading and writing materials. Prisoners were never to serve their disciplinary sentences outside the camps.[193] Article 56 stated that they could not be transferred to prisons, penitentiaries, or other convict establishments.[194]

In conformity with the provisions of the Geneva Convention, each Canadian internment camp was provided with a specific number of detention cells. Any prisoner committing an offence was liable to be imprisoned in such facilities. Regulations stipulated that "any prisoner of war guilty of disobedience to orders or of any act prejudicial to the safety, good order or discipline of the camp will be liable to punishment."[195] The maximum sentence Canadian authorities agreed a prisoner should receive was twenty-eight days of detention, which was less than the maximum allowable by the Geneva Convention. This penalty was usually given for attempted escapes, theft, illicit activities, and smuggling messages. If prisoners disobeyed orders, were absent during inspections, acted insolent, or committed acts of aggression, they were usually sentenced to twenty-one days of detention. Any inmate involved in the destruction of property was given fourteen days. As for prisoners convicted for minor infractions, punishments included confinement to quarters for periods not exceeding fourteen days and extra fatigue duties. Minor infractions included fighting, disobedience of orders, insubordination, and refusal to work. Disciplinary sentences could be imposed only by Canadian officers vested with disciplinary powers, such as camp commandants and responsible officers acting as their substitutes. When cases proved too complicated for camp authorities, they were usually submitted to the military district's commanding officer.[196]

In the early days of southern Quebec's internment operations, camp authorities were uncomfortable when they had to impose sentences on individual prisoners because they had no idea how the other inmates would react. As a result, they tended to give internees short sentences. Despite this leniency, the authorities understood the necessity of showing the prisoners that they were in charge. After arresting their first inmate on 21 July 1940, Camp Île-aux-Noix, authorities claimed, "This will have a very salutary effect on many of the others and it is obvious that the prisoners need some considerable training and discipline."[197] They further stated on 2 August 1940 that "it is necessary to maintain a high degree of discipline among the prisoners and even the smallest infraction of regulations must be immediately checked."[198] This explains why so many internees were arrested for minor infractions in the first months of internment in southern Quebec. Thirty-seven of the forty internees disciplined by southern Quebec camp authorities between July 1940 and March 1941 were given sentences of less than ten days' detention.[199]

The main problem with the civilian internees was their lack of discipline. Because most had never served in the military, they had a hard time adapting to the regimentation of life behind barbed wire, and their discontent gave rise to many cases of insubordination and refusal to obey orders. By contrast, prior military training helped prisoners of war integrate better into camp life. Their respect for authority and understanding of discipline made them in some respects better inmates. However, they were more prone than civilians to trying to escape (see Table 2.2).

Those prisoners who adopted criminal behaviour faced judicial proceedings, in conformity with the Geneva Convention, and Canadian authorities had the right to court martial offenders. These measures were usually taken against such crimes as murder, mutiny, and offences against Canadian personnel. Canadian regulations specified that "military courts shall have power to try any prisoners of war upon any such charges as may be preferred before them for any offence which, if committed in Canada by a person amenable to Canadian law, would be triable before a civil court of criminal jurisdiction, or for any act, conduct, disorder, or neglect prejudicial to the safety or well-being of His Majesty's Dominions, armed forces or subjects, or to the safe custody, control or well-being of any prisoner of war, or to good order and discipline among prisoners of war."[200] On conviction by a military court, punishment was imposed according to the following scale: (1) death; (2) penal servitude for life or for any term not less than three years; (3) imprisonment, with or without hard labour, for any term not exceeding two years; (4) detention for any term not exceeding two years; and (5) field punishment for any period not exceeding three months. In all such cases, prisoners could be sent to local prisons to serve their terms. However, none of these sentences could be carried into effect until they had been confirmed by the governor-general-in-council or the minister of national defence, in accordance with the prisoners' protecting power.[201] In southern Quebec, judicial hearings were very rare. It seems that the only one took place at Camp Sherbrooke on 3 April 1945, when a prisoner of war was tried by a district court martial for "stealing property belonging to a person subject to military law." The fact was that this prisoner had stolen the watch of one of the Canadian guards. The prisoner was eventually sentenced to ninety days' imprisonment without hard labour.[202]

PHERUDA and Political Segregation

The threat of disciplinary action did not always control troublesome political ideologues among the prisoners. Most of the German internee populations held by Allied powers were sharply divided along ideological lines. Some prisoners were Nazis, while others were anti-Nazis or even Communists. This situation created friction that often led to violence. The detaining powers were forced to segregate the prisoners along political and ideological lines. This was no easy task, for there was almost no way of knowing exactly what was going on in a person's mind.

During southern Quebec's phase of civilian internment, Canadian authorities were primarily concerned about the presence of Communist elements. The fear was that Communist activists might entice internees to consolidate themselves against camp authorities and initiate internal disturbances. Communists, explained Eric Koch in *Deemed Suspect*, were in the forefront of those making demands for recognition of refugee status, and of those protesting against prisoner of war status, against facilities unfit for human habitation, against mail delays, and so on. In his opinion, "Communists were activists and trouble-makers."[203] Furthermore, most western powers, including Canada, were staunchly opposed to Communism, despite the fact that the Soviet Union was fighting on their side against Nazi Germany. The doctrine was perceived by many as a "social disease" that had to be annihilated. When Camp Farnham authorities learned in May 1941 that close to 45 percent of their inmates were Communist sympathizers, they responded by stating, "Communists ... declare that they are 'social thinking people' but their social thinking is similar to the attitude the Nazis take regarding their new "Social Order in Europe."[204] This attitude explains why the Camp Farnham authorities wrote the following in September 1941:

> The Communists in this camp have become most active and vocal. Their activities from an administrative standpoint are of course most troublesome and tiresome ... The leaders of this group are doing their best to spread the gospel of Communism ... In a recent election held in this camp some two weeks ago, Communists or Communist sympathizers were selected for most of the posts. This means that they are now in a position to exert a considerable amount of influence over the life of the compound ... This Communist element in the camp will have to be dealt with and more important still it will have to be watched ... It is therefore in its larger aspect a problem of considerable importance as it has a bearing on the present and certainly the future.[205]

Although Communism was perceived as an ideological threat, its supporters rarely resorted to violence. This situation changed with the advent of the prisoner of war phase. At that time, Canadian authorities were focused on countering Nazi dominance in camps across Canada.[206] Nazi prisoners often intimidated and terrorized other inmates to neutralize anti-Nazis and to ensure that no one cooperated with the Canadian authorities. On numerous occasions, Nazis spied on new internees, threatened fellow prisoners, and maltreated or, in extremely rare cases, executed anti-Nazis. Nazis often gathered impressive arsenals of clubs, knives, and other weapons that they used against their opponents. They also blackmailed other inmates by sending their names back to Germany as traitors, using invisible inks for that purpose. Sometimes they held kangaroo courts, where fellow inmates were judged on charges of "treason" for having cooperated with the camp authorities or for openly admitting that they were anti-Nazi. Those who were judged were usually beaten. Prisoners began talking of "Camp Gestapos."[207] Nazis also "waged symbolic war" by defying and taunting the Canadian authorities. They would do so by singing Nazi marching songs, waving Nazi regalia such as homemade swastika banners, and using the Nazi salute among themselves and when they encountered Canadian officers. Celebrations of Nazi holidays, including Hitler's birthday, were also held to provoke camp staff. At Camp Sherbrooke in January 1943, the camp spokesman ordered fellow inmates to place pictures of Adolf Hitler over the prisoners' hut doors along with large "Victory Is with Hitler" signs. Canadian authorities had to pass under these each time they visited the huts. Needless to say, the pictures and signs were immediately removed and the camp spokesman was relieved of his functions. The camp commandant reported that "during the short period of time that Captain Krieger was camp leader, he proved to be a trouble maker of the meanest type."[208]

A system of classification to separate Nazis and anti-Nazis was introduced by the Canadian authorities. Upon approval of Canada's war cabinet, a Psychological Warfare Committee was created in 1943 operating under the aegis of the Department of External Affairs.[209] The purpose of the committee was to collect information and study the presence of Nazism inside the camps, as well as to handle the issue of segregating prisoners of war and re-educating Nazi prisoners (see Chapter 5).[210] Canadian military officials also organized Military Intelligence 7 (MI7) to implement psychological warfare against Nazi prisoners of war.[211]

On 5 August 1944, the Psychological Warfare Committee introduced a system of classification known as PHERUDA to segregate Nazis from anti-Nazis. In conformity with this new scheme, prisoners were interrogated by MI7 and camp intelligence officers, and then classified into three categories: "Black" (Nazis), "Grey" (no strong political interests or convictions), and "White" (anti-Nazis). Each letter of the term PHERUDA referred to the first capital letter of the areas in which prisoners were to be interrogated: (1) **P**olitical leanings (from democrat to rabid Nazi); (2) attitudes towards **H**itler (from anti-Hitler to fanatically pro-Hitler); (3) level of **E**ducation (from university to minimum); (4) **R**eligion (from devout Protestant or Catholic to neo-pagan); (5) **U**sefulness in terms of labour (from willing to cooperate and skilled to refuse to work); (6) **D**ependability (from dependable to undependable); and (7) attitudes towards the **A**llies (from pro- to anti-Allies). Further, each PHERUDA File came with an interrogation report that included five sets of questions covering personal details of the internee's life, such as his general background (education, work, and home life); prisoner of war history (attitudes, work record, and camps where he had been detained); political history (how politically oriented he was in Germany); military history (attitudes, units in which he served, and on which fronts he fought); camp information; and the examiner's remarks (personality, truthfulness, reliability). By combining PHERUDA Files with interrogation reports, intelligence officers were able to segregate inmates into one of the three colour-coded categories.[212]

The government's new colour-coded system enabled camp authorities to reorganize the overall Canadian internment operation according to the political ideas of the internees, which meant a radical transformation of the southern Quebec camps. These were now to specialize in the incarceration of certain types of prisoners. For instance, Sherbrooke and Farnham were "Grey" camps, Grande Ligne was for prisoners labelled "Black," and Sorel was a "White" camp.[213] According to historian Bill Waiser, however, "the [classification] process was so incredibly slow that by war's end, almost two-thirds of the German prisoners held in Canada had yet to be classified."[214] By late September 1945, only 9,172 inmates had been classified by PHERUDA teams out of a total population of some 34,000 prisoners of war.[215]

Despite the introduction of PHERUDA, Nazi elements continued to infiltrate the camps. Such was the problem at Sherbrooke in December 1944, where the arrival from Camp Monteith of sixty-two prisoners, many of them Nazis, created a reign of terror that led to much unrest. Rumours were that the Nazis were planning hangings, beatings, and other forms of brutality. Two Nazi prisoners were even overheard saying, "We have hung some at Monteith; let's erect a gallows here." The aim of these troublemakers was deliberately to create fear among the other prisoners. As a result, numerous internees began approaching the camp authorities for protective custody or for transfer to the anti-Nazi camp they believed existed. Some even made applications for the Pioneer Corps.[216] By February 1945, the problem had become so tense that camp authorities began talking about a "war of nerves inside the enclosure." Prisoners threatened by Nazis feared for their lives; finding a noose in one's bed was extremely traumatizing.[217] So intense were these pressures that, according to the camp's intelligence officer, one prisoner even "broke down and wept while telling his story to the camp commandant."[218] The Sherbrooke "reign of terror" came to an end on 26 March 1945 when forty-nine Nazi troublemakers were transferred to Camp Monteith.[219] A similar situation also took place in late 1944 at Camp Farnham where members of the Waffen-SS had come to dominate the enclosure. Having established their own intelligence section, these Nazis would watch fellow prisoners and search the rooms of anti-Nazis during their absence. They even set up a secret Nazi tribunal "which claims for itself the power of life and death over defeatists and anti-Nazis."[220]

Nazi military training was another problem in southern Quebec camps. Its purpose was secretly to prepare German prisoner of war officers for participation in future Nazi-waged wars. Although such training offered no direct threat to the security of internment camps, it kept the spirit of Nazism and militarism alive among inmates. That Canadian intelligence officers were aware of the problem is evident in a special memorandum submitted to the director of military intelligence:

> Evidence is accumulating that the Nazi government is conducting a systematic campaign amongst POW's in Canada to preserve them as a physically fit, well trained and thoroughly indoctrinated body of soldiers to continue the struggle for power even after a German military defeat. Under conditions existing here this campaign concentrates on: (a) maintaining a strong German sentiment throughout the camps; (b) ensuring that most intensive instruction is given in Nazi doctrines. It is scarcely too much to say that the POW camps here are regarded as special seminaries for future Nazi leaders and workers. The maintenance of German sentiment is achieved mainly by courses in German history, geography and political geography ... The principal emphasis is naturally placed on the dissemination of Nazi ideas and the fostering of Nazi attitudes ... As is well known, educational work is greatly stressed in all camps ... Pressure to attend courses is considerable and apparently stronger in officer than in Other Ranks camps. In the former, nearly 100 per cent of the prisoners attend some course or another; in the latter only between 60 and 70 per cent. Still, in all cases it is remarkably high...The prisoner authorities in most camps endeavour to reduce any possible influence of our press to the minimum ... In view of these facts, it is urged that the need for vigorous and comprehensive counter-action is imperative.[221]

One such military training initiative was introduced at Camp Farnham. There, "Black" prisoners working in the POW orderly room began a census of all Nazi officers incarcerated in the camp. Initiated on 15 October 1944, this census took the form of a "card-index system." Each card represented an individual and indicated his rank; date of entry into the German army; date of last promotion; military position last held; number of years in the field; number of service years at home; date of capture; formation or military unit; military district; and whether he was a regular soldier or a reservist. The purpose of collecting this kind of data "is to build up an underground movement and to re-educate the officers for the next war"; the fact that some German officers were losing their enthusiasm for Nazism also motivated their pro-Nazi brethren.

Officers from all branches of the military were given secret classes connected with their future in the German general staff. Lectures comprised such topics as military science, intelligence, map reading, and battlefield leadership. A secret lecture room was established in one of the camp's huts, and all officers were grouped in the same quarters. The reason for keeping candidates together was to create cohesion and ensure that senior officers had total control. Nevertheless, despite the secrecy, camp authorities learned of this military training program in December 1944 from a "White" prisoner.[222]

Another secret military training program was known as NAPOLA (Nazi Political Learning) and was established by the prisoner of war officers of Camp Grande Ligne. Its purpose was to keep the German officers as well trained and thoroughly indoctrinated as possible. Emphasis was placed on the maintenance of a strong German sentiment, the dissemination of Nazi doctrines, and the fostering of martial attitudes. Members were gathered by invitation. NAPOLA training consisted of series of secret lectures and seminars on topics such as Nazism, German history, political geography, and various subjects related to the art of war. One such class, for instance, studied Adolf Hitler's *Mein Kampf.* Despite NAPOLA's early popularity, the program diminished when Nazi Germany surrendered in May 1945. As camp authorities indicated by June 1945, "NAPOLA activities have either ceased or are being carried on so secretly that our contacts are unable to locate the meeting place."[223] NAPOLA training not only permitted German officers to reaffirm their commitment to the Nazi cause but also gave them an opportunity to test their military skills and knowledge of war.

The HARIKARI Club

Nazis were very well organized, especially at "Black" camps like Grande Ligne. The camp had been constructed to house German prisoner of war officers. Canadian authorities expected Camp Grande Ligne to experience more Nazi activities than any other southern Quebec camp. They were right. In the summer and early autumn of 1944, camp authorities learned how well organized the camp's Nazi officers really were, for they had created their own Gestapo, intelligence, and propaganda sections, as well as an escape committee, all of which operated in utmost secrecy.[224] This organization on the part of the prisoners was a major threat for the security of the camp and the local area. With such a system, there was always the possibility that escapees might be used to collect data or even to commit acts of sabotage. Indeed, it became known that one of the camps' escapees had carried out a reconnaissance of the Dorval airport in Montreal and reported back to the prisoners' intelligence section upon his return. Another did the same in upstate New York. Camp authorities indicated in October 1944 that "the fact that they have an intelligence section which has obtained a mass of information on railroads, bridges and airports in the Montreal area and upper New York State has been known for some time."[225] But although they knew of such actions, they did not understand the prisoners' real purpose.

The answer came in October 1944 when Grande Ligne authorities learned that the camp's most ardent Nazi sympathizers had created a secret organization called the HARIKARI Club.[226] The successful Allied landings in Normandy on D-Day, 6 June 1944 had a tremendous impact on the prisoners of war. The realization that Allied Forces might soon crush Nazi Germany combined with feelings of anger and uselessness, incited the Nazis to become more ruthless and rabid. The HARIKARI Club was created in the early summer of 1944 by some of these prisoners of war as a means of continuing the war behind Canadian barbed wire. Their goal was to prepare a suicidal mass escape that promised to wreak havoc on the region surrounding the camp. They sought to break free in order to slaughter as many Canadians and inflict as much sabotage and destruction as possible before being killed. This rampage was to be launched as soon as the Nazi prisoners regarded the war as absolutely lost or in the event of Germany's unconditional surrender. Director of Military Intelligence Colonel W.W. Murray reported the aim of the plot as follows:

> The HARIKARI Club ... is based on the old German "Twilight of the Gods" (Götterdämerung) philosophy-mythology, wherein the Gods kill off each other in a final orgy of violence. The HARIKARI plan will go into operation when it becomes obvious that the capitulation or destruction of the German Army is imminent and a negotiated peace is beyond hope. When the right moment is decided on by the HARIKARI leaders, members will proceed to murder all fellow POW whom they consider to be "cowards" because of their anti-Nazi sentiments. The HARIKARI POW will then rush some or all of the guard towers, regardless of cost to themselves, and break out of the enclosure. Some will proceed to murder as many of the Camp Staff as possible. In this connection, the Camp Commandant, Camp Intelligence Officer and Camp Sergeant-Major have been singled out for special attention at Grande Ligne. Others will head for the nearest plants, industrial areas, airports, etc., to commit as much damage and sabotage as possible. Their final aim is as much murder and destruction as possible before they themselves are killed. It must be realized that the POW officers involved in the HARIKARI Club are fully aware that a number of innocent people will be killed and that most or all of them will be killed. Nevertheless, their Nazi minds are so transfixed by the Götterdämerung idea that their only thought is to go to their deaths in a final blaze of glory, taking as many of the enemy, and as much of his property, as possible with them to destruction.[227]

Camp authorities learned of the club on 3 October 1944. In a letter addressed to camp intelligence officers, German civilian internee George Felber, the camp's Roman Catholic priest, informed camp officials about the existence of this secret Nazi organization. For several months, Felber and his Catholic followers had been persecuted by anti-Christian Nazi sympathizers, which included several members of the HARIKARI Club. Tired of the harassment and fearing for his life, Felber decided to tell the Canadian authorities about the Nazi prisoners' clandestine activities.[228] In his letter, he warned the camp staff of the true purpose of the HARIKARI Club and requested its immediate dismantlement, emphasizing that "it must be done with extreme care and skill, because otherwise the HARIKARI Club would begin the attack." His solution was to close the camp altogether and divide the prisoner population by transferring it to different internment facilities. Felber also gave the Canadian authorities a list of the ringleaders and other dangerous prisoners. It included some 100 names.[229]

The revelations concerning the HARIKARI Club took camp authorities by surprise. To confirm the authenticity of Felber's story, a "White" German Army officer named Alois Frank was interrogated on 12 October 1944 while in Montreal for an eye treatment. A staunch anti-Nazi, Frank assured camp officials that "the HARIKARI Club is authentic" and that it was "more serious than realized." He gave a detailed account of the Nazi organization's aims and provided a list of some of its targets, which included the munitions dumps at L'Acadie and the St. Jean airport, where the British Commonwealth Air Training Plan (BCATP) No. 9 Air Observation School was located and where a great number of military aircraft were concentrated. Both sites were situated approximately six miles from the camp. "The purpose of the club is to do as much damage and sabotage as possible," Frank told camp officials. "The organization is aware that they will be fired upon by soldiers and that there will be a number of innocent people killed, but some will get out of the wire and proceed to the nearest plants and industrial areas in order to commit sabotage although they do expect to be killed in the act." Frank also confirmed the camp authorities' suspicions that the German prisoners of war operated a secret homemade radio receiver. Canadian authorities perceived this as a serious problem since it meant that the inmates could know the exact date of Germany's capitulation and at this point initiate their own *Götterdämerung*. Frank then furnished camp officials with a list of HARIKARI Club members. It was fairly identical to that provided by Felber and registered approximately 100 names. Frank explained that as a former Bavarian police prefect, he knew many of the prisoners on that list prior to the outbreak of the war and was aware of their Nazi antecedents. To avoid bloodshed and destruction, he recommended the removal of these bad elements from the camp as soon as possible.[230] Because he was determined to help camp authorities eradicate the HARIKARI Club, Frank refused the offer to be sent to another internment camp. In his opinion, "there was much more work for [me] to do within the enclosure" as an informant "so that the camp staff can be advised of the latest information and also of any matter which may be considered of great urgency." Felber, on the other hand, was transferred to the camp at Farnham later that month.[231]

The HARIKARI Club scheme was taken very seriously by the Canadian military authorities. In August 1944, Japanese prisoners of war interned in Cowra, Australia, were involved in a suicidal mass escape that left hundreds of prisoners and several guards dead.[232] Canadian authorities did not want a repetition of these events in Canada. Knowing for several months that the prisoners' intelligence section had collected information on specific objectives within the area from recaptured prisoners of war, the authorities feared that the HARIKARI Club might use these sites as targets for their eventual attack.[233] Department of National Defence officials in Ottawa understood the destructive impact that a similar endeavour could have on the Canadian home front. The proximity of Grande Ligne to Montreal and other urban centres, where important refineries, industrial plants, shipyards, military installations, and transport establishments such as dockyards, railways, and airports were located, made the HARIKARI Club scheme all the more threatening. Attacks against such facilities could seriously affect the Canadian war effort and cause heavy loss of life. Precautionary measures were urgently required to protect the region and its population. Several days after the interrogation of Alois Frank, representatives from the directorates of Prisoners of War and of Military Intelligence, and from the Veterans Guard of Canada, began investigating the HARIKARI Club situation.

The Directorate of Prisoners of War was particularly interested in the level of readiness of the camp staff. On 17 October 1944, Lieutenant-Colonel H.W. Pearson was sent to Military District 4 headquarters in Montreal to discuss the Grande Ligne prisoners' mass escape scheme and to oversee some of the measures taken to protect the camp. That same day, Pearson accompanied several Military District 4 and MI7 officers on a visit to the camp. Lieutenant-Colonel H.W. Hiltz, the camp commandant, informed him that "he was quite able to meet any situation that might arise so long as present conditions were unchanged" but that "he might need additional guard troops as a reserve in the event of insubordination." In his report to Colonel H.N. Streight, the director of Prisoners of War, Pearson concluded that such a mass suicide effort was quite possible and that reinforcements should be ready in the event of trouble.[234] Streight complied with Pearson's request and authorized the immediate mobilization of a reserve force of three platoons from No. 10 Company VGC, stationed at Camp Farnham. These troops were to be placed at the disposal of Military District 4 headquarters. Streight felt very confident in the VGC's ability to cope with a possible mass escape attempt. He also believed that the surrounding landscape would favour the guardsmen. "The country adjacent to the camp is open, flat farm land where concealment is quite difficult," he emphasized. "Past experience has shown that recapture becomes very much more difficult if escaped POW can take concealment in densely wooded areas."[235]

The Directorate of Military Intelligence, on the other hand, was more concerned. On 17 October, Lieutenant-Colonel Eric Acland held several telephone conversations about the HARIKARI Club with MI7 and camp intelligence officers as well as with former camp commandant, Lieutenant-Colonel Eric D.B. Kippen. Based on the information he received, Acland concluded in a report that such a mass suicide effort was quite possible and that, should it occur, "a considerable number of German POW officers will be shot with perhaps unfortunate repercussions on our own POW in Germany; some of the camp staff will be killed; and some of the Nazis will succeed in breaking out and in reaching vulnerable objectives such as the Dorval and St. Hubert air fields." Because the camp was so close to Montreal, Acland suggested that Grande Ligne no longer be used for the detention of officers classified as "Blacks" and that HARIKARI Club members be immediately transferred. As he explained, "The danger of continuing to allow the present rabid clique of Nazi officers to remain at Grande Ligne becomes increasingly more apparent ... It must be considered that any 'Black' officer camp will be a first rate security problem and therefore the locating of such a camp near a metropolitan area or communications centre, as is the case of Grande Ligne ... is not concurred in from the security aspect."[236] Anxious to discuss the possibility of moving the camp's "Black" members to a new "Black" officer camp, Acland arranged an MI7 meeting on 20 October, which was attended by Lieutenant-Colonel Pearson of the Directorate of Prisoners of War. Most intelligence officers agreed with Acland's proposal. They even provided a list of potential internment camps to replace Grande Ligne: No. 33 Petawawa, No. 101 Angler, both in Ontario; No. 70 Fredericton, in New Brunswick; and No. 130 Seebee (formerly Kananaskis), in Alberta. Pearson, on the other hand, emphasized that the segregation of the prisoners of war was the responsibility of the chiefs of the General Staff and "it therefore follows that the General Staff should recommend or suggest the camp which should be used, keeping in mind, in view of the situation in Camp No. 44, security of industry and Army and Air establishments within a reasonable area of the internment camp."[237] Colonel Streight concurred with this view. "The question of establishing a 'Black' camp for officer POW," he explained, "is one that should not be hastily answered. Up to the present, attempts towards segregation have accomplished little of a constructive nature and have added substantially to the confusion and unrest amongst POW. It is my opinion that the number of POWs ... to be found in Camp No. 44 who are not either 'Black' or 'Dark Grey' is almost negligible."[238]

The Veterans Guard of Canada was preoccupied with the protection of VGC personnel. Following a visit to Military District 4 headquarters and the Camp Grande Ligne on 19 October, Colonel C.P. Lavigne, assistant adjutant general of the Veterans Guard of Canada, sent a memorandum to Colonel J.M. Taylor, director of the Veterans Guard of Canada, in which he suggested that the VGC guardsmen be completely re-equipped. Among the items requested were a wheeled armoured vehicle and a Universal Carrier. As he explained, the wheeled armoured vehicle could be used inside the camp's enclosure, while the Universal Carrier would be useful to follow escapees over fields. Lavigne also recommended that the camp be provided with six Vickers heavy machine guns, seven portable No. 58 radio sets, a supply of tear gas, grenades, plus a good quantity of parachute flares and pistol grip lights to be used in the event of an electrical breakdown. He also requested that the British Mk-II steel helmets issued to camp guards be replaced with the American M-1, which could "afford greater protection against clubs, stones, etc."[239] Taylor, however, refused most of the items recommended by Lavigne:

> It is respectfully suggested that the POW personnel of this camp remain as at present, and in addition to, or in place of Vickers machine guns ... which the VGC are not trained in the use of, that sufficient Reising sub-machine guns be made available to place two in each tower instead of one as at present. That tear gas be not supplied, but instead fire hose might be used to rout the POW out of buildings. That an adequate supply of flash and pistol grip lights be kept on hand; and that a supply of wood clubs, say from 2 to 2½ feet in length, be on hand for close combat skirmishing, inside buildings, where it is not possible to use bayonets.[240]

Evidently, Taylor was not as apprehensive of the HARIKARI Club as Lavigne and seemed to believe that a suicidal attack could be quelled in the same manner and with the same tools and weapons as the Bowmanville Riot on 10-12 October 1942, the only serious prisoner of war revolt in a Canadian internment camp during the war. Taylor, then commandant of Camp Bowmanville, suppressed the riot with the help of several hundred Canadian soldiers armed only with unloaded rifles with fixed bayonets, hardwood clubs, and high-pressure fire hoses.[241] In the end, Taylor's comments did not prevent the arrival at Grande Ligne in late October of No. 69 grenades, tear gas generators, Bren light machine guns, as well as other supplies.[242]

In late November, military authorities turned their attention to the protection of the region and its civilian population, and informed the RCMP about the existence of the HARIKARI Club. The threat of sabotage to essential home front installations and the possible danger to civil life and property was taken very seriously by the RCMP. On 29 November, Deputy Commissioner F.J. Mead went to Montreal to discuss the HARIKARI Club threat with Military District 4 officials. Meeting with Major-General E.J. Renaud, the officer commanding Military District 4, and camp commandant Hiltz, he became apprised of the seriousness of the situation and expressed great concern with the danger of sabotage to the important electric power plants at Cèdres and Beauharnois. In the end, all agreed that something serious might soon happen and that measures needed to be taken immediately to counter the threat.[243] Deputy Commissioner Mead then visited the RCMP's "C" Division headquarters in Montreal, where he met with Glen Bethel of the FBI, Commissioner S.T. Wood, and other members of the RCMP. They agreed that there would be the fullest cooperation between the RCMP and Military District 4 authorities and to prepare precautionary plans. Deputy Commissioner F.J. Harvison of "C" Division, RCMP, was sent the next morning to Military District 4 headquarters to work with Renaud and his officers to prepare detailed plans and operational orders to be issued as quickly as possible.[244] In the meantime, RCMP and Military District 4 officials recommended, as a precautionary measure, that additional VGC troops be based in the region. Two platoons from No. 12 Company, VGC, originally stationed at Camp No. 23 Monteith, Ontario, arrived as reinforcements at St. Jean, Quebec, in the late afternoon of 1 December. Their task was to protect the civilians living in the vicinity of the camp in the event of a possible breakout.[245]

Although urgent requests to segregate the camp compound had been issued by the Directorate of Military Intelligence and Camp Grande Ligne officers, higher authorities remained hesitant. The reason was that no one knew whether or not prisoners of war in other camps were aware of the HARIKARI Club's existence or whether similar Nazi organizations had been established in other internment centres. There was the dual possibility that transferring HARIKARI Club leaders might provoke the other "Black" prisoners to initiate the suicide process or trigger the rise of similar groups in other camps.[246] The situation began to change on 1 December, when Major-General Renaud urged the Department of National Defence to move all "Blacks" out of the district and recommended that another camp be chosen for the incarceration of such prisoners. His argument was that "Black" internment camps should not be located near urbanized, industrialized, and densely populated areas, as was the case with Grande Ligne. Instead, they should be established in isolated regions as far removed as possible from vulnerable locales. His reasons were as follows:

> A) The density of the civil population in the neighbouring area; (B) The proximity of Grande Ligne to Montreal District where a considerable number of factories are employed on war work; (C) The easy access to power plants such as Beauharnois, Cèdres, Black River and even Shawinigan, the damage of which would cause great harm to the war effort; (D) The number of airports in the neighbourhood – St. Jean, St. Hubert, Dorval; (E) The proximity to ammunition dumps at L'Acadie and Delson; (F) The difficulty of providing immediate trained reinforcements due to lack of troops in the vicinity. This is particularly so in the winter months when roads to Grande Ligne may become snowbound.[247]

Although Renaud emphasized that all possible precautionary measures had already been taken and that the situation was well in hand, he did warn about the rapidity with which a HARIKARI Club attack might occur and the difficulties that might be encountered by VGC troops if such a scenario ever happened. He was particularly concerned with the older age of VGC guards as well as their poor equipment.[248] Minister of National Defence A.G.L. McNaughton was immediately made aware of the necessity to transfer the "Black" prisoners.

On the morning of 2 December, McNaughton discussed the HARIKARI Club threat with top-ranking Department of National Defence and RCMP officials. He noted that Minister of Justice Louis S. St-Laurent had been briefed on the HARIKARI Club by the RCMP and was particularly concerned with the serious implications of a possible breakout at Grande Ligne. McNaughton made it abundantly clear that the fullest cooperation should continue between military authorities and the RCMP, who were responsible for the protection of civilians.[249] An arrangement was formalized with Commissioner Wood, whereby the RCMP agreed to supply a liaison officer to the Department of National Defence to enhance cooperation.[250] Their greatest concern, however, was the question of transferring approximately 100 HARIKARI Club members to another suitable "Black" camp. After much discussion, McNaughton ordered that "an absolute secure prisoner of war camp be prepared at once to hold from 200 to 250 officers, so that it can be used if it is decided to remove the leaders from Grande Ligne" and also that "full standards of accommodation for officers under the Geneva Convention be observed in order to prevent reprisals in Germany."[251]

When it was pointed out that there was no vacant camp immediately available, all agreed that the most suitable camp was located at Seebee, Alberta, which was fairly isolated in the Rocky Mountains, far from major urban centres or military installations. It was proposed that Seebee be used as a "Super Black" camp for "Black" German officers from all of Canada's prisoner of war camps. After much discussion, it was decided that the 460 German officers and 156 other ranks currently interned at Seebee be moved to the then vacant army training centre at Wainright, Alberta, which would be converted into a prisoner of war camp that could hold approximately 700 officers and 200 other ranks. The drawback was that it would take between six weeks and two months to make the Wainright facilities sufficiently secure. In the end, it was agreed to obtain the concurrence of the chiefs of the General Staff as to the availability of the Wainright training centre, to make arrangements with the quartermaster general for construction and conversion plans, and to select immediately a commanding officer and the required personnel. In the meantime, it was decided to keep the eventual transfer of the "Black" inmates a secret.[252]

On 4 December, the chiefs of the General Staff discussed the transfer of HARIKARI Club members to Seebee. Lieutenant-General J.C. Murchie, the chief of the General Staff, "directed that the hutted accommodation at Wainright would be made immediately available as accommodation for POW removed from Seebee so that in turn the latter could be used to hold officer POW removed from Grande Ligne." He emphasized that the transfer of the "Black" inmates would have to wait until the construction of the new camp, designated No. 135, at Wainright was complete. Only at that time would Grande Ligne no longer be used for the internment of "Black" prisoners.[253] It was now only a matter of time before Canadian authorities could attempt to dismantle the HARIKARI Club.

In the meantime, Military District 4 completed the strengthening of the camp's security system, which had begun a month earlier. Guard towers were reinforced, additional firearms were supplied, a plentiful quantity of pistol-grip spotlights and ground flares were furnished, additional flood lights, searchlights and other lighting equipment were installed, new barbed wire entanglements were erected, and six machine-gun posts were established at strategic points around the camp with weapons facing towards the enclosure.[254] Additional VGC troops, "to the limit of the capacity of the barracks," were stationed in the camp. Reserve VGC forces were also standing by at St. Jean and Farnham. According to operational orders devised by Military District 4 and the RCMP, these troops were to form a "recapture screen" around the camp area in the advent of a mass escape. They were to protect all bridges and railway stations leading to Montreal and intercept all civilian traffic on nearby roads. An agreement was even made with the Canadian National Railway and Canadian Pacific Railway to permit VGC troops to examine all freight trains passing through the region. Men from these units were also to protect vital industrial plants, as well as the Beauharnois and Cèdres electric powerhouses, where "considerable sabotage could be carried out without explosives and other sabotage equipment." Damage to these two power plants, it was believed, "would seriously affect all industries in the Montreal area" and cause delays in war production. It is important to note that VGC guardsmen were to be assisted in their duties around the region by RCMP personnel. Arrangements were also made with the British Commonwealth Air Training Plan (BCATP) No. 9 Air Observation School at St. Jean for military aircraft, which were to be used for aerial reconnaissance and for observing the movements of escapees. The Quebec Provincial Police, the New York State Police, the Vermont State Police, the FBI, and the United States Border Patrol were also to be notified. Canadian Army units were to be used only if VGC and RCMP personnel proved unable to control the situation.[255]

To coordinate a possible recapture operation, a temporary headquarters, commonly referred to as "Bleak House," was established in a vacant building located about a half-mile away from Grande Ligne on the main road leading to the camp. The house also served as a temporary barracks for two well-armed VGC platoons and four RCMP constables. The operational orders stated:

> The first duty of these troops will be to assist the troops at the camp in preventing any actual escape, but the moment an escape occurs, or it appears probable that an attempt may be successful these men will take up previously assigned positions to protect the civilians in the neighbourhood of the camp. There are twenty-five houses in the immediate vicinity of the camp. It is planned to place one Sten sub-machine gun equipped man in each house to remain on duty until relieved, or until instructed that the danger period has passed. They will be under the control of officers picked for this duty who will be working closely with the RCMP personnel also stationed at "Bleak House." ... In discussing the protection of civilians, consideration was given the danger of unduly alarming these people. It was decided that advance warning would not be advisable, but that all Army and RCMP personnel visiting the houses should be French-speaking. It is considered advisable to merely tell the householders that there have been some escapes and to volunteer to safeguard the houses – rather than to handle the approach in a manner that would greatly upset and alarm householders. Constant patrols by Army officers and RCMP personnel would then make sure that proper precautionary measures were in effect at each house.[256]

To ensure that the Canadians benefited from a proper communication system in case prisoners cut telephone lines, radio transmitting and receiving equipment was installed at Camp Grande Ligne, at Bleak House, and at Military District 4 headquarters. A first aid station was also set up at Bleak House. In the meantime, the RCMP began preparing copies of photographs that had been taken of all prisoners upon their arrival in Canada for distribution to newspapers, bridge guards, and other civilian authorities.[257]

On 30 December, an incident occurred that alarmed Canadian military authorities and confirmed the seriousness of the HARIKARI Club plot. The scare began when VGC guardsmen involved in a routine inspection of the prisoner of war living quarters found an anonymous letter addressed to the camp commandant warning him about the preparation of an "act of grave violence and destruction" by some of the camp's inmates. Unaware that the camp staff already knew about the HARIKARI Club, the author of the note, who probably was a "White" prisoner, urgently requested the transfer of all German officers involved in the scheme. The letter provided the names of the most important and dangerous ones.[258]

In light of these revelations, Canadian military officials became certain that HARIKARI Club members planned an escape at the earliest possible moment. On 3 January 1945, four RCMP intelligence officers arrived in the region. One of them was stationed in the camp, while the others were assigned to Bleak House.[259] The Directorate of Prisoners of War also informed the commandants of each Canadian prisoner of war camp about the situation at Grande Ligne. All were asked to keep a vigilant eye for the existence of schemes similar to the HARIKARI Club.[260] Tension rose on 6 January when a VGC guard accidentally discharged his rifle and put a bullet through the electric light conduit, thereby creating a short in the wire and starting a fire in the recreation hut. Fortunately, the local fire department responded rapidly and was able to extinguish the flames without any serious damage. Surprisingly, none of the HARIKARI Club leaders took advantage of the incident to launch an escape.[261]

HARIKARI Club members were finally transferred to the "Super Black" prisoner of war camp at Seebee in Alberta on 6 February 1945. In order not to agitate the prisoners and provoke a pre-emptive HARIKARI Club attack, the move was kept secret. To instil an element of surprise, the operation was done in the early morning hours, when all inmates were asleep. The prisoners of war selected to be transferred were immediately rounded up by armed guards and taken away, along with their belongings. In the end, the Canadians faced no resistance whatsoever. Overall, some 236 "Black" inmates were transferred. The camp was thoroughly searched that evening by RCMP and VGC personnel. The radio receiver and numerous escape tools were found.[262] The HARIKARI Club threat faded away after the surprise transfer. Interestingly, a mass escape scheme similar to that of the HARIKARI Club was planned at Camp Seebee by several of the younger "Black" inmates transferred from Grande Ligne. According to a former inmate, the Seebee group intended to escape and to operate as a commando or guerrilla unit to demolish bridges and dams, cut telephone and power lines, and be as disruptive as possible in the region. Their goal was to instil panic in the civilian population and tie up large numbers of Canadian troops. The plot was apparently dismantled by some of the older German officers.[263]

Despite the lessons learned from the HARIKARI Club experience, Nazi elements continued to flourish in the camps of southern Quebec. Although support for Nazism was weakened when Germany unconditionally surrendered to the Allies on 7 May 1945, "Black" power remained an important force. This caused problems for the Canadian government, which was in the midst of re-educating its war prisoners. At Camp Grande Ligne, authorities pleaded in June 1945 for the transfer out of "Black" prisoners because they were a "stubborn hindrance to the efforts of cooperation which were made by the camp spokesman." The Nazi elements retarded the development of "White" attitudes among other prisoners.[264] The situation worsened in July when many "Whites" were transferred to Camp Sorel to work for the Allied Control Commission. One alarming report stated that "there is now not enough counter-pressure to keep the "Blacks" in check. This situation tends to endanger the success of the policies of re-education that have been laid down by high authority."[265] The culmination of this issue occurred on 7 August 1945, when "Black" prisoners organized a strike to oppose the re-education program that was supported by the camp spokesman. In fact, the latter was "perceived as a traitor and collaborator whose removal by murder was desirable." Ninety percent of the prisoners participated in the strike. Although it ended when camp authorities intervened, the situation demonstrated the considerable power that hardcore Nazi prisoners still held.[266]

Summary

Physical and psychological strain was common among prisoners in the camps of southern Quebec and a source of constant worry to the authorities. Although internees were given numerous opportunities to pursue recreational activities, the pressures imposed by years of internment could not be eradicated. Restricted mobility, sexual deprivation, social alienation, and the lack of material comforts demoralized the prisoners, and their discontent was expressed in acts of dissension, such as strikes, riots, illicit activities, and escape attempts. In response, camp authorities were forced to apply discipline and punish the perpetrators. Conflicting ideologies were another serious problem inside the camps. Both Communism and Nazism prospered among inmates and had to be controlled by the Canadian authorities. Despite the PHERUDA system of prisoner of war classification and intense censorship, such ideological conflicts persisted. Communists and Nazis sometimes used violence to convert fellow inmates, and camp authorities were in a constant state of alert. The HARIKARI Club at Camp Grande Ligne is the most dramatic example of how potentially dangerous some inmates could be.

4
Labour Projects

Labour projects were an important aspect of the internment operation in southern Quebec. Although this scheme included unpaid compulsory services, the bulk of the program was paid. The labour projects' purpose was to employ the internees on a voluntary basis to produce goods that had no direct connection with arms and ammunitions. Most worked on farming operations and in camp workshops. The labour projects eased the pressure of having to billet huge numbers of prisoners on the Canadian home front and contributed to the country's agricultural and industrial production. Although farming was very popular among southern Quebec inmates, the most important internee labour contribution was through the Works Program. This industrial project used internee labour in "camp factories" that produced great quantities of goods, such as camouflage nets, boots, and ammunition boxes. These factories were established in most of the region's camps.

Labour projects gave the internees a constructive pastime and an opportunity to earn money to buy goods from camp canteens. Moreover, they gave the prisoners the ability to practise new trades that they could use after the war. For the camp authorities, labour projects were an effective method for neutralizing unrest. Paying inmates for their labour made authorities hope that they would not dare bite the hand that fed them. Internee labour programs in southern Quebec were introduced in 1940 and lasted well into 1946. Both civilian detainees and prisoners of war were involved in various work schemes.

Regulations governing the employment of civilian internees and prisoners of war were very different. The treatment of prisoners of war was controlled by international conventions, unlike that of civilian prisoners. According to Article 27 of the Geneva Convention, belligerents could employ as workmen prisoners of war who were physically fit, according to their rank and abilities. (Officers and persons of equivalent status were exempt from employment.) Articles 29 and 30 indicated that no prisoners of war were to be employed on work for which they were physically unsuited and that they were not to work excessive hours or longer than was permitted for civilian workers employed on the same work.[1] Article 31 stated that work done by prisoners of war was to have no direct connection with the operations of the war. It was strictly forbidden to employ prisoners in the manufacture or transport of arms and munitions of any kind, or on the transport of materials destined for combatant units. Finally, it was prohibited in Article 32 to employ prisoners of war on unhealthy or dangerous work.[2] In principle, none of these conditions applied to civilian internees, for whom cheap exploitation became a possibility. In Canada enemy combatants and civilian prisoners were originally classified in the same category under the provisions of the Defence of Canada Regulations; prisoners of war were referred to as "prisoners of war Class 1," while so-called enemy aliens were categorized as "prisoners of war Class 2." This system of classification enabled civilian internees to benefit from the same rights as prisoners of war, particularly the Geneva Convention, and to contribute on an equal scale in labour projects.[3]

Compulsory Employment

Life behind barbed wire entailed numerous responsibilities for prisoners. Among them were compulsory camp duties that included paid and unpaid tasks. Daily chores and maintenance work formed the bulk of the unpaid compulsory labour. As stipulated by Article 34 of the Geneva Convention, prisoners of war were not to receive pay for work in connection with the administration, internal arrangement, and maintenance of camps.[4] This was reinforced by the Department of National Defence's *Orders and Instructions, Internment Camps*, which stipulated that civilian internees and prisoners of war below the rank of corporal or the equivalent ratings could be compulsorily employed without pay on maintenance work. Unpaid labour included the upkeep of the camps' roadways; the clearing of snow; the unloading and hauling of rations, fuel, and other camp supplies; the sawing and splitting of wood for fuel; the cutting of hay; the repairing of buildings; and any other similar work approved by the Department of National Defence.[5] In other words, internees were not paid for duties that contributed directly to the maintenance of the camps or their own comfort. When the civilian internees in Camp Sherbrooke were asked to chop 150 elm trees into cords of firewood in the fall of 1941, they were not paid for the task. The reason was that this wood was to be used as fuel for heating the buildings.[6] Only on rare occasions did prisoners receive compensation for camp-related tasks. One such case occurred at Camp Sherbrooke during the civilian internment phase. Rats had nested underneath huts, and camp authorities told inmates they would be paid 40 cents for any rodent that they could catch.[7] Unpaid compulsory work was crucial for the good functioning of the camps and was used for the duration of the region's internment operation.

Paid compulsory labour consisted of tasks connected with camp services and construction work. According to the *Orders and Instructions, Internment Camps*, camp services were vital for the proper functioning of Canadian internment camps. Because internment centres had to be self-sufficient, each camp was equipped with tailor, cobbler, barber and carpenter shops as well as hospital and kitchen facilities. Internees with specific skills and trades were employed for these duties. Aside from doctors and dentists, who were paid 50 cents a day, prisoners involved in trades earned between 20 and 30 cents per day.[8] Such positions were limited and few inmates benefited from this type of employment. By February 1942, for example, out of a camp population of approximately 900 inmates, only the camp leader, the deputy camp leader, and the camp adjutant were paid for their services at Camp Sherbrooke, along with ten accountants and clerks, two doctors, three hospital orderlies, two dentists, two tailors, four barbers, twenty-seven cooks, six stokers, nine cleaners, one electrician, one plumber, one carpenter, and one runner.[9] Despite their limited numbers, these jobs ensured that the prisoners benefited from certain services. Administrative and service-sector work was common in all of southern Quebec's internment camps and these positions remained active throughout the war.

Compulsory paid labour also involved construction duties inside or outside the camp area "involving capital outlay, whereby the state benefited financially." Prisoners were paid to construct new buildings, drains, roads, and any other type of modification to the existing facilities.[10] For example, because camps Farnham and Sherbrooke were unfinished during the early days of internment, authorities used internee labour to accelerate progress and prepare the facilities for winter. For such tasks, prisoners were paid between 20 and 30 cents per day, money that they were happy to earn.[11]

The problem with camp-related work was that internees were either employed in limited numbers or temporarily. What was needed were stable labour projects that could employ more prisoner volunteers. In early 1940, the Canadian authorities began to consider using internee labour for the benefit of Canada's home front.[12] In June 1940, Military District 4 authorities submitted a report entitled *Scheme for the Employment of Interned Aliens* that clearly indicated why the government intended to introduce major work projects within the camps:

> When any group of men, large or small, are forcibly detained in a restricted area removed from their ordinary activities, their morale rapidly deteriorates if they are not given some occupation. This leads to discontent which gives rise to insubordination, a tendency to destroy property wantonly, and renders the group difficult to handle. The result is that an increased number of men are required to guard them. Material of all kinds is destroyed, food is wasted and an internment camp becomes much more expensive than is necessary to operate ... It is therefore of primary necessity to provide some form of labour for those forcibly detained.[13]

It was also mentioned in the document that "conditions have forced us to concentrate into camps a number of men who must be fed, clothed, and housed at our expense ... If we have to detain these people, we should plan to make the best possible use of them." According to the report, agricultural work would be the best means of exploiting internee labour. The objective was to prepare land for future settlement while making the camps self-supporting in the shortest possible time through farming: "While internees are not criminals, they are persons confined for the safety of the state, and, as they cost a certain amount to keep, every effort should be made to make them self-supporting, and, if possible, profitable."[14] Farming was to give the internee an opportunity to raise his self-esteem and to escape the boredom of life behind barbed wire while he contributed to the overall welfare of the camp.

Farming Operations

During the phase of civilian internment in southern Quebec, agricultural work was introduced in two of the region's camps. The first was at Camp Farnham. Located on the property of the Dominion Experimental Farm, it possessed all the necessary assets for such an operation, including infrastructure, tools, livestock and rich arable land. The Directorate of Internment Operations decided to exploit this advantage for the benefit of the internees as early as September 1940. "It is recommended that the present farm foreman and herdsman be employed to take care of the herd, and also harvest the crop," said Brigadier-General Edouard de Bellefeuille Panet, director of Internment Operations. "We understand the cows are being milked and the milk sold to a dairy in Farnham. The foreman and herdsman will have to be employed permanently to supervise the work of the internees while the camp is occupied by them."[15] When the prisoners arrived at Camp Farnham in October 1940, some forty acres of land were made available to them along with twenty-three cows, four horses, a tractor, and numerous tools. Because of the lateness in the season, work on the farm began immediately. As camp authorities indicated, "It is planned to have the farm ploughed and this should be done in the next few weeks."[16] Land had to be prepared for seeding in the spring. Two prisoners skilled in agriculture went to the fields on 27 October 1940 and began preparing twelve acres.[17] In the spring of 1941, the farm's first seeds were planted.[18] A deal was also made with a neighbouring farmer to rent twenty-one acres of land for $150. This increased the size of the camp's farm to some thirty acres.[19]

Soon after, Camp Île-aux-Noix initiated its own farming operation. The process began on 12 May 1941, when representatives from the Dominion Experimental Farm at Ste-Clothilde visited the camp. Immediately, enthusiastic prisoners began preparing the fields with a disc-harrow that they had brought with them.[20] The farming operation at Camp Île-aux-Noix was somewhat smaller than the one in Farnham; only forty-nine internees were employed on the farm at Île-aux-Noix as opposed to between eighty and a hundred inmates working on the one at Farnham.[21] Evidently, Camp Farnham was the most productive. During the 1941 season, the farm produced 38,700 pounds of carrots, 48,900 pounds of turnips, 3,800 pounds of beets, 62,000 pounds of potatoes, and 21 tons of hay.[22] Most of the products cultivated at camps Farnham and Île-aux-Noix were either sold to local grocers or consumed in the camps. According to the Camp Farnham war diary, "The farm was a success. Aside from providing some 150,000 lbs. of vegetables, the farm has paid for the labour of the internees who were utilized."[23]

Farming operations were such a success during the civilian internment phase that when prisoners of war arrived in southern Quebec, the Canadian authorities agreed to let these new inmates work on camp farms. Camp Farnham was the first southern Quebec internment camp to operate a farm during the prisoner of war phase. The process began as soon as the first enemy merchant seamen arrived in the camp in April 1942. Because most of the sailors had never farmed, emphasis was placed on potatoes, which are easy to cultivate. The 1942 camp harvest was less diversified and consisted of 1,500 pounds of beets, 5,760 pounds of cabbage, 4,350 pounds of carrots, 60 pounds of cucumbers, 3,000 pounds of turnips, 9,955 pounds of tomatoes – and 101,625 pounds of potatoes.[24] With the transfer of the seamen to Camp Sherbrooke in November 1942, farming operations at Camp Farnham came to an end.

After November 1942, Farnham was used for the temporary incarceration of prisoner of war officers, who, according to the Geneva Convention, were prevented from doing any kind of work in prison camps. The irony was that the German officers did wish to operate a farm. In January 1943, they asked Ernest L. Maag, delegate in Canada for the International Committee of the Red Cross, if an experimental farm school could be created at Camp Grande Ligne, where they were to be soon transferred. On 21 January 1943, Maag approached Colonel H.N. Streight, director of Prisoners of War, and introduced the demand, to which this latter agreed.[25] Canadian authorities requested a confirmation from the Farnham internees, whose camp spokesman indicated, "I and the officers in Camp 40 are very interested in such an enterprise. There is a great demand for it, and many would take that profession [farmer] after the war." The prisoners emphasized their wish to operate a garden farm with cows, poultry, and hogs. To pay the expenses, the internees approached the German Red Cross for a $5,000 loan, which they were to reimburse with the farm's profits.[26] To ensure that this project was serious and that money was well invested, the Red Cross asked for a written assurance, signed by the officer in charge of internment operations in Military District 4 and by the Camp Farnham spokesman. As the document stipulated, the prisoners "pledge themselves to look after the livestock, regardless of what may happen at the camp ... The officers also are prepared to pledge their word that these schools will not be used to facilitate escapes, all garden and farm workers being strictly on parole."[27] The Grande Ligne farm was finally inaugurated and the prisoners began to buy livestock and farm implements with their loan from the Red Cross. While the internees were still at Camp Farnham in early June 1943, arrangements were made with a local farmer at Grande Ligne to begin work on the farm for $100. As a result, the forty-acre farm was readied for the season, its land disked, harrowed, and seeded.[28]

When the prisoners arrived at Camp Grande Ligne on 28 June 1943, they were very pleased with the farm and immediately began working the fields.[29] The Red Cross delegates who visited the camp on 21 July 1943 were also happy with the camp farm. As Ernest Maag reported,

> We have inspected the fields and gardens where a nice harvest will soon be obtained. The prisoners arrived in this camp on 28 June, at a time when the season was far too advanced to sow or plant; we therefore made arrangements earlier with the camp commandant to have local farmers do the work instead, and everything was done when the prisoners arrived in the camp. Some plants had even started to germinate. Nowadays, the prisoners are busy weeding and spraying the fields with insecticides, and, on the day of our visit, were picking an abundant harvest of radishes ... The German officers work on parole in the fields outside of the camp compound. They all give their word of honour that they will not abuse this privilege to try to escape, nor use the tools at their disposal to prepare escapes ... It is important to mention that work on the farm and gardens contributes more than anything else to maintain the prisoners' morale. They are very interested in the project and are evidently obtaining great satisfaction.[30]

In the end, the Grande Ligne farming operation was a complete success. Production during the first season was profitable. Eighty-two thousand pounds of potatoes were harvested during the 1943 season, along with 28,000 pounds of turnips, 6,500 pounds of red beets, 3,500 pounds of beans, 750 pounds of peas, 2,500 pounds of oats, 800 pounds of barley, 4,000 pounds of hay, 32 square miles of corn, 4,500 cobs of sweet corn, 2,085 pounds of radishes, 20,000 cucumbers, 43 bags of lettuce, and 38 bags of silver beets. Some 350 German prisoner of war officers worked on the farm.[31] Camp Grande Ligne also relied on livestock. When the first animals arrived in September 1943, a department of husbandry was immediately created to coordinate the stables. This meant that farming operations were divided, as some prisoners were assigned to the fields while others to the stable. At the time, the camp's livestock was composed of three milk cows, eight pigs, and 101 chickens.[32] By February 1944, the number of animals in the camp had reached a peak of nine milk cows, twenty-one pigs, 201 chickens, and fifteen geese.[33] The livestock enabled the prisoners to benefit from fresh eggs, meat, and milk. On numerous special occasions, permission was granted by the Canadian authorities for the slaughter of certain animals for camp consumption.[34] In December 1945, for instance, five pigs and one cow were killed for the Christmas dinner.[35]

Camp Grande Ligne also experimented with other staples. In March 1943, when the prisoners expressed their desire to use maple products, an arrangement was concluded with the Grande Ligne Mission, which owned a sugar bush on the camp's site. The mission was to set up the necessary equipment and provide the expert labour while the internees furnished a few men. Maple sugar production was to be divided fifty-fifty between the camp and the mission.[36] Thirteen hundred maple trees were tapped and more than 200 gallons of syrup were produced.[37] So successful was the maple syrup production that it was renewed in 1944.[38] The internees at Grande Ligne also exploited a nearby apple orchard in September 1944.[39] By the end of the month, they had picked two tons. These were stored and apples were given twice a week to the prisoners for as long as stocks lasted.[40] The prisoners at Camp Grande Ligne also produced honey in early 1945. Ten colonies of bees in thriving condition were acquired and a rumour circulated that these bees had been purchased from a farm owned by a brother of American General George S. Patton. The internees nicknamed the insects "Patton's Panzerbees."[41] Initially the production of honey went well, but problems emerged in June 1945 when it was reported that the bees were starving, their natural food sources having been depleted by an early frost.[42] Nevertheless, the colonies survived and in early August the prisoners decided to increase honey production by buying more bees.[43]

In the fall of 1944, farming operations resumed at Camp Farnham after two seasons of inactivity. The function of the thirty-acre farm was to be somewhat different from the one initiated at Camp Farnham during the civilian phase. The new camp farm was to be operated under a sharecropping arrangement. According to this scheme, two-thirds of the production's profits were kept by the internees and one-third was retained by the Canadian authorities. To ensure that this operation was profitable, prisoners were given classes on Canadian farming techniques and even the opportunity to have supervised visits to neighbouring farms.[44] During the winter, three greenhouses located outside the camp enclosure were rented by the prisoners from the Canadian authorities. They were used to seed vegetables that would be transplanted onto the farm's fields in the spring. Prisoners could now work on farm-related duties all year long.[45] By April 1945, the greenhouses proved their worth as some 54,000 cabbage, 54,000 cauliflower, 28,000 red cabbage, and 15,000 tomato plants had been grown during the winter while radishes, lettuce, carrots, celery, horseradishes, and spinach were seeded.[46] In the fall of 1945, as the first season came to an end, the vegetables grown on the camp farm were sent to a local cannery, where they were canned at 6 cents per can. Sixteen prisoners were employed at the cannery. The products were then marketed in Montreal. Total profits for the 1945 season amounted to $15,000: $10,000 for the prisoners and $5,000 for the Canadian authorities.[47] The prisoners also harvested tobacco, some of which they used for their own consumption.[48]

A small farming operation was also initiated at Camp Sherbrooke in the summer of 1945. Prisoners created small gardens where they cultivated flowers, vegetables, strawberries, and raspberries.[49] Alfred Desrochers wrote in Sherbrooke's *La Tribune*, "The barracks are surrounded by victory gardens where hundreds of pounds of vegetables of all kinds are harvested. A large communal garden outside of the enclosure furnishes an abundant harvest of potatoes and cabbages, so popular with the Germans. The prisoners also raise rabbits, permitting them to enjoy civet at least once a month in addition to the more ordinary camp menu."[50] These gardens were very popular and helped to embellish the camp. The camp intelligence officer reported in May 1945 that "nearly all of the prisoners had their sharing lots and were looking after them."[51] So important was gardening at Camp Sherbrooke that greenhouses were established for growing plants in the winter.[52] Expert gardeners even went so far as to cultivate tropical plants in these glass buildings.[53]

Until the repatriation of the prisoners in 1946, the farming operations at camps Farnham, Grande Ligne, and Sherbrooke continued to be active and formed a major part of the labour projects. The prisoners appreciated the opportunity to work the fields and consume their own products. As a Farnham prisoner said, "Planning a better living ... is important – A plentiful supply for our consumption of 'greens' during the summer is assured, as well as extra vegetables for our use next fall and winter. Vegetables are one of the essentials of better and healthier living."[54]

Prisoners of war were also hired by Canadian farmers to work on local farms. On 24 July 1943, Order-in-Council PC 5864 authorized volunteer prisoners to be transferred to farms where they could be billeted with the farmer.[55] Labourers were desperately needed in the Canadian countryside, where manpower shortages had developed because of military recruitment and the movement of young Canadians to cities where better paying industrial jobs were available in war factories. The prisoner of war population in Canada formed a potentially large labour force that Canadian authorities hoped could alleviate some of the rural manpower problems. In the summer of 1943, several Canadian internment camps permitted volunteer prisoners of war to work and be billeted on neighbouring farms.[56] In southern Quebec, however, the process only began with the end of the war in the summer of 1945. This difference had to do with the nature of internment in the region. Camps Farnham and Grande Ligne housed prisoner of war officers who, according to the Geneva Convention, were not supposed to work. As for the enemy merchant seamen detained at Camp Sherbrooke, most had no farming experience. Besides, the sailors were already busy working in the successful Works Program inaugurated at that camp, addressed later in this chapter. The end of the war in 1945 altered the situation. With the threat of retributions against Canadian prisoners of war held by German forces alleviated, Canadian authorities decided to permit all German prisoners of war, including officers, to work.[57] They believed that this decision would keep all internees occupied before repatriation, especially as the German prisoners of war constituted less of a threat now that the Allies had won the war.

In order to benefit from internee labour, a farmer had to produce a certificate from the Department of National Defence's Selective Commission before signing any contracts with the prisoners and the camp authorities. Farmers had to prove to the commission that they had been unable to obtain Canadian civilian labourers.[58] Every time positions opened on local farms, prisoners voluntarily applied in great numbers.[59] For example, when a call was made in Camp Sherbrooke in May 1946 for fourteen volunteers to work on local farms, some 104 inmates applied.[60] So many applications obliged the camp authorities to choose candidates; usually, they chose the prisoners with the best records. As the Camp Sherbrooke intelligence officer noted, "The men were chosen on their good behaviour and their good work attendance."[61] Once chosen, prisoners had to give in writing their promise not to escape or to commit acts prejudicial to Canada, the British Commonwealth, or the United Nations.[62]

Prisoners were lodged and fed on the farms. In some cases, they would work on farms during the day and come back to the internment camp at night. In October 1945, for instance, forty-three Camp Farnham inmates were billeted on farms while seventy-five others left the camp on parole each day for jobs on neighbouring farms.[63] Usually, one prisoner was assigned per farm. In some cases, there were as many as three, depending on the size of the farm and the farmer's needs.[64] The presence of the prisoners of war on southern Quebec farms occasionally worried civilians. According to one farmer, "Certain people in the village were scared of the prisoners. They told us: 'One day, we will find all of you dead in your beds.'"[65] Feeding these fears was the fact that no armed guards accompanied the prisoners on the farms. Prisoners were "on parole" and worked under the supervision of the hiring farmers. Ignorance and the impact of wartime propaganda depicting Germans as dangerous enemies certainly played an important role in Canadians' fears.

The story on the farms was somewhat different. The relationships between farmers and prisoners often evolved from mere tolerance to warm friendship. In *Behind Canadian Barbed Wire*, David Carter wrote that "in some instances, relationships between the farmer and the POW became so positive that the POW would be left for days on end with the farm, livestock and children in his care. Some POWs were sponsored back into Canada after the war by their farmer friends. Some married the farmer's daughter."[66] In most cases, farmers were satisfied with the presence of the prisoners on their farms. One southern Quebec farmer said of the POW billeted on his farm,

> He was an air force officer ... He was fed and lodged on the farm. I kept him for about seven months. He spoke very well in French. We were not scared of him since the war was over. He said he was happy to work on a farm. He spoke very little of the war. He felt very bad about what had happened in his past. When he learned that he would soon be repatriated to Germany along with his comrades, he told me that he was leaving Canada with much sadness, even if he was looking forward to re-joining his family overseas. "I will come back some day," he said.[67]

The popularity of hiring prisoners of war for farm work led more and more farmers to request internee labour. Demands were received daily.[68] The camp with the largest number of prisoners working on local farms was Farnham, growing from four individuals in September 1945[69] to 126 in March 1946.[70] Camp Sherbrooke had the smallest number of prisoners working on parole on farms. Between September 1945 and June 1946, only eleven internees were employed on farms.[71] As for Camp Grande Ligne, by February 1946, some seventy prisoners were employed on farm duties around the region.[72] Working on local farms offered inmates a chance to see for themselves how Canadians lived. In a sense, it contributed to their indoctrination and re-education. By getting acquainted with civilians, the prisoners could see how Canadian society functioned and how it was different from the totalitarianism of the Third Reich. As much as working on farms offered some personal freedom and autonomy to the inmates, it also demonstrated first hand the liberties and benefits of living in democracies like Canada.

Camp Workshops

Aside from farm work, internees contributed voluntarily to Canada's war effort by working in small "camp factories." Known as the Works Program, this industrial scheme was initiated in southern Quebec during the civilian internment phase, in October 1940, because camps Sherbrooke and Île-aux-Noix did not possess the necessary acreage for farming operations. The aim was to offer the internees of these two camps an alternative. Brigadier-General Edouard de Bellefeuille Panet, director of Internment Operations, in cooperation Major D.J. O'Donahoe, the Military District 4 Works Program coordinator, decided to establish a scheme whereby internees could be employed on light manufacturing projects within the camps.[73] The Camp Île-aux-Noix war diary on 5 October 1940 stated, "The idea is to erect a building ... In one end would be housed light manufacturing machinery while the other would be devoted to a wood making plant. It is first of all necessary to have the prisoners erect the building, then to equip it with the necessary machinery. As soon as this is done, prisoners will be employed on manufacturing such articles as army folding tables, benches, chairs, kit bags, bandoliers, prisoner's uniforms, shirts, hold-alls and many other articles."[74]

In charge of the Works Program was the Ordnance Branch of the Department of National Defence, while the Department of Munitions and Supply controlled the contracts.[75] The reason why the Works Program was introduced in southern Quebec instead of other Canadian regions was because most of the prisoners incarcerated in this region at the time were civilians. Civilian internees, unlike enemy combatants, could be employed on work more closely connected with the war effort. Many had backgrounds in science, engineering, and management. Aside from the Works Program managers, controllers, accountants, and department supervisors who were paid 50 cents per day, other employees earned 20 cents, which was raised to 30 cents on 1 October 1941.[76] The Works Program came to include all Military District 4 internment camps. Workshops were built by the inmates at camps Farnham, Île-aux-Noix, and Sherbrooke; the Italian internment centre located on Île Ste-Hélène in Montreal also had one.[77]

Numerous delays affected the program. Some necessary machinery and tools were not received until January 1941, owing to shipping problems. Problems were also encountered with the internees themselves. The initial attitude of the civilian internees was not in favour of the Works Program. Many had no desire to work while being incarcerated. Some believed that the more successful the production was in the workshops the less chance they had of being released. These complications, among many others, retarded the growth of the Works Program's operation in early 1941.[78]

The first workshops were established in Camp Sherbrooke. According to Major D.J. O'Donahoe, Sherbrooke was to be the "starting point of the workshop program." In that sense, Sherbrooke was to act as a prototype camp. Inaugurated on 21 December 1940, the Sherbrooke workshops, which consisted of a woodworking department, a sewing department, a knitting department, a net-making department, and a shoe repair department became operational in January 1941.[79] By July 1941, more than $27,000 worth of goods (which included camouflage nets, kit bags, tables, benches, and wooden ammunition boxes) had been produced.[80] Camp authorities were hoping for a much larger output. As they indicated in the camp's war diary, "Greater results could and should be achieved."[81] Still, some 200 internees were employed in the Works Program at Camp Sherbrooke by July 1941.[82] The workshops remained operational until the civilian internees were transferred in December 1942.

When it was decided on 7 January 1941, to expand the Works Program to include camps Farnham and Île-aux-Noix, workshops were immediately built by the internees. Camp Île-aux-Noix's contribution to the program was somewhat limited; the camp workshop specialized in only one item, camouflage nets.[83] Opened on 15 April 1941,[84] the net-making department employed about 110 internees by July 1941. By that time, some 300 camouflage nets had been produced and shipped to the dyers.[85] The project ended in the fall of 1941 and was replaced with the Canadian Organization for Rehabilitation through Training (ORT) organization's workshop in early 1942.

Camp Farnham's Works Program operation was bigger. Construction of the "camp factories" began in January 1941.[86] Workshops became operational on 17 February 1941, and were divided in a woodworking department, a sewing department, and a knitting department. A net-making department was opened on 15 April 1941, as well as a painting department.[87] By July 1941, approximately 300 men were involved in the Farnham Works Program.[88] When the camp workshops closed on 30 November 1941, prior to the civilian internees' transfer to Camp Sherbrooke, production had been most impressive. The woodworking department had produced 1,200 soldiers' chests, 500 carpenters' tool boxes, 200 razor blade boxes, 300 bayonet racks, 1,457 fly screens and doors, 50 signposts for Camp Farnham (with lettering and painting done in the camp's paintshop), 1,201 Mk-IV folding tables, and 1,500 wooden tables. As for the sewing department, it made 30,720 holdalls, 2,500 kit bags, 700,000 hospital swabs, and 8,337 alterations to the clothing of prisoners from camps Farnham, Île-aux-Noix, and Sherbrooke when their status changed to that of refugees in June 1941. As for the knitting department, it produced 8,880 pairs of army woollen socks, while the net-making department made 3,707 camouflage nets and 2,000 projectile grommets for holding 4.9-inch artillery shells.[89] There was also a lot of recycling in the Works Program. Each day, sawdust was bagged, waste wood was brought to the cookhouse for camp consumption, and waste cloth and wool were bundled and removed to the quartermaster stores.[90]

When the civilian internees' status changed to that of refugees in June 1941, the operation of camp workshops was affected. Although the change in status gave the inmates new privileges, it also created work-related problems at Camp Sherbrooke in October 1941.[91] Two major issues caused the refugees' discontent. First, the inmates made it clear that "the change in designation has not brought about the changes in conditions which the new status suggests and that as refugees, they should be given conditions of living far more closely associated with freedom."[92] Second, the increase in salary from 20 to 30 cents per day for refugees, which took place on 1 October 1941,[93] did not please the internees, who resented the fact that a "fixed and maximum value should be set on all workers and that no opportunity exists for refugees to earn in relation to their production." Most refugees wanted to be paid for what they produced (piece work) instead of a fixed salary. Refugees also wanted to control the internal administration of the Works Program. By doing so, they felt that they "could better determine the value of each individual, both as regards his ability to produce and suitability for work" and that they could thus increase production. Believing that the solution to the present problem was to establish "a system whereby refugees could work happily and create an industry in this camp which could be developed into ever-growing importance to our war effort, rather than await developments of an ugly nature," camp authorities proved willing to grant the refugees what they wanted.[94] However, more senior representatives from Military District 4 headquarters saw the situation as a "natural result of internment" and refused to budge on the inmates' requests.[95] Fortunately, refugee discontent did not culminate in violent incidents.

By late 1941, many refugees were more interested in being released to work in Canadian factories and contribute to the Allied war effort than in labouring in camp workshops. The Canadian government's decision in the spring of 1941 to release refugees if sponsors could be found in Canada gave inmates an opportunity to work on parole for Canadian industries.[96] With the internees no longer being classed as prisoners of war, the restrictions imposed by the Geneva Convention no longer applied. As refugees, inmates could now enjoy more freedom, such as working in war-related functions if Canadian industrialists were willing to sponsor their release. This was not a problem since many industries were desperate for labour. A scheme was developed within the Works Program whereby refugees with certain skills could work voluntarily in Canadian factories for the war effort. Under this scheme, "In response to the reiterated claims on the part of refugees that they are willing and anxious to assist in the war effort, an opportunity has been developed through the Works Program to find employment for certain skilled tradesmen under conditions of freedom within a restricted area."[97] In the fall of 1941, toolmakers, machinists, machine operators, welders, pattern makers, blacksmiths, draughtsmen, and architects were to benefit from this project.

So important was skilled internee labour to Canadian industry that the government promoted it as best it could. In late 1941, an arrangement was made with Camp Farnham authorities to employ refugees for the rebuilding of machine tools at Citadel Merchandising Company Limited, a Crown company located at Ville LaSalle near Montreal. The company had been created by the Canadian government on 3 May 1940 to procure machine tools, which were vital for the production of guns, aircraft, warships, tanks, and countless other items. The company had the task of increasing as rapidly as possible the capacity to build machine tools in Canada and to buy, in the United States and elsewhere, all the machine tools that were available and suitable. These were to be rebuilt and modified for munitions production. In charge of this company was a civilian administrator by the name of T. Arnold.[98] Three Military District 4 personnel including Major D.J. O'Donahoe cooperated with Arnold and tried to find suitable refugees for work at Citadel.[99] The first refugees to be released to work for the Crown company were a group of engineers from Camp Farnham. As one of these refugees recalled, "We were free people working for the Canadian Government for standard normal wages ... We succeeded fairly well. It's not easy within a short time to put up a full fledged machine tool rebuilding operation, but we did ... so we had a successful operation until 1944-1945."[100] Internees from camps Sherbrooke and Île-aux-Noix also found work at Citadel. Another similar operation was initiated near Lachine in late 1941. Known as Machinery Services Limited, this company also employed skilled refugees and engineers on war-related work.[101] According to Eric Koch, some 250 refugees were released by April 1942, mostly for work in Canadian industries.[102] Besides the refugees who worked in Ville LaSalle and Lachine,[103] many others were employed by major factories in Montreal, Toronto, Brantford, and other Canadian cities.[104]

Aside from working in Canadian factories, some refugees cooperated with the Canadian authorities on other war-related work. At Camp Sherbrooke in September 1941, one refugee gave the camp authorities a proposal for the design of a new type of anti-tank and anti-aircraft shell. According to the refugee's rough drafts:

> attached to the base of the bullet or shell there should be a second part filled with magnesium or highly inflammable wire which on percussion would be broken at its connecting neck from the bullet proper and be set on fire. By some device the base of this portion should be made to split outwards so that it would be prevented from passing through the hole made by the bullet on contact with its target and so have the effect of expanding the burning time. It is frequently reported that aeroplanes return riddled with bullet holes and the feeling is that if each bullet left behind it a piece of burning magnesium wire, the effect would be disastrous. Similarly in anti-tank operations an armour piercing bullet passing through the gasoline tank and leaving its trail of burning magnesium would be most effective.[105]

Major W.J.H. Ellwood, Camp Sherbrooke's commandant, was so impressed by this design that he submitted the drawings to the officer commanding Military District 4 "with the recommendation that they be passed on for study and experiment."[106] Moreover, refugee engineers established a design office at Camp Farnham where they made numerous studies related to artillery pieces used by the Canadian Army. As one refugee engineer recalled, "I personally was involved in setting up a design office for gun reamers and tools for the guns in conjunction with industries ... they made the 4-inch naval guns, and out of the camp compound we set up a design office for about 14 or 15 engineers ... under the supervision of a Frenchman from ... Paris, who had come over to help us design these special tools for the guns."[107] One refugee even maintained that the cheeks and fixtures for the famous British-designed 25-pounder field guns, which were built under license in Sorel and used by the Canadian Army, were designed by engineers at Camp Farnham.[108]

Unskilled refugees were less equipped than scientists and engineers to contribute to Canada's war effort and were less likely to be liberated than skilled refugees. To help unskilled refugees develop trades and find jobs, the Canadian authorities agreed to let the Montreal-based Canadian ORT organization erect a mechanical training workshop at Camp Île-aux-Noix. The process began in December 1941 when representatives from this organization visited the camp.[109] In order not to disturb the military authorities and to save time, the ORT decided to construct the building at its own expense.[110] In January 1942, sixty internees began building the workshop,[111] which opened on 29 May 1942.[112] At the time, Camp Île-aux-Noix was the last camp in southern Quebec where refugees were housed. The ORT organization's aim was to "train Jewish young men ... in the industrial and agricultural fields in order to equip them with a trade or calling which will enable them to take their place in life and earn a living in manual occupation."[113] As Major-General Howard Kennedy, quartermaster general, indicated, "The Canadian ORT Organization ... is devoted to the creation of a new occupational existence for refugees and the masses of European Jews through industrial workshops, trade schools, farm colonies."[114] In other words, the task was to prepare highly skilled apprentices for war-related work. The ORT workshop at Camp Île-aux-Noix concentrated on training refugees as mechanics and preparing them for work in machine shops engaged in war production.[115] Employers often visited the facilities to seek new recruits. Three representatives from Machinery Services Limited and a representative from Citadel Merchandising visited the camp's shop and assessed the students in late September 1942. As a result, six refugees were selected for work at Machinery Services. The representatives also indicated that in the next few weeks fifteen other men would be chosen. Further, arrangements were made with the camp's tools controller's office to send old machines from Citadel to Île-aux-Noix for training purposes.[116]

The ORT workshop began experiencing problems in early 1943 due to reductions in the internee population at Camp Île-aux-Noix. As Colonel H.N. Streight, director of Prisoners of War, indicated in a report dated 23 March 1943, "Since the 1st December, camp strength was reduced from 354 to 180. Latter figure will be down to about 138 by reason of releases recently authorized. This will affect the ORT school."[117] As it became evident that Camp Île-aux-Noix was about to close due to the declining number of refugees, the camp's ORT training school was closed, and all the machinery was taken to the ORT technical training school in Montreal on 27 April 1943.[118] As a consequence, the Department of National Defence inherited the ORT workshop facility on the Île-aux-Noix, which continued to operate for six months.[119] Overall, the Canadian ORT organization's workshop at Île-aux-Noix was a success. A considerable number of refugees benefited from this training and were able to find work in various Canadian war industries in the Montreal region, notably Canadian Vickers Limited, Canadian Car and Foundry Company Limited, and Defence Industries Limited. Although the Île-aux-Noix workshop was closed, the Montreal-based office of the ORT organization continued to serve the needs of refugees and had retrained 269 of its 418 trainees by May 1943.[120] According to historian John Joseph Kelly, the operation of the Works Program during the phase of civilian internment was a complete success, in that "it kept refugees gainfully occupied; it permitted them to earn money with which to finance any purchases they deemed necessary from the camp canteen; it did not leave them idle time with which to contemplate their fate; it gave the government materials and crops that it would not have received otherwise; and it provided a profit for the program as a whole."[121] So successful was the Works Program that it paved the way for the larger-scale labour projects initiated by the Canadian authorities in 1943 to compensate for the lack of labour in the country. This included the employment of prisoners of war by mining and lumber companies, wheat farmers, and other contractors.[122]

The Works Program had been such a success during the civilian phase that when prisoners of war arrived at Camp Sherbrooke, in December 1942, the project remained operational. At the time, there was a growing demand for the better allocation of human resources on the home front. Ottawa was beginning to view the immense pool of prisoners of war as a passive labour force that could be exploited for the benefit of Canada. Only a few months later, on 10 May 1943, the Canadian government authorized the departments of Labour and National Defence to employ prisoners of war on a voluntary basis for essential work projects across the country at a rate of 50 cents per day. Some 5,428 prisoners of war were employed on work projects, mainly woodcutting, at the close of the 1943-44 fiscal year; the numbers rose to 8,057 at the end of the 1944-45 fiscal year.[123] In all, some 16,000 prisoners of war were employed in more than 169 different projects in factories, on docks, in mines, on farms, in fields, and in forests throughout Canada between early August 1943 and the time the last inmates left Canada in 1947.[124] The resumption of the Works Program at Camp Sherbrooke was but a mere integration into this wider scheme. As camp authorities indicated, "The continued operation of the Works Program depends upon production. So long as sufficient production is maintained to warrant economical operation, workshops will be maintained otherwise the Works Program will be closed down."[125] Lieutenant-Colonel W.D. Graham, Camp Sherbrooke's commandant, even stated in July 1943, that "the Works Program has been considered to be the main reason for having the camp, and discipline has been a secondary consideration."[126]

To maximize production and create the best work environment possible, most of the camp's "bad elements" were transferred to other camps as of May 1944. These included professional gamblers; manufacturers and dealers of alcoholic drinks; escapees; troublemakers; and fanatical Nazis. This transfer ensured that only those prisoners willing to cooperate with the Works Program remained in the camp. To further alleviate the tensions arising from internment and to raise morale, the prisoners at Camp Sherbrooke were given a great many privileges and liberties. For instance, prisoners could walk out of the camp "on parole" and go fishing on the nearby St. François River.[127] Prisoners appreciated these special privileges and understood that any breach would mean a return to past conditions. As one inmate wrote to his wife, "We have walking privileges in this camp – we can't see a guard armed, and it is up to us, how long we will enjoy these liberties. Anyone should try to escape these liberties will be over."[128] Inmates greatly appreciated what the Canadian authorities were doing by easing camp discipline. One internee wrote to his wife, "This camp is the best camp in this country – which fact has been also established by the protecting power. – All POWs going to work every day in factory, myself working eight hours a day over a year already – and enjoying more privileges over the other POW camps. Therefore I would beg you all neither food stuffs, nor cigarettes to send – as we have everything we need."[129] Another inmate described his Sunday schedule to his wife to allay her anxiety and show her how well he was being treated in Canada: "With beautiful sunshine we started the day at 6 am with concert and coffee outside, then we walked for a long stroll into the bush, by twelve we were back to the camp. After the meal we had moving pictures, 3 o'clock coffee with cakes, then after this – there is a little river around the camp where we are allowed to fish until five. Our dogs are crazy to go in for a swim. Then supper and after super football game with coffee and cakes again outdoors – As you see, we are doing well – I wish you could be here."[130]

The operation of the Works Program at Camp Sherbrooke was divided into three departments: a woodworking department, a sewing department, and a boot and shoe repair department:

> The Works Program functions in much the same way as an industrial enterprise at Camp Sherbrooke ... The woodworking department is the most important part of the program and is divided into two large workshops. The first is used for mass production while the second is more specialized and is used for the making of unique articles in limited quantities ... The woodworking department is so important that in a period of two weeks last summer, eighteen railway cars' worth of merchandise were produced ... Since its creation, it has fulfilled orders for thousands of folding tables and chairs for the Canadian armed forces, thousands of boxes and containers of various sizes and shapes, 20,000 wooden warehouse platforms, 115 stretcher carriers designed at Camp Sherbrooke and said to be a great improvement over similar existing devices, more than 60 pairs of adjustable crutches, and innumerable other objects, ranging from little card filers and fences to the large tables of administrative rooms. In most cases, the prisoners had to design the product, make the drawings, and establish the production process ... The two woodworks are equipped with all the necessary tools, which include electric saws, moulds, sandblasters, and a vast number of hand tools ... In a series of adjoining rooms is located the shoe repair department. About 100 inmates are working there, repairing used Canadian Army shoes and boots for distribution to the populations of Europe. About 2,000 pairs are repaired each week, and it is expected that this number will soon rise to 5,000 pairs. The old shoes and boots are first examined and then plunged in an oily solution from which they come out supple and pliable. The soles and the heels are then flattened and smoothed out. New heels and rubber soles are finally fixed with the help of special sewing machines ... The sewing department consists of about 36 sewing machines and is organized in much the same manner as the other more industrialized departments. It recently completed an order for 200,000 aprons and another for 100,000 ration pockets. At

> the moment, the sewing department is busy making khaki shirts. In addition to the camp's four large production workshops, there is also a metal workshop, which serves for the repair of machines and the fabrication of special metal pieces to be used inside the camp. This workshop includes a forge and all the necessary hand tools used by the machinists and the blacksmiths.[131]

Between 1943 and 1946, these workshops produced a wide array of goods. So great was production that between January and May 1945 the woodworking department produced 23,842 boxes, 15,808 packing cases, 5,000 paint crates, 160 tables, 21,432 flat pallets, 200 razor blade boxes, 300 lane markers, 209,240 shoe trees, and 500 naval lockers. The sewing department produced 19,653 shirts, 17,826 jackets (summer and winter), 22,886 trousers (summer and winter), 961 pyjama trousers, 3,301,650 swabs, 4,200 water bottle covers, 11 ambulance stretchers, 4,500 chemical warfare respirator cases, and 1,853 bags. The boot and shoe repair department made or repaired 93,481 pairs of boots and shoes.[132] Manufacturing work at Camp Sherbrooke resulted in the production of goods valued at approximately $50,000 at the close of the 1943-44 fiscal year, despite a fire that destroyed about half of the accommodation and equipment provided for the purpose.[133] At the end of the next fiscal year, in 1944-45, the output was valued at $625,000.[134] By early 1946, more than 250 prisoners were employed in the program.[135] So successful had been the Works Program that when operations were terminated in June 1946 with the closing of the camp, the Department of Justice took over most of the workshops' machinery with the intention of integrating a similar program into Canadian prisons and penal facilities.[136]

Internee Incomes and Camp Canteens

Labour projects enabled inmates to earn money while being interned. Such programs were not the only way prisoners could gain income. According to the Geneva Convention, prisoner of war officers were to continue receiving their military salaries. As Article 23 stipulated,

> Officers and persons of equivalent status who are prisoners of war shall receive from the Detaining Power the same pay as officers of corresponding rank in the armed forces of that Power, provided, however, that such pay does not exceed that to which they are entitled in the armed forces of the country in whose service they have been. This pay shall be paid to them in full, once a month if possible, and no deduction therefrom shall be made for expenditure devolving upon the Detaining Power, even if such expenditure is incurred on their behalf. An agreement between the belligerents shall prescribe the rate of exchange applicable to this payment; in default of such agreement, the rate of exchange adopted shall be that in force at the moment of the commencement of hostilities.[137]

This meant that the Canadian government was responsible for the service pay of German prisoner of war officers. The exchange rate was fixed at 15 reichsmark to £1 and the Canadian-British exchange rate at $4.43 to £1. A German general received close to $71 per month (240 reichsmark) while a lieutenant earned $21 (72 reichsmark). This changed, however, when a new rate of exchange, 40 reichsmark to £1, was established in September 1945, three months after the unconditional surrender of Germany.[138] The German government took care of the salaries of other prisoners of war. These were paid in the form of monthly allowances that were distributed to the inmates through the Swiss delegation. Non-commissioned officers were paid $11 per month while privates received $6.60. Enemy merchant seamen received quarterly payments of $13.26 from their shipping companies. Civilian internees could also receive an allocation from the German authorities if they declared their loyalty to the Third Reich, to the Swiss consul.[139] Furthermore, internees occasionally received money in letters from friends and relatives and benefited from donations by relief societies.[140]

Because inmates were not allowed to carry money, earned incomes were usually credited to their trust accounts.[141] The main reason for this prohibition was to prevent gambling and bribery. Prisoners were prohibited from using any form of official currency, whether it was cash, money orders, or cheques. In the labour projects, this financial procedure was followed. Pay lists were prepared monthly from daily time sheets by the internees' works office and submitted to the camp's orderly room for double-checking. The lists were then forwarded to the Department of National Defence, which was responsible for printing paycheques. As soon as these cheques were received in each camp, the individual prisoners whose names appeared on the pay list were credited with the amount of wages earned for the month in question. At no point was an inmate to be credited in his account with pay for work until payment had been received from Ottawa.[142] Similar procedures also applied whenever prisoners received allowances from Germany or money from relatives. Trust accounts formed the cornerstone of the camps' monetary system.

Although prisoners were not allowed to carry money, they could use their credit to purchase goods from their canteen. According to Article 12 of the Geneva Convention, canteens were to be established in all camps, and prisoners were to be able to procure, at the local market price, food commodities and ordinary articles. The profits accruing to the administrations of the camps from the canteens were to be used for the benefit of the prisoners.[143] This enabled inmates to reinvest money in their camp's economy. Because internees were not allowed to carry money, an alternative means of purchase had to be adopted. It was with this intention in mind that canteen tickets were issued by camp banks.[144] Whenever an internee wanted to withdraw credit from his account to buy goods from the canteen, he would be provided with this form of currency. A Camp Farnham memorandum of 1941 stated, "These tickets are issued to the internees as required by them against their signature on an Acquittance Roll prepared for this purpose. A cheque for the total amount of these Acquittance Rolls is then made on the Farnham Internment Camp Trust Account in favour of the Camp 'A' Internees Canteen and deposited to the credit of that account in the bank, and each prisoner is then debited with the amount shown opposite his name in the Trust Account ledger."[145] Such a procedure ensured that credit was adequately transferred from an internee's account to the canteen. This could be done only if the prisoner concerned had a sufficient balance in his trust account and if the acquittance roll had been authenticated by both the camp spokesman and the treasurer. The issue and control of canteen tickets was the responsibility of the inmates themselves.[146] Denominations recommended for canteen tickets were a dollar, 50 cents, 25 cents, 10 cents, 5 cents, and a cent.[147] To prevent illegal activities, numerous measures were introduced for the proper administration of canteen tickets. As was indicated in the *Orders and Instructions, Internment Camps*, "Coloured printed tickets only will be used. Tickets will bear the number of the camp, the value, and the period of validity. Colours will be changed semi-annually ... Tickets of different denominations are to be in different colours. At the end of each half year (June 30, December 31) all tickets will be called in and a fresh issue of tickets made of a different colour ... All tickets called in at the end of half-year periods ... are to be cremated in the presence of a responsible officer representing the Commandant."[148] By introducing new canteen tickets every six months, prisoners were prevented from accumulating large sums that could be used for gambling or other illegal activities.[149] When a prisoner was transferred elsewhere, tickets to be redeemed were returned to the camp treasurer and a certificate to this effect was handed over to the camp staff. If funds were available, the appropriate amount was credited to the internee's trust account.[150] Canteen tickets were the only form of currency that inmates could use. Prisoners could buy outside goods only through camp canteens.[151]

The operation of canteens was coordinated by a committee selected by the prisoners.[152] Canteens offered inmates an opportunity to improve their standard of living. They were usually established within a month of a camp's opening.[153] Items were classed in eight categories: (1) TOBACCO: ashtrays, cigars, cigarettes, lighters, matches, pipes, tobacco, etc.; (2) CONFECTIONERY: beer, candies, candles, chewing gum, chocolate bars, soft drinks, etc.; (3) GROCERIES: cakes, coffee, ice cream, fresh fruits and vegetables, sauces, sugar, tea, etc.; (4) TOILET ARTICLES: brushes, hair tonic, mirrors, razors and blades, scissors, shoe polish, soap, toothpaste and toothbrushes, etc.; (5) STATIONERY: books, glue, gramophone needles, ink, music records, paint and brushes, paper, pens and pencils, playing cards, rulers, etc.; (6) CLOTHING: jackets, gloves, pyjamas, shirts, shoes and laces, shower sandals, socks, ties, towels, underwear, etc.; (7) LITERATURE: books, daily, weekly or monthly magazines published in Canada, the United Kingdom, and the United

States, and newspapers; and (8) MISCELLANEOUS: can openers, fly repellents, pillows, remedies, seeds, tumblers, watches, etc.[154]

All these products had to be purchased directly from the suppliers.[155] Numerous Canadian enterprises were involved in such transactions, including the Colgate-Palmolive Company, Imperial Tobacco, and the T. Eaton Company. Canteen merchandise could also be acquired from local businesses. Products were purchased from local dairies, greenhouses, groceries, news companies, and pharmacies. Because commodities were usually purchased in large quantities, canteens contributed notably to the region's economy.[156] However, none of these suppliers could furnish camp canteens with goods that had been rationed for the war effort or were in short supply for the civilian market. For instance, when the Camp Farnham canteen tried to acquire 20 pounds of nuts, 50 pounds of raisins or currants, 300 lemons, 100 pounds of butter, and 60 pounds of coffee for their Christmas festivities in November 1944,[157] the Department of National Defence replied that "any rationed article such as butter will not be approved at any time" and that "the other supplies such as raisins, currants etc. are in short supply for the civilian market and are not approved for that reason."[158]

Although internees were forbidden to buy rationed goods through normal Canadian suppliers, they could do so via international relief organizations. Such neutral organizations were regarded by the Canadian authorities as viable suppliers for camp canteens. Because most relief societies operated worldwide, internees could sometimes purchase products not available in Canada or rationed on the Canadian market. Such was the case in April 1943 when the Camp Farnham spokesman requested the International Red Cross to gather such rationed grocery products as cinnamon, essence of almonds, vanilla, cloves, herbs, paprika, and nuts for the canteen. Furthermore, the camp spokesman indicated, "It should be specially appreciated, if you could find some way in securing oranges and grapefruits in those months when Canadian fresh fruits are not available." Needless to say that such acquisitions were not always appreciated by camp authorities, who had to conform to Canada's rationing policies.[159] Canteen inventories usually varied on a monthly basis: at Camp Sherbrooke, for example, the canteen held $5,954 worth of merchandise in July 1945 and $1,392 the next month.[160]

Canteen committees would send their requests to suppliers and pay upon receipt of the merchandise.[161] To ensure the viability of this procedure, canteen stewards had to make sure "that at all times the cash in bank is sufficient to pay all outstanding commitments; this meant that prisoners had to purchase canteen tickets in advance of the orders placed with suppliers."[162] To help administer canteens, prisoners also borrowed money from relief organizations. Such was the case at Camp Farnham in February 1945, when the canteen committee handed the International Committee of the Red Cross a Canadian Bank of Commerce draft in the amount of $1,600. This was to be the final payment due on an original loan of $5,000 arranged between the Red Cross and the Camp Farnham canteen.[163]

Canteens were allowed to buy products from local suppliers at usual civilian or retail prices and sell them at a higher rate.[164] Prices were controlled and supervised by camp authorities, but profit margins still existed. Coffee was purchased from suppliers at a cost price of 36 cents and sold to the prisoners for 50 cents; playing cards were bought for 29 cents and sold for 33 cents;[165] chocolate bars were acquired for 6 cents and sold for 7 cents; beer was bought at 19 cents and sold at 20 cents; and chewing gum was purchased at 6 cents and sold for 7 cents.[166] Canteens also enabled inmates to earn money by selling handicrafts. Talented prisoners and artists created incredible masterpieces out of wood, stone, and other products found within the camps. Woodcarving was one of the most popular forms of art. Using nothing but small pocket knives and old razor blades, inmates fashioned ashtrays, ships in bottles, chessboards, cigarette holders, and figurines. One Farnham prisoner created a beautiful "hand-carved set of chess figures, complete with board. The figures were most artistically carved out of wood, so carefully done that the very faces of the pawns showed individual expressions."[167] In the fall of 1944, Camp Sherbrooke prisoners even made Christmas toys for poor Canadian children.[168] Artists also created incredible drawings, sketches, paintings, and poems.[169] Numerous subjects, including women, camp life, and landscapes, appeared in these artworks.[170] There were many great artists in the camps of southern Quebec. The most well known was probably Oscar Cahen, who had been interned at Camp Sherbrooke during the civilian phase and who later became one of Canada's leading abstract expressionist painters.[171]

In most cases, canteens kept 10 percent of all sales. Prisoners could also sell their artistic products through the numerous art exhibitions held inside the camps. During such exhibitions, inmates were often given the opportunity to sell their artwork outside of the enclosure. All sales were to be done through the "proper channels" and were to be guided by two conditions: "The price of each article is to be marked plainly and the censor's stamp must be placed on each article before sale; and payment for articles sold outside the enclosure will be made to the accounts officer who credits the individual's trust account with such payments. The securing of handicrafts through the medium of gifts or barter is strictly prohibited."[172] Works could also be sent to Geneva, Switzerland, to be displayed for the International Red Cross prisoners of war art expositions. Such was the case for two Camp Farnham prisoners in January 1945.[173]

In general, canteen profits were used to improve living conditions in the camps of southern Quebec. Kept in a special account, this money gave the inmates enough financial power to service many of their collective needs. Sometimes, profits were used to pay for damage by prisoners to camp property. As was stipulated in the *Orders and Instructions, Internment Camps*, "Fifty percent of canteen profits will be set aside each month to create a reserve for barrack damages, until such time as the said reserve has reached the amount fixed for the camp, on the basis of $2 per prisoner of war, or as follows: $1,000 for a camp not exceeding 500 inmates and $2,000 for a camp detaining between 500 and 1,000 internees."[174] As for the rest of canteen profits, prisoners could use them as they pleased. As was indicated in a 1941 Camp Farnham memorandum issued during the civilian phase, "Profits for the month ... are paid out to various prisoners as decided by the Prisoners' Committee in the form of wages to those who do not receive wages from the Director of Internment Operations ... and also for general camp benefits."[175] Canteen profits were often used for the purchase of recreational and educational materials.[176] When most of the camps closed in 1946, it became very difficult to distribute leftover canteen profits among the prisoners. Because all of the prisoners had been transferred to the United Kingdom, contacting every one of them proved impossible. For this reason, the profits made by all Canadian internment camp canteens were placed in a special trust fund registered by the Receiver General of Canada. This money was then handed over to any international organization willing to use the funds for the benefit and aid of those prisoners of war who had formerly been held in Canada.[177]

Summary

The establishment of labour projects enabled southern Quebec inmates to earn money that they could use to purchase commodities in the camp canteens. This opportunity gave prisoners a sense of autonomy, enabled them to benefit their own camp's economy, and allowed them to contribute to Canada's war effort. Whether they worked on farms or in workshops, internees learned new trades they could use after the war. Labour projects helped camp authorities manage prisoner behaviour and reduced the risk of escape. The simple fact that they worked and were earning money from the Canadian authorities led fewer inmates to adopt rebellious behaviour. Prisoners understood that any act of dissension on their part might mean the end of paid privileges and of the labour projects altogether.

5 Educational Programs

Fostered by the prisoners' thirst for knowledge, educational programs became a characteristic of camp life. These broadened the minds of inmates, helped them maintain their sanity, showed them alternatives to totalitarianism, and prepared them for post-war professions. Initiated in 1940 for civilian internees, camp education was initially organized and coordinated by the inmates themselves. Internees who were trained or expert in various fields of study organized discussions and classes. This intellectual climate eventually led Canadian authorities to authorize younger prisoners to pursue their personal education through correspondence courses with Canadian universities. The arrival of prisoners of war in 1942 dramatically changed the nature of educational programs. As German combatants, most of these inmates had been indoctrinated by Nazi propaganda. As the war progressed, Canadian authorities became aware that the presence of Nazi ideology in internment camps "contaminated" the prisoners. They decided that the German inmates needed to be shown an alternative view, and this was done through a program of re-education. The aim was to have prisoners return to Germany with their Nazi beliefs having been eradicated and replaced by a more democratic outlook. To ensure that the German authorities would not see re-education as "brainwashing," only volunteers were chosen to participate in this program. Re-education eventually became an important tool in the war against Nazi ideology. Through discussion groups, classes, guest speakers, films, and literature, many inmates came to conclude that democracy was a much better system than National Socialism (Nazism). So important was re-education that in 1945 a special camp was set up in Sorel for that specific purpose.

Internee education was not covered by the Geneva Convention; no clauses dealt exclusively with the education of prisoners. Only Article 17, which stipulated that belligerents were to encourage as much as possible the organization of intellectual and sporting activities by prisoners of war, touched upon the issue.[1] The problem with this clause was that detaining powers could interpret it to suit themselves, making it difficult to impose international standards. The only thing that restricted nations from using propaganda methods to indoctrinate prisoners of war was the fear of enemy reprisals, which explains why the re-education of German prisoners of war was not introduced in Canada before the end of the war. The Canadian authorities did agree, however, to introduce general education programs. These began during the civilian phase in southern Quebec and were continued when prisoners of war arrived in the region's camps. According to Canadian regulations, "Educational study courses will be permitted under the direction of the International Red Cross, the International YMCA, and any other organization approved by the Director, Prisoners of War."[2]

Thirst for Knowledge and General Education Programs

During the civilian phase, general education flourished in the camps of southern Quebec. Because there were many academics and former professors among the prisoners, the camps provided an excellent learning environment. In fact, many of these individuals were highly distinguished European scholars who had made important contributions in a variety of disciplines. Some leading German intellectuals, political activists, entertainers, musicians, and professionals were to be found among the internees. As Sherbrooke internee John Newmark recalled, "If you come to think of it, we had everything you can imagine there. Professors of astronomy, architects ... fur traders ... and Cambridge and Oxford students ... musicians, painters and sculptors; all the arts were represented, all the sciences, history ... It was a microcosm in itself, everything was there. That's why I learned such a lot."[3] According to Eric Koch, who was also interned at Camp Sherbrooke, the academic talent assembled in the internment camps of southern Quebec "exceeded that of many Canadian universities."[4] The presence of so many people of different trades and professions behind the barbed wire offered tremendous opportunities to expand horizons. Mechanics, for instance, developed close ties with famous musicians while scientists mingled with lawyers. In other words, internment brought together people who would have never met or developed friendships under normal social circumstances. As one Sherbrooke internee recalled, "Sherbrooke was a highly charged intellectual group ... It was very exciting from that point of view. We had every conceivable profession amongst the inmates and if you wanted to know about anything all you had to do is ask either somebody in the bed above you or near you and you get a very learned lecture on the subject."[5] Thirst for knowledge eventually led some prisoners to lecture others on specific topics. Inmates interested in a specific subject or profession could assemble in one of the barracks and listen to what a prisoner qualified in that particular area had to say about it. This informal intellectual environment was known as the "people's university." The first such people's university appeared at Camp Île-aux-Noix in July 1940,[6] and the concept was soon followed by the other camps.[7] So important were these informal lecture sessions at Camp Farnham that Saturdays were entirely devoted to these classes.[8] On one Saturday, internee Hans Karler, who had commanded International Brigade volunteers during the 1936-39 Spanish Civil War, gave general lectures on the military lessons of that conflict.[9] These lecture sessions proved very popular among southern Quebec inmates. As one internee recalled, "I think ... I learned more in the camp universities than I did at Cambridge before and after [the war]."[10]

Formal camp schools were eventually established at camps Farnham, Île-aux-Noix, and Sherbrooke. These were created and coordinated by the prisoners themselves, upon approval from camp authorities. The first camp school was established at Farnham in November 1940 by William Heckscher, an internee who had taught at Hamburg University. He did so after realizing that there were at least a hundred young boys in the camp between the ages of sixteen and twenty who needed proper guidance and education. These pupils were easy targets for the camp Communists, who were always seeking new recruits. Some thirteen internee teachers were involved in the program. Camp authorities supported the program by offering the use of a hut for classes and exempting students from fatigue duties.[11] The camp's war diary summarized the reasons guiding the authorities' involvement: "The idea behind this is to give internees as much mental activity as possible, as it takes their minds off their many worries and makes them that much easier to control. After all in the running of an internment camp, the expedient thing to do is to run it with as little trouble as possible from the prisoners. If they are given considerable amount of freedom concerning internal affairs in the compound and as much self-government as possible, it has the effect of making them that much easier to control and govern."[12] Camp schools were also created at Île-aux-Noix and Sherbrooke in the spring of 1941.[13] Inmates who participated in camp schools studied topics like chemistry, economics, geography, history, language, mathematics, and music. They were also given the opportunity to participate in junior and senior matriculation examinations held by Montreal's McGill University.[14] This was done at the instigation of T.H. Matthews, the registrar at McGill University, and of the Jewish Committee in Montreal.[15] When the first exams were held in the spring of 1941, some 100 young men from Farnham and Île-aux-Noix had registered.[16] The junior matric could be written anywhere in Quebec as long as McGill approved the exam's supervision; prisoners could write the exam inside their respective camps while being supervised by Canadian officers. The senior matric, which fewer students took, had to be written in Montreal.[17] Candidates were transferred temporarily to the Italian internment camp situated on the Île Ste-Hélène in Montreal and friendships between German and Italian prisoners developed during such visits. "The Italians kept a crew up to feed the students coffee so that they could stay awake while studying. After the exams, we played soccer with them, Germany-Austria versus Italy and at the very end, the night before we left they put on a special ... variety show," one inmate remembered.[18]

Eventually, Queen's University in Kingston and other Canadian institutions of higher learning became involved in the program.[19] Guest speakers from these institutions occasionally visited the camps and lectured inmates on Canadian topics.[20]

Camp schools were highly successful. As Major Eric D.B. Kippen, Camp Farnham's commandant, told William Heckscher, "The results [of the matriculation exams] are fantastic ... and I wish I could send my two sons to your school."[21] So important were camp schools that in September 1941 more than 347 internees were registered in educational programs at Camp Sherbrooke out of a population of approximately 587.[22] Internees registered in camp schools could also prepare for post-war professions. The Camp Sherbrooke education program, for example, included a vocational training school specializing in metal and woodwork, an engineering school, and an agricultural studies school operated in cooperation with McGill's Macdonald College. To suit the educational needs of internees involved in the camp's Works Program during the day, Camp Sherbrooke also offered evening lectures and eventually established a general education program that included English language classes.[23] By the end of the civilian phase in southern Quebec, educational programs were present in all of the camps.

When prisoners of war began arriving in southern Quebec in 1942, the Canadian authorities were hesitant to continue camp schools. The fear was that German authorities might perceive education classes to be a means of indoctrinating German prisoners of war and retaliate on Canadian soldiers held in their custody. It was not until the German prisoners of war themselves made requests to pursue their education that Military District 4 authorities decided to re-establish education programs in the region's camps. This was done in late 1943, when correspondence courses were initiated with the University of Saskatchewan.[24] Again, as during the civilian phase, the prisoners were credited for their work through matriculation examinations. Numerous prisoners of war from camps Farnham, Grande Ligne, and Sherbrooke participated in correspondence courses with the University of Saskatchewan.[25]

The education program initiated at Camp Grande Ligne demonstrated the popularity of correspondence courses among southern Quebec internees. The process began in July 1943, a few weeks after the camp opened, when the German prisoner of war officers made a request through the International Red Cross to pursue their education through correspondence courses.[26] The Canadian authorities acquiesced to the inmates' demand, maintaining that such classes might help boost the morale of the prisoners and leave less time for idleness.[27] Work began on 1 September 1943. The school year was divided into three trimesters: Fall (1 September to 17 December), Winter (17 January to 30 April), and Summer (1 May to 31 August). Matriculation examinations usually took place around Christmas and Easter.[28] Inmates preparing for matriculation examinations studied such subjects as art, biology, chemistry, economics, geography, history, law, mathematics, music, and physics. Those studying foreign languages learned English, French, Italian, Latin, Latvian, Spanish, Russian, and even Japanese.[29] So successful were language classes that 571 Grande Ligne prisoners were registered in them by November 1943.[30]

Vocational classes were also held and included sessions on agriculture, forestry, physiology, public speaking, drafting, music, commercial arithmetic, navigation, commerce, bookkeeping, business management, metallurgy, electricity, geology, engineering, geometry, and railroading.[31] These classes were usually taught by prisoner of war officers who had specialized training. Study circles were also attended each week by some 300 prisoners.[32]

In addition to the University of Saskatchewan correspondence courses, similar arrangements were made with other academic institutions for the prisoners to pursue non-credit courses. In one instance, the European Student Relief Fund registered a Sherbrooke internee for a Spanish class at the University of Toronto in April 1944. A university official responded by writing, "I hope Mr. Herbert Boehme realizes that if such a Spanish course is arranged there will be no university credit given him as in the case of the Saskatchewan courses. However, such an arrangement with the University of Toronto professor will enable him to study the language and to learn it, if that is his main objective."[33] The same situation applied when another Sherbrooke inmate was given the opportunity to pursue a class on ignition engine practice and operation from a technological institute in Great Britain.[34]

Educational Tools: Literature and Motion Pictures

Camp libraries were vital to camp education programs. As Canadian regulations stipulated, "Text books not prohibited ... will be admitted, if supplied by the International Red Cross, the International YMCA, the German Red Cross, Canadians universities and libraries, or from such other institutions or persons as may be authorized by the Director, Prisoners of War."[35] The first camp libraries were created during the civilian phase and continued operating during the prisoner of war phase. Prisoners requested relief organizations, most often the European Student Relief Fund and the YMCA, to purchase specific books, magazines, and newspapers for which they paid upon delivery.[36] These materials included such newspapers as the Montreal *Gazette,* the *Montreal Daily Star, La Presse,* and *The New York Times*. Magazines such as *Time, Newsweek, Illustrated London News, Reader's Digest, Life,* and *Maclean's* were also purchased.[37] Books on democracy, foreign languages, geography, history, law, mathematics, psychology, politics, philosophy, and sports were ordered.[38] It is interesting to note that prisoners ordered books written in English, French, German, Swedish, Spanish, Norwegian, and other languages.[39] Novels were among the most popular forms of literature inside the camps. In Sherbrooke, where the camp library in September 1944 contained some 3,600 volumes, 26 percent of the books were classed as non-fiction, 10 percent dealt with economics, 10 percent addressed history, 15 percent were textbooks, and 39 percent were classified as fiction.[40] Novels helped prisoners to escape the pressures of internment through their imaginations.[41] Prisoners who could not afford to purchase books at their own expense could avail themselves of a travelling library organized by McGill University.[42]

Not all books were approved by camp authorities. Camp censors were strict and forbade inmates to read literature deemed damaging to the Allied cause or that might entice prisoners towards violence or Nazism.[43] Indeed, Canadian authorities decided in September 1944 that "only educational books will be permitted to be purchased by the POW and then only such books as are necessary for the course they are taking within the enclosure." Books dealing with subjects related to Allied armies, navies, and air forces, spies and espionage, map making, weapons and armaments, or formulae for the manufacturing of alcohol or poisons were strictly forbidden. All enemy propaganda documents were to be forwarded to National Defence Headquarters in Ottawa, unless "the propaganda element is of an incidental nature and the scope of the publications chiefly education or recreational."[44] Numerous books and magazines were censored and removed from camp library inventories. Nazi propaganda books such as Adolf Hitler's *Mein Kampf* or training manuals of the German armed forces were restricted. The same applied to volumes promoting Communism, revolution, and social change, such as Karl Marx and Friedrich Engel's *The Communist Manifesto* or Marx's *Das Kapital.* Books dealing with Allied armed forces and current military subjects, such as the *Political and Strategic Interests of the United Kingdom* published by the Royal Institute of the United Kingdom or Cecil King's *His Majesty's Ships* were also prohibited.[45] Although some atlases were tolerated, many were returned by camp censors. The reason was that they contained maps of the United States and Canada whose scale was too big. According to regulations, "Maps of the northern hemisphere or parts of the British Empire are not admissible if the scale exceeds 60 miles to one inch. Maps showing 61 miles or more miles to one inch are good and 59 or less are excluded."[46] Larger-scale maps might be used by the prisoners to plan escapes. Canadian and American magazines were also censored.[47] In some instance, specific articles were removed from publications. Such a case occurred in February 1946 with a *Reader's Digest* article entitled "We Are Bungling the Job in Germany." According to the Directorate of Prisoners of War, "It is considered that said article is apt to arouse misgivings ... and may also serve to encourage the more fanatical pro-Nazi POW in the belief that their cause is not entirely lost. Consequently, it will be necessary to remove pages 87-92, as well as to obliterate line 26 on the cover of this publication, prior to its admission to POW as reading material."[48]

Camp libraries offered southern Quebec inmates an opportunity to learn more about the world and to acclimatize themselves to the North American way of life. As the Camp Sherbrooke spokesman told officials at the travelling library run by Macdonald College in July 1944: "Thank you for the entertainment and educational material provided by your library. This is, apart from newspapers, our only opportunity to keep in touch with the literary and political movements of this continent."[49] According to Eckehart Priebe, who was interned at Farnham and Grande Ligne:

> To me as to many others the opportunity to study the Canadian press and literature became of great importance and of far reaching consequences, not realized before ... What happened here ... was a slow, imperceptible familiarization process, not at all forced down our throats, provided as naturally as food and shelter. You could literally read yourself into the character, history, economy or politics of a nation of which, hitherto, you had known next to nothing. We got acquainted with Canada and the Canadian way of life in a very unobtrusive but equally efficient way. There was no intention to indoctrinate us. Information and reading material was provided as a matter of course. It was of enormous help not only to pass the time away but to understand the inner workings of the democracies allied against our fatherland. The tolerance of the Canadians in providing newspapers, magazines, books and study material amazed me.[50]

Education was also promoted through motion pictures. In addition to entertaining prisoners, movies served as an important means of indoctrination and of relaying Allied propaganda. Films introduced German internees to the norms and values of American, British, and Canadian societies and engendered respect towards these cultures. An authority at Camp Grande Ligne wrote, "One hears that these pictures induce in many prisoners a great inclination towards our way of life. Moving pictures play a tremendous part in the somewhat restricted life of a prisoner, and each detail is thought over and placed under the magnifying glass. Hence, films are an excellent tool of psychology and propaganda."[51] Camp Sorel authorities reported that "English and American films receive the best reception, for the POW emphasize that these give them the best opportunity to learn the English language, while at the same time the films have a very strong influence toward understanding of the Anglo-Saxon way of life."[52] Movie projectors and equipment were furnished by relief organizations, including the Canadian Legion, the Knights of Columbus, and the YMCA.[53] The YMCA was in charge of the general distribution of movies. Working in conjunction with film distributors Twentieth Century Fox, United Artists, and Warner Brothers, the YMCA was able to supply the inmates with one movie per week for which the organization bore the expense.[54] In most cases, prisoners were given movie lists from which they could choose the titles that interested them.[55]

Movies were first presented in southern Quebec during the civilian phase. The process began in early 1941 when camps Sherbrooke and Île-aux-Noix received their first motion picture projectors through relief societies, namely the United Jewish Committee for Interned Refugees.[56] They were followed by Camp Farnham in the summer of 1942,[57] Camp Grande Ligne in the summer of 1944,[58] and Camp

Sorel in the fall of 1945.[59] To help pay for the movies, internees gave 5 cents, usually obtained from the prisoners' canteen funds.[60] American, British, and Canadian movies shown inside the camps included the most popular of the era, among them *Million Dollar Baby* starring Priscilla Land and Ronald Reagan;[61] *The Sun Never Sets* starring Douglas Fairbanks Jr., Basil Rathbone, and Virginia Fields;[62] *South of Suez* starring Brenda Marshall and George Brent;[63] *Algiers* starring Charles Boyer and Hedy Lamarr;[64] *Manpower* starring Marlene Dietrich, Edward G. Robinson, and George Raft;[65] *They Died with Their Boots On* starring Errol Flynn and Olivia de Havilland;[66] and *International Squadron* starring Ronald Reagan.[67] Furthermore, the Canadian government was obligated to screen German-made films. According to historian Ron Robin, "As part of a reciprocal agreement mediated by the Red Cross, the Allies sent a small selection of pre-approved movies to their prisoners in Germany. In exchange, German prisoners in Allied POW camps viewed a limited number of German film productions. All these German movies had been meticulously censored for any overt or covert Nazi propaganda."[68]

The Re-education of German Prisoners of War

The presence of Nazi prisoners of war in Allied internment camps eventually led the American, British, Soviet, and Canadian governments to inaugurate re-education programs.[69] Determined to eradicate Nazism in Germany, Allied officials devised re-education programs designed to induce German prisoners of war to abandon Nazi ideology and embrace democratic or, in the case of the Soviet Union, Communist ideals.[70] The major goal, according to historian Arthur L. Smith, was to "reorient the political thinking of enemy prisoners through a process of re-education with the hope of using these 'graduates' as a vanguard in directing the defeated state [Germany] toward a specific form of government."[71] Officials hoped to eliminate Nazism and German militarism and to reshape the political and ideological fabric of Germany.[72] They feared a repeat of the aftermath of the German surrender during the First World War when disgruntled German soldiers and sailors caused much civil disorder and, ultimately, the 1919 German Revolution. They thought that a similar scenario might result when German prisoners of war were repatriated following the current conflict. Re-education was seen as a means of preparing prisoners for repatriation and, most important, of persuading them to cooperate with Allied authorities who would be occupying post-war Germany.[73]

The problem with re-education, however, was that the Allied powers had very different political ideals. Canada, the United Kingdom, and the United States wanted to re-educate German prisoners along democratic lines, while the Soviet Union hoped to do so using Communist ideology. Each re-education program became a reflection of the political motives of the nation that introduced it. Aside from indoctrinating German prisoners with new political beliefs, re-education offered each Allied nation an opportunity to prepare a vanguard to plant the seeds for a new German government and to collaborate with them in their respective zones of military occupation. It thus permitted each nation to have influence on the political future of Germany.[74] For the Canadian government, which felt shut out of post-war diplomacy by the stronger Allied powers, re-educating prisoners of war was an opportunity to assert Canada's identity in the immediate post-war world.[75]

The process began in 1943 when the British Foreign Office approached the Canadian government on the matter. Canada was detaining thousands of German prisoners of war who had been captured by British and Commonwealth forces and who, by agreement, were the responsibility of the British government. According to a British report sent to the Canadian Chiefs of Staff in May 1943, the re-education of prisoners of war was to be an important contribution to the Allied war effort for the following reasons:

> (1) By providing the means to spread the belief in enemy countries that our prisoners of war are well treated. This belief not only encourages enemy troops to surrender when they are hard pressed but, because it tends to discount Axis home propaganda which maintains that the only alternative to victory is doom, helps to weaken the will to resist of the enemy peoples. The belief that we treat our prisoners kindly, with its implication that the Allies will not be ruthless in victory, will also be spread by repatriated prisoners (when exchanges take place), provided that those who are repatriated have not only been well treated but, because of re-education, are no longer Nazi or Fascist extremists. (2) By providing the means to increase the numbers of listeners to our broadcasts in enemy countries. This is secured by inviting prisoners to broadcast messages to their relatives stating that they are in good health and well treated ... (3) By providing intelligence, particularly the kind of information which is required for the purpose of political warfare. (4) By subversive broadcasts voluntarily given by prisoners who are opposed to the Nazi or Fascist regimes. In this connection it should be noted that such broadcasts can be very effective even if they are anonymous, since the prisoner can, by referring to details which could not well be known to the Allies, convince his listeners that the speaker is in fact an anti-Nazi or anti-Fascist prisoner of war. (5) By providing personnel who, because they are anti-Nazi or anti-Fascist, volunteer for secret service work with the Allies.[76]

In line with this report, the long-term aim of re-education was "to ensure that as many as possible of the prisoners shall return to their respective countries after the war as pro-British advocates of democratic ideals."[77]

Because Canada had the necessary manpower and space, the United Kingdom suggested that a proper re-education program be initiated in that country. Ottawa's initial answer was negative. The Canadian director of internment operations responded that "the government did not countenance any campaign to re-educate and convert the Nazis."[78] Re-educating prisoners of war was perceived as anti-democratic and a waste of resources.[79] British views on Canada's cooperation became very pessimistic; a British Foreign Office report stated, "The Canadians have done virtually nothing to re-educate prisoners ... Indeed, the Canadian camps are a hot-bed of Nazi ideology. The Party regime appears to be fully established amongst prisoners in some camps, and even those on whom we might make a promising beginning in the U.K. would certainly revert to Nazism on arriving in Canada."[80] Canadian intelligence officers were very aware of the problem of Nazism inside internment camps and most were in favour of implementing a re-education program. "The alternative to re-education," wrote Colonel W.W. Murray, the director of military intelligence, "was to return to Germany groups of young men who, through years of incarceration, have become more and more embittered, with their animosity towards non-Germans increased, thus transferring again to Germany the seeds from which another war might in due course germinate."[81]

British patience was finally rewarded in June 1944 when Canada finally agreed to cooperate on a re-education program.[82] The entire project was to be coordinated by the Canadian Psychological Warfare Committee, which had been created in 1943. To ensure the success of such an operation, Nazis had to be properly segregated from anti-Nazis. Segregation was to be the first step in the establishment of the Canadian re-education program. As the May 1943 British report to the Canadian chiefs of staff noted, "Secrecy is imperative not only as a safeguard against reprisals but as cover for propaganda itself; nothing is more fatal in this field than to let the prisoners discover that a deliberate attempt is being made to re-educate them ... Since the most suspicious are the extremists, and since ... they bully any of their fellow prisoners whose loyalty to the regime seems doubtful, the first step would invariably be to segregate the extremists and to ensure that there is no communication between their camp and other camps."[83] The Canadian authorities agreed: "It is a waste of time and effort to try and do any re-education until the rabid Nazis have been segregated."[84] Segregation came with the introduction of the PHERUDA system of classification in 1944 (see Chapter 3). Re-education was intended to make "listeners aware of Canada's separate and distinct identity within the United Nations and underscor[e] its contributions to the Allied effort. The benefits of democracy could be lauded by referring to Canadian achievements and standard of living."[85]

While Canada officially agreed in mid-1944 to initiate its own re-education program, the project was not exploited to its full capacity until the summer of 1945. This was in large part due to the slow progress of the PHERUDA classification system and the difficulties of segregating internment camps. But perhaps the greatest reason was the Canadian authorities' fear that Germany might perceive the

Canadian re-education program as indoctrination and retaliate on Canadian prisoners of war. For this reason, no prisoner was ever forced to participate in the Canadian re-education program. The Canadian government believed that by relying solely on volunteers, the program would be less of a target for the German authorities.[86] It was not until the unconditional surrender of Nazi Germany on 7 May 1945 that the Canadian re-education program intensified. With the war against Germany over and Canada a victorious power, the threat of German retaliation on Canadian prisoners of war became less likely. German prisoners in Canada were also more inclined to abandon National Socialist doctrine now that Nazi Germany was defeated. A Camp Sherbrooke intelligence officer reported, "The wind has been completely knocked out their sails. The rabid Nazis finally realized that their game was up. Strong-arm Gestapo methods are a thing of the past, and to the best of my knowledge complete peace and quietness reigns within the enclosure. The anti-Nazis are now more or less able to hold up their heads and even to a certain extent dictate their own policies."[87] As German prisoners of war became less arrogant and more cooperative, the Canadian authorities became more confident about the re-education program.

Several reasons explain why the internment camps of southern Quebec were chosen to form the basis of the Canadian re-education project. First, these were small camps. Never were there more than a thousand prisoners per camp, making it easier to control the inmate population, sift out the bad elements, and keep the re-education operation as secret as possible. Second, the type of prisoners interned in southern Quebec made it easier to lay the foundation of re-education. As camps for German officers, Farnham and Grande Ligne detained a category of inmate who was fairly educated and very influential on other German prisoners. Third, it seems that the camps were chosen for their strategic position. Proximity to major urban centres such as Quebec City and Montreal made it easier to supply and fulfill the camps' material needs. This helped to ensure that the inmates' morale remained high and that conditions in the camps were optimal. The closeness of Ottawa also made it easier for top military and government officials, as well as American and British diplomats, to visit the camps and work in conjunction with camp authorities and prisoners. It also made it easier to supply the camps with re-education materials, which were often created and provided by National Defence Headquarters and other government sources in Ottawa. Because other re-education materials sometimes arrived in Montreal by ship, rail, or bomber mail from the United Kingdom and the United States, the camps' proximity to the city kept delivery delays to a minimum. Fourth, there was the issue of isolation from other regions. The camps of southern Quebec were far from the large internment camps of Ontario and Western Canada. This made it difficult for "Black" prisoners in the West to be in contact with the "White" and "Grey" inmates in southern Quebec and to know about the re-education program.[88]

Re-education and Camp Sorel

The cornerstone of the re-education program in southern Quebec was Camp Sorel. This camp was purposely designed and built between February and May 1945 as a special re-assessment centre for the re-education of German prisoners of war. This decision was taken at the request of the Psychological Warfare Committee. Sorel was the first and only internment camp in Canada to be constructed solely for re-educational purposes. In fact, the whole re-education project was centralized around Camp Sorel; camps Farnham, Grande Ligne, and Sherbrooke acted as mere subsidiary facilities. Sorel served for both re-educational purposes and as a transit camp for "White" prisoners of war destined to be repatriated to Germany to serve the Allied cause.[89] The camp's functions were as follows: "(A) to assess the prisoners of war for reliability, leadership qualities and suitability for employment in their particular fields either here or in Germany; (B) to strengthen the Anti-Nazi attitudes of the prisoners of war, and familiarize them with certain basic principles and attitudes of the Western Allies; (C) to provide facilities for propaganda work (press, radio) either in Germany or to the other camps; (D) to provide special or refresher training in specific occupations; and (E) to collect data of value for guidance in planning propaganda to Germany and in re-educational work (lectures, films, broadcasts) in other camps."[90] As a re-assessment centre, Camp Sorel selected its "students" meticulously:

> Recommendation for the transfer to this camp of suitable POWs will be made ... by POW camp commandants all over Canada, in consultation with the camp intelligence officers. Such recommendations will only be made after a detailed interrogation according to the PHERUDA system and a statement that the POW desires to work for the reconstruction of Germany and to be transferred to the special camp in Sorel. Such recommendations will be forwarded to the Directorate of Military Intelligence (DMI) for consideration. Final decision as to suitability and time of transfer shall rest with DMI who will make the necessary requests to the Directorate Prisoners of War. In selecting POW, consideration will be given to professions and occupations, partly with a view to the establishment of discussion groups, partly in terms of requests from the U.K., and partly in order to create a well-balanced camp ... An attempt was made to draw men from all camps in Canada in order to show that White attitudes were by no means confined to one or two camps.[91]

Only "White" prisoners were selected for Camp Sorel. All were volunteers and they came from across Canada.[92] Before being sent to Sorel, inmates had to sign a written undertaking whereby they agreed to cooperate with the Allies and to conform to the goals of Canada's re-education project.[93] German officers, other ranks, and enemy merchant sailors were all declared suitable for this scheme. Camp regulations stipulated that "distinction of rank, it is hoped will disappear amongst the

POW when in classes, discussion groups or engaged on psychological warfare work."[94] In fact, all ranks were abolished at Camp Sorel. This was done "to express the idea that all were finding themselves under identical conditions."[95] According to historian Ron Robin, the sudden milling together of prisoners from a wide variety of camps and from all the German armed services effectively removed the trappings of military life from the prisoners' routine, thereby destroying their primary and hitherto sole form of association. To further this goal, the prisoners were required to remove all signs of military association and rank. Robin states that the program directors hoped that the absence of military regalia and the random grouping of prisoners would eliminate some of the unyielding "state consciousness" of the prisoners, and that the lack of a familiar military framework would funnel the innate German respect for authority towards the instructors as symbols of Allied supremacy.[96] Because of its re-education role and the type of internees it contained, conditions at Sorel were very different from those in other Canadian internment camps. Security, for instance, was minimal. As one internee wrote, "We have lawns around our huts and barbed wire has been reduced to a token wire. Living quarters are better for we live three to a room, which we have furnished similar to the one at Seebe (Camp 130). Fortunately, the two counts per day have been abolished."[97] The camp was also guarded by a limited number of VGC personnel. Authorities knew that the "White" prisoners at Sorel constituted no threat to the security of the camp or its surroundings. The Canadian authorities believed that the less the camp looked like a prison, the more open-minded and cooperative the prisoners would be. The director of military intelligence stated in November 1945 that "it has always been my position that guards and administrative personnel could and should be kept at a minimum."[98]

The goal of the screening process was to select prisoners who, according to historian Arthur Smith, "would adapt to the [re-education] program by opening their minds to new ideas and by working hard to understand what was being presented to them. Success or failure rested with the men chosen."[99] Selected prisoners had to express their willingness to cooperate with all of the Allies. Attempts to discriminate among the Allies, and in particular against the Soviet Union, were discouraged.[100] Each internee had to be formally asked "whether he is willing to cooperate actively with the Allied nations, both here and in Europe, in the reconstruction of Germany, in accordance with Allied plans and agree to his proposed transfer to Camp Sorel. It should be made clear to the prisoner that this camp will provide both training and refresher courses for the occupations most needed and that if found suitable the prisoner will be employed to the best advantage."[101]

Inmates were also chosen based on their previous civilian occupations and professions. The aim was to exploit the inmates' trades and special talents for the benefit of the Canadian re-education program. Initially, intellectuals were chosen. They were to form a "brain trust" for the democratization of Germany and of fellow prisoners of war. In the end, the program was expanded to cover a wide variety of job categories. Some prisoners had been interpreters and journalists before the war, while others had been teachers and university professors, technicians, managers, engineers, farmers, lawyers, judges, and doctors. Each Sorel prisoner was assigned a special re-education responsibility connected to his pre-war trade or talent. For example, printers worked the camp press; professors taught re-education classes; journalists wrote re-education literature; cartoonists submitted re-education cartoons for camp newspapers throughout Canada, the United Kingdom, and the United States; bank accountants acted as paymasters; and lawyers and judges worked for the camp's law and administration section.[102] But not all Sorel inmates had special skills; some uneducated "White" internees were brought to the camp to take care of camp chores. Their work freed the other prisoners to concentrate on their re-education duties. This mixing of men of different social backgrounds was also done to "create a well-balanced group" in the camp and "to assess reactions of the common men towards certain re-educational measures."[103]

The main problem with the Camp Sorel segregation system was that "Grey" and "Black" prisoners occasionally lied to interviewers in order to be transferred to Camp Sorel. And sometimes they were successful. One such case occurred in November 1945 when a Sorel inmate was caught smuggling a message to Camp Grande Ligne "in which was written statements prejudicial to the good of Camp Sorel." The man was immediately transferred.[104] This example clearly shows how even the more careful screening could not prevent the inclusion of "students" who were just looking for an easier or more interesting way to spend their internment, and who had no intention of taking re-education seriously.[105] These opportunists believed that participating in the re-education program might accelerate their repatriation. Camp Farnham authorities noted, "There are those who have drastically changed overnight from 'Black' to 'White.' These are naturally recognized as opportunists who are most unreliable and insincere."[106] In the end, numerous internees were refused access to Camp Sorel. Such a case occurred in June 1945 with a Camp Petawawa internee who had applied for transfer to Sorel. According to his interviewers, he was deemed to be "unreliable and unsuitable for any position of trust with the Allied Government in Germany or elsewhere" because "(A) He is not a confirmed Anti-Nazi; (B) He is an opportunist and it is believed he would serve or cooperate with anyone as long as it would be in his own interests to do so; (C) He possesses an unpleasant personality and will 'grovel' at the slightest sign of friendliness or if he is requesting a favour."[107]

Originally, each selected group of prisoners was to stay no longer than three months at Camp Sorel. The idea was to repatriate these men as soon as possible in order that they might serve the Allied occupation forces in Germany. However, this plan proved to be impossible given the chaotic situation that persisted in Germany after the war. Because Sorel prisoners became more and more dissatisfied with the postponement of their transfer home, camp authorities readjusted their operational policies in September 1945. A plan was introduced by MI7 on 26 October, to transform Camp Sorel into a re-educational "production centre." The task of re-educating prisoners of war in Canada had grown considerably since May 1945 and the demand for re-education materials and agents kept increasing. To comply with this situation, Sorel inmates became involved with the production of re-education materials.[108] Because Sorel was strictly a re-education camp where the bulk of prisoners could not benefit from paid labour projects as in the other southern Quebec internment camps, the Canadian authorities decided in November 1945 to pay each prisoner 50 cents per day for producing re-education materials. The main argument was that these inmates were replacing Canadian personnel in this duty.[109]

The production of re-education materials was coordinated by the camp's counter-propaganda committee. It was formed "with the object of producing [German-written] literature, mainly in the form of pamphlets, which will on the one hand refute Nazi ideology and attitudes in various fields and on the other hand produce material designed to help in mental and moral reeducation. These pamphlets are to be sent to all internment camps in Canada."[110] This committee was divided into a number of subcommittees that were headed by prisoners who were experts in a number of disciplines. The following subcommittees were established: law, history, theology, racial theories, forestry, agriculture, economics, education, and "a special section to combat Nazi slogans."[111]

The re-education materials produced at Camp Sorel were quite diversified, and it became necessary to establish radio broadcast sections, press sections, film sections, and even a committee for the reconstruction and rehabilitation of Germany. The radio broadcast section had the important task of cooperating with the international service of the Canadian Broadcasting Corporation (CBC) in the preparation and recording of radio scripts to be broadcast in Canadian internment camps and in Germany.[112]

The press section was in charge of producing the weekly camp newspaper known as *Der Weg*. Articles for this publication were provided not only by Sorel inmates but also by prisoners from other internment camps. The press section also published re-educational bulletins, lecture outlines, newspapers, leaflets, and pamphlets that were distributed to other Canadian internment camps weekly, in cooperation with the camp's translation bureau.[113] From Camp Sorel came three major sources of re-education literature. First, there was the *Bruecke zur Heimat*, which was a weekly publication similar to *Reader's Digest*. Second, there was the *Nachrichten*, which was a weekly bulletin containing the latest news. Third, there was the *Historische Rundbriefe*, which was a fortnightly pamphlet covering aspects of German history.[114] Each week, 130 copies of *Historische Rundbriefe*, 600 copies of *Nachrichten*, 1,850 copies of *Bruecke zur Heimat* and 3,300 pamphlets were produced at Camp Sorel and distributed to all Canadian internment camps.[115] This literature was also "designed for ... prisoners employed in lumber camps and other works projects which could not be reached for re-educational purposes in any other fashion."[116] When production of re-education literature at Camp Sorel ceased on 2 March 1946, twenty-two different types of pamphlets had been produced, as well as eight editions of the *Historische Rundbriefe*, twenty-five editions of the *Nachrichten*, and thirty-four editions of the *Bruecke zur Heimat*.[117]

To facilitate the preparation of re-education materials, Canadian authorities provided Sorel inmates with special documents and literature. In most cases, books illustrating democratic attitudes, experiences, or governmental methods were chosen.[118] Furthermore, unlike in other Canadian internment camps, prisoners were given the opportunity to access Nazi propaganda and books addressing Nazi issues. These books included Adolf Hitler's *Mein Kampf*, Franz L. Neumann's *Behemoth: The Structure and Practice of National Socialism*, Hermann Rauschning's *Germany's Revolution of Destruction* and *The Revolution of Nihilism*, Konrad Heiden's *Hitler: A Bibliography* and *Fuehrer: Hitler's Rise to Power*, and Erika Mann's *School for Barbarians: Education under the Nazis*.[119] This was permitted because the bulk of the Sorel prisoners were known to be staunch anti-Nazis. Camp authorities wrote in November 1945 that "several POWs have emphasized that they have attained a mental freedom and scope which they could not possibly have attained in other camps. All POW here are outspoken opponents of Fascism and other forms of totalitarianism; all are keen learners of the forms of democracy and at least nearly all of them recognize that the difference between totalitarianism and democracy is in the spirit and in the way of life, rather than in the structures of government."[120] Authorities believed that such literature would help internees to understand the flaws of Nazism.

Re-education in Other Southern Quebec Camps

Re-education was also inaugurated on a voluntary basis at Camp Farnham. When the decision was made in the spring of 1945 to create a re-assessment camp in Sorel, Camp Farnham authorities replied by proposing to use their facilities "as a preliminary sifting camp."[121] At the time, the Canadian authorities felt that there was a considerable number of "Grey" prisoners with definite anti-Nazi attitudes who were not ready to be transferred to Camp Sorel owing to their "residues of militaristic sentiment, unwillingness to break with comrades, and oath to Hitler."[122] Camp Farnham authorities described the problem: "That is to say that these people do not denounce democracy but rather that they find it extremely hard to shake off National Socialist doctrines, pumped into them incessantly during the Hitler Regime. Although the earnest endeavour to understand democracy and the sincere attempt to practice it in their own small community is a fact, the younger element at Camp 40, officers and OR's who did belong to the *Jung Volk* and *Hitler*

Jugend, consequently received their one-sided education only in Nazi ideology, find it extremely hard to comprehend many factors about the democratic way of life."[123] As such, the idea of a preparatory camp seemed logical. Farnham was a perfect choice for this program because "White" prisoners there had secretly fostered a democratic movement in the autumn of 1944 that "gradually grew and planted roots throughout this camp, especially after "Blacks" had been sent out."[124] As of late April 1945 Camp Farnham was the "final pre-Sorel screening point"; the authorities reasoned that it "is in the same military district as Sorel, so that transfers between camps could be made with a minimum of difficulty."[125] Prisoners from all over Canada could be transferred to Camp Farnham "without the consent of the prisoners concerned, but simply on suitable recommendations from the camp commandants."[126] Almost immediately, the bulk of the "Black" prisoners incarcerated at Farnham were transferred out to make room for the newcomers.[127]

At Farnham, prisoners were given the opportunity to establish among themselves a democratic form of government to administer their own affairs, which exposed them first-hand to democracy. This process was viewed by Canadian authorities as the perfect way to prepare Camp Farnham inmates for their potential transfer to Camp Sorel.[128] A democratic committee was formed at the camp on 1 July 1945. This eight-man representative council, elected by secret ballot, had the task of coordinating "all POW affairs, administrative as well as political." The democratic committee also became very active in the re-education program. It was noted that "after years of Nazi indoctrination, these POWs are highly propaganda-minded and look for political significance to every newspaper article, lecture or addresses by their own fellow POW. To overcome this attitude it has been the policy of the democratic committee to slowly guide these people into a new channel of thought."[129] The democratic committee began operating a weekly re-education program consisting of newspaper reviews, lectures, and political discussions.[130] By August 1945, the camp's inmates proposed to administer their own affairs through a new form of democratic government. For this purpose, four prisoner of war "lawyers" created a camp constitution that they submitted to the camp authorities on 7 August 1945.[131] An election by secret ballot was then held to find out whether the prisoners were in favour of the constitution and the establishment of an elective assembly or whether they preferred to retain the camp spokesman as their official representative. The election was carried out on 11 August 1945 without any evidence of coercion. The result was clear-cut: 95 percent of the inmates were in favour of the constitution.[132]

The Camp Farnham prisoner of war government, as established through the camp constitution, was divided into two major entities: the representative assembly and the executive committee. The executive committee was the higher echelon of this camp government. Although it consulted with the representative assembly, it was solely charged with negotiating directly with camp authorities. It was made up of three elected members. The chairman, otherwise known as the camp speaker, acted as camp spokesman. Under him were the spiritual and political advisor and the administrative advisor, who were both in charge of their respective sections within the representative assembly. Initially, all of the executive committee's representatives were former officers. This situation changed in February 1946 when one "other ranks" representative was granted permission to sit on the committee.[133] The representative assembly was the lower echelon of this camp system. Every hut elected two prisoners to the representative assembly, with each man being assigned a specific function there. The assembly was divided into three sections: spiritual and political; administration; and medical. All three sections were coordinated by the executive committee. The spiritual and political section was the largest. It was made up of eleven representatives and subdivided into ten subcommittees: radio messages; library; sport; newspaper correspondence; general lectures; film-radio; music; politics and economics; education; and church. The administration section, on the other hand, was made up of seven representatives and subdivided into five subcommittees: paymaster; tools; postal; kitchen; and canteen. Finally, the smallest was the medical section, which was made up of two representatives and subdivided into two subcommittees, medical and dental. Overall, twenty members were elected by the internees for the representative assembly. The assembly's role was to discuss specific camp-related issues and propose new measures to the executive committee.[134] Camp authorities were very pleased with the democratic camp government, writing that "this is an encouraging sign as to their [prisoners'] sincerity to adjust their political bearing."[135]

Re-education was also introduced on a limited scale in camps Grande Ligne and Sherbrooke. The ongoing presence of "Black" elements inside both camps constituted an immense problem as these strong supporters of Nazism seriously delayed Canadian efforts to re-educate the prisoners. Camp Grande Ligne authorities reported that "what a few intelligence officers can do in a week can easily be undone by the insidious propaganda of a highly educated crew of Blacks."[136] A series of transfers was initiated in the fall of 1945. The aim was to segregate the enclosure so that "Grey" prisoners might be more prone to participate in the re-education program without being influenced by "Black" elements. The strategy worked: the remaining prisoners increased their participation in the re-education program. Attempts to initiate re-education at Camp Sherbrooke – the only facility in southern Quebec to still be involved in the Works Program – were weak and unfruitful. Camp authorities noted in December 1945 that "since there is little time during the day for lectures and courses of a re-educational nature due to the Works Program, educational activities are not as advanced as they are in some camps."[137] The camp intelligence officer even admitted that because "every POW in this camp ... is engaged in one kind of work or other, the educational activities here ... are practically nil during day time."[138] Furthermore, the bulk of the camp's inmates were poorly educated merchant seamen who were not greatly interested in reading and studying. Because participation in the Canadian re-education program was voluntary, most prisoners were more inclined to use their spare time for recreational activities.[139] This situation improved in April 1946 when a newly arrived intelligence officer formed an educational committee at Camp Sherbrooke and attracted more inmates to the program.[140]

Lectures and Seminars

Lectures and seminars were an important part of the Canadian re-education program: "a medium for the description and explanation of our way of life," according Camp Grande Ligne authorities.[141] Special re-education classes taught in English formed the bulk of this system. The administrators and teachers employed for this task had professional teaching backgrounds. In most cases, they were humanities and social sciences professors.[142] According to historian Arthur Smith, these teachers were "representatives of the educated genteel middle class who respected education as the foundation of an enlightened democracy."[143] Camp Sorel authorities reasoned that "the impact of intensive contact with outstanding Canadian personalities should have definite educational value. Impressions of the POW gained by the lecturers might also be useful."[144]

Re-education classes were coordinated by the University of Toronto's Canadian Association for Adult Education (CAAE) and began in 1944. In charge of this organization was George W. Brown, a history professor. Each year, the CAAE sent every camp a list of potential lectures from which the internees made selections.[145] Professors from Bishop's University, McGill University, the University of Toronto, and the United Theological College participated in the CAAE program and lectured southern Quebec inmates. Canadian military personnel, priests, members of Canada's National Film Board, and representatives from relief organizations also gave classes.[146] Teachers were paid $7.50 per lecture.[147] Between 1944 and 1946, prisoners were lectured on democracy, constitutional issues, politics, economics, international affairs, American, British, and Canadian history, Western literature, and the Canadian way of life. Class sessions included such topics as "The Development from the League of Nations to the United Nations Charter," "Modern Canadian Art and Literature," "Relations between Canada and the United States in the Course of Canadian History," "The Connections between French Canada and Europe," "The Story of the Royal Canadian Mounted Police," "The History of Great Britain and the Commonwealth," "The Constitutional Revolution of the Seventeenth Century," "Representative and Responsible Government in the British Colonies," "Social Welfare," "Racial Biology," "Canada and Its People," "Canadian Educational Institutions," "Canadian Natural History," "Canadian Political Parties," "The British Parliamentary System," "Commonwealth Relations," "Democracy in the Canadian Army," "The Constitution of Canada," "The Occupation of Germany," "The Canadian Federal and Provincial Governments," "Canadian History, 1500-1946," "Canadian Democracy," and "The Canadian Press."[148] Overall, more than 100 CAAE lectures were given in southern Quebec camps during that period by such professors as John I. Cooper (McGill), D.C. Masters (Bishop's), Anthony Preston (Bishop's), John Hughes (McGill), D.J. McDougall (Toronto), John Dando (McGill), E.F. Beach (McGill), E.H. Yarrill (Bishop's), and Frank R. Scott (McGill).[149]

Because the CAAE largely depended on university professors, lectures were usually discontinued in the summer.[150] Inmates appreciated these weekly lectures and often commented on them. A lecture entitled "Canadian Indians" by history professor D.C. Masters on 20 March 1945 caused the Camp Sherbrooke spokesman to comment, "It must not be overlooked that most of us here read all about Indians in our boys' story books – Indian stories including Cooper's [James Fenimore Cooper, author of *The Last of the Mohicans*] have always been popular with boys in Germany – and their ways and customs are fairly familiar to us. After we all have read so much fiction about Indians in our youth, it would have been interesting to round off the picture with facts e.g. more items taken from their history perhaps with special reference to Cooper's works." Camp intelligence officers were interested in the prisoners' comments because these gave them an insight into the impact of the lectures on the inmates.[151]

The language of instruction was predominantly English as most Canadian professors did not speak German. The only exception was Professor E.H. Yarrill of Bishop's University, who gave lectures in German at Camp Sherbrooke.[152] Interpreters were used, many of them Jewish refugees, and some German prisoners found this objectionable. The language barrier, therefore, proved a serious handicap for Canada's re-education program.[153]

Some re-education seminars and discussion groups were, however, conducted in German. These were "intended not merely for academic information, but to illuminate the present situation and suggest, overtly or by implication the causes of present ills [i.e., Nazism] and a solution to present problems."[154] They also helped prepare the inmates for future cooperation with the Allied occupational forces on German soil.[155] Seminars and discussion groups were deemed useful in providing "assessment material regarding POW in their group relations; studies and reports on practical problems of reconstruction, administrative and technical; and providing opportunities to certain POW to carry on re-educational work amongst their comrades."[156] Such seminars and discussion groups were organized, directed, and taught by "White" prisoners of war officers.[157] In July 1945 Camp Farnham's democratic committee established the basis of a program "for the education and enlightenment and general betterment of the young POW, on democratic principles."[158] The camp intelligence officer wrote:

> The Committee now has appointed some of its members to take charge of various fields. On Monday afternoons an article on current affairs in Europe is read and translated to the prisoners out of *Reader's Digest* ... Saturday afternoons are taken up with a *Wochenschau*, where the events of the past week are discussed from newspaper articles of particular interest. The lecturer, a committee member or one appointed by the Committee, expounds the ides of democratic logic in presenting his review. An open discussion by the audience with the reviewer takes place after the address has been completed ... In order to gradually prepare young POW officers for a more balanced and saner political outlook, to make them familiar with other types of government but National Socialism, two Committee members ... have been appointed to supervise the scheduled lectures on constitutions of Democratic countries. The first lecture will be on the constitution of Switzerland ... There will follow Sweden, British Commonwealth, USA and Canada. On conclusion of this series of lectures one period will be devoted to National Socialism, pointing out its crimes and bad points to the young POW, who do not understand what Nazism meant. Some of the points to be raised will be: The suppression of Religion and infiltration of 'cruelty literature,' thus justifying any crime as long as it was beneficial to National Socialism. Further state autocracy over Individualism. Discussions and lectures are attended by the Camp Intelligence Officer whenever possible.[159]

A similar process was followed at Grande Ligne and Sorel. Because no German prisoner of war officers were residing in Camp Sherbrooke and because there was strong resentment "against combatant officers of the former Nazi army" by the camp's enemy merchant seamen, it was decided to replace seminars and discussion groups by sessions with local civilian speakers.[160] Seminars and group discussions topics at camps Farnham, Grande Ligne, and Sorel included "The Weimar Constitution," "The History of Germany Since 1870," "The Rebirth of a Humane Germany," "Germany and Modern National States," "The European Balance-of-Power under Napoleon," "The Transition from Military to Civil Government in Germany," "Broad Outlines About Future British-German Relationships," "The Nuremberg War Crime Trials," "The Technical Problems in Reconstruction," "Germany's Ultimate Place in Europe and the World," and "The Future of Germany."[161]

Vocational training and trade courses offered in the camps were aimed at preparing German internees for future reintegration into German society. Prisoners of war had to be taught how to make the transition from military to civil life. The main problem was the German officers interned in Camp Farnham and Camp Grande Ligne. Many had never held a civilian profession nor received any preparation for future employment in civil society. Lieutenant-Colonel A.W. De Wolf, Camp Farnham's commandant, warned in 1945, "It is evident that these officers, a great many of whom are very young, will be a source of trouble in Germany, should the opportunity not be afforded to them to prepare themselves for their change over into civil life."[162] Classes were initiated in both camps to teach civilian professions and trades. This program was on balance successful. By 30 May 1945, 438 Grande Ligne officers were registered in civilian employment classes.[163] Prisoners were taught how to become administrators, accountants, architects, bankers, electricians, factory workers, farmers, journalists, lawyers, mechanics, merchants, public servants, and technicians.[164]

Because the goal of re-education was to prepare Germans to cooperate with the future Allied occupation of Germany, great importance was attached to teaching English.[165] English-language classes were inaugurated in all of southern Quebec's internment camps.[166] Eleven such classes were in progress at Camp Sorel by July 1945.[167] The success of English classes was so great that camp authorities estimated that 60 percent of the Sorel prisoners were fluent in English by November 1945.[168] At Camp Farnham, participation in English-language classes was also high. In May 1946, for example, 288 "students" graduated from the camp's English classes.[169] Advanced students could participate in daily English conversation sessions, commonly known as "roundtable conferences." Such discussion groups were inaugurated at Camp Farnham with the goal of preparing "students for future relations with the Allied authorities in Germany, teaching them how to make verbal inquiries, requests, etc."[170] These were normally attended by thirty or so internees, as well as by camp intelligence officers and censors. Prisoners usually chose the topics of conversation for such sessions. Inmates freely discussed the arts, democracy, and politics. These discussions also permitted camp intelligence officers to better understand the inmates' everyday concerns. As the Camp Farnham intelligence officer stated, "It is noteworthy to observe how every conversation wanders away from its original starting point to the fear of the Russians and Communism ... The ever apparent desire to probe deeper into democratic ideologies and practices can clearly be seen by the enthusiastic reception of these conversations and the animated discussions resulting from subjects introduced by the Canadian officers."[171] Eventually, French-language classes were also inaugurated.[172]

Re-education Literature

In all camps, American, British, Canadian, and other Allied-produced re-education literature was distributed to the inmates. Most of the Canadian-made re-education literature, largely newspapers and pamphlets, was written at Camp Sorel. These were read by so many prisoners, according to Camp Grande Ligne authorities, that "in the end they were rags."[173] But not all literature was welcomed in the camps of southern Quebec. For instance, when four issues of the *Information Bulletin* of the Soviet Union's embassy in Washington, D.C., were received at Camp Sorel in November 1945 as "propaganda material from a friendly power," camp censors refused to distribute them. Although they admitted that "these bulletins were very instructive," camp censors explained that "German POWs do not make a distinction between the Soviet Union as such and the Communist party" and that these pamphlets "might introduce party strife in the enclosure."[174]

During the war, most of southern Quebec's internment camps produced camp newspapers. The prisoners of war who participated in such publishing usually attended special "press classes," where they were taught printing and binding. Most of the men involved had formerly been journalists or had demonstrated an interest in becoming journalists once the war ended. At Farnham, the camp newspaper was known as *DKD* (*Deutscher Kriegsgefangenen Dienst*). Its purpose was to stimulate new thoughts in the minds of prisoners. *DKD* was published on the fifteenth and thirtieth of each month.[175] Its first edition was launched on 15 October 1945.[176] Overall, seventeen issues of this newspaper were published at Farnham before production ended on 20 May 1946.[177] Another camp paper, known as *Der Regenpfeifer* was created at Camp Grande Ligne and began to be published in December 1945 in order "to foster a literary forum for discussions on matters political, educational, religious and philosophical and to propagate a humanitarian and Christian moral code."[178] So efficient was the Camp Grande Ligne press group that fifty-six articles were written in February 1946 alone for future publication.[179]

Propaganda Films

Propaganda films were provided by the Military District 4 film library and included numerous newsreels.[180] These short films usually lasted no longer than twenty minutes and were shown on movie nights before the feature presentation. Most of the western Allies created such films. Although they dealt with different subjects, they shared the common goal of initiating the German prisoners of war in democratic values. In January 1946, for instance, around fifteen short re-educational films were shown at Camp Sherbrooke. Five were American-made, two were British and eight were Canadian. They included such evocative titles as *Pincers on Japan*; *Atlantic Patrol (RCN)*; *New Canada*; *Smoke Steel*; *Battle of Europe*; *This Is the Enemy*; *People's War*; and *Price of Victory*.[181]

Special films were shown also to test the prisoners' reaction to specific issues. A Frank Capra film entitled *The Negro Soldier* was shown at Camp Farnham in March 1946 to reveal racist tendencies among the prisoners. This film aroused much criticism, one German colonel even walked out during the performance. Camp authorities reported afterwards that "this picture was chosen by the intelligence officer to probe the racial prejudices of the POW. These are still strong in the majority of the prisoners."[182] Authorities also assessed the prisoners' perspective regarding Communism by presenting pro-Soviet films like *Our Northern Neighbour*.[183]

When the Canadian government learned of the atrocities committed in German concentration camps, they decided to show German prisoners of war short films and photographs that depicted the scenes of barbarism that the Allied forces encountered when they were liberating these camps. The aim was to create a sense of "collective culpability": to make the internees feel responsible for the actions of their government and convince them how evil the Nazis were.[184] All prisoners were forced to attend viewings of official "atrocity films," as they were called. These films depicted gas chambers, crematoria, mass graves, the emaciated prisoners, and other gruesome aspects of the Holocaust. The prisoners' reactions to such films varied considerably. Although most were shocked by what they saw, many refused to believe that such events had actually taken place. In some camps, atrocity films provoked laughter from the German audiences.[185] At Camp Grande Ligne, for example, "White" prisoners accepted the content of such films as being true but most "Blacks" believed them to be Allied propaganda.[186] At Farnham, on the other hand, it was reported that "the prisoners are convinced that the atrocities committed in German concentration camps are true but they state their disbelief that they could have been condoned by the Wehrmacht. They think that arch criminals could only have been responsible for such inhuman deeds."[187] Camp Sorel authorities commented that "the fact that they blame a distinct section, the SS, for atrocities, and another distinct section, the Prussians, for the war indicates that the POW here have a tendency to excuse themselves as a people."[188] Some Farnham prisoners felt so shocked and humiliated by the atrocities that they requested to be allowed to donate their blood to help save lives: "Realizing that they are universally the most hated race, they sense the reluctance with which such an offer may be received by the authorities and ... the public in general if it be known that our boys are being saved with German blood. However, their argument is that if we accept their blood that we might possibly use it for wounded Germans, so that they don't drain our blood banks."[189] Other prisoners asked the Canadian authorities "for consent to work on the land. The produce from their effort, they propose to forward to the needy countries. Alternatively, the produce is to be sold locally and the cash value handed to the authorities for food and supplies."[190]

Radio Broadcasts

In February 1945, the government authorized the International Service of the Canadian Broadcasting Corporation (CBC) to record prisoner of war broadcasts to be diffused throughout Germany. The internees' initially responded to this scheme by asking, "Why should we tell our relatives in Germany that we are well treated here in Canada. Over there our people are thoroughly convinced that we receive the best of everything. In fact, our people are jealous of us being here."[191] The Canadian authorities clarified the situation by telling the inmates that the aim was to tell the German people about the "futility of further resistance, and about the fact that the Canadians do not intend 'harm and destruction' but 'peace and rehabilitation.'"[192] As the CBC added, "Programs ought to indicate that the POW's were conscious of the problems and difficulties of present day Germany and were planning constructively and sympathetically to make what contribution they could to the reconstruction of Germany. A complete break with the past must be indicated. Possible subjects for discussion might be the rebirth of German trade unions or the food problem in Germany, or non-political questions."[193]

Radio groups of fifteen men each were created in most southern Quebec internment camps between May and July 1945.[194] Their purpose was to write political, semi-political, reconstruction, and entertainment scripts for radio broadcasts.[195] For this work prisoners were paid 50 cents per day.[196] Scripts depicting life in the camps of southern Quebec and the treatment of prisoners by Canadian authorities were written, and their titles included: "German Profiteers during the War," "Experiences by a POW at a Canadian Military Hospital," "Faith and Hope in Christianity," "United World," "Sports Should Be to Develop the Body, and Not for Militarist Purposes," and "Jurisdiction Behind the Barb-Wire."[197] Scripts were forwarded to the CBC in Montreal for transmission to Germany.[198] CBC personnel were also authorized to visit the camps with the necessary equipment to record radio transmissions. During such visits, prisoners of war read scripts furnished by the CBC or the camp's radio section. CBC visits were welcomed by the internees because most prisoners were eager to have their voices recorded and broadcast throughout Germany. Many hoped that loved ones might hear them on the radio. The popularity of these recording sessions was so great that more than 150 messages were recorded during one single CBC visit at Camp Farnham in May 1945.[199] Prisoners of war were also brought to the CBC studios in Montreal to record their messages whenever portable equipment was unavailable.[200]

Positive messages came from individual prisoners and sometimes camp orchestras were even recorded to reinforce the upbeat mood.[201] Prisoners targeted certain German regions in their messages. As one Camp Farnham inmate explained, "We should address different areas in Germany separately ... Bavaria must be addressed by a Bavarian, who knows the people there and who does not speak with a Prussian accent while the Sudetenland must be addressed by prisoners with Czech accents, and so on."[202] Participants in camp radio sections were also supplied with Nazi propaganda speeches so that they could mimic them to confuse listeners in Germany. Copies of speeches made by Nazi officials such as Paul Joseph Goebbels and Alfred Rosenberg were ordered by the Camp Farnham radio group in December 1945. "We understand these speeches have appeared in pamphlet form," wrote camp authorities. "Such material could in our opinion prove very useful. The leader of the radio group, Lt. Karl Gass, can imitate the voice of Goebbels to perfection. With access to the above mentioned material we should be able to produce some very effective radio scripts. We therefore request that such material be placed at our disposal."[203]

Prearranged discussions among inmates were also recorded, and in these camp life was again depicted positively. The men also spoke about democracy, their return to civil life, cooperation with the Allies, and the reconstruction of Germany.[204] One such broadcast entitled *What Do We Want?* was nothing more than a conversation among three German prisoners of war on the future of democracy in Germany. They openly rejected Nazism and preached cooperation with the western Allies.[205] In the end, the CBC deemed it necessary to fix weekly quotas for all camps participating in radio production; Camp Sorel (twenty scripts), Camp Farnham (eight scripts), and Camp Grande Ligne (three scripts).[206] Camp Sherbrooke became involved in the program as of January 1946 and produced eighteen scripts. Camp Sherbrooke's late contribution to the writing of radio scripts was explained by the camp commandant: "The reason for this is the low standard of education of enemy merchant seamen (who comprise 99 per cent of the POW strength) and that they are fairly busy under the Works Program."[207]

The CBC broadcasts usually brought immense happiness to the internees' relatives in Germany. A Camp Sorel prisoner's sister wrote in November 1945, "Your radio report from the camp was a great event for us in these days as it was the first time we ourselves were able to hear you speak from abroad. You cannot imagine our joy ... Now we feel fully relieved about you."[208] In another instance, a mother told her son, "Since I heard you on the radio, I am not worried about your fate."[209]

Following Germany's capitulation in May 1945, radio receivers were allowed for re-educational purposes in "Grey" and "White" camps.[210] Southern Quebec inmates also grew fond of the CBC's *Verchères* transmissions. These were fifteen-minute German- language news broadcasts that aired daily at 5:45 pm.[211] So popular was this show that 75 percent of Camp Farnham's internees listened to it each day.[212] Because most prisoners took for granted that the *Verchères* broadcasts were "intended primarily for the prisoners of war in Canada and only secondly for all German-speaking circles," camp radio groups often sent suggestions to the CBC regarding the show. Such was the case when the Farnham, Grande Ligne, and Sorel radio groups requested CBC officials to abolish all topics regarding "the collective responsibility of the German people for the misfortune that has befallen them" from the *Verchères* format.[213]

Results of the Canadian Re-education Program

As time went on, the Canadian re-education program sometimes met with a lack of enthusiasm among the prisoners. Delays in the repatriation of inmates preoccupied the men. "The question of going home absorbs most of the prisoners' thoughts," wrote Camp Sherbrooke's intelligence officer in December 1945.[214] Rumours circulating that the prisoners were to be sent to the United Kingdom for reconstruction work prior to repatriation also alarmed the internees. Camp Grande Ligne authorities wrote in February 1946 that "re-education is now 'over the hump.' The whole educational and re-educational work has become overshadowed in the minds of the prisoners of war by the question of their return to the UK. One factor which has contributed to the decrease in enthusiasm is the unconfirmed rumor that the prisoners will have to do reconstruction work in England, before returning home."[215] Worries about the fate of relatives, especially those living in the Soviet zone of occupation in Germany, also afflicted most inmates. These concerns were exacerbated when newly captured prisoners arrived in the camps with firsthand news about the harsh Soviet treatment of civilians in Germany. Such a case took place when the commander of the German submarine *U-889* was interned at Camp Farnham in May 1945 after having surrendered his boat to the Royal Canadian Navy in the aftermath of Germany's capitulation.[216] He told fellow internees, "Russians rape young German girls and make slave labourers out of German workers."[217] Such comments aroused much discontent inside the camps and made prisoners less inclined to participate in re-education. The only remedy was the arrival of letters from the Soviet zone of occupation, "thus relieving the exaggerated fears which many POW had maintained with regard to Russian treatment of civilians."[218] It was estimated by 1946 that 95 percent of southern Quebec inmates were anti-Communists.[219]

Canadian policies towards food rations in 1945-46 also helped to diminish the gains of re-education. Historian Chris Madsen writes that "during the war, Canadian authorities, hoping for reciprocal treatment towards Canadian prisoners of war in German custody, had kept rations artificially high for German POW's. Interned Germans received many food items denied or strictly rationed to Canadian civilians such as butter, sugar, and meat. However, the end of the war brought an official Canadian policy to reduce the food supply. The defeat of Germany and the liberation of Allied POWs removed any need for reciprocity."[220] The reduced rations provoked some resentment towards Canadian authorities, particularly within the large internment camps in Alberta. This meant less cooperation and more bitterness on the part of the prisoners.

Canadian planners were forced to ask themselves whether re-educational methods were achieving their ends. Some commentators have argued that brutal Soviet methods were more successful during the early years of re-education. According to historian Arthur Smith, "The western Allied planners of re-education may well have asked themselves at some point if the severe deprivation encountered by the German prisoners in Russia was a stronger inducement to study than the more national arguments presented by the United States and Britain. If terrible living conditions could be improved by studying Communism, many prisoners would conclude that they had nothing to lose; if camp conditions were tolerable or even quite good as in some American and British camps, prisoners did not have the same incentive. However, Western planners could console themselves that the prisoners who chose their offer to study democracy did so because of a genuine interest in learning about it."[221]

The temptation to abandon the program altogether became evident on numerous occasions. Ultimately, it was the fear that Nazi ideology might prevail behind Canadian barbed wire and in post-war Europe that persuaded Canadian authorities to pursue re-education despite the problems they encountered. Camp Farnham authorities argued, "Re-education must stay active. It is held by this office that, should work in this field be terminated now it is rumored the success and progress already achieved here will slowly disintegrate. The desire to learn is there, the sincerity and eagerness to help those young ones solely educated under the Nazi regime is there. To neglect this fertile ground now would be an indication of lack of imagination and vision."[222] Also persuading the Canadian authorities to maintain re-educational efforts was the fear that the Soviet program might have greater influence on post-war Germany.[223]

Despite occasional setbacks, the Canadian re-education program had positive results in southern Quebec. "Confidence in the strength and sincerity of purpose of the western world" was said to have increased by 70 percent at Camp Grande Ligne in 1945, for instance.[224] The camp's intelligence officer reported in November of that year that "all indications confirm that the process of re-orientation has become substantial, in this camp. It now becomes evident how successful has been this somewhat conservative policy of morally providing the means whereby the POW can exercise their own faculties and develop their own thoughts, and by so doing gain an appreciation of our ideals."[225] So strong was re-education at Camp Farnham that prisoners even disavowed their ties to the German military: "Significant indication of the anti-militaristic feeling in camp 40 are the remarks passed on arrival here of 200 new uniforms through the Red Cross. Some officers and OR's [Other Ranks] stated as follows: 'We are done with militarism. We don't want them.'"[226]

Re-education also contributed to creating a climate of cooperation between German inmates and the Canadian authorities. Indeed, the names of approximately 300 people in Germany "considered to be willing and trustworthy to cooperate with the Allied Control Commission" were obtained from southern Quebec inmates and submitted to the Directorate of Military Intelligence.[227] In the end, many southern Quebec internees were pleased with the education they received in the region's camps. Said one former Sorel inmate after having been transferred to the United Kingdom in early 1946, "I have written this letter to you [Major L.L. Brunton, former Camp Sorel commandant], Sir, because you should know that I, as well as many other POW returned from Canada, have brought back from there a conception of life whereby we can still hold our heads high, in spite of the propaganda directed against all Germans; because this conception will help along those who still have a home and will provide a healthy foundation for the future."[228]

Although the aim of re-education was to prepare a vanguard who would establish democracy in Germany, numerous internees began to express deep resentments about going back to the "fatherland." According to one observer, "many POW's expressed their reluctance to leave Canada and hoped they would be allowed to immigrate to Canada in the near future."[229] The Camp Grande Ligne intelligence officer wrote,

> A somewhat unexpected byproduct of re-education crops up in the attitude of the many POW who have fallen under its influence and who now know so much about the affairs and life on this continent, that the idea of returning to Germany has become utterly distasteful to them. Of course, the main objective of re-orientation is to make a contribution towards the creation of a strong democratic element in Germany. However, many of the POW who for 5 years read Canadian newspapers, accepted Canadian views and are gradually shedding their inner allegiance to the "Fatherland." In one respect it is discouraging to find that after many months of work on a prospective proponent of democratic ideas in Germany, the POW in question appears one day at the office with a long dissertation in which he sets forth that he is through with Germany. Instead, he wants to immigrate to Canada.[230]

Intending to immigrate to Canada, numerous prisoners attempted to accelerate the process by demonstrating how essential could be their contribution to the Canadian economy. At Camp Grande Ligne, two prisoners wrote an agricultural study entitled *Summary Dealing with Barnyard Manure* after the Department of Agriculture had given inmates pamphlets, bulletins, and publications depicting the great differences between farming in Canada and in Germany. The government's goal was to help internees working on the camp farm, but some internees took this information to mean that the Canadian government was seeking new immigrant farmers. As the two prisoners indicated, "Our one and only intention is to show you our gratitude for furnishing us with Canadian farmer's literature. We do hope, that our essay may be worth reading for you, though we are fully aware of the fact that Canadian farming-conditions differ greatly from those in Germany ... but we would like to give you a specimen of our interest in farming, which we hope to prove practically in case our petitions to immigrate into Canada as farmers ... should be granted."[231]

Other prisoners attempted to gain permission to immigrate by promoting their scientific knowledge. Since the capitulation of Germany in May 1945, most Allied powers had been racing against one another to gain access to German scientists and German technology. Southern Quebec prisoners read about this situation in American and Canadian newspapers. Such was the case, for example, for a Sorel inmate who was a specialist in aircraft jet engines. Having read that "the United

States is going to transfer German engineers and scientists to that country in order to let them continue their experiment and that England also approached German scientists of chemical and plastic plants for the same purpose and that Russia also engaged many German scientists and engineers to continue their research, he became interested to be employed as such in Canada."[232] The internee claimed that he had worked as a gas-turbine engineer in Berlin between 1935 and 1939. He offered his services to the Canadian government by enclosing a detailed report and the sketch drawing of an aircraft combustion turbine that he had worked on before the war, and added,

> Before the war, the German Reich asked engineers to build a new kind of engine which could use many kinds of fuel, especially alcohol, acetylene, hydrogen and the like which can be produced in Germany. For unknown reasons, the production of high economic turbines was delayed for the duration of the war in favour of other kinds of engines to be used in planes and for V-weapons. The combustion turbine was designed to create an engine with a low consumption of fuel. It is propelled by two rotors which are geared together. Through this, the effect is almost the same as that of a standard reaction-turbine. On each side of the two rotors are air inlets channels. Shortly before the blades of both the rotors run into one another fuel is added into the air inlet to rotor No. 2. The blades compress the mixture and at the climax ignition elements explode the charge. The expanding gases drive the blades by applying their power to the rotors.[233]

These immigration attempts proved that instead of wishing to return home to implant the basic principles of democracy, internees had "fallen in love" with their detaining power. However, Canada's strict immigration policies and the Geneva Convention's emphasis on repatriation meant that no prisoners were allowed to immigrate to Canada in the immediate aftermath of the war.

Overall, the success of Canada's re-education program was limited. According to historian Andrew Rettig, April 1946 PHERUDA statistics revealed that the Canadian re-education program was less effective than expected:

> The statistical results of Canadian reeducation compared unfavourably to the American and British figures. Canada placed 18.7 per cent in the White anti-Nazi groups, 44 in the Grey undecided groups, and 30 in the Nazi section, while the Americans claimed an incredible breakdown of 15 per cent, 70 per cent and 15 per cent. Britain felt that only 10 per cent of its POWs became tolerant anti-Nazis, that 80 per cent were "conformists," and that the remainder defended intolerant Nazism. The result showed that Canada-taught POWs learned least, perhaps reflecting the fact that Canada originally received so many enthusiastic Nazi POWs."[234]

The strong expressions of Nazi loyalty among some Canadian-held prisoners of war led Colonel Henry Faulk, head of the British re-education program, to claim that "Canada undertook a 'limited re-educational effort' that was far too 'intellectual' to affect the rank and file of the POWs."[235]

In the end, the Allies' re-education of prisoners of war had almost no impact on post-war Germany. According to historian Ron Robin, "Neither British nor American re-education officials were able to secure pivotal government positions for their graduates. There is no evidence of large numbers of POWs from either program serving as apostles of democracy in their home country."[236]

Summary

Despite the programs' shortcomings, it would be erroneous to believe that education and re-education had no impact on prisoners or benefits for authorities. Education programs enabled prisoners to satisfy their thirst for knowledge. They kept inmates busy learning, making them less prone to concentrate on their captivity. During the prisoner of war phase, the situation was more complex. During this period, Nazism prevailed in the camps of southern Quebec and violence was frequent. This situation led the Canadian government to initiate a re-education program aimed at indoctrinating prisoners along democratic lines. The goal was to modify the internees' beliefs so that when they were repatriated to Germany Nazi thoughts would be eradicated. By using lectures and seminars, literature, films, and radio broadcasts as re-educational tools, Canadian officials were indeed able to open the minds of prisoners towards democratic ideals.

6

Canada's Internment Experience: A Home Front Victory

The internment operation initiated on the south shore of the St. Lawrence River during the Second World War was an integral part of the Canadian internment experience and, as such, reflected how internment camps functioned and how prisoners were treated in Canada. The fact that the Canadian government strictly abided by the provisions of the Geneva Convention in its treatment of both German civilians and prisoners of war shows that inmates were adequately treated in this country. Compared with the internment operations of other belligerent powers, namely those of Germany and Japan, conditions in southern Quebec camps and in other Canadian internment facilities during the war were generally good. No prisoners were executed by Canadian guards, nor were any sadistic medical experiments conducted on the prisoners. Inmates were never beaten or tortured. They were allowed to work, but only on a voluntary basis, and they were paid for their services. Living conditions in the camps were also more than adequate. Inmates were given plentiful portions of food and permitted all sorts of recreational activities. Never were they refused contact with humanitarian societies, nor were they refused the opportunity to pursue their education. Despite a difficult start in 1940, the internment operation in southern Quebec grew to become one of Canada's most important. The decision to use the region's camps as the basis for the Canadian re-education program serves as a testimony of the importance southern Quebec camps attained throughout the war. Southern Quebec's internment operations typify the drastic measures that may be adopted by belligerents in times of war. Aside from the approximately 38,000 Germans interned in Canada during the war, the country also incarcerated other "enemy ethnic groups." These included civilians of Italian, Japanese, Finnish, Hungarian, and Romanian descent, as well as other individuals whose ethnic backgrounds lay with countries that supported Axis forces or were at war against the Allies.[1] In addition to these groups, Canada detained homegrown Fascist sympathizers, Communists, and civilians perceived to be subversives.[2] The treatment of these internees resembled, in many ways, that of German prisoners.

Canada also detained thousands of Italian and German prisoners of war overseas. Most were captured by Canadian troops during the Italian and Northwestern European campaigns. It is estimated that following VE Day, British and Canadian armed forces detained close to three million "surrendered" German prisoners of war in Europe alone. Similar numbers were also held by the United States Army.[3]

Needless to say, Allied forces in Europe found themselves suddenly overwhelmed by an astounding number of surrendered enemy soldiers. This created important logistical problems that made it difficult for Allied troops to provide German prisoners with adequate food, shelter, and medical assistance. On many occasions, German prisoners were scattered in open field camps where they had to dig holes in the ground and use whatever means possible to protect themselves from inclement weather. As a result, numerous prisoners died. The most critical account of conditions in these camps, which maintains that American and French captors deliberately neglected prisoners, puts the German death toll at over one million.[4] This is certainly a gross exaggeration but, according to author Joan Beaumont, "even the fiercest defenders of the American authorities – who attribute the deaths to the logistic problems of handling several million prisoners rather than malice – put the minimum number of deaths at 56,000."[5] Clearly, the treatment of German prisoners in Europe following the surrender of Germany was not as good as that in Canada.

Canada's Fair Treatment of German Internees

The treatment of German prisoners in Canada was always done in conformity with the rules of the Geneva Convention. There are many reasons why the country chose to abide by this convention, the most important being the nature of the enemies themselves. Because Germany and Japan had little interest in treating prisoners of war adequately in the interests of humanity, Canada had to pin its hopes on the concept of reciprocity. Historian Jonathan Vance argues that the proper treatment of German prisoners in Canada was inextricably linked to the treatment of Canadians in enemy hands. The Canadian government believed that as long as German prisoners were well cared for and Canada continued to abide to the provisions of the Geneva Convention, Canadian prisoners of war would be adequately treated by the enemy. Only by linking the treatment of prisoners in Canada to that of Canadians in enemy hands could the government attempt to exert some influence over the enemy. However, as Vance explains, even this sensible position was weakened by the fact that reciprocity functioned only when the enemy valued its citizens in captivity as much as Canada did.[6] Nonetheless, the principle of reciprocity played an important role and the Canadian government usually lodged a protest when conditions affecting Canadians in German hands were markedly worse than those experienced by prisoners in Canada.[7]

The proper treatment of German inmates in Canada, which was often better than what the articles of the Geneva Convention stipulated, came as a shock to both German prisoners and Canadian civilians. It was a known fact that rations in Canadian internment camps were quite generous and sometimes consisted of items such as sugar and butter that were rationed on the Canadian home front. As Vance describes in *Objects of Concern*, a groups of German prisoners of war arriving at

Halifax were delighted to discover that their first meal consisted of white bread with butter, fried potatoes, scrambled eggs, ham, baked beans, peaches, and coffee. Many Canadians felt that conditions inside the camps were better than they should be. Some even lodged complaints with camp authorities. Most prisoners gained weight and were heavier when they were repatriated than when they arrived in Canada. Rations were only one of many amenities that German prisoners benefited from while in Canada. Such amenities ranged from the indoor swimming pool at Camp Bowmanville to the freedom to order almost anything they wanted from the T. Eaton Company's catalogue.[8]

Canadian prisoners of war sometimes found themselves the recipients of privileges as a result of the conditions enjoyed by German prisoners of war held in Canada. Jonathan Vance notes an announcement made by German authorities to Canadian prisoners of war: "Our Führer has been very impressed with the official reports of the treatment received by German prisoners in Canada. He has therefore authorized that preferential treatment be given to Canadian prisoners of war ... a new all-Canadian camp is being prepared near Stettin. There Canadians will be allowed the freedom of the town. They will be able to mix among the civilian population, and go to shows and other entertainment. Their food will be increased to double ration."[9]

While the Canadian prisoners were never transferred to this so-called "Canadian" camp, this announcement clearly shows how German authorities were well aware of the proper conditions in internment camps in Canada. A comparison between the number of German prisoners of war who died in Canadian hands versus Canadian prisoners in German and Japanese custody provides evidence of the proper treatment inmates received in Canada. Of the nearly 10,000 Canadians who fell into enemy hands, 670 died in captivity (380 in Europe and 290 on the Pacific theatre).[10] It is estimated that more than 150 Canadian prisoners of war were murdered by German troops in the Normandy campaign alone.[11] On the other hand, of the more than 34,000 German prisoners of war in Canada, only 162 died in captivity, most of them from uncontrollable diseases such as tuberculosis, pneumonia, cancer, diabetes, and heart failure.[12]

Still, despite the good treatment German prisoners received in Canada, camp life created severe physical and psychological strains. Although internees were protected by the provisions of the Geneva Convention and benefited from numerous privileges, the sheer reality of being held captive was enough to generate stress. Restricted mobility, sexual deprivation, social alienation, and the scarcity of material comforts all affected the morale of prisoners. As a consequence, internees became occasionally restless and uncooperative. They sometimes expressed their discontent through dissension that led to strikes, riots, illicit activities, and escape attempts. This reality forced camp authorities to apply discipline and punish the perpetrators. Another major problem had to do with the prisoners' political and ideological tendencies. For the Canadian authorities, the dominance of Nazism inside internment camps constituted a major problem, especially when Nazis acted in insubordinate ways or when they terrorized anti-Nazi fellow prisoners. Despite attempts to segregate camp populations with the introduction of the PHERUDA method of prisoner of war classification in 1943, Canadian authorities were unable to eradicate the presence of Nazism inside the camps. The rise of the Camp Grande Ligne HARIKARI Club, for instance, clearly shows the power Nazi prisoners held in several Canadian internment camps in the last months of the war.

Hoping to minimize the consequences of physical and psychological strains, the Canadian government introduced two major schemes in the camps of southern Quebec: labour projects and educational programs. The belief was that both these projects would keep inmates occupied and force them to spend less time plotting against camp authorities. The aim was to broaden the mind of the prisoners, help them maintain sanity, show them alternatives to Nazism, and prepare them for post-war professions. To ensure that the German authorities would not see these projects as "brainwashing," the Canadian government chose only volunteers to participate. Because the treatment of prisoners remained adequate in southern Quebec camps, acts of dissension on the part of the inmates were rare. Instead, prisoners actively participated in recreational and educational activities organized within the camps.

All of southern Quebec's internees were repatriated by the end of 1946, but the return to civilian life took its toll on them. Most had been interned for several years, and the transition from internment to civilian life was no easy task. Former civilian internee Eric Koch says in *Deemed Suspect* that release was a bittersweet experience for many; they felt lonely and confused at first, having become accustomed to camp life where all decisions were made for them and everything was predictable and safe. Crossing a busy city street could be an unnerving experience for recently released inmates, as was suddenly sleeping alone in a room after years of having heard the "comfortable sound" of men snoring. According to Koch, it was "like being exiled to some distant, unfamiliar and boring island."[13] Although some prisoners maintained hard grudges about their internment, many others confessed to having derived immeasurable benefits from the experience. "Most of us feel that the years spent in this compression chamber between Europe and North America, between Hitler and the post-war world, taught us a great deal about ourselves and about the way a community works," said Koch.[14] In fact, for those prisoners held in Canada, captivity offered numerous benefits, including an asylum from death and destruction in Europe.

German Internees and Their Recollections of Internment

Probably the best indicator of the success of the Canadian internment operation are the feelings expressed by the German prisoners themselves. Several took the opportunity after the war to write to the Canadian authorities to give their thanks for the treatment they received. One former Grande Ligne officer wrote in 1957, "I also keep in best memory the time I spent in Grande Ligne as far as one may keep in best memory a time spent behind barbed wire."[15] Another former prisoner wrote to Colonel Eric D.B. Kippen in 1947,

> It is now more than a year ago since I left Canada as a POW in your charge ... Having regained individual freedom, I may be allowed to remember the years I had to spend in your country, and doing so, I should like to let you know, you as a representative of the Canadian nation, how very much I shall always appreciate the ever so correct and considerate attitude of the government of Canada and the military authorities towards POWs. This is meant to be a simple act of gratitude to fairness met in enemy hands. I honestly believe that many of the former POWs will agree with me, if I say, that your country has done a lot to show Germans in Canadian custody the value of democratic life. The results of this attitude, I hope, will prove to be of stimulating value in rebuilding our own country.[16]

Although such correspondence represents an inadequate sampling of the views expressed by most former German prisoners of war interned in Canada, it confirms that Canadian authorities obeyed the Geneva Convention throughout the war and carried out their responsibilities in a very responsible manner.

In the end, hundreds of former German internees, influenced by the good treatment they received in Canadian internment camps during the war, immigrated to Canada. The process began in the latter part of the civilian phase, when many of the German refugees chose to remain in the country instead of returning to Germany or the United Kingdom. In the course of writing *Deemed Suspect*, Eric Koch was able to locate 478 ex-refugees. Of these, 283 immigrated to Canada, 80 to the United States, 18 to the United Kingdom, 17 to other countries, and 80 chose to remain anonymous for various reasons.[17] Koch explains, "The war had turned Canada into a far more open and receptive society. Everything was there to help our integration ... Canada's relaxed attitude toward its nationhood suited us perfectly. For ... many reasons most of us chose to remain in Canada after the war, even if we could have gone to the United States or returned to Europe; we quickly grew roots in Canadian society. Many of us even passed the ultimate test of true Canadianism: a passionate interest in hockey."[18]

As for the German prisoners of war, many wanted to stay in Canada but the terms of the Geneva Convention demanded that they be repatriated to Germany.[19] It is estimated that at least 6,000 German prisoners of war made applications in various forms for permission to remain in Canada. Their applications were placed on Department of National Defence Files for future reference. Eventually, a large number did immigrate to Canada in post-war years.[20] Influenced by the fair treatment they had received in the country during the war and by the difficult economic conditions that existed in post-war Germany, these individuals chose Canada as their new home. While there are no exact figures as to how many former German prisoners came back to Canada after the war, author David Carter speculates that at least a thousand immigrated to the country. Many were sponsored by Canadian farmers.[21] In *Escape from Canada*, John Melady provides interesting accounts of some of the prisoners who came back to Canada. "I and a lot of others wanted to stay in Canada when the war was over," one former German prisoner of war told Melady. "We had grown so attached to this country that we had no wish to leave it. I had been working on a farm, along with several others I knew. The farmers were glad of the help and they really tried to convince the authorities to allow us to stay. It was no use, however; we were all sent back. But as soon as I could, I applied to return here."[22] Another former inmate recalled how he became friends with some of the former guards in the internment camp where he was detained: "I could not complain about the guards I had. After the war I came back to Canada to live and I went to see some of them. We became friends and talked of old times when we were together on different sides."[23] Yet another remarked, "I like Canadians. They made my life as pleasant as possible from the day I came here as a prisoner. Later, when I returned as a landed immigrant, I knew this was my country."[24]

German former prisoners who chose Canada as their new home did so because they firmly believed that the treatment they received in Canada was reflective of the Canadian way of life. The camps of southern Quebec, like all of Canada's Second World War internment camps, played an important role in this process. Despite the occasional setbacks and complaints on the part of the prisoners themselves – an important aspect of any properly functioning internment operation – the administration and treatment of inmate populations in Canadian Second World War internment camps was humane and in complete accordance to the Geneva Convention. It is fair to say that the internment operation in southern Quebec, as an integral part of the Canadian internment operation, must be regarded as a major victory and accomplishment of the Canadian home front.

Appendix

Table A.1

Canadian permanent internment camps for German prisoners, 1939-47

ID Letter (1939-41)	ID Number (1941-46)	Camp name	Province	Open	Closed
A	40	Farnham	Quebec	1940	1946
B	70	Fredericton	New Brunswick	1940	1946
C	20	Gravenhurst	Ontario	1940	1946
E	21	Espanola	Ontario	1940	1943
F	31	Kingston	Ontario	1940	1943
H	32	Hull	Quebec	1941	1947
I	41	Île-aux-Noix	Quebec	1940	1943
K	130	Kananaskis-Seebee	Alberta	1939	1946
L	–	Cove Fields (Quebec City)	Quebec	1940	1941
M	22	Mimico (New Toronto)	Ontario	1940	1944
N	42	Sherbrooke (Newington)	Quebec	1940	1946
P	33	Petawawa	Ontario	1939	1946
Q	23	Monteith	Ontario	1940	1946
R	–	Red Rock	Ontario	1940	1941
S	43	Île Ste-Hélène	Quebec	1940	1943
T	–	Trois-Rivières	Quebec	1940	1940
W	100	Neys	Ontario	1941	1946
X	101	Angler	Ontario	1941	1946
–	10	Chatham	Ontario	1944	1946
–	30	Bowmanville	Ontario	1941	1945
–	44	Grande Ligne	Quebec	1943	1946
–	45	Sorel	Quebec	1945	1946
–	132	Medicine Hat	Alberta	1943	1946
–	133	Lethbridge-Ozada	Alberta	1942	1946
–	135	Wainright	Alberta	1944	1946

Sources: Yves Bernard and Caroline Bergeron, *Trop loin de Berlin: Des prisonniers allemands au Canada (1939-1946)* (Sillery, QC: Éditions du Septentrion, 1995), 17-19; Chris M.V. Madsen and R.J. Henderson, *German Prisoners of War in Canada and Their Artifacts* (Regina: Hignell Printing, 1993), 98-101.

Table A.2

Number of prisoners interned at Camp Farnham, 1940-46

	1940	1941	1942	1943	1944	1945	1946
1-15 January	0	446	445	234	0	656	431
16-31 January	0	459	445	234	0	656	427
1-15 February	0	446	0	332	0	656	427
16-28 February	0	366	0	233	0	555	394
1-15 March	0	458	0	334	0	553	394
16-31 March	0	458	0	334	0	553	394
1-15 April	0	467	0	334	0	553	492
16-30 April	0	467	597	334	0	501	799
1-15 May	0	466	597	235	0	501	733
16-31 May	0	487	598	235	0	507	4
1-15 June	0	490	598	235	0	471	0
16-30 June	0	534	599	467	0	400	0
1-15 July	0	564	597	0	0	400	0
16-31 July	0	564	599	0	0	401	0
1-15 August	0	573	597	0	0	401	0
16-31 August	0	573	598	6	0	401	0
1-15 September	0	573	600	7	0	401	0
16-30 September	0	566	600	1	596	401	0
1-15 October	0	566	600	0	602	403	0
16-31 October	523	566	594	0	657	405	0
1-15 November	523	493	594	0	657	405	0
16-30 November	556	493	597	0	657	407	0
1-15 December	545	494	229	0	656	429	0
16-31 December	446	488	234	0	656	429	0

Sources: Library and Archives Canada (LAC), RG-24, Vol. 11,254, File 13-3-5, "Strength Returns, Camp Farnham," 1940-41; LAC, RG-24, Reel: C-5374, File HQS 7236-1-10-40, "Strength Returns, Camp Farnham," 1941-46.

Table A.3

Number of prisoners interned at Camp Île-aux-Noix, 1940-43

	1940	1941	1942	1943
1-15 January	0	324	234	305
16-31 January	0	321	233	195
1-15 February	0	319	212	195
16-28 February	0	282	212	179
1-15 March	0	276	205	179
16-31 March	0	263	199	154
1-15 April	0	263	190	151
16-30 April	0	263	172	151
1-15 May	0	265	156	147
16-31 May	0	265	137	139
1-15 June	0	261	114	135
16-30 June	0	374	113	122
1-15 July	0	333	103	115
16-31 July	273	330	93	100
1-15 August	273	330	84	95
16-31 August	273	330	76	89
1-15 September	273	330	76	88
16-30 September	273	330	64	83
1-15 October	273	249	59	81
16-31 October	373	249	50	52
1-15 November	375	241	44	42
16-30 November	325	241	343	0
1-15 December	323	236	315	0
16-31 December	324	234	305	0

Sources: Library and Archives Canada (LAC), RG-24, Vol. 11,254, File 13-3-10, "Strength Returns, Camp Île-aux-Noix," 1940-41; LAC, RG-24, Reel: C-5374, File HQS 7236-1-10-41, "Strength Returns, Camp Île-aux-Noix," 1941-43.

Table A.4

Number of prisoners interned at Camp Sherbrooke, 1940-46

	1940	1941	1942	1943	1944	1945	1946
1-15 January	0	565	508	630	628	444	412
16-31 January	0	639	921	629	628	445	412
1-15 February	0	639	897	630	628	445	412
16-28 February	0	592	897	630	627	445	404
1-15 March	0	594	889	630	627	445	405
16-31 March	0	594	841	630	623	396	405
1-15 April	0	594	792	630	623	394	405
16-30 April	0	605	749	630	622	394	405
1-15 May	0	605	668	629	473	380	395
16-31 May	0	598	656	705	473	380	395
1-15 June	0	598	583	706	473	380	362
16-30 June	0	636	557	706	473	376	0
1-15 July	0	635	543	706	470	376	0
16-31 July	0	635	498	698	470	369	0
1-15 August	0	635	487	698	400	369	0
16-31 August	0	635	437	677	397	369	0
1-15 September	0	587	420	677	397	369	0
16-30 September	0	587	392	677	397	369	0
1-15 October	618	552	356	677	397	369	0
16-31 October	736	552	321	677	397	369	0
1-15 November	736	527	299	677	397	369	0
16-30 November	721	527	299	629	392	412	0
1-15 December	721	508	594	629	392	412	0
16-31 December	565	508	594	628	449	412	0

Sources: Library and Archives Canada (LAC), RG-24, Vol. 15,399 and 15,400, vols. 1 to 26, War Diary of Internment Camp Sherbrooke, 1940-42; LAC, RG-24, Reel: C-5374, File HQS 7236-1-10-42, "Strength Returns, Camp Sherbrooke," 1941-46.

Table A.5

Number of prisoners interned at Camp Grande Ligne, 1943-46

	1943	1944	1945	1946
1-15 January	0	596	708	593
16-31 January	0	623	708	564
1-15 February	0	624	472	564
16-28 February	0	724	472	508
1-15 March	0	725	471	508
16-31 March	0	723	472	508
1-15 April	0	715	634	239
16-30 April	0	715	634	12
1-15 May	0	718	634	0
16-31 May	0	718	635	0
1-15 June	0	718	637	0
16-30 June	464	718	624	0
1-15 July	467	718	610	0
16-31 July	603	718	610	0
1-15 August	603	718	610	0
16-31 August	603	713	612	0
1-15 September	603	713	601	0
16-30 September	601	713	599	0
1-15 October	601	712	599	0
16-31 October	621	711	597	0
1-15 November	621	711	600	0
16-30 November	596	711	600	0
1-15 December	596	711	593	0
16-31 December	596	711	593	0

Source: Library and Archives Canada, RG-24, Reel: C-5374, File HQS 7236-1-10-44, "Strength Returns, Camp Grande Ligne," 1943-46.

Table A.6

Number of prisoners interned at Camp Sorel, 1945-46

	1945	1946
1-15 January	0	212
16-31 January	0	212
1-15 February	0	212
16-28 February	0	185
1-15 March	0	184
16-31 March	0	0
1-15 April	0	0
16-30 April	0	0
1-15 May	0	0
16-31 May	0	0
1-15 June	0	0
16-30 June	121	0
1-15 July	225	0
16-31 July	225	0
1-15 August	226	0
16-31 August	223	0
1-15 September	207	0
16-30 September	208	0
1-15 October	208	0
16-31 October	232	0
1-15 November	229	0
16-30 November	227	0
1-15 December	234	0
16-31 December	213	0

Source: Library and Archives Canada, RG-24, Reel: C-5374, File HQS 7236-1-10-45, "Strength Returns, Camp Sorel," 1945-46.

Notes

Chapter 1: A History of Internment

1 Department of National Defence, Directorate of History and Heritage [DHH], 113.3P4 (D2), "Directorate Narrative, Directorate of Prisoners of War," 5 September 1945. See also Yves Bernard and Caroline Bergeron, *Trop loin de Berlin: Des prisonniers allemands au Canada (1939-1946)* (Sillery, QC: Éditions du Septentrion, 1995), 357; John Joseph Kelly, "The Prisoner of War Camps in Canada, 1939-1947" (MA thesis, University of Windsor, 1976), 209; Chris M.V. Madsen and R.J. Henderson, *German Prisoners of War in Canada and Their Artifacts* (Regina: Hignell Printing, 1993), 1.

2 On women internees, see Andrée Laprise, "Des civils internés pendant la deuxième guerre mondiale: Le camp des femmes de Kingston, 1939-1943" (MA thesis, Université de Montréal, 2000); Michelle McBride, "The Curious Case of Female Internees," in *Enemies Within: Italian and Other Internees in Canada and Abroad,* ed. Franca Iacovetta, Roberto Perin, and Angelo Principe (Toronto: University of Toronto Press, 2000), 148-70.

3 William E.S. Flory, *Prisoners of War: A Study in the Development of International Law* (Washington, DC: American Council of Public Affairs, 1942), 24-38.

4 Joël Kotek and Pierre Rigoulot, *Le siècle des camps: Détention, concentration, extermination: Cent ans de mal radical* (Paris: JC Lattès, 2000), 11-46; Philippe Masson and Alain Melchior-Bonnet, eds., *Dictionnaire de la Seconde guerre mondiale,* vol. 1 (Paris: Librairie Larousse, 1979), 527-31.

5 Jonathan F. Vance, ed., *Encyclopedia of Prisoners of War and Internment* (Santa Barbara: ABC-CLIO, 2000), 1-349.

6 A.J. Barker, *Behind Barbed Wire* (London: B.T. Batsford, 1974), 5-6; Flory, *Prisoners of War,* 10-18.

7 Barker, *Behind Barbed Wire,* 6-7; Geoffrey Best, *Humanity in Warfare* (New York: Columbia University Press, 1980), 78-79; Vance, ed., *Encyclopedia,* 199-201.

8 Mark Mayo Boatner, *The Civil War Dictionary* (New York: David McKay Company, 1988), 15; Kotek and Rigoulot, *Le siècle des camps,* 26-27; Vance, ed., *Encyclopedia,* 9-10, 297-9; Steven E. Woodworth, ed., *The American Civil War: A Handbook of Literature and Research* (Westport, CT: Greenwood, 1996), 466-75. See also William Marvel, *Andersonville: The Last Depot* (Chapel Hill: University of North Carolina Press, 1994).

9 Barker, *Behind Barbed Wire,* 13-15; Best, *Humanity in Warfare,* 155-56.

10 Canada, *Red Cross and Prisoners of War Conventions* (Ottawa: Edmond Cloutier, 1942), 42-47; John F. Hutchinson, *Champions of Charity: War and the Rise of the Red Cross* (Boulder, CO: Westview Press, 1996), 11-56; Vance, ed., *Encyclopedia,* 109-10.

11 Barker, *Behind Barbed Wire,* 15; Best, *Humanity in Warfare* 156-57; Flory, *Prisoners of War,* 19-20; Vance, ed., *Encyclopedia,* 34.

12 Michael Howard, George J. Andreopoulos, and Mark R. Shulman, eds., *The Laws of War: Constraints on Warfare in the Western World* (New Haven, CT: Yale University Press, 1994), 119-39; Robert Jackson, *The Prisoners, 1914-18* (London and New York: Routledge, 1989), 5-6; Vance, ed., *Encyclopedia,* 125-26.

13 Richard Shelly Hartigan, *The Forgotten Victim: A History of the Civilian* (Chicago: Precedent Publishing, 1982), 93-115.

14 Best, *Humanity in Warfare*, 190-200. See also Walter Laqueur, *Guerrilla: A Historical and Critical Study* (Boston: Little, Brown and Company, 1976).

15 Brad K. Berner, *The Spanish-American War: A Historical Dictionary* (Lanham, MD: The Scarecrow Press, 1998), 309; Donald H. Dyal, *Historical Dictionary of the Spanish American War* (Westport, CT: Greenwood Press, 1996), 275; Kotek and Rigoulot, *Le siècle des camps*, 48-59; Vance, ed., *Encyclopedia*, 63. See also Philip S. Foner, *The Spanish-Cuban-American War and the Birth of American Imperialism, 1895-1902* (New York: Monthly Review Press, 1972); Joseph Smith, *The Spanish-American War: Conflict in the Caribbean and the Pacific, 1895-1902* (London: Longman, 1994).

16 Kotek and Rigoulot, *Le siècle des camps*, 56-57; G.J.A. O'Toole, *The Spanish War: An American Epic, 1898* (New York: W.W. Norton and Company, 1984), 57-58.

17 Benjamin R. Beede, ed., *The War of 1898 and U.S. Interventions, 1898-1934: An Encyclopedia* (New York: Garland Publishing, 1994), 31-34; Max Boot, *The Savage Wars of Peace: Small Wars and the Rise of American Power* (New York: Basic Books, 2002), 125; Vance, ed., *Encyclopedia*, 63. See also Brian McAllister Linn, *The Philippine War, 1899-1902* (Lawrence: University Press of Kansas, 2000); Brian McAllister Linn, *The U.S. Army and Counterinsurgency in the Philippine War, 1899-1902* (Chapel Hill: University of North Carolina Press, 1989); and Stuart Creighton Miller, *"Benevolent Assimilation": The American Conquest of the Philippines, 1899-1903* (New Haven, CT: Yale University Press, 1982).

18 Kotek and Rigoulot, *Le siècle des camps*, 62-79; G.H.L. Le May, *British Supremacy in South Africa, 1899-1907* (Oxford: Clarendon Press, 1965), 91-110; Bernard Lugan, *La Guerre des Boers, 1899-1902* (Paris: Perrin, 1998), 203-10; Bill Nasson, *The South African War, 1899-1902* (London: Arnold, 1999), 219-24; Thomas Pakenham, *The Boer War* (New York: Random House, 1979), 533-49. See also S.B. Spies, *Methods of Barbarism? Roberts and Kitchener and Civilians in the Boer Republics, January 1900-May 1902* (Cape Town: Barber and Rousseau, 1977).

19 Le May, *British Supremacy*, 106-10; Lugan, *La Guerre des Boers*, 210-12; Nasson, *The South African War*, 223-24; Vance, ed., *Encyclopedia*, 29.

20 Pakenham, *The Boer War*, 535.

21 Helmut Bley, *South-West Africa under German Rule, 1894-1914* (Evanston, IL: Northwestern University Press, 1971), 149-73; Kotek and Rigoulot, *Le siècle des camps*, 82-94; Bruce Vandervort, *Wars of Imperial Conquest in Africa, 1830-1914* (Bloomington and Indianapolis: Indiana University Press, 1998), 202. See also Horst Drechsler, *Let Us Die Fighting: The Struggle of the Herero and Nama against German Imperialism (1884-1915)* (London: Zed Press, 1980).

22 Jackson, *The Prisoners*, 134-50; Ronald Stent, *A Bespattered Page? The Internment of His Majesty's "Most Loyal Enemy Aliens"* (London: Andre Deutsch, 1980), 16-18. See also David Cesarani and Tony Kushner, eds., *The Internment of Aliens in Twentieth Century Britain* (London: F. Cass, 1993); Gerhard Fischer, *Enemy Aliens: Internment and the Homefront Experience in Australia, 1914-1920* (St. Lucia, Australia: University of Queensland Press, 1989); Gerhard Fischer, "Integration, 'Negative Integration,' Disintegration: The Destruction of the German-Australian Community during the First World War," in *Alien Justice: Wartime Internment in Australia and North America*, ed. Kay Saunders and Roger Daniels (St. Lucia, Australia: University of Queensland Press, 2000), 1-27.

23 David Edward Smith, "Emergency Government in Canada," *Canadian Historical Review* 50, 4 (December 1969): 430-31.

24 Jeffrey A. Keshen, *Propaganda and Censorship behind Canada's Great War* (Edmonton: University of Alberta Press, 1996), 9-11; Lubomyr Luciuk, *In Fear of the Barbed Wire Fence: Canada's First National Internment Operations and the Ukrainian Canadians, 1914-1920* (Kingston, ON: Kashtan Press, 2001), 3-4; Desmond Morton, "Sir William Otter and Internment Operations in Canada during the First World War," *Canadian Historical Review* 55, 1 (March 1974): 35-38.

25 Luciuk, *In Fear of the Barbed Wire Fence,* 6; John Herd Thompson, *Les minorités ethniques pendant les guerres mondiales* (Ottawa: Société historique du Canada, 1991), 7.
26 Morton, "Sir William Otter," 38-39. See also Desmond Morton, *The Canadian General: Sir William Otter* (Toronto: Hakkert, 1974).
27 William Otter, *Report on Internment Operations: Canada, 1914-1920* (Ottawa: Thomas Mulvey, 1921), 4-6, reproduced in Luciuk, *In Fear of the Barbed Wire Fence,* 123-43.
28 Otter, *Report on Internment Operations,* 6. See also David J. Carter, *Behind Canadian Barbed Wire: Alien, Refugee and Prisoners of War Camps in Canada, 1914-1946* (Calgary: Tumbleweed Press, 1980), 19-23. Carter's book was republished recently under the title *P.O.W. behind Canadian Barbed Wire: Alien, Refugee and Prisoner of War Camps in Canada, 1914-1946* (Elkwater, AB: Eagle Butte Press, 1998).
29 Luciuk, *In Fear of the Barbed Wire Fence,* 12.
30 Carter, *Behind Canadian Barbed Wire,* 20-21; Morton, "Sir William Otter," 35-37.
31 Otter, *Report on Internment Operations,* 6. See also Morton, "Sir William Otter," 46-47.
32 Jackson, *The Prisoners,* 134-41.
33 Carter, *Behind Canadian Barbed Wire,* 28-29.
34 Hutchinson, *Champions of Charity,* 279-85; Jackson, *The Prisoners,* 62-66.; Vance, ed., *Encyclopedia,* 143-45. See also Caroline Moorehead, *Dunant's Dream: War, Switzerland and the History of the Red Cross* (London: Harper Collins, 1998).
35 Carter, *Behind Canadian Barbed Wire,* 29.
36 Bill Waiser, *Park Prisoners: The Untold Story of Western Canada's National Parks, 1915-1946* (Saskatoon: Fifth House Publishers, 1995), 10.
37 Carter, *Behind Canadian Barbed Wire,* 25-26; Waiser, *Park Prisoners,* 10-47.
38 Morton, "Sir William Otter," 48.
39 Carter, *Behind Canadian Barbed Wire,* 29-30.
40 Ibid., 26-27; Luciuk, *In Fear of the Barbed Wire Fence,* 24.
41 Otter, *Report on Internment Operations,* 17.
42 Waiser, *Park Prisoners,* 46.
43 Morton, "Sir William Otter," 56-57.
44 Otter, *Report on Internment Operations,* 17. See also Morton, "Sir William Otter," 57-58.
45 Otter, *Report on Internment Operations,* 15-17.
46 For more information on Canada's First World War internment operation, see Joseph A. Boudreau, "Western Canada's 'Enemy Aliens' in World War One," *Alberta Historical Review* 12 (Winter 1964): 1-9; Georgia Green Fooks, *Prairie Prisoners: POWs in Lethbridge during Two World Conflicts* (Lethbridge, AB: Lethbridge Historical Society, 2003); Bohdan S. Kordan, *Enemy Aliens, Prisoners of War: Internment in Canada during the Great War* (Montreal and Kingston: McGill-Queen's University Press, 2002); Bohdan S. Kordan and Peter Melnycky, *In the Shadow of the Rockies, Diary of the Castle Mountain Internment Camp, 1915-1917* (Edmonton: Canadian Institute of Ukrainian Studies Press, 1991); Jean Laflamme, *Les camps de détention au Québec durant la première guerre mondiale* (Montreal: n.p., 1973); Brenda Lee-Whiting, "'Enemy Aliens': German-Canadians on the Home Front," *The Beaver* 69, 5 (1989): 53-58; Lubomyr Luciuk, *Internment Operations: The Role of the Old Fort Henry in World War I* (Kingston, ON: Delta, 1980); Lubomyr Luciuk, ed., *Righting an Injustice: The Debate over Redress for Canada's First National Internment Operations* (Toronto: Justinian Press, 1994); and *Roll Call: Remembering the Internees* (Kingston, ON: Kashtan Press, 1999).
47 Barker, *Behind Barbed Wire,* 16; Kotek and Rigoulot, *Le siècle des camps,* 96-129; Vance, ed., *Encyclopedia,* 49-51. See also Jean Claude Farcy, *Les camps de concentration français de la Première guerre mondiale, 1914-1920* (Paris: Anthropos, 1995); Michael Moynihan, *Black Bread and Barbed Wire: Prisoners in the First World War* (London: Leo Cooper, 1978); Jörg Nagler,

"Internment of German Enemy Aliens in the United States during the First and Second World War," in *Alien Justice*, ed. Saunders and Daniels, 66-79; Panikos Panyani, *Minorities in Wartime: National and Racial Groupings in Europe, North America, and Australia during the Two World Wars* (Oxford: Berg, 1993); Alon Rachamimov, *POWs and the Great War: Captivity on the Eastern Front* (Oxford: Berg, 2002); Richard B. Speed, *Prisoners, Diplomats and the Great War: A Study in the Diplomacy of Captivity* (New York: Greenwood Press, 1990); Samuel R. Williamson and Peter Pastor, eds., *Essays on World War I: Origins and Prisoners of War* (New York: Columbia University Press, 1983).

48 Jonathan F. Vance, *Objects of Concern: Canadian Prisoners of War through the Twentieth Century* (Vancouver: UBC Press, 1994), 254. See also Desmond Morton, *Silent Battle: Canadian Prisoners of War in Germany, 1914-1919* (Toronto: Lester Publisher, 1992).

49 Vance, *Objects of Concern*, 88.

50 Barker, *Behind Barbed Wire*, 16-17; Flory, *Prisoners of War*, 23; Vance, ed., *Encyclopedia*, 107-8.

51 Jackson, *The Prisoners*, 7.

52 Kotek and Rigoulot, *Le siècle des camps*, 110-29; Guy Richard, *L'Histoire inhumaine: massacres et genocides des origins à nos jours* (Paris: Armand Colin, 1992), 107-9. See also D. Boyanian, *Armenia: The Case for a Forgotten Genocide* (Westwood, NJ: Educational Book Crafters, 1972); Israel W. Charny, ed., *Encyclopedia of Genocide* (Santa Barbara: ABC-CLIO, 2000); G.S. Graber, *Caravans to Oblivion: The Armenian Genocide* (New York: John Wiley and Sons, 1996).

53 Hartigan, *The Forgotten Victim*, 117-20.

54 Kotek and Rigoulot, *Le siècle des camps*, 238-60.

55 Ibid.,132-235; Jean-Jacques Marie, *Le goulag* (Paris: Presses Universitaires de France, 1999), 20-36; Richard, *L'Histoire inhumaine*, 121-22; Vance, ed., *Encyclopedia*, 123, 258-59. See also Anne Applebaum, *Gulag: A History* (New York: Doubleday, 2003); David J. Dallin and Boris I. Nicolaevsky, *Forced Labor in Soviet Russia* (New Haven, CT: Yale University Press, 1955) and Michael Jakobson, *Origins of the Gulag: The Soviet Prison Camp System, 1917-1934* (Lexington: University Press of Kentucky, 1993); Aleksandr Isaevich Solzhenitsyn, *The Gulag Archipelago, 1918-1956* (New York: Harper and Row, 1985).

56 Dallin and Nicolaevsky, *Forced Labor*, 206-16, 299-305; Marie, *Le goulag*, 23-26.

57 Kotek and Rigoulot, *Le siècle des camps*, 170-76; Richard, *L'Histoire inhumaine*, 114-15.

58 Richard, *L'Histoire inhumaine*, 116. See also Applebaum, *Gulag*.

59 Konnilyn G. Feig, *Hitler's Death Camps: The Sanity of Madness* (New York: Holmes and Meier Publishers, 1981), 23-24; Kotek and Rigoulot, *Le siècle des camps*, 296-338; William L. Shirer, *The Rise and Fall of the Third Reich: A History of Nazi Germany* [1950] (New York: Fawcett Crest, 1992), 374-76; Vance, ed., *Encyclopedia*, 64. See also Eugen Kogon, *The Theory and Practice of Hell: The German Concentration Camps and the System behind Them* (New York: Farrar, Straus and Cudahy, 1950).

60 Feig, *Hitler's Death Camps*, 25-26; Kotek and Rigoulot, *Le siècle des camps*, 339-467.

61 Feig, *Hitler's Death Camps*, 32-33; Richard, *L'Histoire inhumaine*,143-44. See also Shirer, *Rise and Fall*, 1234-40.

62 Feig, *Hitler's Death Camps*, 27-28. See also Kotek and Rigoulot, *Le siècle des camps*, 430-58; Richard, *L'Histoire inhumaine*,144-46; Shirer, *Rise and Fall*, 1259-69; Vance, ed., *Encyclopedia*, 90-91.

63 Feig, *Hitler's Death Camps*, 32; Shirer, *Rise and Fall*, 1264.

64 Feig, *Hitler's Death Camps*, 26; Vance, ed., *Encyclopedia*, 15-16. See also Yisrael Gutman and Michael Berenbaum, eds., *Anatomy of the Auschwitz Death Camp* (Bloomington: Indiana University Press, 1994).

65 Feig, *Hitler's Death Camps*, 38; Masson and Melchior-Bonnet, *Dictionnaire de la Seconde guerre mondiale*, vol. 1, 531; Shirer, *Rise and Fall*, 1274-88; Vance, ed., *Encyclopedia*, 306-7. See also Gotz Aly, Peter Chroust, and Christian Pross, *Cleansing the Fatherland: Nazi Medicine*

and Racial Hygiene (Baltimore, MD: Johns Hopkins University Press, 1994); Philippe Aziz, *Doctors of Death* (Geneva: Ferni Publishers, 1976); Benno Muller-Hill, *Murderous Science: Elimination by Scientific Selection of Jews, Gypsies, and Others: Germany 1933-1945* (Oxford: Oxford University Press, 1988); Arthur L. Caplan, *When Medicine Went Mad: Bioethics and the Holocaust* (Totowa, NJ: Humana Press, 1992); Robert J. Lifton, *The Nazi Doctors: Medical Killing and the Psychology of Genocide* (New York: Basic Books, 1986); Robert Proctor, *Racial Hygiene: Medicine under the Nazis* (Cambridge: Harvard University Press, 1988); Lore Shelley, ed., *Criminal Experiments on Human Beings in Auschwitz and War Research Laboratories: Twenty Prisoners' Accounts* (San Francisco: Mellen Research University Press, 1991).

66 Feig, *Hitler's Death Camps,* 26. For more information on the Holocaust consult Gotz Aly, *The Final Solution: Nazi Population Policy and the Murder of the European Jews* (London: Oxford University Press, 2000); Doris Bergen, *War and Genocide: A Concise History of the Holocaust* (Lanham, MD: Rowman and Littlefield, 2002); Lucy Dawidowicz, *The War against the Jews, 1933-1945* (New York: Rinehart, 1975); Deborah Dwork and Robert Jan van Pelt, *Holocaust: A History* (New York: W.W. Norton, 2002); Jack R. Fischel, *Historical Dictionary of the Holocaust* (Lanham, MD: Scarecrow Press, 1999); Henry Friedlander, *The Origins of Nazi Genocide: From Euthanasia to the Final Solution* (Chapel Hill: University of North Carolina Press, 1995); Martin Gilbert, *The Holocaust: A History of the Jews of Europe during the Second World War* (New York: Henry Holt and Company, 1986); Donald M. McKale, *Hitler's Shadow War: The Holocaust and World War II* (New York: Cooper Square Press, 2002); Gerhard Schoenberner, *The Yellow Star: The Persecution of the Jews in Europe, 1933-1945* (New York: Fordham University Press, 2005); and Leni Yahil, *The Holocaust: The Fate of European Jewry, 1932-1945* (New York: Oxford University Press, 1990).

67 Vance, ed., *Encyclopedia,* 51-57, 329-42.

68 Vance, *Objects of Concern,* 4-5; Vance, ed., *Encyclopedia,* 201-3. See also Carl Geiser, *Prisoners of the Good Fight: The Spanish Civil War, 1936-1939* (Westport, CT: Lawrence Hill and Company, 1986); Stephen P. Halbrook, *Target Switzerland: Swiss Armed Neutrality in World War II* (Rockville Centre, MD: Sarpedon, 1998); Alfred A. Häsler, *The Lifeboat Is Full: Switzerland and the Refugees, 1933-1945* (New York: Funk and Wagnalls, 1969); Ralph Keefer, *Grounded in Eire: The Story of Two RAF Fliers Interned in Ireland during World War II* (Montreal: McGill-Queen's University Press, 2001); Andre Lasserre, *Frontières et camps: Le refuge en Suisse de 1933 à 1945* (Lausanne: Payot, 1995); Charles D'Ydewalle, *An Interlude in Spain* (London: Readers Union and Macmillan, 1946).

69 Bob Moore and Kent Fedorowich, "Prisoners of War in the Second World War: An Overview," in *Prisoners of War and Their Captors in World War II,* ed. Bob Moore and Kent Fedorowich (Oxford: Berg, 1996), 1.

70 Vance, *Objects of Concern,* 99, 255-56. See also Daniel G. Dancocks, *In Enemy Hands: Canadian Prisoners of War, 1939-45* (Edmonton: Hurtig Publishers, 1983); Roy MacLaren, *Canadians behind Enemy Lines, 1939-1945* (Vancouver: University of British Columbia Press, 1981).

71 C.P. Stacey, *Arms, Men and Governments: The War Policies of Canada, 1939-1945* (Ottawa: Department of National Defence, 1970), 590; C.P. Stacey, *Canada and the Age of Conflict, Volume 2* (Toronto: University of Toronto Press, 1981), 370-73.

72 Jonathan Vance, "The Trouble with Allies: Canada and the Negotiation of Prisoner of War Exchanges," in *Prisoners of War and Their Captors,* ed. Moore and Fedorowich, 81. See also Noel Barber, *Prisoner of War: The Story of British Prisoners Held by the Enemy* (London: George G. Harrap, 1944); Hugh V. Clarke, *Barbed Wire and Bamboo: Australian POWs in Europe, North Africa, Singapore, Thailand and Japan* (St. Leonard, Australia: Allen and Unwin, 1992); D.A. Foy, *For You the War Is Over: American Prisoners of War in Nazi Germany* (New York: Stein and Day, 1984); Maxwell Leigh, *Captives Courageous: South African Prisoners of*

War in World War II (Johannesburg: Ashanti Publishing, 1992); David Rolf, "'Blind Bureaucracy': The British Government and POWs in German Captivity, 1939-45," in *Prisoners of War and Their Captors,* ed. Moore and Fedorowich, 47-67.

73 Richard, *L'Histoire inhumaine,* 124-25; Vance, ed., *Encyclopedia,* 157-58. See also Allen Paul, *Katyn: Stalin's Massacre and the Seeds of Polish Resurrection* (Annapolis, MD: Naval Institute Press, 1991); J.K. Zawodny, *Death in the Forest: The Story of the Katyn Forest Massacre* (Notre Dame IN: University of Notre Dame Press, 1962).

74 Joan Beaumont, "Protecting Prisoners of War, 1939-95," in *Prisoners of War and Their Captors,* ed. Moore and Fedorowich, 279; John Keegan, *A History of Warfare* (New York: Vintage Books, 1994), 373; Shirer, *Rise and Fall,* 1240-41; Gerhard L. Weinberg, *A World at Arms: A Global History of World War II* (Cambridge: Cambridge University Press, 1994), 894; Vance, ed., *Encyclopedia,* 329. See also Omer Bartov, *The Eastern Front, 1941-45: German Troops and the Barbarization of Warfare* (New York: St. Martin's Press, 1986); Hannes Heer et al., *The German Army and Genocide: Crimes against War Prisoners, Jews and Other Civilians in the East, 1939-1944* (New York: New Press, 1999); S.P. Mackenzie, "The Treatment of Prisoners of War in World War II," *Journal of Modern History,* 66 (1994): 487-520.

75 Dancocks, *In Enemy Hands,* xii-xiii; Ikuhiko Hata, "From Consideration to Contempt: The Changing Nature of Japanese Military and Popular Perceptions of Prisoners of War through the Ages," in *Prisoners of War and Their Captors,* ed. Moore and Fedorowich, 253-76; John Keegan and Richard Holmes, *Soldiers: A History of Men in Battle* [1985] (Toronto: Prospero Books, 1999), 50-51. See also William A. Berry, *Prisoner of the Rising Sun* (Norman: University of Oklahoma Press, 1993); Van Waterford, *Prisoners of the Japanese in World War II* (Jefferson, NC: McFarland, 1994).

76 Vance, *Objects of Concern,* 255. See also Dave McIntosh, *Hell on Earth: Aging Faster, Dying Sooner, Canadian Prisoners of the Japanese during World War II* (Toronto: McGraw-Hill Ryerson, 1996); Charles G. Roland, *Long Night's Journey into Day: Prisoners of War in Hong Kong and Japan, 1941-1945* (Waterloo: Wilfrid Laurier University Press, 2001); Carl Vincent, *No Reason Why: The Canadian Hong Kong Tragedy: An Examination* (Stittsville, ON: Canada's Wings, 1981).

77 Richard, *L'Histoire inhumaine,* 263-66.

78 Ibid., 265; Vance, ed., *Encyclopedia,* 23-24; Weinberg, *A World at Arms,* 315. See also Stanley L. Falk, *Bataan: The March of Death* (New York: Norton, 1962); Adrian R. Martin, *Brothers from Bataan: POWs, 1942-1945* (Manhattan, KS: Sunflower University Press, 1992); Donald Knox, ed., *Death March: The Survivors of Bataan* (New York: Harcourt Brace Jovanovich, 1981).

79 Barker, *Behind Barbed Wire,* 106-12; Sibylla Jane Flower, "Captors and Captives on the Burma-Thailand Railway," in *Prisoners of War and Their Captors,* ed. Moore and Fedorowich, 227-52; Richard, *L'Histoire inhumaine,* 266-67; Vance, ed., *Encyclopedia,* 36-37. See also E.R. Hall, *The Burma-Thailand Railway of Death* (Armadale, Australia: Graphic Books, 1981); Clifford Kinvig, *Death Railway* (New York: Ballantine Books, 1973); Clifford Kinvig, *River Kwai Railway: The Story of the Burma-Siam Railroad* (Herndon, VA: Brassey's, 1998); Gavan McCormack and Hank Nelson, eds., *The Burma-Thailand Railway: Memory and History* (Chiang Mai, Thailand: Silkworm Books, 1993).

80 Richard, *L'Histoire inhumaine,* 267-68; Charles G. Roland, "Human Vivisection: The Intoxication of Limitless Power in Wartime," in *Prisoners of War and Their Captors,* ed. Moore and Fedorowich, 149-79; Weinberg, *A World at Arms,* 560. See also Hal Gold, *Unit 731: Testimony* (Tokyo: Yenbooks, 1996); Sheldon Harris, *Factories of Death: Japanese Biological Warfare, 1932-45 and the American Cover-up* (London: Routledge, 1994); Peter Williams and David Wallace, *Unit 731: The Japanese Army's Secret of Secrets* (London: Hodder and Stoughton, 1989).

81 Beaumont, "Protecting Prisoners of War," 280. See also Gavan Daws, *Prisoners of the Japanese: POW's in World War II in the Pacific* (New York: W. Morrow, 1994).

82 Richard, *L'Histoire inhumaine,* 261-73.

83 Kotek and Rigoulot, *Le siècle des camps,* 486; Richard, *L'Histoire inhumaine,* 261-73. For more information on Japanese atrocities against civilian populations, consult Iris Chang, *The Rape of Nanking: The Forgotten Holocaust of World War II* (New York: Basic Books, 1997); Laurence Rees, *Horror in the East: Japan and the Atrocities of World War II* (New York: Da Capo Press, 2002); Edward F.L. Russell, *Knights of Bushido: A Short History of Japanese War Crimes* (Mechanicsburg, PA: Stackpole Books, 2002); Yuki Tanaka, *Hidden Horrors: Japanese War Crimes in World War II* (Boulder, CO: Westview Press, 1998).

84 Keegan and Holmes, *Soldiers,* 50; Richard, *L'Histoire inhumaine* 263.

85 Vance, ed., *Encyclopedia,* 37.

86 Ibid., 305-6. See also Daniel Barenblatt, *A Plague upon Humanity: The Secret Genocide of Axis Japan's Germ Warfare Operation* (New York: HarperCollins, 2004).

87 Ibid., 268-69. See also George L. Hicks, *The Comfort Women: Japan's Brutal Regime of Enforced Prostitution in the Second World War* (New York: Norton, 1995); Margaret D. Stetz and Bonnie Oh, eds., *Legacies of the Comfort Women of World War II* (Amonk, NY: M.E. Sharpe, 2001); Yuki Tanaka, *Japan's Comfort Women: The Military and Involuntary Prostitution during War and Occupation* (London: Routledge, 2001); Yoshimi Yoshiaki, *Comfort Women: Sexual Slavery in the Japanese Military during World War II* (New York: Columbia University Press, 1995).

88 Beaumont, "Protecting Prisoners of War," 278-79. See also David Rolf, *Prisoners of the Reich: Germany's Captives, 1939-1945* (London: Leo Cooper, 1988).

89 Roger Daniels, "Incarcerating Japanese Americans: An Atrocity Revisited," in *Alien Justice,* ed. Saunders and Daniels, 168-84; Geoffrey S. Smith, "The Japanese Canadians and World War II," in *Alien Justice,* ed. Saunders and Daniels, 93-113; Sandra C. Taylor, "From Incarceration to Freedom: Japanese Americans and the Departure from the Concentration Camps," in *Alien Justice,* ed. Saunders and Daniels, 205-20. See also Allan R. Bosworth, *America's Concentration Camps* (New York: Norton, 1967); Roger Daniels, *Concentration Camps: North American Japanese in the United States and Canada* (Malabar, FL: Krieger, 1989); Page Smith, *Democracy on Trial: The Japanese American Evacuation and Relocation in World War II* (New York: Simon and Schuster, 1995).

90 Barker, *Behind Barbed Wire,* 204-21; Beaumont, "Protecting Prisoners of War," 280-85; Vance, ed., *Encyclopedia,* 108-9.

91 Hartigan, *The Forgotten Victim,* 5-6.

92 This book is based on Martin F. Auger, "Prisoners of the Home Front: A Social Study of the German Internment Camps of Southern Quebec, 1940-1946" (MA thesis, University of Ottawa, 2000).

Chapter 2: Organizing and Developing Southern Quebec's Internment Operation

1 Library and Archives of Canada [LAC], RG-2, Vol. 1592, File 1429G, Order-in-Council PC 2097, 20 August 1936. See also John Joseph Kelly, "The Prisoner of War Camps in Canada, 1939-1947" (MA thesis, University of Windsor, 1976), 1-4; Daniel Robinson, "Planning for the 'Most Serious Contingency': Alien Internment, Arbitrary Detention, and the Canadian State, 1938-39," *Journal of Canadian Studies* 28, 2 (1993): 6.

2 LAC, RG-2, Vol. 2003, Order-in-Council PC 531, 14 March 1938. See also Kelly, "Prisoner of War Camps," 5-7; Robinson, "Planning for the 'Most Serious Contingency,'" 7-16; John Stanton, "Government Internment Policy, 1939-1945," *Labour/Le Travail* 31 (Spring 1993): 222.

3 LAC, RG-2, Vol. 1653, File 1948G, Order-in-Council PC 2483, 3 September 1939. See also Stanton, "Government Internment Policy," 210.

4 Cornelia Bartl, "The Loss of the German-Canadian Image," in *German-Canadian Yearbook,* vol. 13, ed. Georg K. Weissenborn (Toronto: University of Toronto Press, 1994), 313.

5 Canada, *Debates of the House of Commons*, vol. 1 (1940), 23 May 1940, 144. See also Reg Whitaker and Gregory S. Kealey, "A War on Ethnicity? The RCMP and Internment," in *Enemies Within: Italians and Other Internees in Canada and Abroad,* ed. Franca Iacovetta, Roberto Perin, and Angelo Principe (Toronto: University of Toronto Press, 2000), 129; K.M. McLaughlin, *The Germans in Canada* (Ottawa: Canadian Historical Association, 1985), 16; Stanton, "Government Internment Policy," 219-21.

6 Canada, *Defence of Canada Regulations* (Ottawa: Edmond Cloutier, 1941), 30.

7 Canada, *Debates of the House of Commons*, vol. 1 (1940), 11 June 1940, 663. See also Robert H. Keyserlingk, "'Agents within the Gates': The Search for Nazi Subversives in Canada during World War II," *Canadian Historical Review* 66, 2 (June 1985): 214-15; Robert H. Keyserlingk, "Breaking the Nazi Plot: Canadian Government Attitudes toward German Canadians, 1939-1945," in *On Guard for Thee: War, Ethnicity, and the Canadian State, 1939-1945,* ed. Norman Hilmer, Bohdan Kordan, and Lubomyr Luciuk (Ottawa: Minister of Supply and Services Canada, 1988), 53-70; Robert H. Keyserlingk, "The Canadian Government's Attitude toward Germans and German Canadians in World War II," *Canadian Ethnic Studies* 16, 1 (1984): 18-19; Whitaker and Kealey, "A War on Ethnicity?" 137.

8 Kelly, "Prisoner of War Camps," 47-50; John Melady, *Escape from Canada! The Untold Story of German POWs in Canada, 1939-1945* (Toronto: Macmillan of Canada, 1981), 28. See also Roy R. Maddocks, "A.G.L. McNaughton, R.B. Bennett and the Unemployment Relief Camps, 1932-1935" (MA thesis, Carleton University, 1974).

9 François Lafitte, *The Internment of Aliens* (New York: Penguin Books, 1940), 36-37.

10 Irving Abella and Harold Troper, *None Is Too Many: Canada and the Jews of Europe, 1933-1948* (Toronto: Lester and Orpen Dennys, 1982), 3-5; Paula J. Draper, "The 'Camp Boys': Interned Refugees from Nazism," in *Enemies Within,* ed. Iacovetta, Perin, and Principe, 171. See also Walter W. Igersheimer and Ian Darragh, *Blatant Injustice: The Story of a Jewish Refugee from Nazi Germany Imprisoned in Britain and Canada during World War II* (Montreal and Kingston: McGill-Queen's University Press, 2005).

11 LAC, MG-30, C 192, Vol. 3, "Interview of Emil Fackenheim," [1980s], 25.

12 Eric Koch, *Deemed Suspect: A Wartime Blunder* (Toronto: Methuen Publications, 1980), 9; Lafitte, *Internment of Aliens,* 37, 63; Ronald Stent, *A Bespattered Page? The Internment of His Majesty's "Most Loyal Enemy Aliens"* (London: Andre Deutsch, 1980), 35.

13 Miriam Kochan, *Britain's Internees in the Second World War* (London: Macmillan, 1983), 10-18; Lafitte, *Internment of Aliens,* 62-65; Stent, *A Bespattered Page?* 35-37.

14 Kochan, *Britain's Internees,* 59; Stent, *A Bespattered Page?* 69-72. For more information on the British internment operation during the Second World War, see also Miriam Kochan, *Prisoners of England* (London: Macmillan, 1980); Peter and Lilly Gillman, *'Collar the Lot!': How Britain Interned and Expelled its Wartime Refugees* (London: Quartet Books, 1980); A.W. Brian Simpson, *In the Highest Degree Odious: Detention without Trial in Wartime Britain* (Oxford: Clarendon Press, 1992).

15 LAC, MG-30, C 192, Vol. 3, "Interview of Dr. Ernst Waengler," [1980s], 13-14.

16 Koch, *Deemed Suspect,* 33; Chris M.V. Madsen and R.J. Henderson, *German Prisoners of War in Canada and Their Artifacts* (Regina: Hignell Printing, 1993), 6; Bob Moore, "Axis Prisoners in Britain during the Second World War: A Comparative Survey," in *Prisoners of War and Their Captors in World War II,* ed. Bob Moore and Kent Fedorowich, (Oxford: Berg, 1996), 22; Stent, *A Bespattered Page?* 97.

17 Kochan, *Britain's Internees,* 19-20, 59; Stent, *A Bespattered Page?* 48-52, 69-72.

18 Koch, *Deemed Suspect,* 27.

19 Ibid., 28.

20 LAC, RG-2, 7c, Reel: C-11,789, File 1, Minutes of the Cabinet War Committee, 5 June 1940.

21 LAC, RG-2, 7c, Reel: C-11,789, File 1, Minutes of the Cabinet War Committee, 10 June 1940.

22 Paula Jean Draper, "The Accidental Immigrants: Canada and the Interned Refugees," Part 1, *Canadian Jewish Historical Society Journal* 2, 1 (1978): 15; Koch, *Deemed Suspect,* 34; Kochan, *Britain's Internees,* 58-59. See also Paula J. Draper, "The Accidental Immigrants: Canada and the Interned Refugees" (PhD diss., University of Toronto, 1983).
23 Koch, *Deemed Suspect,* 40-64; Lafitte, *Internment of Aliens,* 123-43; Moore, "Axis Prisoners in Britain," in *Prisoners of War and Their Captors,* ed. Moore and Fedorowich, 25-26; Stent, *A Bespattered Page?* 96-113.
24 Koch, *Deemed Suspect,* 65-68; Stent, *Internment of Aliens,* 96-97. See also Paul R. Bartrop and Gabrielle Eisen, eds., *The Dunera Affaire: A Documentary Resource Book* (Melbourne, Australia: Schwartz and Wilkinson, 1990); R.J.B. Bosworth, "The Internment of Italians in Australia," in *Enemies Within,* ed. Iacovetta, Perin, and Principe, 227-55; Kay Saunders, "A Difficult Reconciliation: Civil Liberties and Internment Policy in Australia during World War II," in *Alien Justice,* ed. Saunders and Daniels, 114-37; Kay Saunders, "'Taken Away to Be Shot?': The Process of Incarceration in Australia in World War II," in *Alien Justice,* ed. Saunders and Daniels, 152-67.
25 Kelly, "Prisoner of War Camps," 54.
26 Lafitte, *Internment of Aliens,* 13.
27 Ibid., 143.
28 Ibid., 135.
29 Yves Bernard and Caroline Bergeron, *Trop loin de Berlin: Des prisonniers allemands au Canada (1939-1946)* (Sillery, QC: Éditions du Septentrion, 1995), 28-40.
30 Kelly, "Prisoner of War Camps," 57.
31 LAC, RG-2, 7c, Reel: C-11,789, File 1, Minutes of the Cabinet War Committee, 14 June 1940.
32 Kelly, "Prisoner of War Camps," 50-51.
33 Ibid., 51-57; Koch, *Deemed Suspect,* 77-117; Eckehart J. Priebe, *Thank You, Canada: From Messerschmitt Pilot to Canadian Citizen* (West Vancouver: Condor Publishing, 1990), 176-77. See also Ted Jones, *Both Sides of the Wire: The Fredericton Internment Camp* (Fredericton, NB: New Ireland Press, 1989); Cecil Porter, *The Gilded Cage: Gravenhurst German Prisoner of War Camp 20, 1940-1946* (Huntsville, ON: Fox Meadow Creations, 1999); William Repka and Kathleen Repka, *Dangerous Patriots: Canada's Unknown Prisoners of War* (Vancouver: New Star Books, 1982).
34 David J. Carter, *Behind Canadian Barbed Wire: Alien Refugee and Prisoner of War Camps in Canada, 1914-1946* (Calgary: Tumbleweed Press, 1980), 117; Paula Jean Draper, "The Accidental Immigrants," Part 2, *Canadian Jewish Historical Society Journal* 2, 2 (1978): 91; Kelly, "Prisoner of War Camps," 58-59; Melady, *Escape from Canada!* 32; C.P. Stacey, *Six Years of War: The Army in Canada, Britain, and the Pacific* (Ottawa: Queen's Printer, 1966), 151.
35 LAC, MG-30, C 192, Vol. 3, "Interview of Colonel Eric Kippen," [1980s], 9-11.
36 LAC, RG-24, Vol. 15,399, vol. 1 (July 1940), War Diary of Internment Camp Île-aux-Noix, 1 July 1940, 1.
37 LAC, RG-24, Vol. 15,399, vol. 1 (July 1940), War Diary of Internment Camp Île-aux-Noix, 5 July 1940, 1.
38 LAC, MG-30, C 192, Vol. 3, "Interview of Colonel Eric Kippen," [1980s], 11-12.
39 LAC, RG-24, Vol. 15,399, vol. 1 (July 1940), War Diary of Internment Camp Île-aux-Noix, 15 July 1940, 3.
40 LAC, RG-24, Vol. 15,399, vol. 2 (August 1940), War Diary of Internment Camp Île-aux-Noix, 1 August 1940, 1.
41 LAC, RG-24, Vol. 15,399, vol. 1 (July 1940), War Diary of Internment Camp Île-aux-Noix, 15 July 1940, 3.
42 LAC, RG-24, Vol. 15,399, vol. 1 (July 1940), War Diary of Internment Camp Île-aux-Noix, 15 July 1940-16 July 1940, 3-4.

43 LAC, RG-24, Reel: C-5377, File HQS 7236-18, Vol. 1-2, "List of POW Missing Articles – Internment Camp I," 16 June 1941.
44 LAC, RG-24, Vol. 15,399, vol. 2 (August 1940), War Diary of Internment Camp Île-aux-Noix, 31 August 1940, 8.
45 LAC, RG-24, Vol. 15,399, vol. 3 (September 1940), War Diary of Internment Camp Île-aux-Noix, 25 September 1940, 8.
46 LAC, RG-24, Reel: C-5377, File HQS 7236-18, Vol. 1-2, "Findings of the Court of Inquiry," 19 February 1941.
47 LAC, RG-24, Reel: C-5377, File HQS 7236-18, Vol. 1-2, "Detective Léon Pronovost to the Director of the Quebec Provincial Police," 11 July 1941.
48 LAC, RG-24, Reel: C-5377, File HQS 7236-18, Vol. 1-2, "Voluntary Statement of Hermas Labonté of St. Jean," 10 June 1941.
49 LAC, RG-24, Reel: C-5377, File HQS 7236-18, Vol. 1-2, "Voluntary Statement of René Trochei of St. Jean," 10 June 1941.
50 Kelly, "Prisoner of War Camps," 55-57.
51 LAC, RG-24, Reel: C-5378, File HQS 7236-20, "Brigadier-General Edouard de Bellefeuille Panet (Director of Internment Operations) to the Adjutant-General," 5 September 1940.
52 LAC, RG-24, Reel: C-5378, File HQS 7236-20, "Brigadier-General Edouard de Bellefeuille Panet (Director of Internment Operations) to the Secretary of State," 8 August 1940.
53 LAC, RG-24, Vol. 15,397, vol. 1 (October 1940), War Diary of Internment Camp Farnham, 9 October 1940, 1.
54 LAC, MG-30, C 192, Vol. 3, "Interview of Colonel Eric Kippen," [1980s], 16-17.
55 LAC, RG-24, Vol. 15,397, vol. 1 (October 1940), War Diary of Internment Camp Farnham, 10 October 1940, 11 October 1940, and 15 October 1940, 1-4.
56 LAC, RG-24, Vol. 15,397, vol. 1 (October 1940), War Diary of Internment Camp Farnham, 15 October 1940, 4.
57 LAC, RG-24, Vol. 15,397, vol. 1 (October 1940), War Diary of Internment Camp Farnham, 16 October 1940, 5.
58 LAC, RG-24, Vol. 15,397, vol. 1 (October 1940), War Diary of Internment Camp Farnham, 18 October 1940, 6.
59 LAC, RG-24, Vol. 11,253, File 11-2-40, "Report on Inspection of Camp 'A'," 22 October 1940.
60 LAC, RG-24, Vol. 15,397, vol. 1 (October 1940), War Diary of Internment Camp Farnham, 21 October 1940, 9.
61 LAC, RG-24, Vol. 15,397, vol. 1 (October 1940), War Diary of Internment Camp Farnham, 18 October 1940, 6.
62 LAC, RG-24, Vol. 15,397, vol. 1 (October 1940), War Diary of Internment Camp Farnham, 20 October 1940, 8.
63 LAC, RG-24, Vol. 11,253, File 11-2-40, "Report on Inspection of Camp 'A,'" 22 October 1940.
64 LAC, RG-24, Vol. 15,399, vol. 1 (October 1940), War Diary of Internment Camp Sherbrooke, 5 October 1940, 1.
65 Ibid., 1.
66 Ibid., 2.
67 Ibid., 3.
68 Koch, *Deemed Suspect,* 126.
69 LAC, MG-30, C 192, Vol. 3, "Interview of Emil Fackenheim," [1980s], 40-41.
70 LAC, MG-30, C 192, Vol. 3, "Interview of Fred Wolff," [1980s], 31-32.
71 LAC, MG-30, C 192, Vol. 3, "Interview of Emil Fackenheim," 40-41; LAC, RG-24, Vol. 15,399, vol. 1 (October 1940), War Diary of Internment Camp Sherbrooke, 15 October 1940, 3.
72 LAC, RG-24, Vol. 15, 399, vol. 5 (February 1941), War Diary of Internment Camp Sherbrooke, "Internee Statement," 21 February 1941, Appendix 2, 2.

73 LAC, MG-30, C 192, Vol. 3, "Interview of Emil Fackenheim," [1980s], 40-41.
74 LAC, RG-24, Vol. 15,399, vol. 1 (October 1940), War Diary of Internment Camp Sherbrooke, 15 October 1940, 3.
75 LAC, RG-24, Vol. 15,399, vol. 1 (October 1940), War Diary of Internment Camp Sherbrooke, 16 October 1940, 3.
76 Koch, *Deemed Suspect,* 128.
77 Ibid., 129-30.
78 LAC, RG-24, Vol. 15,399, vol. 1 (October 1940), War Diary of Internment Camp Sherbrooke, 18 October 1940, 4.
79 LAC, RG-24, Vol. 15,399, vol. 1 (October 1940), War Diary of Internment Camp Sherbrooke, 21 October 1940, 4.
80 LAC, RG-24, Vol. 15,399, vol. 1 (October 1940), War Diary of Internment Camp Sherbrooke, 19 October 1940, 4.
81 Canada, *Regulations Governing the Maintenance of Discipline among and Treatment of Prisoners of War* (Ottawa: J.O. Patenaude, 1939), 3.
82 LAC, RG-2, Vol. 1675, File 2089G, Order-in-Council PC 2322, 31 May 1940.
83 Stanton, "Government Internment Policy," 223-24.
84 LAC, MG-30, C 192, Vol. 3, "Interview of Colonel Eric Kippen," [1980s], 12-13.
85 LAC, RG-24, Vol. 6576, File 1-2-4, "Office of the High Commissioner for Canada in London to the Secretary of State for External Affairs in Ottawa," 1 February 1941.
86 Kochan, *Britain's Internees,* 117.
87 LAC, RG-2, Vol. 1721, File PC 4568, Order-in-Council PC 4568, 25 June 1941.
88 LAC, RG-24, Vol. 6576, File 1-2-4, "Colonel H. Stethem (Commissioner of Internment Operations) to H. D. Scully (Commissioner of Customs)," 23 July 1941.
89 LAC, RG-2, Vol. 1724, File PC 5246, Order-in-Council PC 5246, 15 July 1941.
90 Draper, "The Accidental Immigrants," Part 2, 85; Priebe, *Thank You, Canada,* 178.
91 LAC, MG-30, C 192, Vol. 3, "Interview of Rabbi Erwin Schild," [1980s], 11-12.
92 LAC, RG-24, Vol. 15,399, vol. 10 (July 1941), War Diary of Internment Camp Sherbrooke, 23 July 1941, 24 July 1941, 25 July 1941, and 28 July 1941, 5-6.
93 Bartl, "The Loss of the German-Canadian Image," 14; Koch, *Deemed Suspect,* 230.
94 Stent, *A Bespattered Page?,* 242-43.
95 Ibid., 249.
96 LAC, MG-30, C 192, Vol. 3, "Interview of Ernst Waengler," [1980s], 5-18; Kochan, *Britain's Internees,* 165-66.
97 LAC, RG-24, Vol. 15,399, vol. 18 (December 1941), War Diary of Internment Camp Île-aux-Noix, 7 December 1941, 1. See also Draper, "The Accidental Immigrants," Part 2, 94; Koch, *Deemed Suspect,* 230.
98 LAC, MG-30, C 192, Vol. 3, "Interview of Constance Hayward," [1980s], 10-15.
99 LAC, MG-30, C 192, Vol. 3, "Interview of Kurt Swinton," [1980s], 15-16. See also LAC, RG-24, Vol. 15,397, vol. 13 (October 1941), War Diary of Internment Camp Farnham, 13 October 1941, 3.
100 Iacovetta, "The 'Camp Boys,'" in *Enemies Within,* ed. Iacovetta, Perin, and Principe, 189.
101 LAC, RG-24, Reel: C-5420, File HQS 7236-96-41, "Major- General H.F.G. Letmon (Adjutant-General) to District Officer Commanding Military District 4," 30 October 1943.
102 LAC, RG-24, Vol. 15,399, vol. 41 (November 1943), War Diary of Internment Camp Île-aux-Noix, 4 November 1943, 2.
103 LAC, RG-24, Reel: C-5377, File HQS 7236-18, Vol. 1-2, "Deputy Minister of National Defence to V. I. Grossman (Executive Secretary of the Canadian ORT Organization," 20 April 1944; LAC, RG-24, Reel: C-5377, File HQS 7236-18, Vol. 1-2, "Lieutenant-Colonel F. H. Collins (Engineer Accounts and Stores to Financial Superintendent, Department of National Defence)," 7 February 1946.

104 LAC, RG-24, Vol. 6576, File 1-2-4, "Office of the High Commissioner for Canada in London to the Secretary of State for External Affairs in Ottawa," 1 February 1941.
105 Canada, *Red Cross and Prisoners of War Conventions* (Ottawa: Edmond Cloutier, 1942), 90-91.
106 Bill Waiser, *Park Prisoners: The Untold Story of Western Canada's National Parks, 1915-1946* (Saskatoon: Fifth House Publishers, 1995), 217-18.
107 LAC, RG-24, Vol. 6576, File 1-2-4, "Office of the High Commissioner for Canada in London to the Secretary of State for External Affairs in Ottawa," 1 February 1941.
108 Madsen and Henderson, *German Prisoners of War*, 6.
109 Carter, *Behind Canadian Barbed Wire*, 137.
110 LAC, RG-24, Reel: C-5378, File HQS 7236-20, "K.H. Coleman (Under-Secretary of State) to Colonel H. Desrosiers (Acting Deputy Minister of National Defence)," 16 September 1941; LAC, RG-24, Vol. 15,397, vol. 13 (October 1941), War Dairy of Internment Camp Farnham, 10 October 1941, 3.
111 LAC, RG-24, Vol. 15,397, vol. 16 (January 1942), War Diary of Internment Camp Farnham, 23 January 1942, 5.
112 LAC, RG-24, Reel: C-5378, File HQS 7236-20, "Memorandum of the Director of Organization and Administration to the Chief Treasury Officer (Army Service)," 27 January 1942.
113 LAC, RG-24, Vol. 15,397, vol. 19 (April 1942), War Diary of Internment Camp Farnham, 18 April 1942, 3.
114 LAC, RG-24, Vol. 15,400, vol. 26 (November 1942), War Diary of Internment Camp Sherbrooke, 25 November 1942, 4.
115 LAC, RG-24, Reel: C-5374, File HQS 7236-1-10-42, "Strength Returns, Camp Sherbrooke," 1942-1946.
116 LAC, RG-24, Vol. 15,398, vol. 27 (December 1942), War Diary of Internment Camp Farnham, 2 December 1942, 1. See also Priebe, *Thank You, Canada*, 181.
117 Canada, *Red Cross and Prisoners*, 96-97.
118 LAC, RG-24, Vol. 15,398, vol. 27 (December 1942), War Diary of Internment Camp Farnham, 6 December 1942, 3.
119 Canada, *Red Cross and Prisoners*, 96-97; Bill Waiser, *Park Prisoners*, 219-20.
120 LAC, RG-24, Vol. 11,247, File 9-1-3 (40), "Oberstleutnant Schlichting (Camp Spokesman) to the Consul General of Switzerland in Canada," 6 December 1942.
121 LAC, RG-24, Vol. 11,247, File 9-1-3 (40), "Telegram by Oberstleutnant Schlichting (Camp Spokesman) to the Consul General of Switzerland in Canada," 6 December 1942.
122 LAC, RG-24, Vol. 15,398, vol. 27 (December 1942), War Diary of Internment Camp Farnham, 6 December 1942, 3.
123 LAC, RG-24, Vol. 15,398, vol. 27 (December 1942), War Diary of Internment Camp Farnham, 10 December 1942 and 12 December 1942, 5-6.
124 LAC, RG-24, Reel: C-5420, File HQS 7236-96-44, "Lieutenant-Colonel R.W. Catto (Veterans Guard of Canada) to Director of Administration (Veterans Guard of Canada)," 19 October 1942, Appendix "D."
125 Ibid.
126 LAC, RG-24, Reel: C-5420, File HQS 7236-96-44, "Lieutenant-Colonel R.W. Catto (Veterans Guard of Canada) to Director of Administration (Veterans Guard of Canada)," 19 October 1942, Appendix "B."
127 LAC, RG-24, Reel: C-5420, File HQS 7236-96-44, "Lieutenant-Colonel R.W. Catto (Veterans Guard of Canada) to Director of Administration (Veterans Guard of Canada)," 19 October 1942, Appendix "A."
128 LAC, RG-24, Reel: C-5420, File HQS 7236-96-44, "Brigadier-General N.B. MacDonald (District Quartermaster-General) to DAG," 23 September 1942.

129 LAC, RG-24, Reel: C-5420, File HQS 7236-96-44, "Lieutenant-Colonel R.W. Catto (Veterans Guard of Canada) to Director of Administration (Veterans Guard of Canada)," 19 October 1942, Appendix "D."

130 LAC, RG-24, Reel: C-5420, File HQS 7236-96-44, "Brigadier-General N.B. MacDonald (District Quartermaster-General) to DAG," 23 September 1942; LAC, RG-24, Vol. 15,403, vol. 1 (January 1943), War Diary of Internment Camp Grande Ligne, "Minutes of a Meeting of the Committee of the Privy Council, PC 10854," 1 December 1942, Appendix 1, 1-3.

131 LAC, RG-24, Vol. 15,403, vol. 1 (January 1943), War Diary of Internment Camp Grande Ligne, "Minutes of a Meeting of the Committee of the Privy Council, PC 10854," 1 December 1942, Appendix 1, 1-3; LAC, RG-24, Reel: C-5396, File HQS 7236-79, "General Secretary of the Grande Ligne Mission to the Secretary (Department of National Defence)," 12 January 1943.

132 LAC, RG-24, Vol. 15,403, vol. 1 (January 1943), War Diary of Internment Camp Grande Ligne, 15 January 1943, 1; LAC, RG-24, Reel: C-5396, File HQS 7236-79, "Lieutenant-Colonel E.J. Underwood (Director of Postal Services and Chief Superintendent of Post Office Service) to Director of Prisoners of War," 5 February 1943.

133 LAC, RG-24, Vol. 15,403, vol. 1 (January 1943), War Diary of Internment Camp Grande Ligne, 17 January 1943, 1.

134 LAC, RG-24, Reel: C-5413, File HQS 7236-91-1-40, "Memorandum of the Consulate General of Switzerland in Canada in charge of German interests," 11 May 1943.

135 LAC, RG-24, Reel: C-5413, File HQS 7236-91-1-40, "Schlichting (Camp Spokesman) to the Consul General of Switzerland (Protecting Power)," 8 April 1943.

136 LAC, RG-24, Reel: C-5413, File HQS 7236-91-1-40, "Consul General of Switzerland to the Department of External Affairs," 31 May 1943.

137 LAC, RG-24, Reel: C-5413, File HQS 7236-91-1-44, "O. Jaccard (Consul General of Switzerland in Canada) to Colonel H.N. Streight (Director of Prisoners of War)," 18 June 1943.

138 LAC, RG-24, Reel: C-5378, File HQS 7236-20, "Memorandum of J.A. Lacombe (Military District 4 Treasury Officer)," 24 January 1944; LAC, RG-24, Vol. 15,398, vol. 41 (February 1944), War Diary of Internment Camp Farnham, 6 February 1944, 2.

139 LAC, RG-24, Vol. 15,398, vol. 37 (October 1943), War Diary of Internment Camp Farnham, 17 October 1943 and 18 October 1943, 3.

140 LAC, RG-24, Vol. 15,398, vol. 39 (December 1943), War Diary of Internment Camp Farnham, "Syllabus of Training: Scout School – Veterans Guard of Canada," 1 December 1943, Appendix 4, 1-4.

141 LAC, RG-24, Vol. 15,398, vol. 41 (February 1944), War Diary of Internment Camp Farnham, 25 February 1944, 5.

142 LAC, RG-24, Vol. 15,398, vol. 42 (March 1944), War Diary of Internment Camp Farnham, 1 March 1944, 1; vol. 43 (April 1944), War Diary of Internment Camp Farnham, "Department of National Defence Parade State for Camp Farnham," 19 April 1944, Appendix 3, 1.

143 LAC, RG-24, Vol. 15,398, vol. 44 (May 1944), War Diary of Internment Camp Farnham, 13 May 1944, 3.

144 LAC, RG-24, Vol. 15,398, vol. 44 (May 1944), War Diary of Internment Camp Farnham, 15 May 1944, 4.

145 LAC, RG-24, Reel: C-5378, File HQS 7236-20, "Letter Addressed to Colonel H.N. Streight (Director of Prisoners of War)," 21 September 1944; LAC, RG-24, Reel: C-5365, File HQS 9139-4-40, "Colonel H.N. Streight (Director of Prisoners of War) to Chief Postal Censor," 22 September 1944; LAC, RG-24, Reel: C-5378, File HQS 7236-20, "Major- General H.F.G. Letbon (Adjutant-General) to the District Officer Commanding Military District 4," 23 September 1944.

146 LAC, RG-24, Reel: C-5413, File HQS 7236-91-4-40, "Colonel Hans Jay (Camp Spokesman) to the Consul General of Switzerland," 22 October 1944; LAC, RG-24, Reel: C-5413, File HQS

7236-91-4-40, "Colonel H.N. Streight (Director of Prisoners of War) to the Department of External Affairs (Special Section POW)," 28 October 1944; LAC, RG-24, Reel: C-5413, File HQS 7236-91-4-40, "Under-Secretary of State for External Affairs to Department of National Defence," 19 December 1944.

147 Daniel Costelle, *Les Prisonniers* (Paris: Flammarion, 1975), 236. See also Lewis H. Carlson, *We Were Each Other's Prisoners: An Oral History of World War II American and German Prisoners of War* (New York: Basic Books, 1997); Judith Gansberg, *Stalag U.S.A.: The Remarkable Story of German POWs in America* (New York: Crowell, 1977); Arnold Krammer, *Nazi Prisoners of War in America* (New York: Stein and Day, 1979).

148 Timothy J. Holian, *The German-Americans and World War II: An Ethnic Experience* (New York: Peter Lang Publishing, 1996), 137-38, 156. See also John Christgau, *"Enemies": World War II Alien Internment* (Ames: Iowa State University Press, 1985); John Joel Culley, "Enemy Alien Control in the United States during World War II: A Survey," in *Alien Justice,* ed. Saunders and Daniels, 138-51; Arnold Krammer, *Undue Process: The Untold Story of America's German Alien Internees* (Lanham: Rowman and Littlefield, 1997).

149 External Affairs Documents [EAD], "Extract from Minutes of Cabinet War Committee," 23 September 1944 in *Documents on Canadian External Relations,* vol. 10, ed. John F. Hilliker (Ottawa: Canadian Government Publishing, 1987), 1102.

150 EAD, "Extract from Minutes of Cabinet War Committee," 11 December 1944 in *Documents,* ed. Hilliker, 1103; EAD, "Memorandum by High Commissioner of Great Britain," January 1945 in *Documents,* ed. Hilliker, 1104-5. See also Stacey, *Six Years of War,* 151.

151 Kelly, "Prisoner of War Camps," 158. See also Margaret Bevege, *Behind Barbed Wire: Internment in Australia during World War II* (St. Lucia, Australia: University of Queensland Press, 1993); Alan Fitzgerald, *Italian Farming Soldiers: Prisoners of War in Australia, 1941-1947* (Carlton, Australia: Melbourne University Press, 1981); W. Wynne Mason, *Prisoners of War: Official History of New Zealand in the Second World War, 1939-1945* (Wellington, New Zealand: War History Branch, Department of Internal Affairs, 1954); Bob Moore and Kent Fedorowich, *The British Empire and Its Italian Prisoners of War, 1940-47* (Basingstoke, UK: Palgrave, 2002); Moore, "Axis Prisoners in Britain," in *Prisoners of War and Their Captors,* ed. Moore and Fedorowich, 19-46; Barbara Winter, *Stalag Australia: German Prisoners of War in Australia* (North Ryde, Australia: Angus and Robertson, 1986).

152 EAD, "Memorandum by High Commissioner of Great Britain," January 1945, in *Documents,* ed. Hilliker, 1104-5.

153 EAD, "Extract from Minutes of Cabinet War Committee," 11 December 1944, in *Documents,* ed. Hilliker, 1103.

154 LAC, MG-26, J-13, William Lyon Mackenzie King Diaries, 11 December 1944, 2.

155 EAD, "Extract from Minutes of Cabinet War Committee," 11 December 1944, in *Documents,* ed. Hilliker, 1102-3.

156 EAD, "Norman A. Robertson (Canadian Under-Secretary of State for External Affairs) to General A.G.L. McNaughton (Minister of National Defence)," 16 January 1945, in *Documents,* ed. Hilliker, 1104.

157 EAD, "Norman A. Robertson (Canadian Under-Secretary of State for External Affairs) to High Commissioner in Great Britain," 22 January 1945, in *Documents,* ed. Hilliker, 1106-9.

158 EAD, "Canadian Secretary of State for External Affairs to High Commissioner in Great Britain," 22 January 1945, in *Documents,* ed. Hilliker, 1106-9.

159 EAD, "High Commissioner in Great Britain to Norman A. Robertson (Canadian Under-Secretary of State for External Affairs)," 18 January 1945, in *Documents,* ed. Hilliker, 1105-6.

160 Carter, *Behind Canadian Barbed Wire,* 139; John Joseph Kelly, "Der Deutsche Kriegsgefangener auf Alberta: Alberta and the Keeping of German Prisoners of War, 1939-1947," in *For King*

and Country: Alberta in the Second World War, ed. K.W. Tingley (Edmonton: Reidmore Books, 1995), 285-302; Kelly, "Prisoner of War Camps," 124-25; Jake MacDonald, "The Beast of War and the Beautiful Lake," *The Beaver* 76, 2 (1996): 29-30; Madsen and Henderson, *German Prisoners of War,* 98-99; Melady, *Escape from Canada!* 18, 22; Priebe, *Thank You, Canada,* 178.

161 LAC, RG-24, Reel: C-5366, File HQS 9139-9, "Lieutenant Colonel H.V. Dicks (Royal Army Medical Centre) to Director of Army Psychiatry," 24 February 1945.

162 LAC, RG-24, Reel: C-5366, File HQS 9139-9, "Colonel H.N. Streight (Director of Prisoners of War) to Director of Intelligence," 16 March 1945.

163 LAC, RG-24, Reel: C-5366, File HQS 9139-9, "Certified Minutes of a Meeting of the Treasury Board (Privy Council), Approved by His Excellency the Governor General in Council," 16 May 1945.

164 LAC, RG-24, Reel: C-5421, File HQS 7236-99, "Memorandum by Colonel H.N. Streight (Director of Prisoners of War)," 20 April 1945; LAC, RG-24, Vol. 15,404, vol. 1 (May 1945), War Diary of Internment Camp Sorel, 9 May 1945, 10 May 1945 to 16 May 1945, 1; LAC, RG-24, Vol. 15,404, vol. 2 (June 1945), War Diary of Internment Camp Sorel, 22 June 1945 to 29 June 1945, 2-3.

165 LAC, RG-24, Vol. 15,404, vol. 2 (June 1945), War Diary of Internment Camp Sorel, 22 June 1945 to 29 June 1945, 2-3.

166 LAC, RG-24, Reel: C-5421, File HQS 7236-99, "Recommendation for Camp Sorel by the Director of Prisoners of War," 19 May 1945; LAC, RG-24, Reel: C-5421, File HQS 7236-99, "Major General A.E. Welford (Adjutant-General) to the District Officers Commanding Military Districts 2, 3, 4, and 13," 24 May 1945.

167 LAC, RG-24, Reel: C-5374, File HQS 7236-1-10-45, "Strength Returns, Camp Sorel," 1945-1946.

168 Canada, *Red Cross and Prisoners,* 116-17.

169 LAC, RG-24, Reel: C-5365, File HQS 9139-4-40, "Lieutenant-Colonel A.W. De Wolf (Camp Commandant) to District Officer Commanding Military District 4," 26 June 1945. See also Howard Margolian, *Conduct Unbecoming: The Story of the Murder of Canadian Prisoners of War in Normandy* (Toronto: University of Toronto Press, 1998).

170 EAD, "Canadian Secretary of State for External Affairs to Acting High Commissioner in Great Britain," 29 September 1945, in *Documents,* ed. Hilliker, 1116-17.

171 LAC, RG-24, Reel: C-5366, File HQS 9139-9, "Major G.W. Hamilton (British War Office) to Colonel Raymont (Office of the High Commissioner for Canada in the United Kingdom)," 29 November 1946; LAC, RG-24, Reel: C-5366, File HQS 9139-9, "Department of National Defence Enquiry re. Employment, Usefulness and Repatriation of German POWs transferred from Canada to the United Kingdom," 4 December 1946.

172 LAC, RG-24, Vol. 15,404, vol. 11 (March 1946), War Diary of Internment Camp Sorel, 4 March 1946, 5 March 1946, and 6 March 1946, 1; LAC, RG-24, Reel: C-5421, File HQS 7236-99, "Major-General E.G. Weeks (Adjutant-General) to District Officer Commanding Military District 4," 6 March 1946.

173 LAC, RG-24, Vol. 15,404, vol. 12 (April 1946), War Diary of Internment Camp Sorel, "Daily Orders by Major L.L. Brunton (Camp Commandant)," 17 April 1946, Appendix 1, 19; LAC, RG-24, Vol. 15,404, vol. 12 (April 1946), War Diary of Internment Camp Sorel, 17 April 1946.

174 LAC, RG-24, Reel: C-5366, File HQS 9139-44, "Major-General E.G. Weeks (Adjutant-General) to District Officers Commanding Military Districts 2 and 4," 2 April 1946; LAC, RG-24, Reel: C-5396, File HQS 7236-79, "Major-General E.G. Weeks (Adjutant-General) to the District Officer Commanding Military District 4," 10 April 1946; LAC, RG-24, Vol. 15,404, vol. 40 (April 1946), War Diary of Internment Camp Grande Ligne, 10 April 1946, 12 April 1946, 15 April 1946, and 16 April 1946, 2.

175 LAC, RG-24, Vol. 15,404, vol. 40 (April 1946), War Diary of Internment Camp Grande Ligne, 30 April 1946, 4.

176 LAC, RG-24, Reel: C-5420, File HQS 7236-96-44, "D.W. Jerry (President of the Grande Ligne Mission) to the Department of National Defence," 16 August 1945.

177 LAC, RG-24, Reel: C-5420, File HQS 7236-96-44, "Major-General H.A. Young (Quartermaster-General) to Deputy Minister of National Defence," 28 February 1946; LAC, RG-24, Vol. 15,404, vol. 40 (April 1946), War Diary of Internment Camp Grande Ligne, 30 April 1946, 4.

178 LAC, RG-24, Reel: C-5378, File HQS 7236-20, "Memorandum by Lieutenant-Colonel H.W. Pearson (Assistant Director of Prisoners of War)," 14 May 1946; LAC, RG-24, Reel: C-5378, File HQS 7236-20, "Memorandum by Colonel J.M. Taylor (Director, Veterans Guard of Canada)," 17 May 1946; LAC, RG-24, Vol. 15,398, vol. 64 (May 1946), War Diary of Internment Camp Farnham, 22 May 1946, 3.

179 LAC, RG-24, Vol. 15,398, vol. 65 (June 1946), War Diary of Internment Camp Farnham, 6 June 1946, 1.

180 LAC, RG-24, Vol. 15,398, vol. 65 (June 1946), War Diary of Internment Camp Farnham, 17 June 1946, 2.

181 "Le camp d'internement Newington cédé à la corporation des biens de guerre," *La Tribune de Sherbrooke*, 2 December 1946; "Délégation de Sherbrooke auprès de la Corporation des biens de guerre," *La Tribune de Sherbrooke*, 23 April 1946; LAC, RG-24, Vol. 15,401, vol. 69 (June 1946), War Diary of Internment Camp Sherbrooke, 11 June 1946 and 14 June 1946, 2; "Les internés allemands au camp Newington," *La Tribune de Sherbrooke*, 30 January 1947.

182 Carter, *Behind Canadian Barbed Wire,* 228; Bernard and Bergeron, *Trop loin de Berlin,* 350; Priebe, *Thank You, Canada,* 190-91.

183 Carter, *Behind Canadian Barbed Wire,* 229; Kelly, "Prisoner of War Camps," 209-10.

Chapter 3: Life behind Barbed Wire

1 Canada, *Red Cross and Prisoners of War Conventions* (Ottawa: Edmond Cloutier, 1942), 104-5.

2 Canada, *Defence of Canada Regulations (Consolidation)* (Ottawa: Edmond Cloutier, 1941), 5.

3 Library and Archives Canada [LAC], RG-24, Vol. 15,399, vol. 3 (September 1940), War Diary of Internment Camp Île-aux-Noix, 14 September 1940, 5-6.

4 LAC, RG-24, Vol. 15,399, vol. 9 (June 1941), War Diary of Internment Camp Sherbrooke, 9 June 1941, 2.

5 Canada, *Regulations,* 5.

6 Translated by Martin Auger. See Mario Duliani, *La ville sans femmes* (Montreal: Société des Éditions Pascal, 1945), 48-49.

7 Canada, *Regulations Governing the Maintenance of Discipline among and Treatment of Prisoners of War* (Ottawa: J.O. Patenaude, 1939), 5.

8 Canada, *Red Cross and Prisoners,* 120-23.

9 Canada, *Orders and Instructions, Internment Camp* (Ottawa: Department of National Defence, 1945), 62.

10 LAC, RG-24, Reel: C-5413, File HQS 7236-91-4-42, "The Consul General of Switzerland to Prisoner of War Hans Knups," 6 March 1945.

11 Paula Jean Draper, "The Accidental Immigrants: Canada and the Interned Refugees," Part 1, *Canadian Jewish Historical Society Journal* 2, 1 (1978): 25-26.

12 Canada, *Red Cross and Prisoners,* 118-19.

13 Jonathan F. Vance, "Canadian Relief Agencies and Prisoners of War, 1939-45," *Journal of Canadian Studies* 31, 2 (1996): 133-47; Jonathan F. Vance, *Objects of Concern: Canadian Prisoners of War through the Twentieth Century* (Vancouver: UBC Press, 1994), 149-56.

14 John O. Buffinga, "The War Prisoners' Aid of the YMCA and Hermann Boeschenstein's Role as an Ethnic Mediator (1943-1947)," *Canadian Ethnic Studies* 20, 2 (1988): 57; John Melady, *Escape from Canada! The Untold Story of German POWs in Canada, 1939-1945* (Toronto: Macmillan of Canada, 1981), 51-52.
15 Draper, "The Accidental Immigrants" Part 1, 25-26.
16 LAC, RG-24, Reel: C-5416, File HQS 7236-94-6-40, "March 1943 Intelligence Summary," 1 April 1943.
17 LAC, RG-24, Vol. 15, 399, vol. 6 (March 1941), War Diary of Internment Camp Sherbrooke, 5 March 1941, 1.
18 Canada, *Red Cross and Prisoners,* 93.
19 Ibid.
20 Ibid.
21 Vance, *Objects of Concern,* 131.
22 LAC, MG-30, C 192, Vol. 3, "Interview of Colonel Eric Kippen," [1980s], 8-7.
23 Buffinga, "War Prisoners' Aid," 57.
24 LAC, RG-24, Reel: C-5376, File HQS 7236-1-11, "Instructions for Completing Form I.O. 32 [Monthly Return Form of Parcels Received in Camps]," [n.d.]; LAC, RG-24, Reel: C-5365, File HQS 9139-4-40, "January 1946 Interpreter's Report," 31 January 1946.
25 Canada, *Orders and Instructions,* 60; LAC, RG-24, Vol. 15,399, vol. 5 (February 1941), War Diary of Internment Camp Sherbrooke, "Camp Standing Orders for Internees," 5 March 1941, Appendix A.
26 LAC, RG-24, Reel: C-5376, File HQS 7236-1-11, "Consulate General of Switzerland in Canada to Department of External Affairs," 8 August 1941.
27 LAC, RG-24, Reel: C-5376, File HQS 7236-1-11, "Under-Secretary of State for External Affairs to Internment Operations," 23 August 1941.
28 LAC, RG-24, Reel: C-5376, File HQS 7236-1-11, "Colonel H. Stethem (Commissioner of Internment Operations) to the Camp Commandants," 26 August 1941; LAC, RG-24, Reel: C-5376, File HQS 7236-1-11, "Lieutenant-Colonel E.H. Minns (A/Commissioner of Internment Operations) to the Camp Commandants," 9 October 1941.
29 LAC, MG-30, C 192, Vol. 3, "Interview of Emil Fackenheim," [1980s], 43; LAC, RG-24, Vol. 15,399, vol. 3 (December 1940), War Diary of Internment Camp Sherbrooke, 23 December 1940, 3; LAC, RG-24, Reel: C-5403, File HQS 7236-83-7-40, "Colonel Jay (Camp Spokesman) to the Ladies of the Red Cross of Argentina in Buenos Aires," 25 February 1945; LAC, RG-24, Reel: C-5416, File HQS 7236-94-6-42, "November 1944 Intelligence Report," November 1944; LAC, RG-24, Reel: C-5375, File HQS 7236-1-11-42, "Statement of Parcels Received at Camp Sherbrooke," October 1945 to January 1946.
30 Draper, "The Accidental Immigrants" Part 2, 90.
31 LAC, MG-30, C 192, Vol. 3, "Interview of Helmut Blume," [1980s], 37-9.
32 LAC, RG-24, Vol. 11,249, File 9-5-3-41, "Report of the 28 August 1940 visit by Ernest L. Maag (Delegate in Canada for the International Red Cross)," September 1940; LAC, RG-24, Vol. 15,399, vol. 3 (December 1940), War Diary of Internment Camp Sherbrooke, 18 December 1940, 2.
33 LAC, RG-24, Vol. 15,399, vol. 3 (September 1940), War Diary of Internment Camp Île-aux-Noix, 4 September 1940, 1.
34 Eric Koch, *Deemed Suspect: A Wartime Blunder* (Toronto: Methuen, 1980), 155-56.
35 Yves Bernard and Caroline Bergeron, *Trop loin de Berlin: Des prisonniers allemands au Canada (1939-1946)* (Sillery, QC: Éditions du Septentrion, 1995), 163; Gilles Dallaire, "Partis d'Allemagne en conquérants ... ils sont prisonniers à Sherbrooke," *La Tribune de Sherbrooke,* 12 October 1985.
36 LAC, RG-24, Reel: C-5416, File HQS 7236-94-6-44, "December 1943 Intelligence Summary," December 1943; LAC, RG-24, Reel: C-5365, File HQS 9139-4-42, "February 1945 Intelligence

Report," 4 March 1945; LAC, RG-24, Reel: C-5419, File HQS 7236-94-14-40, "Lieutenant-Colonel A.W. De Wolf (Camp Commandant) to District Officer Commanding Military District 4," 12 March 1945.

37 LAC, RG-24, Reel: C-5365, File HQS 9139-4-44, "December 1945 Information Summary," 5 January 1946.

38 LAC, RG-24, Vol. 15,399, vol. 3 (September 1940), War Diary of Internment Camp Île-aux-Noix, 4 September 1940, 1; LAC, RG-24, Reel: C-5365, File HQS 9139-4-44, "May 1945 Intelligence Report," May 1945; LAC, RG-24, Reel: C-5365, File HQS 9139-4-42, "May 1945 Intelligence Report," 15 June 1945; LAC, RG-24, Reel: C-5365, File HQS 9139-4-42, "January 1946 Intelligence Report," January 1946.

39 LAC, MG-30, C 192, Vol. 3, "Interview of John Newmark," [1980s], 11-3, 11-4.

40 LAC, RG-24, Vol. 15,399, vol. 6 (March 1941), War Diary of Internment Camp Sherbrooke, 5 March 1941, 1; LAC, RG-24, Vol. 15,399, vol. 10 (July 1941), War Diary of Internment Camp Sherbrooke, 22 July 1941, 5; LAC, RG-24, Vol. 15,399, vol. 12 (September 1941), War Diary of Internment Camp Sherbrooke, 13 September 1941 and 14 September 1941, 3; LAC, RG-24, Reel: C-5365, File HQS 9139-4-44, "May 1945 Intelligence Report," May 1945; LAC, RG-24, Reel: C-5365, File HQS 9139-4-42, "May 1945 Intelligence Report," 15 June 1945; LAC, RG-24, Reel: C-5365, File HQS 9139-4-44, "December 1945 Information Summary," 5 January 1946; LAC, RG-24, Reel: C-5365, File HQS 9139-4-42, "February 1946 Intelligence Report," February 1946.

41 LAC, RG-24, Reel: C-5365, File HQS 9139-4-42, "January 1945 Intelligence Report," 4 February 1945; LAC, RG-24, Reel: C-5419, File HQS 7236-94-14-42, "Broadcast Information on Camp to Headquarters Military District 4," 20 February 1945.

42 LAC, RG-24, Vol. 15,399, vol. 4 (January 1941), War Diary of Internment Camp Sherbrooke, 1 January 1941, 1; LAC, RG-24, Vol. 15,399, vol. 10 (July 1941), War Diary of Internment Camp Sherbrooke, 1 July 1941, 2; LAC, RG-24, Vol. 15,403, vol. 7 (July 1943), War Diary of Internment Camp Grande Ligne, 23 July 1943, 6; LAC, RG-24, Reel: C-5416, File HQS 7236-94-6-44, "December 1943 Intelligence Summary," December 1943.

43 LAC, MG-30, C 192, Vol. 3, "Interview of Ernest Shield," [1980s], 38-10, 18-15.

44 LAC, RG-24, Reel: C-5416, File HQS 7236-94-6-44, "May 1944 Intelligence Summary," May 1944.

45 LAC, RG-24, Vol. 15,404, vol. 6 (October 1945), War Diary of Internment Camp Sorel, "Camp Daily Orders," 22 October 1945, Appendix 1, 25.

46 LAC, RG-24, Reel: C-5416, File HQS 7236-94-6-44, "June 1944 Intelligence Summary," June 1944.

47 LAC, RG-24, Reel: C-5416, File HQS 7236-94-6-42, "November 1944 Intelligence Report," November 1944.

48 LAC, RG-24, Reel: C-5365, File HQS 9139-4-42, "April 1945 Intelligence Report," 3 May 1945.

49 LAC, RG-24, Reel: C-5419, File HQS 7236-94-14-40, "Lieutenant-Colonel A.W. De Wolf (Camp Commandant) to District Officer Commanding Military District 4," 10 April 1945.

50 LAC, RG-24, Vol. 15,403, vol. 13 (January 1944), War Diary of Internment Camp Grande Ligne, 17 January 1944, 4.

51 LAC, RG-24, Reel: C-5419, File HQS 7236-94-14-40, "Lieutenant-Colonel A.W. De Wolf (Camp Commandant) to District Officer Commanding Military District 4," 7 March 1945.

52 Jean Cazeneuve, *Essai sur la psychologie du prisonnier de guerre* (Paris: Presses Universitaires de France, 1945), vii.

53 Translated by Martin Auger. See Ibid., 15-16, 18.

54 Translated by Martin Auger. See Ibid., 20.

55 Ibid., 22-23.

56 LAC, MG-30, C 192, Vol. 3, "Interview of John Newmark," [1980s], 11-12, 11-13.

57 Jonathan Vance, ed. *Encyclopedia of Prisoners of War and Internment* (Santa Barbara: ABC-CLIO, 2000), 20. See also A.L. Vischer, *Barbed Wire Disease: A Psychological Study of the Prisoners of War* (London: John Bale, Sons, and Danielsson, 1919).
58 Vance, ed., *Encyclopedia,* 20-21.
59 Translated by Martin Auger. See Cazeneuve, *Essai,* 35.
60 Translated by Martin Auger. See Ibid., 34-35.
61 Koch, *Deemed Suspect,* 143.
62 LAC, MG-30, C 192, Vol. 3, "Interview of Ernest Guter," [1980s], 34-12, 34-13.
63 LAC, RG-24, Reel: C-5416, File 7236-94-6-42, "October 1944 Intelligence Report," 1 November 1944.
64 LAC, RG-24, Vol. 15,398, vol. 29 (February 1943), War Diary of Internment Camp Farnham, 26 February 1943 and 27 February 1943, 8-9.
65 LAC, RG-24, Vol. 15,399, vol. 3 (September 1940), War Diary of Internment Camp Île-aux-Noix, 14 September 1940, 5-6.
66 Translated by Martin Auger. See Cazeneuve, *Essai,* 39-41.
67 Mario Duliani, *La ville sans femmes* (Montreal: Société des Éditions Pascal, 1945), 205-6.
68 Translated by Antonino Mazza. See Mario Duliani, *The City without Women: A Chronicle of Internment Life in Canada during the Second World War* (Oakville, ON: Mosaic Press, 1994), 99-100, 108. Original version can be found in Duliani, *La ville sans femmes,* 219.
69 LAC, MG-30, C 192, Vol. 3, "Interview of Mrs. Ann Cowan," [1980s], 11-14.
70 Translated by Martin Auger. See Bernard and Bergeron, *Trop loin de Berlin,* 292.
71 Translated by Martin Auger. See Cazeneuve, *Essai,* 45-50.
72 Translated by Antonino Mazza. See Duliani, *The City without Women,* 101. The original version can be found in Duliani, *La ville sans femmes,* 209.
73 LAC, MG-30, C 192, Vol. 3, "Interview of John Newmark," [1980s], 11-1.
74 Koch, *Deemed Suspect,* 137.
75 LAC, RG-24, Vol. 15,399, vol. 4 (January 1941), War Diary of Internment Camp Sherbrooke, 25 January 1941, 1.
76 LAC, MG-30, C 192, Vol. 3, "Interview of Josef Kates," [1980s], 1-2, 21-22.
77 Melady, *Escape from Canada!* 60; LAC, MG-30, C 192, Vol. 3, "Interview of Gerry Waldston," [1980s], 22.
78 Koch, *Deemed Suspect,* 157.
79 Ibid., 158-59.
80 Chris M.V. Madsen and R.J. Henderson, *German Prisoners of War in Canada and Their Artifacts* (Regina: Hignell Printing, 1993), 72-73.
81 Translated by Martin Auger. See Cazeneuve, *Essai,* 55.
82 Translated by Martin Auger. See Ibid., 57-58.
83 Eastern Townships Research Centre [ETRC], Eastern Townships Collection [ETC], 98-003, Box No. 121, File 2.4, "Interview of Norma Beattie," 21 August 1991; LAC, RG-24, Vol. 15,400, vol. 40 (January 1944), War Diary of Internment Camp Sherbrooke, 8 January 1944 and 9 January 1944, 2-3; LAC, RG-24, Vol. 15,400, vol. 45 (June 1944), War Diary of Internment Camp Sherbrooke, 15 June 1944 and 16 June 1944, 1.
84 Canada, *Red Cross and Prisoners,* 88-89.
85 ETRC, ETC, 98-003, Box No. 121, File 2.12, "Interview of Shirley Hall," 2 August 1991.
86 Carol Gaskell, *Women's Words: Eastern Township Anglophone Women Remember the Second World War* (Lennoxville, QC: n.p., 1995), 105.
87 LAC, RG-24, Vol. 15, 397, vol. 7 (April 1941), War Diary of Internment Camp Farnham, 25 April 1941, 6-7.
88 Vance, *Objects of Concern,* 130-31.
89 J.L. Granatstein and Desmond Morton, *A Nation Forged in Fire: Canadians and the Second World War, 1939-1945* (Toronto: Lester and Orpen Dennys, 1989), 54; John F. Hilliker,

ed., *Documents on Canadian External Relations,* Vol. 9, *1942-1943* (Ottawa: Canadian Government Publishing, 1980), 473-525; C.P. Stacey, *Arms, Men and Governments: The War Policies of Canada, 1939-1945* (Ottawa: Department of National Defence, 1970), 152-53; Vance, ed., *Encyclopedia,* 270-71; Vance, *Objects of Concern,* 134-37; Jonathan F. Vance, "Men in Manacles: The Shackling of Prisoners of War, 1942-1943," *Journal of Military History* 59, 3 (July 1995): 485-97. See also S.P. Mackenzie, "The Shackling Crisis: A Case-Study in the Dynamics of Prisoner-of-War Diplomacy in the Second World War," *International History Review* 17 (1995): 78-98.

90 Bernard and Bergeron, *Trop loin de Berlin,* 174-78; David J. Carter, *Behind Canadian Barbed Wire: Alien, Refugee and Prisoner of War Camps in Canada, 1914-1946* (Calgary: Tumbleweed, 1980), 107-14; Melady, *Escape from Canada!* 62-70; Eckehart J. Priebe, *Thank You, Canada: From Messerschmitt Pilot to Canadian Citizen* (West Vancouver: Condor, 1990), 107-17; Vance, *Objects of Concern,* 136-37.

91 External Affairs Documents [EAD], "Dominions Secretary to Secretary of State for External Affairs," 8 December 1942, in *Documents,* ed. Hilliker, 512; Vance, "Men in Manacles," 496.

92 LAC, RG-24, Reel: C-5413, File HQS 7236-91-1-44, "Memorandum of the Consul General of Switzerland in Canada in charge of German Interests," 30 November 1943.

93 EAD, "Dominions Secretary to Secretary of State for External Affairs," 30 November 1943, in *Documents,* ed. Hilliker, 525; Vance, "Men in Manacles," 497-98.

94 Canada, *Red Cross and Prisoners,* 118-19.

95 LAC, RG-24, Vol. 11,247, File 9-1-3 (40), "Consul General of Switzerland in Canada to Captain K. Krieger (Camp Spokesman)," 1 October 1942.

96 Priebe, *Thank You, Canada,* 89.

97 LAC, MG-30, C 192, Vol. 3, "Interview of Helmut Pokorny," [1980s], 3-8, 3-9.

98 Priebe, *Thank You, Canada,* 89.

99 LAC, RG-24, Reel: C-5409, File HQS 7236-87-5-42, "Carl Witt (Camp Spokesman) to Captain M.J. O'Brien (A/Camp Commandant)," 3 September 1943.

100 LAC, RG-24, Reel: C-5409, File HQS 7236-87-5-42, "Major D.J. O'Donahoe (Works Program) to the Director of Prisoners of War," 6 September 1943.

101 LAC, RG-24, Vol. 15,397, vol. 12 (September 1941), War Diary of Internment Camp Farnham, 2 September 1941, 1.

102 LAC, RG-24, Vol. 15,397, vol. 12 (September 1941), War Diary of Internment Camp Farnham, 11 September 1941, 3.

103 LAC, RG-24, Vol. 15,397, vol. 12 (September 1941), War Diary of Internment Camp Farnham, 16 September 1941, 19 September 1941, and 21 September 1941, 4-5.

104 LAC, RG-24, Vol. 15,397, vol. 12 (September 1941), War Diary of Internment Camp Farnham, "Major E.D.B. Kippen (Camp Commandant) to District Officer Commanding Military District 4," 30 September 1941, Appendix 5.

105 LAC, RG-24, Vol. 15,397, vol. 12 (September 1941), War Diary of Internment Camp Farnham, 25 September 1941 and 26 September 1941, 6.

106 LAC, RG-24, Vol. 15,397, vol. 12 (September 1941), War Diary of Internment Camp Farnham, "Major E.D.B. Kippen (Camp Commandant) to District Officer Commanding Military District 4," 30 September 1941, Appendix 5.

107 Ibid.

108 Canada, *Orders and Instructions,* 20-21; LAC, RG-24, Reel: C-5398, File HQS 7236-81-40, "Camp Spokesman to Ernest L. Maag (Delegate in Canada for the International Committee of the Red Cross)," 19 April 1943.

109 Priebe, *Thank You, Canada,* 149.

110 Ibid., 150.

111 LAC, RG-24, Vol. 15,397, vol. 12 (September 1941), War Diary of Internment Camp Farnham, 13 September 1941, 4.

112 LAC, RG-24, Vol. 15,400, vol. 40 (January 1944), War Diary of Internment Camp Sherbrooke, 22 January 1944, 23 January 1944, and 24 January 1944, 5-6; LAC, RG-24, Vol. 15,400, vol. 41 (February 1944), War Diary of Internment Camp Sherbrooke, 29 February 1944, 5; LAC, RG-24, Vol. 15,400, vol. 42 (March 1944), War Diary of Internment Camp Sherbrooke, 4 March 1944 and 6 March 1944, 1.

113 Priebe, *Thank You, Canada,* 143.

114 LAC, RG-24, Vol. 15,397, vol. 6 (March 1941), War Diary of Internment Camp Farnham, "Colonel H. Stethem (Director of Internment Operations) to the Commandants of all Internment Camps," 19 March 1941, Appendix 11.

115 Priebe, *Thank You, Canada,* 143-44.

116 Ibid., 145.

117 LAC, RG-24, Reel: C-5365, File HQS 9139-4-44, "February 1945 Intelligence Summary," February 1945.

118 Canada, *Red Cross and Prisoners,* 102-3.

119 Translated by Martin Auger. See Daniel Costelle, *Les Prisonniers* (Paris: Flammarion, 1975), 178.

120 Canada, *Orders and Instructions,* 52.

121 Priebe, *Thank You, Canada,* 180-81.

122 LAC, RG-24, Vol. 11,250, File 10-2-3-40, "Intelligence Report," 16 September 1942; LAC, RG-24, Reel: C-5410, File HQS 7236-88-5-44, "Colonel of the Directorate of Military Intelligence to the Director of Prisoners of War," 24 April 1945; LAC, RG-24, Reel: C-5409, File HQS 7236-88-5-40, "Lieutenant-Colonel A.W. De Wolf (Camp Commandant) to District Officer Commanding Military District 4," 25 March 1945; LAC, RG-24, Reel: C-5410, File HQS 7236-88-5-42, "Lieutenant-Colonel H.W. Pearson (A/Director Prisoners of War) to Camp Commandant," 8 November 1945. See also Melady, *Escape from Canada!* 70-71; Don Page, "Tommy Stone and Psychological Warfare in World War Two: Transforming a POW Liability into an Asset," *Journal of Canadian Studies* 16, 3-4 (1981): 112.

123 LAC, RG-24, Vol. 15,400, vol. 16 (January 1942), War Diary of Internment Camp Sherbrooke, "Instructions for the Censor," January 1942, Appendix 4, 21-23.

124 John Joseph Kelly, "Intelligence and Counter-Intelligence in German Prisoner of War Camps in Canada during World War II," *Dalhousie Review* 58, 2 (1978): 289-90.

125 Canada, *Orders and Instructions,* 54.

126 LAC, RG-24, Vol. 15,398, vol. 31 (April 1943), War Diary of Internment Camp Farnham, 29 April 1943, 11.

127 Kelly, "Intelligence," 289-90.

128 LAC, RG-24, Reel: C-5409, File; HQS 7236-87-5-42, "H.D. Hedley (Camp Commandant) to Military District 4 Headquarters," 6 March 1945.

129 Canada, *Regulations,* 4.

130 LAC, MG-30, C 192, Vol. 3, "Interview of Thomas Gold," [1980s], 29-12, 29-13.

131 LAC, RG-24, Vol. 15,399, vol. 35 (May 1943), War Diary of Internment Camp Île-aux-Noix, 24 May 1943, 4-5.

132 LAC, RG-24, Vol. 15,398, vol. 31 (April 1943), War Diary of Internment Camp Farnham, 22 April 1943, 8.

133 LAC, RG-24, Vol. 15,398, vol. 29 (February 1943), War Diary of Internment Camp Farnham, 13 February 1943, 16 February 1943, and 18 February 1943, 4-5.

134 Carter, *Behind Canadian Barbed Wire,* 122.

135 LAC, RG-24, Vol. 15,401, vol. 66 (March 1946), War Diary of Internment Camp Sherbrooke, "Major A.R. Turner (Camp Commandant) to Military District 4 Headquarters," 24 March 1946, Appendix 3, 1.

136 LAC, RG-24, Vol. 15,397, vol. 2 (November 1940), War Diary of Internment Camp Farnham, "Escapes – What to Look For," November 1940, Appendix 7, 1.

137 Ibid., 2; LAC, RG-24, Vol. 15,403, vol. 15 (March 1944), War Diary of Internment Camp Grande Ligne, 21 March 1944, 6.

138 LAC, RG-24, Vol. 15,397, vol. 2 (November 1940), War Diary of Internment Camp Farnham, "Escapes – What to Look For," November 1940, Appendix 7, 1.

139 LAC, RG-24, Reel: C-5416, File HQS 7236-94-6-40, "January 1943 Intelligence Summary," 4 February 1943; LAC, RG-24, Vol. 15,398, vol. 28 (January 1943), War Diary of Internment Camp Farnham, 26 January 1943, 27 January 1943, 28 January 1943, and 29 January 1943, 8-9.

140 LAC, RG-24, Reel: C-5389, File HQS 7236-44-44, "Royal Canadian Mounted Police Commissioner to the Director of Administration," 21 December 1948.

141 LAC, RG-24, Vol. 15,397, vol. 2 (November 1940), War Diary of Internment Camp Farnham, "Escapes – What to Look For," November 1940, Appendix 7, 2.

142 LAC, RG-24, Reel: C-5389, File HQS 7236-44-42, "Lieutenant- Colonel B.B.W. Minard (Camp Commandant) to Military District 4 Headquarters," 22 April 1943; "Police Dragnet Spread Through District for Two Escaped Nazis," *Sherbrooke Daily Record*, 16 April 1943; "Two Escaped German Prisoners of War Are Found Hiding Inside Camp," *Sherbrooke Daily Record*, 17 April 1943.

143 LAC, RG-24, Vol. 15,403, vol. 21 (September 1944), War Diary of Internment Camp Grande Ligne, 13 September 1944, 4-5.

144 LAC, RG-24, Vol. 15,403, vol. 21 (September 1944), War Diary of Internment Camp Grande Ligne, 15 September 1944, 5.

145 LAC, RG-24, Vol. 15,397, vol. 1 (October 1940), War Diary of Internment Camp Farnham, 25 October 1940, 11; LAC, RG-24, Vol. 15,397, vol. 1 (October 1940), War Diary of Internment Camp Farnham, "Camp Standing Orders," 25 October 1940, Appendix 2; LAC, RG-24, Vol. 15,397, vol. 5 (February 1941), War Diary of Internment Camp Farnham, "Notes on Prevention of Escapes," 24 December 1940, Appendix A, 1-4.

146 LAC, RG-24, Vol. 15,403, vol. 21 (September 1944), War Diary of Internment Camp Grande Ligne, 14 September 1944, 5.

147 LAC, RG-24, Reel: C-5413, File HQS 7236-91-4-44, "Camp Spokesman to the Consul General of Switzerland in Canada," 17 October 1944.

148 LAC, RG-24, Vol. 15,397, vol. 2 (November 1940), War Diary of Internment Camp Farnham, "Escapes – What to Look For," November 1940, Appendix 7, 2.

149 LAC, RG-24, Reel: C-5389, File HQS 7236-44-44, "Lieutenant-Colonel E.D.B. Kippen (Camp Commandant) to the District Officer Commanding Military District 4," 31 August 1943; LAC, RG-24, Reel: C-5389, File HQS 7236-44-40, "Sergeant F.J. Devereaux (Veterans Guard of Canada) to Lieutenant-Colonel A.W. De Wolf (Camp Commandant)," 18 December 1944; Priebe, 187.

150 Costelle, *Les prisonniers*, 13-16; Madsen and Henderson, *German Prisoners of War*, 65; Priebe, *Thank You, Canada*, 187. See also Kendal Burt and James Leasor, *The One That Got Away* (London: Collins, 1956); Fritz Wentzel, *Single or Return: The Story of a German POW in British Camps and the Escape of Lieutenant Franz von Werra* (London: William Kimber, 1954).

151 Priebe, *Thank You, Canada*, 122; Bernard and Bergeron, *Trop loin de Berlin*, 75.

152 Translated by Martin Auger. See "Recherches des 2 évadés," *La Tribune de Sherbrooke*, 26 November 1942.

153 "Les deux évadés de Sherbrooke sont repris à Newport, Vermont," *La Tribune de Sherbrooke*, 11 December 1942, 3; "Two Escaped German Prisoners Are Recaptured at Newport, Vt.," *Sherbrooke Daily Record*, 11 December 1942.

154 Madsen and Henderson, *German Prisoners of War*, 65. See also Michael L. Hadley, *U-Boats against Canada: German Submarines in Canadian Waters* (Montreal and Kingston: McGill-Queen's University Press, 1985).

155 LAC, RG-24, Vol. 15,397, vol. 5 (February 1941), War Diary of Internment Camp Farnham, "Notes on Prevention of Escapes," 24 December 1940, Appendix A, 1-4.
156 LAC, RG-24, Vol. 15,399, vol. 1 (July 1940), War Diary of Internment Camp Île-aux-Noix, 19 July 1940, 5.
157 LAC, RG-24, Vol. 15,399, vol. 2 (August 1940), War Diary of Internment Camp Île-aux-Noix, 15 August 1940, 4.
158 LAC, RG-24, Vol. 15,397, vol. 1 (October 1940), War Diary of Internment Camp Farnham, 24 October 1940, 10.
159 LAC, RG-24, Vol. 15,397, vol. 2 (November 1940), War Diary of Internment Camp Farnham, 25 November 1940, 8-9; LAC, RG-24, Vol. 15,397, vol. 4 (January 1941), War Diary of Internment Camp Farnham, "No. 4 Active Company – Veterans Guard of Canada – Syllabus of Training," 27 January 1941, Appendix F, 1; LAC, RG-24, Vol. 15,400, vol. 20 (May 1942), War Diary of Internment Camp Sherbrooke, "Camp Orders," 5 May 1942, 6 May 1942, and 11 May 1942, Appendix 1, 5-6, 11.
160 LAC, RG-24, Vol. 15,397, vol. 5 (February 1941), War Diary of Internment Camp Farnham, "Notes on Prevention of Escapes," 24 December 1940, Appendix A, 1-4.
161 LAC, RG-24, Vol. 15,397, vol. 2 (November 1940), War Diary of Internment Camp Farnham, "Escapes – What to Look For," November 1940, Appendix 7, 3.
162 LAC, RG-24, Vol. 15,399, vol. 2 (August 1940), War Diary of Internment Camp Île-aux-Noix, 26 August 1940, 6-7; LAC, MG-30, C 192, Vol. 3, "Interview of Ernest Guter," [1980s], 24-7.
163 LAC, RG-24, Vol. 15,399, vol. 2 (November 1940), War Diary of Internment Camp Sherbrooke, 29 November 1940, 2; LAC, RG-24, Vol. 15,397, vol. 3 (December 1940), War Diary of Internment Camp Farnham, 29 December 1940, 7; LAC, RG-24, Vol. 15,397, vol. 11 (August 1941), War Diary of Internment Camp Farnham, 8 August 1941, 3; LAC, MG-30, C 192, Vol. 3, "Interview of Ernst Waengler," [1980s], 1-17; See also Carter, *Behind Canadian Barbed Wire,* 82; Kelly, "Prisoner of War Camps," 92-94; Melady, *Escape from Canada!* 54; Priebe, *Thank You, Canada,* 173, 188.
164 LAC, RG-24, Vol. 15,399, vol. 2 (August 1940), War Diary of Internment Camp Île-aux-Noix, 3 August 1940, 1.
165 LAC, RG-24, Reel: C-5416, File HQS 7236-94-6-44, "Lieutenant-Colonel E.D.B. Kippen (Camp Commandant) to the Director of Prisoners of War," 7 July 1943; LAC, RG-24, Vol. 15,403, vol. 7 (July 1943), War Diary of Internment Camp Grande Ligne, 7 July 1943, 2.
166 LAC, RG-24, Vol. 15,403, vol. 8 (August 1943), War Diary of Internment Camp Grande Ligne, 14 August 1943, 15 August 1943, and 19 August 1943, 4-5; LAC, RG-24, Reel: C-5389, File HQS 7236-44-44, "Lieutenant-Colonel E.D.B. Kippen (Camp Commandant) to the District Officer Commanding Military District 4," 31 August 1943.
167 LAC, RG-24, Vol. 15,403, vol. 8 (August 1943), War Diary of Internment Camp Grande Ligne, 27 August 1943, p 8.
168 LAC, RG-24, Reel: C-5389, File HQS 7236-44-44, "Major-General R.J. Renaud (District Officer Commanding Military District 4) to the Secretary (Department of National Defence)," 31 August 1943; LAC, RG-24, Vol. 15,403, vol. 8 (August 1943), War Diary of Internment Camp Grande Ligne, 31 August 1943, 9.
169 LAC, RG-24, Vol. 15,403, vol. 9 (September 1943), War Diary of Internment Camp Grande Ligne, 2 September 1943 and 3 September 1943, 1.
170 LAC, RG-24, Vol. 15,403, vol. 9 (September 1943), War Diary of Internment Camp Grande Ligne, 6 September 1943, 2.
171 LAC, RG-24, Vol. 15,403, vol. 10 (October 1943), War Diary of Internment Camp Grande Ligne, 13 October 1943 and 21 October 1943, 3, 5; LAC, RG-24, Vol. 15,403, vol. 10 (October 1943), War Diary of Internment Camp Grande Ligne, "Part 1 Orders," 28 October 1943, Appendix 1, 25.

172 LAC, RG-24, Vol. 15,403, vol. 14 (February 1944), War Diary of Internment Camp Grande Ligne, 16 February 1944 and 26 February 1944, 4, 8.

173 LAC, RG-24, Vol. 15,403, vol. 14 (February 1944), War Diary of Internment Camp Grande Ligne, 27 February 1944 and 29 February 1944, 8-9; LAC, RG-24, Reel: C-5389, File HQS 7236-44-44, "Lieutenant-Colonel E.D.B. Kippen (Camp Commandant) to Military District 4 Headquarters," 3 March 1944.

174 LAC, RG-24, Reel: C-5416, File HQS 7236-94-6-44, "March 1944 Intelligence Summary," March 1944.

175 LAC, RG-24, Vol. 15,403, vol. 19 (July 1944), War Diary of Internment Camp Grande Ligne, 13 July 1944 and 17 July 1944, 4-5.

176 LAC, RG-24, Vol. 15,403, vol. 19 (July 1944), War Diary of Internment Camp Grande Ligne, 30 July 1944, 8; LAC, RG-24, Reel: C-5389, File HQS 7236-44-44, "Lieutenant-Colonel E.D.B. Kippen (Camp Commandant) to the District Officer Commanding Military District 4," 8 August 1944.

177 LAC, RG-24, Vol. 15,403, vol. 20 (August 1944), War Diary of Internment Camp Grande Ligne, 8 August 1944, 3.

178 LAC, RG-24, Vol. 15,403, vol. 20 (August 1944), War Diary of Internment Camp Grande Ligne, 26 August 1944, 9.

179 LAC, RG-24, Vol. 15,403, vol. 21 (September 1944), War Diary of Internment Camp Grande Ligne, 4-15 September 1944, 1-5; LAC, RG-24, Vol. 15,403, vol. 21 (September 1944), War Diary of Internment Camp Grande Ligne, "Lieutenant-Colonel E.D.B. Kippen (Camp Commandant) to Major-General R.J. Renaud (District Officer Commanding Military District 4)," 7 September 1944, Appendix 5, 1-2; LAC, RG-24, Vol. 15,403, vol. 21 (September 1944), War Diary of Internment Camp Grande Ligne, "Lieutenant-Colonel E.D.B. Kippen (Camp Commandant) to Major-General R.J. Renaud (District Officer Commanding Military District 4)," 13 September 1944, Appendix 7, 1; LAC, RG-24, Reel: C-5416, File HQS 7236-94-6-44, "Colonel W.W. Murray (Director of Military Intelligence) to Deputy Chief of the General Staff," 18 October 1944; LAC, RG-24, Vol. 15,403, vol. 21 (September 1944), War Diary of Internment Camp Grande Ligne, 26 September 1944, 9; LAC, RG-24, Vol. 15,403, vol. 21 (September 1944), War Diary of Internment Camp Grande Ligne, 27 September 1944, Appendix 8, 1.

180 LAC, RG-24, Vol. 15,403, vol. 21 (September 1944), War Diary of Internment Camp Grande Ligne, 28 September 1944, 9.

181 LAC, RG-24, Reel: C-5389, File HQS 7236-44-40, "Escape Standing Orders," 10 January 1941.

182 LAC, RG-24, Vol. 15,397, vol. 2 (November 1940), War Diary of Internment Camp Farnham, 8 November 1940, 4 and 11 November 1940, 5; LAC, RG-24, Vol. 15,397, vol. 9 (June 1941), War Diary of Internment Camp Farnham, 25 June 1941, 5.

183 LAC, RG-24, Reel: C-5389, File HQS 7236-44-41, "Escape Plan," 12 December 1940 and 26 February 1941; LAC, RG-24, Reel: C-5389, File HQS 7236-44-40, "Escape Operation Order No. 3," 1 October 1941; LAC, RG-24, Reel: C-5389, File HQS 7236-44-42, "Recapture Operation Order No. 2, Appendix B," 23 November 1943; LAC, RG-24, Reel: C-5389, File HQS 7236-44-42, "Recapture Operation Order No. 2, Appendix D," 23 November 1943; LAC, RG-24, Reel: C-5389, File HQS 7236-44-40, "Recapture Operation Order No. 1, Appendix B," 24 August 1944.

184 LAC, RG-24, Reel: C-5389, File HQS 7236-44-42, "Escape Orders, Internment Camp Sherbrooke," 22 February 1941.

185 "Les évadés sont encore en liberté," *La Tribune de Sherbrooke*, 10 November 1942; "Recherches des 2 évadés," *La Tribune de Sherbrooke*, 26 November 1942; "Les deux évadés du camp sont repris à Sand Hill," *La Tribune de Sherbrooke*, 30 November 1942; "Les deux évadés de Sherbrooke sont repris à Newport, Vermont," *La Tribune de Sherbrooke*, 11 December 1942;

"Les deux évadés de Newington," *La Tribune de Sherbrooke*, 9 April 1943; "Les deux évadés de Newington sont retrouvés à Ascot Corner," *La Tribune de Sherbrooke*, 10 April 1943; "Deux autres prisonniers s'échappent, hier soir, du camp de Newington," *La Tribune de Sherbrooke*, 15 April 1943; "Les évadés sont retrouvés dans le camp," *La Tribune de Sherbrooke*, 17 April 1943; "Évasion du camp de Newington," *La Tribune de Sherbrooke*, 6 August 1943; "L'Allemand est repris à St-Malo," *La Tribune de Sherbrooke*, 7 August 1943; "Un violent incendie rase un vaste bâtiment du camp d'internement," *La Tribune de Sherbrooke*, 16 October 1943; "Deux journalistes, un photographe au camp d'internement," *La Tribune de Sherbrooke*, 16 October 1943; "Un vieil incendie, une photo neuve," *La Tribune de Sherbrooke*, 14 January 1944; "Un prisonnier Nazi s'évade puis se rend," *La Tribune de Sherbrooke*, 31 July 1944; "Un commandant nouveau au camp d'internement," *La Tribune de Sherbrooke*, 20 September 1944; "Deuxième grand incendie en moins d'un an au camp d'internement," *La Tribune de Sherbrooke*, 23 September 1944; "Un prisonnier boche s'évade de Newington," *La Tribune de Sherbrooke*, 14 May 1945; "Les recherches se poursuivent pour Friedriech," *La Tribune de Sherbrooke*, 15 May 1945; "Le prisonnier évadé est capturé près de Coaticook," *La Tribune de Sherbrooke*, 16 May 1945; "Une journée avec les prisonniers allemands du camp Newington," *La Tribune de Sherbrooke*, 29 October 1945; "Évadé du camp de Newington," *La Tribune de Sherbrooke*, 25 March 1946; "Le prisonnier boche évadé a été capturé," *La Tribune de Sherbrooke*, 28 March 1946; "Délégation de Sherbrooke auprès de la corporation des biens de guerre," *La Tribune de Sherbrooke*, 23 April 1946; "Le camp d'internement Newington cédé à la corporation des biens de guerre," *La Tribune de Sherbrooke*, 2 December 1946; "Les internés à Sherbrooke vécurent avec confort mais dans l'angoisse jusqu'à la victoire alliée," *La Tribune de Sherbrooke*, 3 February 1947.

186 "Les évadés sont encore en liberté," *La Tribune de Sherbrooke*, 10 November 1942. Quotation translated by Martin Auger from "Les deux évadés du camp sont repris à Sand Hill," *La Tribune de Sherbrooke*, 30 November 1942.

187 "Widespread Search Continues for Escaped Prisoners of War," *Sherbrooke Daily Record*, 8 December 1942; "East Angus-Weedon Area Searched for Two Escaped German Seamen," *Sherbrooke Daily Record*, 10 December 1942; "Les deux évadés de Sherbrooke sont repris à Newport, Vermont," *La Tribune de Sherbrooke*, 11 December 1942; "Two Escaped German Prisoners are Recaptured at Newport, Vt.," *Sherbrooke Daily Record*, 11 December 1942.

188 LAC, RG-24, Vol. 15,401, vol. 66 (March 1946), War Diary of Internment Camp Sherbrooke, "Major A.R. Turner (Camp Commandant) to Military District 4 Headquarters," 29 March 1946, Appendix 4, 1.

189 LAC, RG-24, Vol. 15,398, vol. 33 (June 1943), War Diary of Internment Camp Farnham, 28 June 1943 and 29 June 1943, 8-9.

190 Canada, *Red Cross and Prisoners*, 106.

191 Ibid., 106-8.

192 Ibid., 108-9.

193 Ibid., 110-11.

194 Ibid., 110.

195 Canada, *Regulations*, 4.

196 Bernard and Bergeron, *Trop loin de Berlin*, 313; Canada, *Regulations*, 8-11. For specific cases in southern Quebec see, LAC, RG-24, Vol. 15,400, vol. 16 (January 1942), War Diary of Internment Camp Sherbrooke," 24 January 1942, 6; LAC, RG-24, Vol. 15,400, vol. 18 (March 1942), War Diary of Internment Camp Sherbrooke, 10 March 1942, 11 March 1942, 12 March 1942, 13 March 1942, and 14 March 1942, 2-3; LAC, RG-24, Vol. 15,400, vol. 18 (March 1942), War Diary of Internment Camp Sherbrooke, 24 March 1942, 4; LAC, RG-24, Vol. 15,400, vol. 43 (April 1944), War Diary of Internment Camp Sherbrooke, 3 April 1944, 4 April 1944, 5 April 1944, 6 April 1944, 7 April 1944, 8 April 1944, 20 April 1944, and 24 April 1944, 1-4; LAC, RG-24, Reel:

C-5389, File HQS 7236-44-40, "Major-General E.J. Renaud (District Officer Commanding Military District 4) to the Secretary (Department of National Defence)," 21 December 1944; LAC, RG-24, Reel: C-5421, File HQS 7236-99, "Major-General E.J. Renaud (District Officer Commanding Military District 4) to the Secretary (Department of National Defence)," 17 November 1945; LAC, MG-30, C 192, Vol. 3, "Interview of Edgar Steinberg, [1980s], 23; LAC, MG-30, C 192, Vol. 3, "Interview of Ernest Guter," [1980s], 34-10.

197 LAC, RG-24, Vol. 15,399, vol. 1 (July 1940), War Diary of Internment Camp Île-aux-Noix, 21 July 1940, 6.

198 LAC, RG-24, Vol. 15,399, vol. 2 (August 1940), War Diary of Internment Camp Île-aux-Noix, 2 August 1940, 1.

199 LAC, RG-24, Vol. 15,399, vol. 2 (August 1940), War Diary of Internment Camp Île-aux-Noix, 16 August 1940 and 17 August 1940, 4; LAC, RG-24, Vol. 15,399, vol. 3 (September 1940), War Diary of Internment Camp Île-aux-Noix, 4 September 1940, 1; LAC, RG-24, Vol. 15,399, vol. 3 (September 1940), War Diary of Internment Camp Île-aux-Noix, 7 September 1940, 3; LAC, RG-24, Vol. 15,397, vol. 1 (October 1940), War Diary of Internment Camp Farnham, 30 October 1940, 12; LAC, RG-24, Vol. 15,397, vol. 2 (November 1940), War Diary of Internment Camp Farnham, 8 November 1940, 4; LAC, RG-24, Vol. 15,397, vol. 3 (December 1940), War Diary of Internment Camp Farnham, 23 December 1940, 5; LAC, RG-24, Vol. 15,397, vol. 4 (January 1941), War Diary of Internment Camp Farnham, 10 January 1941, 3; LAC, RG-24, Vol. 15,397, vol. 5 (February 1941), War Diary of Internment Camp Farnham, 13 February 1941, 16 February 1941, 17 February 1941, and 20 February 1941, 4-6; LAC, RG-24, Vol. 15,397, vol. 6 (March 1941), War Diary of Internment Camp Farnham, 11 March 1941, 22 March 1941, 23 March 1941, 24 March 1941, and 25 March 1941, 3-7; LAC, MG-30, C 192, Vol. 3, "Interview of Helmut Blume," [1980s], 37-15.

200 Canada, *Red Cross and Prisoners,* 110-13; Canada, *Regulations,* 11-15.

201 Canada, *Red Cross and Prisoners,* 110-13; Canada, *Regulations,* 11-15.

202 LAC, RG-24, Vol. 15,401, vol. 55 (April 1945), War Diary of Internment Camp Sherbrooke, "Camp Orders," 17 April 1945, Appendix 1, 15; LAC, RG-24, Reel: C-5365, File HQS 9139-4-42, "April 1945 Intelligence Report," 3 May 1945.

203 Koch, *Deemed Suspect,* 163.

204 LAC, RG-24, Vol. 11,250, File 10-2-3-40, "Captain F.W. Staff (Directorate of Military Intelligence) to Officer Commanding Internment Camp Farnham," 27 May 1941.

205 LAC, RG-24, Vol. 15,397, vol. 12 (September 1941), War Diary of Internment Camp Farnham, "Major E.D.B. Kippen (Camp Commandant) to Commissioner of Refugee Camps," 19 September 1941.

206 Martin F. Auger, "The Problem of Nazism in the German POW Officer Camps of Southern Quebec, 1942-1945" (14th Military History Colloquium, London, 10 May 2003).

207 Department of National Defence, Directorate of History and Heritage [DHH], 193.009 (D29), Vol. 28, "Memorandum on Prisoners of War Intelligence Directorate," 27 March 1944; LAC, RG-24, Vol. 15,398, vol. 26 (November 1942), War Diary of Internment Camp Farnham, 13 November 1942, 4; LAC, RG-24, Vol. 15,400, vol. 40 (January 1944), War Diary of Internment Camp Sherbrooke, 21 January 1944, 5. See also Kelly, "Intelligence," 285-286; Macdonald, 30.

208 LAC, RG-24, Vol. 11,247, File 9-1-3 (42), "Lieutenant-Colonel B.B.W. Minard (Camp Commandant) to the Commissioner of Internment Operations," 21 January 1943.

209 DHH, 193.009 (D29), Vol. 28, "Chiefs of Staff Memorandum on Political Warfare – Directorate of Prisoners of War Intelligence," 23 March 1944.

210 DHH, 193.009 (D29), Vol. 28, "Thomas A. Stone (Chairman of the Psychological Warfare Committee) to the Chief of the General Staff," 22 July 1943.

211 Andrew Rettig, "A De-programming Curriculum: Allied Reeducation and the Canadian-American Psychological Warfare Program for German POWs, 1943-47," *American Review of Canadian Studies* 29, 4 (1999): 602.

212 Carter, *Behind Canadian Barbed Wire*, 143; Kelly, "Intelligence," 285, 293; Page, "Tommy Stone," 115.
213 Bernard and Bergeron, *Trop loin de Berlin*, 304.
214 Bill Waiser, *Park Prisoners: The Untold Story of Western Canada's National Parks, 1915-1916* (Saskatoon: Fifth House, 1995), 226.
215 Kelly, "Intelligence," 291.
216 LAC, RG-24, Reel: C-5366, File HQS 9139-42, "Report of a visit to Camp Sherbrooke by Lieutenant E. Davidson (RCNVR)," 15-16 December 1944; LAC, RG-24, Reel: C-5416, File HQS 7236-94-6-42, "December 1944 Intelligence Report," December 1944; LAC, RG-24, Reel: C-5365, File HQS 9139-4-42, "February 1945 Intelligence Report," 4 March 1945.
217 LAC, RG-24, Reel: C-5365, File HQS 9139-4-42, "January 1945 Intelligence Report," 4 February 1945; LAC, RG-24, Reel: C-5366, File HQS 9139-42, "Lieutenant-Colonel H.D. Hedley (Camp Commandant) to Military District 4 Headquarters," 7 February 1945.
218 LAC, RG-24, Reel: C-5365, File HQS 9139-4-42, "February 1945 Intelligence Report," 4 March 1945.
219 LAC, RG-24, Reel: C-5365, File HQS 9139-4-42, "March 1945 Intelligence Report," 2 April 1945.
220 LAC, RG-24, Reel: C-5365, File HQS 9139-4-40, "December 1944 Intelligence Report," December 1944; LAC, RG-24, Reel: C-5365, File HQS 9139-4-40, "January 1945 Intelligence Report," 29 January 1945.
221 DHH, 193.009 (D29), Vol. 28, "Memorandum by Major R.H. Pender (Directorate of Military Intelligence)," 23 February 1944.
222 LAC, RG-24, Reel: C-5366, File HQS 9139-40, "Major H.H. Cuning (A/Camp Commandant) to Major-General E.J. Renaud (District Officer Commanding Military District 4)," 26 December 1944.
223 LAC, RG-24, Reel: C-5365, File HQS 9139-4-44, "Lieutenant-Colonel H.W. Hiltz (Camp Commandant) to District Officer Commanding Military District 4," 17 June 1945.
224 LAC, RG-24, Reel: C-5366, File HQS 9139-44, "Chief of the General Staff to the District Officer Commanding Military District 4," 15 September 1944; LAC, RG-24, Reel: C-5416, File HQS 7236-94-6-44, "Director of Military Intelligence to the Deputy Chief of the General Staff," 18 October 1944.
225 LAC, RG-24, Reel: C-5365, File HQS 9139-4-44, "Director of Military Intelligence to MI3," 17 October 1944.
226 For more information on the HARIKARI Club, see Martin F. Auger, "The HARIKARI Club: German Prisoners of War and the Mass Escape Scare of 1944-45 at Internment Camp Grande Ligne, Quebec," *Canadian Military History* 13, 3 (2004): 49-67.
227 LAC, RG-24, Reel: C-5416, File HQS 7236-94-6-44, "Colonel W.W. Murray (Director of Military Intelligence) to all Canadian Prisoner of War Camp Intelligence Officers," 14 November 1944.
228 LAC, RG-24, Reel: C-5416, File HQS 7236-94-6-44, "Roman Catholic Priest George Felber (Civilian Internee) to Captain Jungbluth (Camp Intelligence Officer)," 3 October 1944; LAC, RG-24, Reel: C-5416, File HQS 7236-94-6-44, "Director of Military Intelligence to Deputy Chief of the General Staff," 18 October 1944.
229 LAC, RG-24, Reel: C-5416, File HQS 7236-94-6-44, "Roman Catholic Priest George Felber (Civilian Internee) to Captain Jungbluth (Camp Intelligence Officer)," 3 October 1944.
230 LAC, RG-24, Reel: C-5416, File HQS 7236-94-6-44, "W. Fisher (Assistant Camp Censor) to the Lieutenant-Colonel H.W. Hiltz (Camp Commandant)," 16 October 1944.
231 LAC, RG-24, Reel: C-5416, File HQS 7236-94-6-44, "Memorandum by Major Lieven (Military Intelligence 7)," 25 October 1944.
232 Gavin Long, *The Final Campaigns: Australia in the War of 1939-1945* (Canberra: Australian War Memorial, 1963), 623-24; Vance, ed., *Encyclopedia*, 64-65, 97-98. See also Teruhiko Asada,

Night of a Thousand Suicides: The Japanese Outbreak at Cowra (Sydney: Angus and Robertson, 1970); Charlotte Carr-Gregg, *Japanese Prisoners of War in Revolt: The Outbreaks of Featherston and Cowra during World War II* (New York: St. Martin's Press, 1978), Ian Dear, *Escape and Evasion: POW Breakouts in World War II* (London: Cassell and Company, 2000).

233 LAC, RG-24, Reel: C-5416, File HQS 7236-94-6-44, "Director of Military Intelligence to the Deputy Chief of the General Staff," 18 October 1944.

234 LAC, RG-24, Reel: C-5416, File HQS 7236-94-6-44, "Memorandum by Major Lieven (Military Intelligence 7)," 25 October 1944; LAC, RG-24, Reel: C-5416, File HQS 7236-94-6-44, "Colonel H.N. Streight (Director of Prisoners of War) to DAG," 31 October 1944.

235 LAC, RG-24, Reel: C-5416, File HQS 7236-94-6-44, "Colonel H.N. Streight (Director of Prisoners of War) to Brigadier G.A. Ferguson (Deputy Adjutant-General, Department of National Defence)," 31 October 1944.

236 LAC, RG-24, Reel: C-5365, File HQS 9139-4-44, "Lieutenant-Colonel Eric Acland (Directorate of Military Intelligence) to MI3 (Department of National Defence)," 17 October 1944.

237 LAC, RG-24, Reel: C-5416, File HQS 7236-94-6-44, "Lieutenant-Colonel H.W. Pearson (Assistant Adjutant-General, Directorate of Prisoners of War) to Colonel H.N. Streight (Director of Prisoners of War)," 27 October 1944.

238 LAC, RG-24, Reel: C-5416, File HQS 7236-94-6-44, "Colonel H.N. Streight (Director of Prisoners of War) to Brigadier G.A. Ferguson (Deputy Adjutant-General, Department of National Defence)," 31 October 1944.

239 LAC, RG-24, Reel: C-5416, File HQS 7236-94-6-44, "Colonel C.P. Lavigne (Assistant Adjutant-General, Veterans Guard of Canada) to Colonel J.M. Taylor (Director, Veterans Guard of Canada)," 27 October 1944.

240 LAC, RG-24, Reel: C-5416, File HQS 7236-94-6-44, "Report of Colonel J.M. Taylor (Director, Veterans Guard of Canada)," 27 October 1944.

241 Carter, *Behind Canadian Barbed Wire,* 107-14; Melady, *Escape from Canada!* 62-70.

242 LAC, RG-24, Vol. 15,403, vol. 22 (October 1944), War Diary of Internment Camp Grande Ligne, 23 October 1944, 6.

243 LAC, RG-24, Reel: C-5416, File HQS 7236-94-6-44, "Brigadier Marcel Noel (Vice Adjutant-General, Department of National Defence) to Brigadier G.A. Ferguson (Deputy Adjutant-General, Department of National Defence), 1 December 1944.

244 LAC, RG-24, Reel: C-5416, File HQS 7236-94-6-44, "Inspector C.W. Harvison ('C' Division, RCMP) to Commissioner S.T. Wood (RCMP)," 4 December 1944.

245 LAC, RG-24, Reel: C-5416, File HQS 7236-94-6-44, "Telegram from the Commandant of Internment Camp Monteith," 30 November 1944; LAC, RG-24, Reel: C-5416, File HQS 7236-94-6-44, "Brigadier Marcel Noel (Vice Adjutant-General, Department of National Defence) to Brigadier G.A. Ferguson (Deputy Adjutant-General, Department of National Defence)," 1 December 1944.

246 LAC, RG-24, Reel: C-5416, File HQS 7236-94-6-44, "Director of Military Intelligence to all camp Intelligence Officers," 14 November 1944.

247 LAC, RG-24, Reel: C-5416, File HQS 7236-94-6-44, "Major General E.J. Renaud (District Officer Commanding Military District 4) to the Secretary (Department of National Defence)," 1 December 1944.

248 LAC, RG-24, Reel: C-5416, File HQS 7236-94-6-44, "Brigadier Marcel Noel (Vice Adjutant-General, Department of National Defence) to Brigadier G.A. Ferguson (Deputy Adjutant-General, Department of National Defence)," 1 December 1944.

249 LAC, RG-24, Reel: C-5416, File HQS 7236-94-6-44, "Minutes of a Meeting Held in the Office of General A.G.L. McNaughton (Minister of National Defence)," 2 December 1944.

250 LAC, RG-24, Reel: C-5416, File HQS 7236-94-6-44, "Minutes of a Conference Held in the Office of Brigadier Marcel Noel (Vice Adjutant-General, Department of National Defence) to Deal with POW Camp No. 44 Grande Ligne," 2 December 1944.

251 LAC, RG-24, Reel: C-5416, File HQS 7236-94-6-44, "Minutes of a Meeting Held in the Office of General A.G.L. McNaughton (Minister of National Defence)," 2 December 1944.
252 LAC, RG-24, Reel: C-5416, File HQS 7236-94-6-44, "Minutes of a Conference Held in the Office of Brigadier Marcel Noel (Vice Adjutant-General, Department of National Defence) to Deal with POW Camp No. 44 Grande Ligne," 2 December 1944.
253 LAC, RG-24, Reel: C-5416, File HQS 7236-94-6-44, "Record of Decisions Taken at a Meeting Held in the Office of the Chief of the General Staff in Regard to Prisoners of War Accommodation," 4 December 1944; LAC, RG-24, Reel: C-5416, File HQS 7236-94-6-44, "Major-General A.E. Walford (Adjutant-General, Department of National Defence) to District Officer Commanding Military District 4," 6 December 1944.
254 LAC, RG-24, Reel: C-5416, File HQS 7236-94-6-44, "Minutes of a Conference Held in the Office of Brigadier Marcel Noel (Vice Adjutant-General, Department of National Defence) to Deal with POW Camp No. 44 Grande Ligne," 2 December 1944; LAC, RG-24, Reel: C-5416, File HQS 7236-94-6-44, "Inspector C.W. Harvison ('C' Division, RCMP) to Commissioner S.T. Wood (RCMP)," 4 December 1944; LAC, RG-24, Reel: C-5416, File HQS 7236-94-6-44, "Major-General A.E. Walford (Adjutant-General, Department of National Defence) to District Officer Commanding Military District 4," 6 December 1944.
255 LAC, RG-24, Reel: C-5416, File HQS 7236-94-6-44, "Inspector C.W. Harvison ('C' Division, RCMP) to Commissioner S.T. Wood (RCMP)," 4 December 1944.
256 LAC, RG-24, Reel: C-5416, File HQS 7236-94-6-44, "Inspector C.W. Harvison ('C' Division, RCMP) to Commissioner S.T. Wood (RCMP)," 4 December 1944.
257 LAC, RG-24, Reel: C-5416, File HQS 7236-94-6-44, "Deputy Commissioner F.J. Mead (RCMP) to Brigadier Marcel Noel (Vice Adjutant-General, Department of National Defence)," 9 December 1944.
258 LAC, RG-24, Vol. 15,403, vol. 24 (December 1944), War Diary of Internment Camp Grande Ligne, 30 December 1944, 6.
259 LAC, RG-24, Vol. 15,403, vol. 25 (January 1945), War Diary of Internment Camp Grande Ligne, 3 January 1945, 1.
260 Bernard and Bergeron, *Trop loin de Berlin*, 295.
261 LAC, RG-24, Vol. 15,403, vol. 25 (January 1945), War Diary of Internment Camp Grande Ligne, 6 January 1945, 2.
262 LAC, RG-24, Reel: C-5365, File HQS 9139-4-44, "February 1945 Intelligence Summary," February 1945; LAC, RG-24, Reel: C-5374, File HQS 7236-1-10-44, Strength Returns, Camp Grande Ligne, 10 February 1945.
263 Carter, *Behind Canadian Barbed Wire*, 100, 113.
264 LAC, RG-24, Reel: C-5366, File HQS 9139-44, "Lieutenant-Colonel H.W. Hiltz (Camp Commandant) to District Officer Commanding Military District 4," 6 June 1945; LAC, RG-24, Reel: C-5365, File HQS 9139-4-44, "June 1945 Intelligence Summary," June 1945.
265 LAC, RG-24, Reel: C-5366, File HQS 9139-44, "Lieutenant-Colonel H.W. Hiltz (Camp Commandant) to District Officer Commanding Military District 4," 31 July 1945.
266 LAC, RG-24, Reel: C-5419, File HQS 7236-94-14-44, "Lieutenant-Colonel H.W. Hiltz (Camp Commandant) to District Officer Commanding Military District 4," 9 August 1945.

Chapter 4: Labour Projects

1 Canada, *Red Cross and Prisoners of War Conventions* (Ottawa: Edmond Cloutier, 1942), 98-99.
2 Ibid., 100-1.
3 Canada, *Defence of Canada Regulations (Consolidation)* (Ottawa: Edmond Cloutier, 1941), 3.
4 Canada, *Red Cross and Prisoners*, 100-1.
5 Canada, *Orders and Instructions, Internment Camps* (Ottawa: Department of National Defence, 1945), 43-44.

6 Library and Archives Canada [LAC], RG-24, Vol. 15,400, vol. 14 (November 1941), War Diary of Internment Camp Sherbrooke, "Major W.J.H. Ellwood (Camp Commandant) to District Officer Commanding Military District 4," 20 November 1941, Appendix 1, 8.

7 LAC, MG-30, C 192, Vol. 3, "Interview of Edgar Steinberg," [1980s], 1-2.

8 Canada, *Orders and Instructions,* 44. See also LAC, RG-24, Vol. 15,400, vol. 13 (October 1941), War Diary of Internment Camp Sherbrooke, "Report by Major W.J.H. Ellwood (Camp Commandant)," 23 October 1941, Appendix 1, 32-33.

9 LAC, RG-24, Vol. 15,400, vol. 17 (February 1942), War Diary of Internment Camp Sherbrooke, "Major W.J.H. Ellwood (Camp Commandant) to Commissioner of Refugee Camps," 6 February 1942, Appendix 1, 2-3; LAC, RG-24, Vol. 15,400, vol. 17 (February 1942), War Diary of Internment Camp Sherbrooke, "Major W.J.H. Ellwood (Camp Commandant) to Commissioner of Refugee Camps," 10 February 1942, Appendix 1, 9.

10 Canada, *Orders and Instructions,* 44.

11 LAC, RG-24, Vol. 11,249, File 9-5-3-40, "Report of the Red Cross visit to Camp Farnham by Ernest L. Maag (Delegate in Canada for the International Committee of the Red Cross)," 26 November 1940; LAC, RG-24, Vol. 15,397, vol. 2 (November 1940), War Diary of Internment Camp Farnham, 23 November 1940, 8; LAC, RG-24, Vol. 15,399, vol. 2 (November 1940), War Diary of Internment Camp Sherbrooke, 18 October 1940 and 21 October 1940, 4; LAC, RG-24, Vol. 15,399, vol. 5 (February 1941), War Diary of Internment Camp Sherbrooke, "Internee Statement," 21 February 1941, Appendix 2, 3.

12 John Joseph Kelly, "The Prisoner of War Camps in Canada, 1939-1947" (MA thesis, University of Windsor, 1976), 89-90.

13 LAC, RG-24, Vol. 6576, File 1-1-5, "Scheme for the Employment of Interned Aliens," 11 June 1940.

14 Ibid.

15 LAC, RG-24, Reel: C-5378, File HQS 7236-20, "Brigadier-General Edouard de Bellefeuille Panet (Director of Internment Operations), to the Adjutant-General (Department of National Defence)," 5 September 1940.

16 LAC, RG-24, Vol. 15,397, vol. 1 (October 1940), War Diary of Internment Camp Farnham, 18 October 1940, 6.

17 LAC, RG-24, Vol. 15,397, vol. 1 (October 1940), War Diary of Internment Camp Farnham, 27 October 1940, 11.

18 LAC, RG-24, Vol. 15,397, vol. 8 (May 1941), War Diary of Internment Camp Farnham, 14 May 1941 and 15 May 1941, 3.

19 LAC, RG-24, Vol. 15,397, vol. 8 (May 1941), War Diary of Internment Camp Farnham, 19 May 1941, 4.

20 LAC, RG-24, Vol. 15,399, vol. 11 (March 1941), War Diary of Internment Camp Île-aux-Noix, 12 May 1941, 3.

21 LAC, RG-24, Vol. 11,253, File 11-2-41, "Inspection Report," 25 June 1941; LAC, RG-24, Vol. 15,399, vol. 27 (September 1942), War Diary of Internment Camp Île-aux-Noix, 11 September 1942, 1.

22 LAC, RG-24, Vol. 15,397, vol. 13 (October 1941), War Diary of Internment Camp Farnham, 7 October 1941 and 14 October 1941, 2, 4.

23 LAC, RG-24, Vol. 15,397, vol. 12 (September 1941), War Diary of Internment Camp Farnham, 8 September 1941, 3.

24 LAC, RG-24, Vol. 15,397, vol. 23 (August 1942), War Diary of Internment Camp Farnham, "Farm Produce Works Program," August 1942, 8.

25 LAC, RG-24, Reel: C-5403, File HQS 7236-83-7-40, "Ernest L. Maag (Delegate in Canada for the International Committee of the Red Cross) to S. Marley Scott (Department of External Affairs)," 23 March 1943.

26 LAC, RG-24, Reel: C-5396, File HQS 7236-79, "Schlichting (Camp Farnham Spokesman) to Ernest L. Maag (Delegate in Canada for the International Committee of the Red Cross)," 21 January 1943.

27 LAC, RG-24, Reel: C-5403, File HQS 7236-83-7-40, "Ernest L. Maag (Delegate in Canada for the International Committee of the Red Cross) to S. Marley Scott (Department of External Affairs)," 23 March 1943.

28 LAC, RG-24, Vol. 15,403, vol. 6 (June 1943), War Diary of Internment Camp Grande Ligne, 1 June 1943, 5 June 1943, and 6 June 1943, 1.

29 LAC, RG-24, Vol. 15,403, vol. 6 (June 1943), War Diary of Internment Camp Grande Ligne, 28 June 1943, 29 June 1943, and 30 June 1943, 5.

30 Translated by Martin Auger. See LAC, RG-24, Reel: C-5413, File HQS 7236-91-1-44, "Report by E.L. Maag (Delegate in Canada for the International Committee of the Red Cross)," 21 July 1943.

31 LAC, RG-24, Reel: C-5416, File HQS 7236-94-6-44, "September 1943 Intelligence Summary," 11 October 1943; LAC, RG-24, Vol. 15,403, vol. 9 (September 1943), War Diary of Internment Camp Grande Ligne, "Lieutenant-Colonel E.D.B. Kippen (Camp Commandant) to Director of Prisoners of War," 30 September 1943, Appendix 3.

32 LAC, RG-24, Vol. 15,403, vol. 9 (September 1943), War Diary of Internment Camp Grande Ligne, 22 September 1943, 23 September 1943, and 24 September 1943, 6; LAC, RG-24, Reel: C-5416, File HQS 7236-94-6-44, "September 1943 Intelligence Summary," 11 October 1943.

33 LAC, RG-24, Vol. 15,403, vol. 13 (January 1944), War Diary of Internment Camp Grande Ligne, 13 January 1944, 3; LAC, RG-24, Vol. 15,403, vol. 14 (February 1944), War Diary of Internment Camp Grande Ligne, 11 February 1944, 3.

34 LAC, RG-24, Vol. 15,403, vol. 12 (December 1943), War Diary of Internment Camp Grande Ligne, 6 December 1943, 2; LAC, RG-24, Vol. 15,403, vol. 21 (September 1944), War Diary of Internment Camp Grande Ligne, 12 September 1944, 4.

35 LAC, RG-24, Reel: C-5365, File HQS 9139-4-44, "December 1945 Information Summary," 5 January 1946.

36 LAC, RG-24, Vol. 15,403, vol. 3 (March 1943), War Diary of Internment Camp Grande Ligne, 24 March 1943, 6.

37 LAC, RG-24, Vol. 15,403, vol. 4 (April 1943), War Diary of Internment Camp Grande Ligne, 1 April 1943, 3 April 1943, and 21 April 1943, 1, 4.

38 LAC, RG-24, Vol. 15,403, vol. 15 (March 1944), War Diary of Internment Camp Grande Ligne, 19 March 1944 and 21 March 1944, 5-6; LAC, RG-24, Vol. 15,403, vol. 17 (April 1944), War Diary of Internment Camp Grande Ligne, 14 April 1944 and 21 April 1944, 4, 6.

39 LAC, RG-24, Vol. 15,403, vol. 21 (September 1944), War Diary of Internment Camp Grande Ligne, 12 September 1944, 4.

40 LAC, RG-24, Vol. 15,403, vol. 21 (September 1944), War Diary of Internment Camp Grande Ligne, 21 September 1944, 7.

41 LAC, RG-24, Reel: C-5365, File HQS 9139-4-44, "June 1945 Intelligence Summary," June 1945.

42 LAC, RG-24, Vol. 15,403, vol. 30 (June 1945), War Diary of Internment Camp Grande Ligne, 4 June 1945, 1.

43 LAC, RG-24, Vol. 15,404, vol. 32 (August 1945), War Diary of Internment Camp Grande Ligne, 7 August 1945, 1.

44 LAC, RG-24, Reel: C-5365, File HQS 9139-4-40, "July 1945 Interpreter's Report," 1 August 1945.

45 LAC, RG-24, Reel: C-5419, File HQS 7236-94-14-40, "Lieutenant-Colonel A.W. De Wolf (Camp Commandant) to District Officer Commanding Military District 4," 15 March 1945.

46 LAC, RG-24, Reel: C-5419, File HQS 7236-94-14-40, "Lieutenant-Colonel A.W. De Wolf (Camp Commandant) to District Officer Commanding Military District 4," 12 April 1945.

47 LAC, RG-24, Reel: C-5365, File HQS 9139-4-40, "August 1945 Interpreter's Report," 31 August 1945.
48 Ibid.
49 Carol Gaskell, *Women's Words: Eastern Township Anglophone Women Remember the Second World War* (Lennoxville, QC: n.p., 1995), 105.
50 Translated by Martin Auger. See Alfred Desrochers, "Une journée avec les prisonniers allemands du camp Newington," *La Tribune de Sherbrooke*, 29 October 1945, 10.
51 LAC, RG-24, Reel: C-5365, File HQS 9139-4-42, "April 1945 Intelligence Report," 3 May 1945.
52 LAC, RG-24, Reel: C-5365, File HQS 9139-4-42, "February 1945 Intelligence Report," 4 March 1945; LAC, RG-24, Reel: C-5365, File HQS 9139-4-40, "July 1945 Interpreter's Report," 1 August 1945.
53 LAC, RG-24, Reel: C-5365, File HQS 9139-4-42, "March 1945 Intelligence Report," 2 April 1945.
54 LAC, RG-24, Reel: C-5419, File HQS 7236-94-14-40, "Lieutenant-Colonel A.W. De Wolf (Camp Commandant) to District Officer Commanding Military District 4," 12 April 1945.
55 Kelly, "Prisoner of War Camps," 164.
56 Jeffrey A. Keshen, *Saints, Sinners, and Soldiers: Canada's Second World War* (Vancouver and Toronto: UBC Press, 2004), 68; Kelly, *Prisoner of War Camps,* 164-65.
57 Yves Bernard and Caroline Bergeron. *Trop loin de Berlin: Des prisonniers allemands au Canada (1939-1946)* (Sillery, QC: Éditions du Septentrion, 1995), 321.
58 LAC, RG-24, Reel: C-5365, File HQS 9139-4-40, "March 1946 Interpreter's Report," 5 April 1946.
59 Kelly, "Prisoner of War Camps," 189.
60 LAC, RG-24, Reel: C-5366, File HQS 9139-42, "May 1946 Intelligence Report," May 1946.
61 LAC, RG-24, Reel: C-5365, File HQS 9139-4-42, "February 1945 Intelligence Report," 4 March 1945.
62 Canada, *Orders and Instructions,* 18.
63 LAC, RG-24, Reel: C-5365, File HQS 9139-4-40, "October 1945 Interpreter's Report," 31 October 1945.
64 LAC, RG-24, Reel: C-5374, File HQS 7236-1-10-40, "State of POW Employed on Works Projects," May 4, 1946, 11 May 1946, and 25 May 1946; LAC, RG-24, Reel: C-5374, File HQS 7236-1-10-44, "State of POW Employed on Work Projects," 23 February 1946.
65 Translated by Martin Auger. See Bernard and Bergeron, *Trop loin de Berlin,* 322.
66 John Melady, *Escape from Canada! The Untold Story of German POWs in Canada, 1939-1945* (Toronto: Macmillan of Canada, 1981), 59.
67 Translated by Martin Auger. See Bernard and Bergeron, *Trop loin de Berlin,* 322.
68 LAC, RG-24, Reel: C-5365, File HQS 9139-4-40, "October 1945 Interpreter's Report," 31 October 1945.
69 LAC, RG-24, Reel: C-5365, File HQS 9139-4-40, "September 1945 Interpreter's Report," 30 September 1945; LAC, RG-24, Reel: C-5376, File HQS 7236-1-13-40, "Return of POWs and Internees on Strength of Camp No. 40 Who Are Quartered and Rationed outside Camp," 30 September 1945 and 30 November 1945.
70 LAC, RG-24, Reel: C-5365, File HQS 9139-4-40, "March 1946 Interpreter's Report," 5 April 1946; LAC, RG-24, Reel: C-5376, File HQS 7236-1-13-40, "Return of POWs and Internees on Strength of Camp No. 40 Who Are Quartered and Rationed outside Camp," 30 March 1946 and 31 May 1946.
71 LAC, RG-24, Reel: C-5376, File HQS 7236-1-13-42, "Return of POWs and Internees on Strength of Camp No. 42 Quartered and Rationed Outside Camp, 1944-1946," 30 September 1945, 30 October 1945, 1 December 1945, 2 January 1946, 31 January 1946, 28 February 1946, 31 March

1946, 30 April 1946, and 2 June 1946; LAC, RG-24, Reel: C-5365, File HQS 9139-4-42, "February 1946 Intelligence Report," February 1946.

72 LAC, RG-24, Reel: C-5374, File HQS 7236-1-10-44, "State of POW Employed on Work Projects," 23 February 1946.

73 Kelly, "Prisoner of War Camps," 75-76.

74 LAC, RG-24, Vol. 15,399, vol. 4 (October 1940), War Diary of Internment Camp Île-aux-Noix, 5 October 1940, 2.

75 Kelly, "Prisoner of War Camps," 78; Eric Koch, *Deemed Suspect: A Wartime Blunder* (Toronto: Methuen, 1980), 219.

76 LAC, RG-24, Vol. 15,400, vol. 13 (October 1941), War Diary of Internment Camp Sherbrooke, "Report by Major W.J.H. Ellwood (Camp Commandant)," 23 October 1941, Appendix 1, 32-33.

77 Kelly, "Prisoner of War Camps," 76-77; Eckehart J. Priebe, *Thank You, Canada: From Messerschmitt Pilot to Canadian Citizen* (West Vancouver: Condor, 1990), 183.

78 Kelly, "Prisoner of War Camps," 76-77; Priebe, *Thank You, Canada*, 83.

79 LAC, RG-24, Vol. 15,399, vol. 3 (December 1940), War Diary of Internment Camp Sherbrooke, 21 December 1940, 2.

80 LAC, RG-24, Vol. 15,399, vol. 10 (July 1941), War Diary of Internment Camp Sherbrooke, 20 July 1941, 5.

81 LAC, RG-24, Vol. 15,399, vol. 10 (July 1941), War Diary of Internment Camp Sherbrooke, 21 July 1941, 5.

82 Kelly, "Prisoner of War Camps," 79.

83 LAC, RG-24, Vol. 11,253, File 11-2-41, "Inspection Report," 25 June 1941.

84 LAC, RG-24, Vol. 15,399, vol. 10 (April 1941), War Diary of Internment Camp Île-aux-Noix, 15 April 1941, 2.

85 LAC, RG-24, Vol. 15,399, vol. 13 (July 1941), War Diary of Internment Camp Île-aux-Noix, 6 July 1941, 1.

86 LAC, RG-24, Vol. 15,397, vol. 4 (January 1941), War Diary of Internment Camp Farnham, 7 January 1941, 8 January 1941, 22 January 1941, and 27 January 1941, 2-10; LAC, RG-24, Vol. 15,397, vol. 5 (February 1941), War Diary of Internment Camp Farnham, 11 February 1941, 13 February 1941 and 24 February 1941, 2-7.

87 LAC, RG-24, Vol. 15,397, vol. 14 (November 1941), War Diary of Internment Camp Farnham, November 1941, Appendix 4.

88 LAC, RG-24, Vol. 11,249, File 9-5-3-40, "Report of the 7 April 1941 Red Cross visit to Camp Farnham," 2 July 1941.

89 LAC, RG-24, Vol. 11,253, File 11-2-40, "Inspection Report," 24 June 1941; LAC, RG-24, Vol. 15,397, vol. 14 (November 1941), War Diary of Internment Camp Farnham, November 1941, Appendix 4.

90 LAC, RG-24, Vol. 15,397, vol. 6 (March 1941), War Diary of Internment Camp Farnham, "Shop Rules and Regulations Governing Internal Discipline for the Successful Operation of the Factory by Major E.D.B. Kippen (Camp Commandant)," 3 March 1941, Appendix 3.

91 LAC, RG-24, Vol. 15,400, vol. 13 (October 1941), War Diary of Internment Camp Sherbrooke, "Camp Spokesman Statement," 15 October 1941, Appendix 2, 1-3.

92 LAC, RG-24, Vol. 15,400, vol. 13 (October 1941), War Diary of Internment Camp Sherbrooke, "Major W.J.H. Ellwood (Camp Commandant) to the District Officer Commanding Military District 4," 24 October 1941, Appendix 1, 36-37.

93 LAC, RG-24, Vol. 15,400, vol. 13 (October 1941), War Diary of Internment Camp Sherbrooke, 1 October 1941, 1.

94 LAC, RG-24, Vol. 15,400, vol. 13 (October 1941), War Diary of Internment Camp Sherbrooke, "Major W.J.H. Ellwood (Camp Commandant) to the District Officer Commanding Military District 4," 24 October 1941, Appendix 1, 36-37.

95 LAC, RG-24, Vol. 15,400, vol. 13 (October 1941), War Diary of Internment Camp Sherbrooke, 28 October 1941, 5.
96 Koch, *Deemed Suspect,* 230.
97 LAC, RG-24, Vol. 15,400, vol. 13 (October 1941), War Diary of Internment Camp Sherbrooke, "Major W.J.H. Ellwood (Camp Commandant) to the Camp Spokesman," 20 October 1941, Appendix 1, 28.
98 J. de N. Kennedy, *History of the Department of Munitions and Supply,* vol. 1 (Ottawa: Edmond Cloutier, 1950), 323-27.
99 LAC, MG-30, C 192, Vol. 3, "Interview of Helmut Pokorny," [1980s], 11-13, 22-23.
100 Ibid., 11-13.
101 LAC, RG-24, Vol. 15,397, vol. 12 (September 1941), War Diary of Internment Camp Farnham, 14 September 1941, 4.
102 Koch, *Deemed Suspect,* 230.
103 LAC, RG-24, Vol. 15,400, vol. 16 (January 1942), War Diary of Internment Camp Sherbrooke, 27 January 1942 and 30 January 1942, 7-8; LAC, RG-24, Vol. 15,400, vol. 17 (February 1942), War Diary of Internment Camp Sherbrooke, 2 February 1942, 1.
104 LAC, RG-24, Vol. 15,400, vol. 21 (June 1942), War Diary of Internment Camp Sherbrooke, "Refugees Leaving Camp," 26 June 1942, Appendix 2, 5; LAC, RG-24, Vol. 15,400, vol. 22 (July 1942), War Diary of Internment Camp Sherbrooke, "Nominal Roll of Refugees Leaving Camp," 7 July 1942 and 18 July 1942, Appendix 2, 2-6.
105 LAC, RG-24, Vol. 15,400, vol. 13 (September 1941), War Diary of Internment Camp Sherbrooke, "Major W.J.H. Ellwood (Camp Commandant) to District Officer Commanding Military District 4," 8 September 1941, Appendix 1, 18.
106 Ibid.
107 LAC, MG-30, C 192, Vol. 3, "Interview of Helmut Pokorny," [1980s], 10-11.
108 LAC, MG-30, C 192, Vol. 3, "Interview of Toni Obert," [1980s], 3.
109 LAC, RG-24, Vol. 15,399, vol. 18 (December 1941), War Diary of Internment Camp Île-aux-Noix, 18 December 1941, 3.
110 LAC, RG-24, Reel: C-5420, File HQS 7236-96-41, "Louis Fitch (President of the Canadian ORT Organization) to Lieutenant-Colonel R.S.W Fordham (Commissioner of Refugee Camps, Department of the Secretary of State)," 18 May 1942; LAC, RG-24, Reel: C-5420, File HQS 7236-96-41, "Report by V.I. Grossman (Executive Secretary of the Canadian ORT Organization)," 20 May 1943.
111 LAC, RG-24, Vol. 15,399, vol. 19 (January 1942), War Diary of Internment Camp Île-aux-Noix, 17 January 1942, 2.
112 LAC, RG-24, Vol. 15,399, vol. 23 (May 1942), War Diary of Internment Camp Île-aux-Noix, 29 May 1942, 4; LAC, RG-24, Reel: C-5420, File HQS 7236-96-41, "Colonel H.N. Streight (Director of Prisoners of War) to the Adjutant-General," 1 November 1943.
113 LAC, RG-24, Reel: C-5420, File HQS 7236-96-41, "Louis Fitch (President of the Canadian ORT Organization) to Lieutenant-Colonel R.S.W Fordham (Commissioner of Refugee Camps, Department of the Secretary of State)," 18 May 1942.
114 LAC, RG-24, Reel: C-5420, File HQS 7236-96-41, "Major-General Howard Kennedy (Quartermaster-General) to the Deputy Minister of National Defence," 9 November 1943.
115 LAC, RG-24, Reel: C-5420, File HQS 7236-96-41, "Louis Fitch (President of the Canadian ORT Organization) to Lieutenant-Colonel R.S.W Fordham (Commissioner of Refugee Camps, Department of the Secretary of State)," 18 May 1942.
116 LAC, RG-24, Reel: C-5420, File HQS 7236-96-41, "V.I. Grossman (Executive Secretary of the Canadian ORT Organization) to Lieutenant-Colonel R.S.W. Fordham (Commissioner of Refugee Camps, Department of the Secretary of State)," 22 September 1942.

117 LAC, RG-24, Reel: C-5420, File HQS 7236-96-41, "Colonel H.N. Streight (Director of Prisoners of War) to Director of Works and Construction (National Defence Headquarters)," 23 March 1943.

118 LAC, RG-24, Vol. 15,399, vol. 34 (April 1943), War Diary of Internment Camp Île-aux-Noix, 27 April 1943, 4.

119 LAC, RG-24, Reel: C-5420, File HQS 7236-96-41, "V.I. Grossman (Executive Secretary of the Canadian ORT Organization) to Major J. Renaud (District Officer Commanding Military District 4)," 21 September 1943; LAC, RG-24, Reel: C-5420, File HQS 7236-96-41, "Colonel H.N. Streight (Director of Prisoners of War) to the Adjutant-General," 1 November 1943.

120 LAC, RG-24, Reel: C-5420, File HQS 7236-96-41, "Report by V.I. Grossman (Executive Secretary of the Canadian ORT Organization)," 20 May 1943.

121 Kelly, "Prisoner of War Camps," 79.

122 Bernard and Bergeron, *Trop loin de Berlin,* 241; Kelly, "Prisoner of War Camps," 162.

123 Canada, DND, *Report of the Department of National Defence for the Fiscal Year Ending 31 March 1944* (Ottawa: Edmond Cloutier, 1944), 39; Canada, DND, *Report of the Department of National Defence for the Fiscal Year Ending 31 March 1945* (Ottawa: Edmond Cloutier, 1946), 52.

124 David J. Carter, *Behind Canadian Barbed Wire: Alien, Refugee and Prisoner of War Camps in Canada, 1914-1946* (Calgary: Tumbleweed, 1980), 135; Bill Waiser, *Park Prisoners: The Untold Story of Western Canada's National Parks, 1915-1946* (Saskatoon: Fifth House, 1995), 220. See also Stefania H. Cepuch, "'Our Guests Are Busy': The Internment and Labour of German Prisoners of War in Ontario, 1940-1946" (MA thesis, Queen's University, 1992).

125 LAC, RG-24, Vol. 15,400, vol. 18 (March 1942), War Diary of Internment Camp Sherbrooke, "Works Program," March 1942, Appendix 1, 36.

126 LAC, RG-24, Reel: C-5420, File HQS 7236-96-42, "Lieutenant-Colonel W.D. Graham (Camp Commandant) to the Director of Prisoners of War," 3 July 1943.

127 LAC, RG-24, Reel: C-5416, File HQS 7236-94-6-42, "May 1944 Intelligence Report," May 1944.

128 LAC, RG-24, Reel: C-5416, File HQS 7236-94-6-42, "June 1944 Intelligence Report," June 1944.

129 LAC, RG-24, Reel: C-5416, File HQS 7236-94-6-42, "May 1944 Intelligence Report," May 1944.

130 Ibid.

131 Translated by Martin Auger. See Alfred Desrochers, "Une journée avec les prisonniers allemands du camp Newington," *La Tribune de Sherbrooke,* 29 October 1945.

132 LAC, RG-24, Reel: C-5365, File HQS 9139-4-42, "January 1945 Intelligence Report," 4 February 1945; LAC, RG-24, Reel: C-5365, File HQS 9139-4-42, "February 1945 Intelligence Report," 4 March 1945; LAC, RG-24, Reel: C-5365, File HQS 9139-4-42, "March 1945 Intelligence Report," 2 April 1945; LAC, RG-24, Reel: C-5365, File HQS 9139-4-42, "April 1945 Intelligence Report," 3 May 1945; LAC, RG-24, Reel: C-5365, File HQS 9139-4-42, "May 1945 Intelligence Report," 15 June 1945.

133 Canada, DND, *Report of the Department of National Defence for the Fiscal Year Ending 31 March 1944,* 38-39.

134 Canada, DND, *Report of the Department of National Defence for the Fiscal Year Ending 31 March 1945,* 52.

135 LAC, RG-24, Reel: C-5365, File HQS 9139-4-42, "February 1946 Intelligence Report," February 1946.

136 LAC, RG-24, Vol. 15,401, vol. 68 (May 1946), War Diary of Internment Camp Sherbrooke, 9 May 1946, 1.

137 Canada, *Red Cross and Prisoners,* 96-97.

138 Kelly, "Prisoner of War Camps," 118-19.

139 Ibid., 120.

140 LAC, RG-24, Vol. 15,397, vol. 6 (March 1941), War Diary of Internment Camp Farnham, "Memorandum Covering the Operations of the Farnham Internment Trust Account," March

1941, Appendix 4, 2; LAC, RG-24, Vol. 15,397, vol. 6 (March 1941), War Diary of Internment Camp Farnham, 5 March 1941, 2; LAC, RG-24, Vol. 15,398, vol. 27 (December 1942), War Diary of Internment Camp Farnham, 3 December 1942, 2.

141 LAC, MG-30, C 192, Vol. 3, "Interview of Harry Greenfield," [1980s], 16.

142 LAC, RG-24, Vol. 15,397, vol. 6 (March 1941), War Diary of Internment Camp Farnham, "Memorandum Covering the Operations of the Farnham Internment Trust Account," March 1941, Appendix 4, 1-3.

143 Canada, *Red Cross and Prisoners,* 92-93.

144 Priebe, *Thank You, Canada,* 185-86.

145 LAC, RG-24, Vol. 15,397, vol. 6 (March 1941), War Diary of Internment Camp Farnham, "Memorandum Regarding the Procedure Followed in Operating the Camp 'A' Internees Canteen, Camp Farnham," March 1941, Appendix 5, 1.

146 Canada, *Orders and Instructions,* 26.

147 Ibid., 30; LAC, RG-24, Vol. 15,397, vol. 6 (March 1941), War Diary of Internment Camp Farnham, "Memorandum Regarding the Procedure Followed in Operating the Camp 'A' Internees Canteen, Camp Farnham," March 1941, Appendix 5, 1.

148 Canada, *Orders and Instructions,* 30.

149 Priebe, *Thank You, Canada,* 185-86.

150 Canada, *Orders and Instructions,* 31.

151 Ibid., 20.

152 Ibid., 19.

153 LAC, RG-24, Vol. 15,399, vol. 2 (August 1940), War Diary of Internment Camp Île-aux-Noix, 4 August 1940, 2; LAC, RG-24, Vol. 15,399, vol. 2 (November 1940), War Diary of Internment Camp Sherbrooke, 2 November 1940, 1.

154 Canada, *Orders and Instructions,* 21-25. See also LAC, RG-24, Vol. 15,399, vol. 2 (August 1940), War Diary of Internment Camp Île-aux-Noix, 4 August 1940, 2; LAC, RG-24, Vol. 15,399, vol. 5 (February 1941), War Diary of Internment Camp Sherbrooke, 22 February 1941, 1; LAC, RG-24, Reel: C-5398, File HQS 7236-81-40, "Inventory Stock on Hand, POW Canteen, Camp Farnham," 30 June 1942; LAC, RG-24, Reel: C-5398, File HQS 7236-81-42, "Inventory Stock on Hand, Camp Sherbrooke Canteen," 31 August 1944; LAC, RG-24, Reel: C-5398, File HQS 7236-81-40, "Inventory Stock on Hand POW Canteen, Camp Farnham," 31 August 1945; LAC, RG-24, Reel: C-5398, File HQS 7236-81-40, "General Expenses List," 20 May 1946.

155 Canada, *Orders and Instructions,* 19.

156 LAC, RG-24, Reel: C-5398, File HQS 7236-81-42, "Abstract of Receipts and Disbursements for the Canteen of Camp Sherbrooke," 31 August 1944; LAC, RG-24, Reel: C-5398, File HQS 7236-81-40, "Accounts Payable for the Current Month of May 1946," May 1946.

157 LAC, RG-24, Reel: C-5398, File HQS 7236-81-40, "Lieutenant-Colonel A.W. De Wolf (Camp Commandant) to Director of Prisoners of War," 23 November 1944.

158 LAC, RG-24, Reel: C-5398, File HQS 7236-81-40, "Colonel H.W. Streight (Director of Prisoners of War) to Lieutenant- Colonel A.W. De Wolf (Camp Commandant)," 24 November 1944.

159 LAC, RG-24, Reel: C-5398, File HQS 7236-81-40, "Camp Spokesman to Ernest L. Maag (Delegate in Canada for the International Committee of the Red Cross)," 19 April 1943.

160 LAC, RG-24, Reel: C-5398, File HQS 7236-81-42, "Abstract of Receipts and Disbursements for the Canteen of Camp Sherbrooke," 31 August 1945.

161 Canada, *Orders and Instructions,* 28-29.

162 LAC, RG-24, Vol. 15,397, vol. 6 (March 1941), War Diary of Internment Camp Farnham, "Memorandum Regarding the Procedure Followed in Operating the Camp 'A' Internees Canteen, Camp Farnham," March 1941, Appendix 5, 2.

163 LAC, RG-24, Reel: C-5398, File HQS 7236-81-40, "Colonel H.N. Streight (Director of Prisoners of War) to Ernest L. Maag (Delegate in Canada for the International Committee of the Red Cross," 3 February 1945.

164 Canada, *Orders and Instructions,* 30; See also LAC, RG-24, Reel: C-5398, File HQS 7236-81-40, "Major-General K.G. Weeks (Adjutant-General) to District Officer Commanding Military District 4," 30 November 1946.

165 LAC, RG-24, Reel: C-5398, File HQS 7236-81-40, "Inventory Stock on Hand, POW Canteen, Camp Farnham," 30 June 1942.

166 LAC, RG-24, Reel: C-5398, File HQS 7236-81-40, "Inventory Stock on Hand, POW Canteen," 31 March 1946; LAC, RG-24, Reel: C-5398, File HQS 7236-81-40, "Inventory Stock on Hand, POW Canteen," 30 April 1946.

167 LAC, RG-24, Reel: C-8436, File HQS 9139-2-40, "Major G.H. Cuning (A/Camp Commandant) to District Officer Commanding Military District 4," 22 December 1944.

168 LAC, RG-24, Reel: C-5416, File HQS 7236-94-6-42, "November 1944 Intelligence Report," November 1944.

169 Ibid.; LAC, RG-24, Reel: C-5419, File HQS 7236-94-14-40, "Report on Camp Farnham by Lieutenant-Colonel A.W. De Wolf (Camp Commandant)," January 1945; LAC, RG-24, Reel: C-5365, File HQS 9139-4-40, "May 1945 Intelligence Report," 31 May 1945; LAC, RG-24, Reel: C-5365, File HQS 9139-4-42, "January 1946 Intelligence Report," January 1946.

170 LAC, RG-24, Reel: C-8436, File HQS 9139-2-44, "Lieutenant-Colonel E.D.B. Kippen (Camp Commandant) to District Officer Commanding Military District 4," 17 August 1944.

171 Koch, *Deemed Suspect,* 156.

172 Canada, *Orders and Instructions,* 67; LAC, RG-24, Vol. 15,400, vol. 47 (August 1944), War Diary of Internment Camp Sherbrooke, "Camp Orders," 31 August 1944, Appendix 1, 27; LAC, RG-24, Reel: C-5416, File HQS 7236-94-6-42, "November 1944 Intelligence Report," November 1944; LAC, RG-24, Vol. 15,404, vol. 35 (November 1945), War Diary of Internment Camp Grande Ligne, "Camp Daily Orders," 22 November 1945, Appendix 1, 21.

173 LAC, RG-24, Reel: C-5419, File HQS 7236-94-14-40, "Report on Camp Farnham by Lieutenant-Colonel A.W. De Wolf (Camp Commandant)," January 1945.

174 Canada, *Orders and Instructions,* 20.

175 LAC, RG-24, Vol. 15,397, vol. 6 (March 1941), War Diary of Internment Camp Farnham, "Memorandum Regarding the Procedure Followed in Operating the Camp 'A' Internees Canteen, Camp Farnham," March 1941, Appendix 5, 2.

176 Bernard and Bergeron, *Trop loin de Berlin,* 22; Canada, *Orders and Instructions,* 32.

177 LAC, RG-24, Reel: C-5398, File HQS 7236-81-40, "Deputy Minister of National Defence to Carl Müller (United States zone in Germany)," 11 August 1948.

Chapter 5: Educational Programs

1 Canada, *Red Cross and Prisoners of War Conventions* (Ottawa: Edmond Cloutier, 1942), 94-95.

2 Canada, *Orders and Instructions, Internment Camps* (Ottawa: Department of National Defence, 1945), 66.

3 Library and Archives Canada [LAC], MG-30, C 192, Vol. 3, "Interview of John Newmark," [1980s], 11.

4 Eric Koch, *Deemed Suspect: A Wartime Blunder* (Toronto: Methuen, 1980), 146.

5 LAC, MG-30, C 192, Vol. 3, "Interview of Walter Loevinsohn," [1980s], 13.

6 LAC, RG-24, Vol. 11,249, File 9-5-3-41, "Report of the 28 August 1940 visit to Camp Île-aux-Noix by Ernest L. Maag (Delegate in Canada for the International Committee of the Red Cross)," September 1940.

7 LAC, MG-30, C 192, Vol. 3, "Interview of Emil Fackenheim," [1980s], 6-7. See also Paula Jean Draper, "The 'Camp Boys,'" in *Enemies Within: Italian and Other Internees in Canada and Abroad,* ed. Franca Iacovetta, Roberto Perin, and Angelo Principe (Toronto: University of Toronto Press, 2000), 178-79; Mario Duliani, *La ville sans femmes* (Montreal: Société des Éditions Pascal, 1945), 200-1.

8 Duliani, *La ville sans femmes,* 201.
9 LAC, MG-30, C 192, Vol. 3, "Interview of Walter Loevinsohn," [1980s], 13.
10 LAC, MG-30, C 192, Vol. 3, "Interview of Thomas Gold," [1980s], 7.
11 LAC, MG-30, C 192, Vol. 3, "Interview of William Heckscher," [1980s], 27-5, 27-6.
12 LAC, RG-24, Vol. 15,397, vol. 2 (November 1940), War Diary of Internment Camp Farnham, 7 November 1940, 3.
13 Koch, *Deemed Suspect,* 151; LAC, MG-30, C 192, Vol. 3, "Interview of Emil Fackenheim," [1980s], 6-7; LAC, MG-30, C 192, Vol. 3, "Interview of Fred Schlessinger," [1980s], 34.
14 LAC, RG-24, Vol. 11,249, File 9-5-3-40, "Report of the 26 November 1940 Red Cross visit to Camp Farnham by Ernest L. Maag (Delegate in Canada for the International Committee of the Red Cross)," 26 November 1940. See also Paula Jean Draper, "The Accidental Immigrants," Part 2, *Canadian Jewish Historical Society Journal,* 2, 2 (1978): 86-87.
15 Koch, *Deemed Suspect,* 150.
16 LAC, RG-24, Vol. 11,253, File 11-2-41, "Inspection Report," 25 June 1941.
17 LAC, RG-24, Vol. 15,399, vol. 15 (September 1941), War Diary of Internment Camp Île-aux-Noix, 7 September 1941 and 18 September 1941, 1, 3; LAC, MG-30, C 192, Vol. 3, "Interview of Josef Kates," [1980s], 17-20.
18 LAC, MG-30, C 192, Vol. 3, "Interview of Josef Kates," [1980s], 17-20.
19 LAC, RG-24, Reel: C-5401, File HQS 7236-83-6-41, "Lieutenant-Colonel R.S.W. Fordham to Major Bruce Thompson (Camp Commandant)," 1 April 1943.
20 LAC, RG-24, Vol. 15,399, vol. 22 (April 1942), War Diary of Internment Camp Île-aux-Noix, 13 April 1942, 21 April 1942, and 28 April 1942, 2-4.
21 LAC, MG-30, C 192, Vol. 3, "Interview of William Heckscher," [1980s], 27-8.
22 Koch, *Deemed Suspect,* 151-52.
23 Ibid.
24 John O. Buffinga, "The War Prisoners' Aid of the YMCA and Hermann Boeschenstein's Role as an Ethnic Mediator (1943-1947)." *Canadian Ethnic Studies* 20, 2 (1988): 66.
25 LAC, RG-24, Reel: C-5400, File HQS 7236-83-3-42, "Rolf Hertsel (Prisoner of War) to the Secretary (University of Saskatchewan)," 30 June 1944; LAC, RG-24, Reel: C-5400, File HQS 7236-83-3-40, "Lieutenant-Colonel A.W. De Wolf (Camp Commandant) to Director of Prisoners of War," 8 December 1944.
26 LAC, RG-24, Reel: C-5413, File HQS 7236-91-1-44, "E.L. Maag (Delegate in Canada for the International Committee of the Red Cross)," 21 July 1943.
27 LAC, RG-24, Reel: C-5416, File HQS 7236-94-6-44, "November 1943 Intelligence Summary," November 1943.
28 LAC, RG-24, Reel: C-5400, File HQS 7236-83-3-44, "Report of Camp Spokesman Schlichting," 1 May 1944.
29 LAC, RG-24, Reel: C-5416, File HQS 7236-94-6-44, "October 1943 Intelligence Summary," 5 November 1943; LAC, RG-24, Reel: C-5416, File HQS 7236-94-6-44, "November 1943 Intelligence Summary," November 1943; LAC, RG-24, Reel: C-5400, File HQS 7236-83-3-44, "Report of Camp Spokesman Schlichting," 1 May 1944.
30 LAC, RG-24, Reel: C-5416, File HQS 7236-94-6-44, "November 1943 Intelligence Summary," November 1943.
31 LAC, RG-24, Reel: C-5416, File HQS 7236-94-6-44, "October 1943 Intelligence Summary," 5 November 1943; LAC, RG-24, Reel: C-5416, File HQS 7236-94-6-44, "November 1943 Intelligence Summary," November 1943.
32 LAC, RG-24, Reel: C-5400, File HQS 7236-83-3-44, "Report of Camp Spokesman Schlichting," 1 May 1944.
33 LAC, RG-24, Reel: C-5400, File HQS 7236-83-3-42, "Dale Brown (European Student Relief Fund) to Carl Witt (Camp Spokesman)," 27 April 1944.
34 Ibid.

35 Canada, *Orders and Instructions,* 66.

36 LAC, RG-24, Reel: C-5400, File HQS 7236-83-3-42, "Alfred Pauli (Camp Spokesman) to Dale Brown (European Student Relief Fund)," 5 October 1944; LAC, RG-24, Reel: C-5410, File HQS 7236-88-5-45, "Lieutenant-Colonel B.B.W. Minard (Camp Commandant) to the Director of Prisoners of War," 20 July 1945; LAC, RG-24, Reel: C-5401, File HQS 7236-83-6-40, "Colonel Jay (Camp Spokesman) to H. Boeschenstein (Director in Canada for the War Prisoners' Aid of the YMCA)," 28 November 1945. See also Buffinga, "The War Prisoners' Aid," 59.

37 LAC, RG-24, Reel: C-8436, File HQS 9139-1-45, "List of Papers Subscribed to by POW Canteen," August 1945.

38 LAC, RG-24, Reel: C-5401, File HQS 7236-83-6-40, "Colonel Jay (Camp Spokesman) to H. Boeschenstein (Director in Canada for the War Prisoner's Aid of the YMCA)," 28 November 1945.

39 LAC, RG-24, Reel: C-5400, File HQS 7236-83-3-42, "Alfred Pauli (Camp Spokesman) to McGill University (Redpath Library)," 10 October 1944.

40 LAC, RG-24, Reel: C-8436, File HQS 9139-1-42, "Department of National Defence Report," 6 September 1944.

41 LAC, RG-24, Reel: C-5400, File HQS 7236-83-3-42, "Alfred Pauli (Camp Spokesman) to the Travelling Library Department (Macdonald College)," 12 July 1944.

42 Ibid.

43 LAC, RG-24, Reel: C-5400, File HQS 7236-83-3-44, "Lieutenant-Colonel E.D.B. Kippen (Camp Commandant) to the District Officer Commanding Military District 4," 18 August 1944.

44 LAC, RG-24, Reel: C-5400, File HQS 7236-83-3-44, "Colonel H.N. Streight (Director of Prisoners of War) to Lieutenant-Colonel E.D.B. Kippen (Camp Commandant)," 12 September 1944. See also Canada, *Orders and Instructions,* 60.

45 LAC, RG-24, Reel: C-5400, File HQS 7236-83-3-44, "Colonel H.N. Streight (Director of Prisoners of War) to Dale Brown (European Student Relief Fund)," 2 June 1944; LAC, RG-24, Reel: C-5410, File HQS 7236-88-5-45, "Lieutenant-Colonel B.B.W. Minard (Camp Commandant) to the Director of Prisoners of War," 20 July 1945.

46 Canada, *Orders and Instructions,* 58. See also LAC, RG-24, Reel: C-5400, File HQS 7236-83-3-42, "Colonel H.N. Streight (Director of Prisoners of War) to Dale Brown (Secretary of the European Student Relief Fund)," 19 February 1945.

47 LAC, RG-24, Reel: C-5410, File HQS 7236-88-5-42, "Lieutenant-Colonel H.D. Hedley (Camp Commandant) to Director of Prisoners of War," 19 November 1945.

48 LAC, RG-24, Reel: C-5410, File HQS 7236-88-5-42, "Lieutenant-Colonel H.W. Pearson (A/Director Prisoners of War) to Camp Commandant," 5 February 1946.

49 LAC, RG-24, Reel: C-5400, File HQS 7236-83-3-42, "Alfred Pauli (Camp Spokesman) to the Travelling Library Department (Macdonald College)," 12 July 1944.

50 Eckehart Priebe, *Thank You, Canada: From Messerschmitt Pilot to Canadian Citizen* (West Vancouver: Condor, 1990), 142.

51 LAC, RG-24, Reel: C-5365, File HQS 9139-4-44, "September 1945 Intelligence Report," 4 October 1945.

52 LAC, RG-24, Reel: C-5365, File HQS 9139-4-45, "November 1945 Intelligence Report," 2 December 1945.

53 LAC, RG-24, Vol. 15,397, vol. 24 (September 1942), War Diary of Internment Camp Farnham, 12 September 1942, 4; LAC, RG-24, Vol. 6583, File 3-3-5 (40), "Jerome Davis (YMCA) to Major H.W. Pearson (Internment Operations)," 19 January 1943.

54 Buffinga, "The War Prisoners' Aid," 59.

55 LAC, RG-24, Reel: C-5401, File HQS 7236-83-6-40, "Colonel Jay (Camp Spokesman) to H. Boeschenstein (Director in Canada for the War Prisoners' Aid of the YMCA)," 29 August 1945.

56 LAC, RG-24, Vol. 15,399, vol. 6 (March 1941), War Diary of Internment Camp Sherbrooke, 25 March 1941, 28 March 1941, and 29 March 1941, 2-3; LAC, RG-24, Vol. 15,399, vol. 10 (April 1941), War Diary of Internment Camp Île-aux-Noix, 30 April 1941, 4.

57 LAC, RG-24, Vol. 6583, File 3-3-5 (40), "K. Krieger (Camp Leader) to Dr. Davis (YMCA)," 30 August 1942; LAC, RG-24, Reel: C-5401, File HQS 7236-83-6-40, "Lieutenant-Colonel H.W. Pearson (Director of Prisoners of War) to Dr. H. Boeschenstein (Director in Canada for the War Prisoners' Aid of the YMCA)," 24 April 1946.

58 LAC, RG-24, Reel: C-5396, File HQS 7236-79, "Lieutenant-Colonel E.D.B. Kippen (Camp Commandant) to Director of Prisoners of War," 5 August 1944.

59 LAC, RG-24, Reel: C-5365, File HQS 9139-4-45, "September 1945 Intelligence Report," September 1945.

60 LAC, RG-24, Vol. 15,400, vol. 22 (July 1942), War Diary of Internment Camp Sherbrooke, "Camp Orders," 7 July 1942, Appendix 1, 8.

61 LAC, RG-24, Vol. 15,400, vol. 22 (July 1942), War Diary of Internment Camp Sherbrooke, "Camp Orders," 8 July 1942, Appendix 1, 9.

62 LAC, RG-24, Vol. 15,400, vol. 22 (July 1942), War Diary of Internment Camp Sherbrooke, "Camp Orders," 28 July 1942, Appendix 1, 29.

63 LAC, RG-24, Vol. 15,400, vol. 22 (July 1942), War Diary of Internment Camp Sherbrooke, "Camp Orders," 29 July 1942, Appendix 1, 30.

64 LAC, RG-24, Vol. 15,400, vol. 24 (September 1942), War Diary of Internment Camp Sherbrooke, "Camp Orders," 4 September 1942, Appendix 1, 4.

65 LAC, RG-24, Vol. 15,400, vol. 24 (September 1942), War Diary of Internment Camp Sherbrooke, "Camp Orders," 22 September 1942, Appendix 1, 12.

66 LAC, RG-24, Vol. 15,400, vol. 25 (October 1942), War Diary of Internment Camp Sherbrooke, "Camp Orders," 12 October 1942, Appendix 1, 9.

67 LAC, RG-24, Vol. 15,400, vol. 26 (November 1942), War Diary of Internment Camp Sherbrooke, "Camp Orders," 17 November 1942, Appendix 1, 9.

68 Ron Robin, *The Barbed-Wire College: Reeducating German POWs in the United States during World War II* (Princeton, NJ: Princeton University Press, 1995), 109.

69 For more information on American, British, and Soviet efforts to re-educate German prisoners of war, see Henry Faulk, *Group Captives: The Re-education of German Prisoners of War in Britain, 1945-1948* (London: Chatto and Windus, 1977); Nicholas Pronay and Keith Wilson, eds., *The Political Re-education of Germany and Her Allies* (London: Croom Helm, 1985); Matthias Reiss, "The Nucleus of a New German Ideology? The Re-education of German Prisoners of War in the United States during World War II," in *Prisoners of War, Prisoners of Peace: Captivity, Homecoming and Memory in World War II,* ed. Bob Moore and Barbara Hately-Broad (Oxford: Berg, 2005), 91-102; Robin, *Barbed-Wire College*; Arthur L. Smith Jr., *The War for the German Mind: Re-educating Hitler's Soldiers* (Providence, RI: Berghahn Books, 1996).

On the Canadian re-education program, consult C.R. Kilford, "The Re-education of German Prisoners of War in Canada during World War II," Master of Defence Studies Research Project, Canadian Forces College, 2003.

70 Jonathan Vance, *Encyclopedia of Prisoners of War and Internment* (Santa Barbara: ABC-CLIO, 2000), 240.

71 Smith Jr., *The War for the German Mind,* viii.

72 Vance, ed., *Encyclopedia,* 240.

73 Andrew Rettig, "A De-programming Curriculum: Allied Reeducation and the Canadian-American Psychological Warfare Program for German POWs, 1943-47," *American Review of Canadian Studies* 29, 4 (1999): 593.

74 Robin, *Barbed-Wire College,* 172.

75 Rettig, "A De-programming Curriculum," 593.
76 Department of National Defence, Directorate of History and Heritage (DHH), 193.009 (D29), Vol. 28, "The Re-education of Prisoners of War," 15 May 1943.
77 Ibid.
78 Smith Jr., *The War for the German Mind,* 23.
79 Rettig, "A De-programming Curriculum," 599.
80 Smith Jr., *The War for the German Mind,* 23.
81 DHH, 193.009 (D29), Vol. 28, "Colonel W.W. Murray (Director of Military Intelligence) to the Chief of the General Staff," 15 November 1943.
82 Smith Jr., *The War for the German Mind,* 24.
83 DHH, 193.009 (D29), Vol. 28, "The Re-Education of Prisoners of War," 15 May 1943.
84 Smith Jr., *The War for the German Mind,* 24.
85 Don Page, "Tommy Stone and Psychological Warfare in World War Two: Transforming a POW Liability into an Asset," *Journal of Canadian Studies* 16, 3-4 (1981): 116.
86 Rettig, "A De-programming Curriculum," 603; Smith Jr., *The War for the German Mind,* 21.
87 LAC, RG-24, Reel: C-5365, File HQS 9139-4-42, "May 1945 Intelligence Report," 15 June 1945.
88 Martin F. Auger, "L'université barbelée: La rééducation de prisonniers de guerre allemands dans les camps d'internement du sud du Québec, 1943-1946," (Ottawa: 54e Congrès de l'Institut d'Histoire de l'Amérique Française [IHAF], 27 October 2001).
89 LAC, RG-24, Reel: C-5421, File HQS 7236-99, "Lieutenant-Colonel H.W. Pearson (Director of Prisoners of War) to the Adjutant-General (Camp Sorel)," 25 September 1945.
90 LAC, RG-24, Reel: C-5419, File HQS 7236-94-14-45, "Assessment Camp Sorel," 3 May 1945; LAC, RG-24, Reel: C-5366, File HQS 9139-45, "Confidential Report on Camp Sorel by Lieutenant-Colonel R.G. Wygard (MI7)," 15 February 1946.
91 LAC, RG-24, Reel: C-5419, File HQS 7236-94-14-45, "Assessment Camp Sorel," 3 May 1945; LAC, RG-24, Reel: C-5366, File HQS 9139-45, "Confidential Report on Camp Sorel by Lieutenant-Colonel R.G. Wygard (MI7)," 15 February 1946.
92 LAC, RG-24, Reel: C-5421, File HQS 7236-99, "Colonel E.D.B. Kippen (Commandant of Camp Lethbridge) to Director of Prisoners of War," 5 September 1945.
93 LAC, RG-24, Reel: C-5421, File HQS 7236-99, "Colonel H.N. Streight (Director of Prisoners of War) to the Officer Commanding No. 8 Company of the Veterans Guard of Canada," 5 July 1945; LAC, RG-24, Reel: C-5421, File HQS 7236-99, "Colonel E.D.B. Kippen (Commandant of Camp Lethbridge) to Headquarters Military District 13," 5 June 1945; LAC, RG-24, Reel: C-5421, File HQS 7236-99, "Colonel H.N. Streight (Director of Prisoners of War) to Colonel E.D.B. Kippen (Commandant of Camp Lethbridge)," 13 June 1945.
94 LAC, RG-24, Reel: C-5419, File HQS 7236-94-14-45, "Assessment Camp Sorel," 3 May 1945.
95 LAC, RG-24, Reel: C-5366, File HQS 9139-9, "Baron von Schlothein (Prisoner of War) to Lieutenant-Colonel B.B.W. Minard (Camp Commandant)," 17 October 1945.
96 Robin, *Barbed-Wire College,* 151-52.
97 LAC, RG-24, Reel: C-5365, File HQS 9139-4-45, "July 1945 Interpreter's Report," 1 August 1945.
98 LAC, RG-24, Reel: C-5366, File HQS 9139-45, "Director of Military Intelligence to Deputy Chief of the General Staff," 27 November 1945.
99 Smith Jr., *The War for the German Mind,* 64.
100 LAC, RG-24, Reel: C-5421, File HQS 7236-99, "Colonel H.N. Streight (Director of Prisoners of War) to Colonel E.D.B. Kippen (Commandant Camp Lethbridge)," 13 June 1945.
101 LAC, RG-24, Reel: C-5421, File HQS 7236-99, "Colonel H.N. Streight (Director of Prisoners of War) to the Officer Commanding No. 8 Company of the Veterans Guard of Canada," 5 July 1945.
102 LAC, RG-24, Reel: C-5366, File HQS 9139-45, "Concise Assessment of POW in Special Camp Sorel," 15 February 1946.

103 Ibid.
104 LAC, RG-24, Reel: C-5421, File HQS 7236-99, "Major-General E.J. Renaud (District Officer Commanding Military District 4) to the Secretary (Department of National Defence)," 17 November 1945.
105 Smith Jr., *The War for the German Mind*, 64.
106 LAC, RG-24, Reel: C-5365, File HQS 9139-4-40, "Lieutenant-Colonel A.W. De Wolf (Camp Commandant) to District Officer Commanding Military District 4," 7 July 1945.
107 LAC, RG-24, Reel: C-5421, File HQS 7236-99, "Brigadier V.C. Thackray (Commandant of Camp Petawawa) to National Defence Headquarters (NDHQ)," 15 June 1945.
108 LAC, RG-24, Reel: C-5366, File HQS 9139-45, "Confidential Report on Camp Sorel by Lieutenant-Colonel R.G. Wygard (MI7)," 15 February 1946.
109 LAC, RG-24, Reel: C-8436, File HQS 9139-1-45, "Director of Military Intelligence to the Secretary (Prisoners of War Committee)," 7 November 1945.
110 LAC, RG-24, Reel: C-5366, File HQS 9139-9, "Report of the Counter Propaganda Committee," 1945.
111 Ibid.; LAC, RG-24, Reel: C-8436, File HQS 9139-1-45, "Synopsis of Re-Educational Pamphlets by the Director of Military Intelligence," 6 February 1945.
112 LAC, RG-24, Reel: C-5419, File HQS 7236-94-14-45, "Assessment Camp Sorel," 3 May 1945.
113 Ibid.
114 LAC, RG-24, Reel: C-5365, File HQS 9139-4-45, "January 1946 Intelligence Report," 31 January 1946.
115 LAC, RG-24, Reel: C-8436, File HQS 9139-1-45, "Report: Stock and Consumption for Printing Supplies," 16 January 1946.
116 LAC, RG-24, Reel: C-5366, File HQS 9139-45, "Confidential Report on Camp Sorel by Lieutenant-Colonel R.G. Wygard (MI7)," 15 February 1946.
117 LAC, RG-24, Reel: C-5365, File HQS 9139-4-45, "February 1946 Intelligence Report," 7 March 1946.
118 LAC, RG-24, Reel: C-5365, File HQS 9139-4-45, "August 1945 Intelligence Report," August 1945.
119 LAC, RG-24, Reel: C-8436, File HQS 9139-1-45, "German Books," September 1945.
120 LAC, RG-24, Reel: C-5365, File HQS 9139-4-45, "November 1945 Intelligence Report," 2 December 1945.
121 LAC, RG-24, Reel: C-5366, File HQS 9139-40, "Director of Military Intelligence to Director of Prisoners of War," 3 April 1945.
122 LAC, RG-24, Reel: C-5366, File HQS 9139-40, "Lieutenant-Colonel G.F. Armstrong (Camp Commandant) to the District Officer Commanding Military District 4 for transmission to MI7 and NI3," 8 November 1945.
123 LAC, RG-24, Reel: C-5366, File HQS 9139-40, "Lieutenant-Colonel G.F. Armstrong (Camp Commandant) to the District Officer Commanding Military District 4 for transmission to MI7 and NI3," 8 November 1945.
124 LAC, RG-24, Reel: C-5365, File HQS 9139-4-40, "July 1945 Intelligence Report," 1 August 1945; LAC, RG-24, Reel: C-5365, File HQS 9139-4-40, "Camp Commandant De Wolf to District Officer Commanding Military District 4," 20 March 1945.
125 LAC, RG-24, Reel: C-5419, File HQS 7236-94-14-45, "Assessment Camp Sorel," 3 May 1945.
126 Ibid.
127 LAC, RG-24, Reel: C-5365, File HQS 9139-4-40, "April 1945 Intelligence Report," 1 May 1945.
128 Ibid.
129 LAC, RG-24, Reel: C-5365, File HQS 9139-4-40, "July 1945 Intelligence Report," 1 August 1945.
130 Ibid.
131 LAC, RG-24, Reel: C-5365, File HQS 9139-4-40, "Camp Constitution for POW, Camp 40, Canada," 11 August 1945.

132 LAC, RG-24, Reel: C-5365, File HQS 9139-4-40, "Lieutenant-Colonel A.W. De Wolf (Camp Commandant) to District Officer Commanding Military District 4," 11 August 1945.
133 LAC, RG-24, Reel: C-5365, File HQS 9139-4-40, "January 1946 Intelligence Report," 2 February 1946; LAC, RG-24, Reel: C-5365, File HQS 9139-4-40, "February 1946 Intelligence Report," 6 March 1946.
134 LAC, RG-24, Reel: C-5365, File HQS 9139-4-40, "Camp Executive Committee and Representative Assembly," 11 August 1945; LAC, RG-24, Reel: C-5365, File HQS 9139-4-40, "Administrative Chart of the POW Representative Assembly at Camp Farnham," 20 September 1945.
135 LAC, RG-24, Reel: C-5365, File HQS 9139-4-40, "August 1945 Intelligence Report," 1 September 1945.
136 LAC, RG-24, Reel: C-5365, File HQS 9139-4-44, "September 1945 Intelligence Report," 4 October 1945.
137 LAC, RG-24, Reel: C-5365, File HQS 9139-4-42, "December 1945 Intelligence Report," December 1945.
138 LAC, RG-24, Reel: C-8436, File HQS 9139-1-42, "Lieutenant-Colonel H.D. Hedley (Camp Commandant) to District Officer Commanding Military District 4," 26 December 1945.
139 LAC, RG-24, Reel: C-5365, File HQS 9139-4-42, "January 1946 Intelligence Report," January 1946.
140 LAC, RG-24, Reel: C-5365, File HQS 9139-4-42, "April 1946 Intelligence Report," April 1946.
141 LAC, RG-24, Reel: C-5365, File HQS 9139-4-44, "November 1945 Intelligence Report," 3 December 1945.
142 LAC, RG-24, Reel: C-5419, File HQS 7236-94-14-45, "Assessment Camp Sorel," 3 May 1945.
143 Smith Jr., *The War for the German Mind*, 30.
144 LAC, RG-24, Reel: C-5419, File HQS 7236-94-14-45, "Assessment Camp Sorel," 3 May 1945.
145 LAC, RG-24, Reel: C-8436, File HQS 9139-1-42, "Lieutenant-Colonel H.D. Hedley (Camp Commandant) to Director of Prisoners of War," 14 November 1944; LAC, RG-24, Reel: C-5400, File HQS 7236-83-3-40, "Camp Spokesman Jay to the Canadian Association for Adult Education," 6 December 1944; LAC, RG-24, Reel: C-5419, File HQS 7236-94-14-40, "Lieutenant-Colonel A.W. De Wolf (Camp Commandant) to District Officer Commanding Military District 4," 10 January 1945; LAC, RG-24, Reel: C-5400, File HQS 7236-83-3-40, "George Brown (Chairman of Special Committee of the Canadian Association for Adult Education) to Colonel H.N. Streight (Director of Prisoners of War)," 23 February 1945.
146 LAC, RG-24, Reel: C-8436, File HQS 9139-1-40, "Lieutenant-Colonel G.F. Armstrong (Camp Commandant) to District Officer Commanding Military District 4," 16 November 1945; LAC, RG-24, Reel: C-5365, File HQS 9139-4-44, "February 1946 Intelligence Report," 5 March 1946.
147 LAC, RG-24, Reel: C-8436, File HQS 9139-1-42, "Lieutenant-Colonel A.G. Wygard (for Chief of the General Staff) to District Officer Commanding Military District 4," 21 January 1946.
148 LAC, RG-24, Reel: C-8436, File HQS 9139-1-44, "Lieutenant-Colonel H.W. Hiltz (Camp Commandant) to District Officer Commanding Military District 4," 11 January 1945; LAC, RG-24, Reel: C-5419, File HQS 7236-94-14-40, "Lieutenant-Colonel A.W. De Wolf (Camp Commandant) to District Officer Commanding Military District 4," 26 March 1945; LAC, RG-24, Reel: C-8436, File HQS 9139-1-40, "Lieutenant-Colonel A.W. De Wolf (Camp Commandant) to District Officer Commanding Military District 4," 26 March 1945; LAC, RG-24, Reel: C-8436, File HQS 9139-1-42, "Alfred Pauli (Camp Spokesman) to Sergeant-Major MacFarlane (Camp Interpreter)," 3 April 1945; LAC, RG-24, Reel: C-5400, File HQS 7236-83-3-40, "Schedule of Lectures," 9 April 1945; LAC, RG-24, Reel: C-5400, File HQS 7236-83-3-40, "Schedule of Lectures," 10 April 1945; LAC, RG-24, Reel: C-5400, File HQS 7236-83-3-40, "Jay (Camp Spokesman) to the Canadian Association for Adult Education," 24 May 1945; LAC, RG-24, Reel: C-8436, File HQS 9139-1-40, "Lieutenant-Colonel A.W. De Wolf (Camp Commandant) to District Officer Commanding Military District 4," 25 August 1945; LAC, RG-24, Reel: C-8436, File HQS 9139-1-45, "Lieutenant-Colonel B.B.W. Minard (Camp

Commandant) to District Officer Commanding Military District 4," 21 September 1945; LAC, RG-24, Reel: C-5365, File HQS 9139-4-44, "September 1945 Intelligence Report," 4 October 1945; LAC, RG-24, Reel: C-8436, File HQS 9139-1-40, "F.R. Scott (McGill University) to Lieutenant Henning Sorensen (Camp Farnham)," 10 December 1945; LAC, RG-24, Reel: C-5400, File HQS 7236-83-3-42, "Major A.H. Turner (Camp Commandant) to Military District 4 Headquarters," 6 February 1946; LAC, RG-24, Reel: C-8436, File HQS 9139-1-45, "First Lieutenant W. Ratzlaffral (Camp Sorel) to District Officer Commanding Military District 4," 25 February 1946; LAC, RG-24, Reel: C-5400, File HQS 7236-83-3-42, "Major A.H. Turner (Camp Commandant) to Military District 4 Headquarters," 1 March 1946.

149 LAC, RG-24, Reel: C-5416, File HQS 7236-94-6-44 "March 1944 Intelligence Summary," March 1944; LAC, RG-24, Reel: C-5400, File HQS 7236-83-3-42, "G.R.E. MacFarlane (Camp Censor) to Lieutenant-Colonel H.D. Hedley (Camp Commandant)," February 1945; LAC, RG-24, Reel: C-5400, File HQS 7236-83-3-44, "Timetable of Lectures by the Canadian Association for Adult Education at Camp Grande Ligne," 19 February 1945; LAC, RG-24, Reel: C-5400, File HQS 7236-83-3-42, "Timetable of Lectures offered by the Canadian Association for Adult Education for Camp Sherbrooke," 22 February 1945; LAC, RG-24, Reel: C-5419, File HQS 7236-94-14-40, "Lieutenant-Colonel A.W. De Wolf (Camp Commandant) to District Officer Commanding Military District 4," 5 March 1945; LAC, RG-24, Reel: C-8436, File HQS 9139-1-42, "Alfred Pauli (Camp Spokesman) to Sergeant-Major MacFarlane (Camp Interpreter)," 18 March 1945; LAC, RG-24, Reel: C-5365, File HQS 9139-4-42, "March 1945 Intelligence Report," 2 April 1945; LAC, RG-24, Reel: C-5400, File HQS 7236-83-3-40, "Schedule of Lectures," 9 April 1945; LAC, RG-24, Reel: C-5400, File HQS 7236-83-3-40, "Schedule of Lectures," 10 April 1945; LAC, RG-24, Reel: C-8436, File HQS 9139-1-45, "Lieutenant-Colonel B.B.W. Minard (Camp Commandant) to Major A. Wygard (MI7)," 15 September 1945; LAC, RG-24, Reel: C-8436, File HQS 9139-1-40, "Lieutenant Henning Sorensen (Royal Canadian Naval Volunteer Reserve) to Camp Commandant," 27 November 1945; LAC, RG-24, Reel: C-5400, File HQS 7236-83-3-45, "Major-General A.E. Welford (Adjutant General) to the District Officer Commanding Military District 4," 30 November 1945; LAC, RG-24, Reel: C-5400, File HQS 7236-83-3-40, "Major-General E.G. Weeks (Adjutant-General) to the District Officer Commanding Military District 4," 8 January 1946; LAC, RG-24, Reel: C-8436, File HQS 9139-1-44, "Major A.J. Reid (Camp Commandant) to District Officer Commanding Military District 4," 20 February 1946.

150 LAC, RG-24, Reel: C-5400, File HQS 7236-83-3-40, "George W. Brown (Chairman of Special Committee of the Canadian Association for Adult Education) to Colonel H.N. Streight (Director of Prisoners of War)," 21 June 1945.

151 LAC, RG-24, Reel: C-8436, File HQS 9139-1-42, "R. Hertzel (Prisoner of War) to the Camp Censor," 23 March 1945.

152 LAC, RG-24, Reel: C-5400, File HQS 7236-83-3-42, "Major A.R. Turner (Camp Commandant) to Military District 4 Headquarters," 6 February 1946; LAC, RG-24, Reel: C-5400, File HQS 7236-83-3-42, "Major A.H. Turner (Camp Commandant) to Military District 4 Headquarters," 1 March 1946.

153 LAC, RG-24, Reel: C-8436, File HQS 9139-1-42, "R. Hertzel (Prisoner of War) to the Camp Censor," 23 March 1945; Smith Jr., 31.

154 LAC, RG-24, Reel: C-5419, File HQS 7236-94-14-45, "Assessment Camp Sorel," 3 May 1945.

155 Ibid.; LAC, RG-24, Reel: C-5365, File HQS 9139-4-45, "August 1945 Intelligence Report," August 1945; LAC, RG-24, Reel: C-5365, File HQS 9139-4-45, "September 1945 Intelligence Report," September 1945; LAC, RG-24, Reel: C-5366, File HQS 9139-45, "Confidential Report on Camp Sorel by Lieutenant-Colonel R.G. Wygard (MI7)," 15 February 1946; LAC, RG-24, Reel: C-5366, File HQS 9139-45, "Concise Assessment of POW in Special Camp Sorel," 15 February 1946.

156 LAC, RG-24, Reel: C-5419, File HQS 7236-94-14-45, "Assessment Camp Sorel," 3 May 1945.

157 LAC, RG-24, Reel: C-8436, File HQS 9139-1-40, "Lieutenant- Colonel A.W. De Wolf (Camp Commandant) to District Officer Commanding Military District 4," 15 February 1945; LAC, RG-24, Reel: C-8436, File HQS 9139-1-40, "Lieutenant-Colonel A.W. De Wolf (Camp Commandant) to District Officer Commanding Military District 4," 23 February 1945; LAC, RG-24, Reel: C-8436, File HQS 9139-1-40, "Lieutenant-Colonel A.W. De Wolf (Camp Commandant) to District Officer Commanding Military District 4," 5 March 1945.

158 LAC, RG-24, Reel: C-8436, File HQS 9139-1-40, "Lieutenant-Colonel A.W. De Wolf (Camp Commandant) to District Officer Commanding Military District 4," 19 July 1945.

159 LAC, RG-24, Reel: C-8436, File HQS 9139-1-40, "Lieutenant-Colonel A.W. De Wolf (Camp Commandant) to District Officer Commanding Military District 4," 19 July 1945.

160 LAC, RG-24, Reel: C-8436, File HQS 9139-1-42, "Lieutenant-Colonel H.D. Hedley (Camp Commandant) to District Officer Commanding Military District 4," 27 December 1945.

161 LAC, RG-24, Reel: C-5419, File HQS 7236-94-14-45, "Assessment Camp Sorel," 3 May 1945; LAC, RG-24, Reel: C-8436, File HQS 9139-1-40, "Lieutenant-Colonel A.W. De Wolf (Camp Commandant) to District Officer Commanding Military District 4," 30 July 1945; LAC, RG-24, Reel: C-5365, File HQS 9139-4-45, "August 1945 Intelligence Report," August 1945; LAC, RG-24, Reel: C-5365, File HQS 9139-4-45, "September 1945 Intelligence Report," September 1945; LAC, RG-24, Reel: C-5365, File HQS 9139-4-45, "November 1945 Intelligence Report," 2 December 1945; LAC, RG-24, Reel: C-5365, File HQS 9139-4-44, "November 1945 Intelligence Report," 3 December 1945; LAC, RG-24, Reel: C-5365, File HQS 9139-4-45, "January 1946 Intelligence Report," 31 January 1946; LAC, RG-24, Reel: C-5366, File HQS 9139-45, "Confidential Report on Camp Sorel by Lieutenant-Colonel R.G. Wygard (MI7)," 15 February 1946; LAC, RG-24, Reel: C-5400, File HQS 7236-83-3-45, "Flight Lieutenant W. Ratzlaff (A/Camp Commandant) to the District Officer Commanding Military District 4," 25 February 1946; LAC, RG-24, Reel: C-8436, File HQS 9139-1-45, "Major L.L. Brunton (Camp Commandant) to District Officer Commanding Military District 4," 28 February 1946.

162 LAC, RG-24, Reel: C-5365, File HQS 9139-4-40, "Lieutenant-Colonel A.W. De Wolf (Camp Commandant) to District Officer Commanding Military District 4," 18 June 1945.

163 LAC, RG-24, Reel: C-8436, File HQS 9139-1-44, "Lieutenant-Colonel H.W. Hiltz (Camp Commandant) to District Officer Commanding Military District 4," 30 May 1945.

164 LAC, RG-24, Reel: C-5365, File HQS 9139-4-44, "May 1945 Intelligence Report," May 1945; LAC, RG-24, Vol. 15,403, vol. 29 (May 1945), War Diary of Internment Camp Grande Ligne, 14 May 1945, 15 May 1945, 24 May 1945, 25 May 1945, and 26 May 1945, 3-5; LAC, RG-24, Reel: C-5400, File HQS 7236-83-3-40, "Lieutenant-Colonel G.F. Armstrong (Camp Commandant) to the District Officer Commanding (D.O.C.) Military District 4," 28 December 1945; LAC, RG-24, Reel: C-5400, File HQS 7236-83-3-40, "Lieutenant-Colonel G.F. Armstrong (Camp Commandant) to the District Officer Commanding Military District 4," 16 January 1946.

165 LAC, RG-24, Reel: C-8436, File HQS 9139-1-44, "Report on Educational Activities during the Winter Term, 1945-1946 at Internment Camp 44," [n.d.]

166 LAC, RG-24, Reel: C-5419, File HQS 7236-94-14-45, "Assessment Camp Sorel," 3 May 1945; LAC, RG-24, Reel: C-5365, File HQS 9139-4-45, "September 1945 Intelligence Report," September 1945.; LAC, RG-24, Reel: C-5365, File HQS 9139-4-45, "November 1945 Intelligence Report," 2 December 1945; LAC, RG-24, Reel: C-5365, File HQS 9139-4-45, "January 1946 Intelligence Report," 31 January 1946; LAC, RG-24, Reel: C-5366, File HQS 9139-45, "Confidential Report on Camp Sorel by Lieutenant-Colonel R.G. Wygard (MI7)," 15 February 1946; LAC, RG-24, Reel: C-8436, File HQS 9139-1-45, "Major L.L. Brunton (Camp Commandant) to District Officer Commanding Military District 4," 28 February 1946.

167 LAC, RG-24, Reel: C-5365, File HQS 9139-4-45, "August 1945 Intelligence Report," August 1945.
168 LAC, RG-24, Reel: C-5365, File HQS 9139-4-45, "November 1945 Intelligence Report," 2 December 1945.
169 LAC, RG-24, Reel: C-5400, File HQS 7236-83-3-40, "E. Boeschenstein (YMCA) to Colonel E. Jay (Camp Spokesman)," 13 May 1946.
170 LAC, RG-24, Reel: C-5365, File HQS 9139-4-40, "November 1945 Intelligence Report," 30 November 1945.
171 LAC, RG-24, Reel: C-5365, File HQS 9139-4-40, "May 1945 Intelligence Report," 29 May 1945; LAC, RG-24, Reel: C-5419, File HQS 7236-94-14-40, "Lieutenant-Colonel G.F. Armstrong (Camp Commandant) to District Officer Commanding Military District 4," 16 November 1945.
172 LAC, RG-24, Reel: C-5365, File HQS 9139-4-45, "October 1945 Intelligence Report," 31 October 1945.
173 LAC, RG-24, Reel: C-5365, File HQS 9139-4-44, "November 1945 Intelligence Report," 3 December 1945.
174 LAC, RG-24, Reel: C-5410, File HQS 7236-88-5-45, "Lieutenant-Colonel B.B.W. Minard (Camp Commandant) to the Director of Prisoners of War," 21 November 1945.
175 LAC, RG-24, Reel: C-5419, File HQS 7236-94-14-40, "Lieutenant-Colonel A.W. De Wolf (Camp Commandant) to District Officer Commanding Military District 4," 12 October 1945; LAC, RG-24, Reel: C-5365, File HQS 9139-4-40, "October 1945 Intelligence Report," 31 October 1945.
176 LAC, RG-24, Vol. 15,398, vol. 57 (October 1945), War Diary of Internment Camp Farnham, 15 October 1945, 2.
177 LAC, RG-24, Vol. 15,398, vol. 64 (May 1946), War Diary of Internment Camp Farnham, "DKD, Number 17," 20 May 1946, Appendix 3, 1-28.
178 LAC, RG-24, Reel: C-5365, File HQS 9139-4-44, "December 1945 Information Summary," 5 January 1946.
179 LAC, RG-24, Reel: C-5365, File HQS 9139-4-44, "February 1946 Intelligence Report," 5 March 1946.
180 LAC, RG-24, Reel: C-5365, File HQS 9139-4-44, "December 1945 Intelligence Report," 7 January 1946.
181 LAC, RG-24, Reel: C-5419, File HQS 7236-94-14-42, "Major A.R. Turner (Camp Commandant) to Headquarters, Military District 4," 29 January 1946.
182 LAC, RG-24, Reel: C-5365, File HQS 9139-4-40, "March 1946 Intelligence Report," 9 April 1946.
183 LAC, RG-24, Reel: C-5365, File HQS 9139-4-44, "May 1945 Intelligence Report," May 1945; LAC, RG-24, Reel: C-5365, File HQS 9139-4-45, "January 1946 Intelligence Report," 31 January 1946.
184 LAC, RG-24, Reel: C-5365, File HQS 9139-4-40, "May 1945 Intelligence Report," 29 May 1945; LAC, RG-24, Reel: C-5365, File HQS 9139-4-42, "September 1945 Intelligence Report," 1 October 1945.
185 Chris M.V. Madsen and R.J. Henderson, *German Prisoners of War in Canada and Their Artifacts* (Regina: Hignell Printing, 1993), 87.
186 LAC, RG-24, Reel: C-5365, File HQS 9139-4-44, "July 1945 Intelligence Report," 3 August 1945.
187 LAC, RG-24, Reel: C-5365, File HQS 9139-4-40, "May 1945 Intelligence Report," 29 May 1945.
188 LAC, RG-24, Reel: C-5365, File HQS 9139-4-45, "July 1945 Intelligence Report," 4 August 1945.
189 LAC, RG-24, Reel: C-5365, File HQS 9139-4-40, "May 1945 Intelligence Report," 29 May 1945.
190 Ibid.

191 LAC, RG-24, Reel: C-8436, File HQS 9139-2-40, "Lieutenant-Colonel A.W. De Wolf (Camp Commandant) to District Officer Commanding Military District 4," 16 February 1945.

192 Ibid.

193 LAC, RG-24, Reel: C-8436, File HQS 9139-2-45, "Report on a Visit to Camp Sorel by H.G. Skilling (Supervisor for the Central European Section of the CBC)," 12 July 1945.

194 Ibid.; LAC, RG-24, Reel: C-8436, File HQS 9139-2-40, "Lieutenant-Colonel A.W. De Wolf (Camp Commandant) to District Officer Commanding Military District 4," 30 July 1945; LAC, RG-24, Reel: C-5365, File HQS 9139-4-40, "July 1945 Intelligence Report," 1 August 1945.

195 LAC, RG-24, Reel: C-8436, File HQS 9139-2-40, "Lieutenant-Colonel A.W. De Wolf (Camp Commandant) to District Officer Commanding Military District 4," 11 September 1945.

196 LAC, RG-24, Reel: C-5365, File HQS 9139-4-40, "October 1945 Intelligence Report," 31 October 1945.

197 LAC, RG-24, Reel: C-8436, File HQS 9139-2-40, "Lieutenant-Colonel G.F. Armstrong (Camp Commandant) to District Officer Commanding Military District 4," 1 March 1946.

198 LAC, RG-24, Reel: C-8436, File HQS 9139-2-40, "Lieutenant-Colonel A.W. De Wolf (Camp Commandant) to District Officer Commanding Military District 4," 16 May 1945.

199 LAC, RG-24, Reel: C-5365, File HQS 9139-4-40, "May 1945 Intelligence Report," 29 May 1945.

200 LAC, RG-24, Reel: C-8436, File HQS 9139-2-40, "Lieutenant-Colonel A.W. De Wolf (Camp Commandant) to Director of Prisoners of War," 4 October 1945; LAC, RG-24, Reel: C-8436, File HQS 9139-2-40, "Report on the Recording of POW messages from Camp Farnham at Montreal Studios of the CBC International Service by Helmut Blume (Chief Editor of the German Section of the CBC International Service)," 6 October 1945.

201 LAC, RG-24, Reel: C-5365, File HQS 9139-4-40, "May 1945 Intelligence Report," 29 May 1945; LAC, RG-24, Reel: C-5365, File HQS 9139-4-44, "June 1945 Intelligence Summary," June 1945; LAC, RG-24, Reel: C-8436, File HQS 9139-2-42, "Adjutant-General to District Officer Commanding Military District 4," 23 April 1946.

202 LAC, RG-24, Reel: C-5419, File HQS 7236-94-14-40, "Lieutenant-Colonel A.W. De Wolf (Camp Commandant) to District Officer Commanding Military District 4," 16 February 1945.

203 LAC, RG-24, Reel: C-5419, File HQS 7236-94-14-40, "Lieutenant-Colonel G.F. Armstrong (Camp Commandant) to District Officer Commanding Military District 4," 10 December 1945.

204 LAC, RG-24, Reel: C-8436, File HQS 9139-2-40, "Lieutenant-Colonel A.W. De Wolf (Camp Commandant) to District Officer Commanding Military District 4," 30 July 1945; LAC, RG-24, Reel: C-5419, File HQS 7236-94-14-40, "Lieutenant-Colonel G.F. Armstrong (Camp Commandant) to District Officer Commanding Military District 4," 2 November 1945.

205 LAC, RG-24, Reel: C-8436, File HQS 9139-2-40, "Lieutenant-Colonel A.W. De Wolf (Camp Commandant) to District Officer Commanding Military District 4," 11 September 1945.

206 LAC, RG-24, Reel: C-8436, File HQS 9139-2-44, "Report of a Visit to Camp Grande Ligne by Helmut Blume (Chief Editor of the German Section of the CBC)," 2 October 1945; LAC, RG-24, Reel: C-5365, File HQS 9139-4-44, "September 1945 Intelligence Report," 4 October 1945; LAC, RG-24, Reel: C-8436, File HQS 9139-2-45, "Report of a Visit to Camp Sorel by Helmut Blume (Chief Editor of the German Section of the CBC)," 18 October 1945; LAC, RG-24, Reel: C-8436, File HQS 9139-2-45, "Report on a visit of five POW's from Sorel Camp at International Service Studios by Helmut Blume (Chief Editor of the German Section of the CBC)," 26 October 1945.

207 LAC, RG-24, Reel: C-8436, File HQS 9139-2-42, "Major A.R. Turner (Camp Commandant) to Military District 4 Headquarters," 22 January 1946.

208 LAC, RG-24, Reel: C-8436, File HQS 9139-2-45, "A. Small (A/Camp Commandant) to District Officer Commanding Military District 4," 19 January 1946.

209 Ibid.
210 Kelly, " Prisoner of War Camps," 190.
211 LAC, RG-24, Reel: C-8436, File HQS 9139-2-44, "Lieutenant-Colonel C.G. Kerr (Camp Commandant) to District Officer Commanding Military District 4," 23 October 1945; LAC, RG-24, Reel: C-5419, File HQS 7236-94-14-40, "Lieutenant-Colonel G.F. Armstrong (Camp Commandant) to District Officer Commanding Military District 4," 7 December 1945; LAC, RG-24, Reel: C-5365, File HQS 9139-4-40, "February 1946 Interpreter's Report," 1 March 1946.
212 LAC, RG-24, Reel: C-8436, File HQS 9139-2-40, "Lieutenant-Colonel G.F. Armstrong (Camp Commandant) to District Officer Commanding Military District 4," 19 December 1945.
213 LAC, RG-24, Reel: C-8436, File HQS 9139-2-40, "Report by Helmut Blume (Chief Editor of the German Section of the CBC)," December 1945.
214 LAC, RG-24, Reel: C-5365, File HQS 9139-4-42, "December 1945 Intelligence Report," December 1945.
215 LAC, RG-24, Reel: C-5365, File HQS 9139-4-44, "January 1946 Intelligence Report," 4 February 1946.
216 LAC, RG-24, Reel: C-5369, File HQS 7236-1-6-40, "May 1945 Nominal Roll," 23 May 1945; LAC, RG-24, Reel: C-5365, File HQS 9139-4-40, "June 1945 Intelligence Report," 1 July 1945.
217 LAC, RG-24, Reel: C-5365, File HQS 9139-4-40, "June 1945 Intelligence Report," 1 July 1945.
218 LAC, RG-24, Reel: C-5365, File HQS 9139-4-40, "March 1946 Intelligence Report," 9 April 1946.
219 LAC, RG-24, Reel: C-5365, File HQS 9139-4-45, "February 1946 Intelligence Report," 7 March 1946; LAC, RG-24, Reel: C-5365, File HQS 9139-4-40, "Lieutenant-Colonel G.F. Armstrong (Camp Commandant) to District Officer Commanding Military District 4," 27 March 1946.
220 Madsen and Henderson, *German Prisoners of War,* 88.
221 Smith Jr., *The War for the German Mind,* 63.
222 LAC, RG-24, Reel: C-5365, File HQS 9139-4-40, "September 1945 Intelligence Report," 1 October 1945.
223 Rettig, "A De-programming Curriculum," 599.
224 LAC, RG-24, Reel: C-5365, File HQS 9139-4-44, "July 1945 Intelligence Report," 3 August 1945.
225 LAC, RG-24, Reel: C-5365, File HQS 9139-4-44, "November 1945 Intelligence Report," 3 December 1945.
226 LAC, RG-24, Reel: C-5365, File HQS 9139-4-40, "September 1945 Intelligence Report," 1 October 1945.
227 LAC, RG-24, Reel: C-5365, File HQS 9139-4-40, "June 1945 Intelligence Report," 1 July 1945.
228 LAC, RG-24, Reel: C-5366, File HQS 9139-45, "Richard Marchfelder (Prisoner of War) to Lieutenant-Colonel R.G. Wygard (MI7)," August 1946.
229 LAC, RG-24, Reel: C-5365, File HQS 9139-4-45, "February 1946 Intelligence Report," 7 March 1946.
230 LAC, RG-24, Reel: C-5365, File HQS 9139-4-44, "November 1945 Intelligence Report," 3 December 1945.
231 LAC, RG-24, Reel: C-8436, File HQS 9139-1-44, "Summary Dealing with Barnyard Manure," 28 March 1946, 1-16; LAC, RG-24, Reel: C-8436, File HQS 9139-1-44, "Rud Bohnisch and Ernst Breiler (Prisoners of War) to Major T.L. Reid (Camp Commandant)," 29 March 1946.
232 LAC, RG-24, Reel: C-5366, File HQS 9139-45, "Richard Marchfelder (Prisoner of War) to Lieutenant-Colonel B.B.W. Minard (Camp Commandant)," 19 September 1945.
233 Ibid.
234 Rettig, "A De-programming Curriculum," 612-13.
235 Faulk, *Group Captives,* 179; Rettig, "A De-programming Curriculum,"593.
236 Robin, *Barbed-Wire College,* 176.

Chapter 6: Canada's Internment Experience

1 On the internment of civilians of Italian origin, see J.A. Ciccocelli, "The Innocuous Enemy Alien: Italians in Canada during World War II" (MA thesis, University of Western Ontario, 1977); Enrico Carlson Cumbo, "'Uneasy Neighbours': Internment and Hamilton's Italians," in *Enemies Within: Italian and Other Internees in Canada and Abroad,* ed. Franca Iacovetta, Roberto Perin, and Angelo Principe (Toronto: University of Toronto Press, 2000), 99-119; Franca Iacovetta and Roberto Perin, "Italians and Wartime Internment: Comparative Perspectives on Public Policy, Historical Memory, and Daily Life," in *Enemies Within,* ed. Iacovetta, Perin, and Principe, 3-21; Luigi Bruti Liberati, "The Internment of Italian Canadians," in *Enemies Within,* ed. Iacovetta, Perin, and Principe, 76-98; Luigi G. Pennacchio, "Exporting Fascism to Canada: Toronto's Little Italy," in *Enemies Within,* ed. Iacovetta, Perin, and Principe, 52-75; Angelo Principe, "A Tangled Knot: Prelude to 10 June 1940," in *Enemies Within,* ed. Iacovetta, Perin, and Principe, 27-51; Bruno Ramirez, "Ethnicity on Trial: The Italians of Montreal and the Second World War," in *On Guard for Thee: War, Ethnicity, and the Canadian State, 1939-1945,* ed. Norman Hilmer, Bohdan Kordan, and Lubomyr Luciuk (Ottawa: Ministry of Supply and Services Canada, 1988), 71-84.

On the internment of Japanese Canadians, see Ken Adachi, *The Enemy That Never Was: A History of Japanese Canadians* (1976; Toronto: McClelland and Stewart, 1991); Barry Broadfoot, *Years of Sorrow, Years of Shame: The Story of Japanese Canadians in World War II* (Toronto: Doubleday Canada, 1977); J.L. Granatstein and Gregory A. Johnson, "The Evacuation of the Japanese Canadians, 1942: A Realist Critique of the Received Version," in *On Guard for Thee,* ed. Hilmer, Kordan, and Luciuk, 101-21; Desmond Morton, *A Military History of Canada* (Toronto: McClelland and Stewart, 1992); Robert Katsumasa Okazaki, *The Nisei Mass Evacuation Group and P.O.W. Camp 101, Angler, Ontario* (Scarborough, ON: Markham Litho, 1995); Patricia Roy, J.L. Granatstein, Masako Lino, and Hiroko Takamura, *Mutual Hostages: Canadians and Japanese during the Second World War* (Toronto: University of Toronto Press, 1990); Ann Gomer Sunhara, *Politics of Racism: The Uprooting of Japanese Canadians during the Second World War* (Toronto: Lorimer, 1981); Mary Taylor, *Black Mark: The Japanese-Canadians in World War II* (Toronto: Oberon Press, 2004); and W. Peter Ward, "British Columbia and the Japanese Evacuation," *Canadian Historical Review* 57, 3 (1976): 289-309.

On the internment of other ethnic groups, see N.F. Dreisziger, "7 December 1941: A Turning Point in Canadian Wartime Policy toward Enemy Ethnic Groups?" *Journal of Canadian Studies* 32, 1 (1997): 93-105; Robert H. Keyserlingk, "The Canadian Government's Attitude toward Germans and German Canadians in World War II," *Canadian Ethnic Studies* 16, 1 (1984): 18; Daniel Robinson, "Planning for the 'Most Serious Contingency': Alien Internment, Arbitrary Detention, and the Canadian State, 1938-1939." *Journal of Canadian Studies* 28, 2 (1993): 10; John Herd Thompson, *Les minorités ethniques pendant les guerres mondiales* (Ottawa: Société historique du Canada, 1991), 11-18.

2 On homegrown Fascist sympathizers, see Lita-Rose Betcherman, *The Swastika and the Maple Leaf: Fascist Movements in Canada in the Thirties* (Toronto: Fitzhenry and Whiteside, 1975), 145-47. See also Michelle McBride, "From Internment to Indifference: An Examination of RCMP Response to Fascism and Nazism in Canada from 1934 to 1941" (MA thesis, Memorial University, 1997); Martin Robin, *Shades of Right: Nativist and Fascist Politics in Canada, 1920-1940* (Toronto: University of Toronto Press, 1992); Jonathan F. Wagner, *Brothers Beyond the Sea: National Socialism in Canada* (Waterloo, ON: Wilfrid Laurier Press, 1981); Jonathan F. Wagner, "The Deutscher Bund Canada, 1934-1939," *Canadian Historical Review* 58 (June 1977): 176-200.

On Communists, see Ian Radforth, "Political Prisoners: The Communist Internees," in *Enemies Within,* ed. Iacovetta, Perin, and Principe, 194-224; Reg Whitaker, "Official Repression of Communism during World War II," *Labour-Le Travail* 17 (Spring 1986): 135-66.

On civilians perceived as subversives, see Robinson, "Planning for the 'Most Serious Contingency,'" 14. See also J.L. Granatstein and J.M. Hitsman, *Broken Promises: A History of Conscription in Canada* (Toronto: Oxford University Press, 1977).

3 James Bacque, *Other Losses: An Investigation into the Mass Deaths of German Prisoners at the Hands of the French and Americans after World War II* (1989; Bolton: Little, Brown and Company, 1999), 208-9.

4 Joan Beaumont, "Protecting Prisoners of War, 1939-95," in *Prisoners of War and Their Captors,* ed. Kent Moore and Bob Fedorowich (Oxford: Berg, 1996), 279.

5 Ibid. See also Günter Bischof and Stephen E. Ambrose, eds., *Eisenhower and the German POWs: Facts against Falsehood* (Baton Rouge: Louisiana State University, 1992).

6 Jonathan Vance, *Objects of Concern: Canadian Prisoners of War through the Twentieth Century* (Vancouver: UBC Press, 1994), 248-49.

7 Ibid., 131.

8 Ibid., 131-32.

9 Ibid., 133-34.

10 Jeffrey A. Keshen, *Saints, Sinners, and Soldiers: Canada's Second World War* (Vancouver and Toronto: UBC Press, 2004), 240; Vance, *Objects of Concern,* 256.

11 Vance, *Objects of Concern,* 253.

12 John Joseph Kelly, "The Prisoner of War Camps in Canada, 1939-1947" (MA thesis, University of Windsor, 1976), 210.

13 Eric Koch, *Deemed Suspect: A Wartime Blunder* (Toronto: Methuen, 1980), 233.

14 Koch, *Deemed Suspect,* 166, 168; Library and Archives Canada [LAC], MG-30, C 192, Vol. 3, "Harry Rasky, *The Spies Who Never Were,* Part 2 (CBC, 1981)," II-29-II-30.

15 "Letter to Colonel E.D.B. Kippen," 30 January 1957, reproduced in Kelly, "Prisoner of War Camps," 211.

16 "Letter to Colonel E.D.B. Kippen," 26 March 1947, reproduced in Kelly, "Prisoner of War Camps," 212.

17 Koch, *Deemed Suspect,* 256, 264-72.

18 Ibid., 258-9.

19 John Melady, *Escape from Canada! The Untold Story of German POWs in Canada, 1939-1945* (Toronto: Macmillan of Canada, 1981), 182.

20 Ted Jones, *Both Sides of the Wire: The Fredericton Internment Camp* (Fredericton, NB: New Ireland Press, 1989), 711; Kelly, "Prisoner of War Camps," 209.

21 David J. Carter, *Behind Canadian Barbed Wire: Alien, Refugee and Prisoner of War Camps in Canada, 1914-1946,* (Calgary: Tumbleweed, 1980), 291.

22 Melady, *Escape from Canada!* 197.

23 Ibid., 185.

24 Ibid., 196-97.

Bibliography

Archival Sources

Library and Archives of Canada (LAC)

Cabinet War Committee. Reel C-11,789, File 1. Minutes of the Cabinet War Committee, December 9, 1939, to July 15, 1940.

Manuscripts of the First Half of the Twentieth Century, MG-30. C 192, Vol. 3, Collection Eric Koch, "Interviews by Harry Rasky (CBC)," [1980s].

Records of the Privy Council Office, RG-2.

Orders-in-Council

Vol. 1592, File 1429G. Order-in-Council PC 2097, 20 August, 1936.

Vol. 2003. Order-in-Council PC 531, 14 March, 1938.

Vol. 1653, File 1948G. Order-in-Council PC 2483, 3 September, 1939.

Vol. 1675, File 2089G. Order-in-Council PC 2322, 31 May, 1940.

Vol. 1721, File P.C. 4568. Order-in-Council PC 4568, 25 June, 1941.

Vol. 1724, File P.C. 524. Order-in-Council PC 5246, 15 July, 1941.

Records of the Department of National Defence, RG-24

Reel C-5365, File HQS 9139-4-40. Camp Intelligence, Camp Farnham, 1944-46.

Reel C-5365, File HQS 9139-4-42. Camp Intelligence, Camp Sherbrooke, 1944-46.

Reel C-5365, File HQS 9139-4-44. Camp Intelligence, Camp Grande Ligne, 1944-46.

Reel C-5365, File HQS 9139-4-45. Camp Intelligence, Camp Sorel, 1945-46.

Reel C-5366, File HQS 9139-9. Administration, Camp Sorel, 1945-46.

Reel C-5366, File HQS 9139-40. Classification of POW, Camp Farnham, 1944-46.

Reel C-5366, File HQS 9139-42. Classification of POW, Camp Sherbrooke, 1944-46.

Reel C-5366, File HQS 9139-44. Classification of POW, Camp Grande Ligne, 1944-46.

Reel C-5366, File HQS 9139-45. Classification of POW, Camp Sorel, 1945-46.

Reel C-5369, File HQS 7236-1-6-40. Nominal Rolls Prepared on Arrival, Camp Farnham, 1942-45.

Reel C-5374, File HQS 7236-1-10-40. Strength Returns, Camp Farnham, 1941-46.

Reel C-5374, File HQS 7236-1-10-41. Strength Returns, Camp Île-aux-Noix, 1941-43.

Reel C-5374, File HQS 7236-1-10-42. Strength Returns, Camp Sherbrooke, 1941-46.

Reel C-5374, File HQS 7236-1-10-44. Strength Returns, Camp Grande Ligne, 1943-46.

Reel C-5374, File HQS 7236-1-10-45. Strength Returns, Camp Sorel, 1945-46.

Reel C-5375, File HQS 7236-1-11-42. Parcels, Letters to External Affairs, IRC, and Swiss Consul, Camp Sherbrooke, 1942-46.

Reel C-5376, File HQS 7236-1-11-40. Parcels, Letters to External Affairs, IRC, and Swiss Consul, Camp Farnham, 1942-46.

Reel C-5376, File HQS 7236-1-11-44. Parcels, Letters to External Affairs, IRC, and Swiss Consul, Camp Grande Ligne, 1943-46.

Reel C-5376, File HQS 7236-1-11-45. Parcels, Letters to External Affairs, IRC, and Swiss Consul, Camp Sorel, 1945-46.

Reel C-5376, File HQS 7236-1-13-40. Monthly Return of POW Quartered and Rationed Outside Camp, Camp Farnham, 1944-46.
Reel C-5376, File HQS 7236-1-13-42. Monthly Return of POW Quartered and Rationed Outside Camp, Camp Sherbrooke, 1944-46.
Reel C-5377, File HQS 7236-18, Vols. 1-2. Administration, Camp Île-aux-Noix, 1940-46.
Reel C-5378, File HQS 7236-20. Organization and Administration, Camp Farnham, 1940-46.
Reel C-5389, File HQS 7236-44-40. Escape Plans and Correspondence, Camp Farnham, 1941-45.
Reel C-5389, File HQS 7236-44-41. Escape Plans and Correspondence, Camp Île-aux-Noix, 1944-45.
Reel C-5389, File HQS 7236-44-42. Escape Plans and Correspondence, Camp Sherbrooke, 1944-45.
Reel C-5389, File HQS 7236-44-44. Escape Plans and Correspondence, Camp Grande Ligne, 1943-48.
Reel C-5396, File HQS 7236-79. Officers, Grande Ligne, 1942-46.
Reel C-5398, File HQS 7236-81-40. Canteens, Camp Farnham, 1942-48.
Reel C-5398, File HQS 7236-81-42. Canteens, Camp Sherbrooke, 1944-46.
Reel C-5400, File HQS 7236-83-3-40. Educational Facilities, Camp Farnham, 1943-46.
Reel C-5400, File HQS 7236-83-3-42. Educational Facilities, Camp Sherbrooke, 1943-46.
Reel C-5400, File HQS 7236-83-3-44. Educational Facilities, Camp Grande Ligne, 1943-46.
Reel C-5400, File HQS 7236-83-3-45. Educational Facilities, Camp Sorel, 1945-46.
Reel C-5401, File HQS 7236-83-6-40. YMCA Reports on Welfare Matters, Camp Farnham, 1943-46.
Reel C-5401, File HQS 7236-83-6-41. YMCA Reports on Welfare Matters, Camp Île-aux-Noix, 1943.
Reel C-5403, File HQS 7236-83-7-40. IRC Correspondence, Camp Farnham, 1943-44.
Reel C-5409, File HQS 7236-87-5-42. Correspondence re. Mail, Camp Sherbrooke, 1943-46.
Reel C-5409, File HQS 7236-88-5-40. Correspondence, Instructions re. Censorship, Camp Farnham, 1943-46.
Reel C-5410, File HQS 7236-88-5-42. Correspondence, Instructions re. Censorship, Camp Sherbrooke, 1943-45.
Reel C-5410, File HQS 7236-88-5-44. Correspondence, Instructions re. Censorship, Camp Grande Ligne, 1943-45.
Reel C-5410, File HQS 7236-88-5-45. Correspondence, Instructions re. Censorship, Camp Sorel, 1945.
Reel C-5413, File HQS 7236-91-1-40. Visits by Representatives of Protecting Power, Camp Farnham, 1943-45.
Reel C-5413, File HQS 7236-91-1-44. Visits by Representatives of Protecting Power, Camp Grande Ligne, 1943-45.
Reel C-5413, File HQS 7236-91-4-40. Complaints by POW, Camp Farnham, 1943-45.
Reel C-5413, File HQS 7236-91-4-42. Complaints by POW, Camp Sherbrooke, 1944-45.
Reel C-5413, File HQS 7236-91-4-44. Complaints by POW, Camp Grande Ligne, 1943-45.
Reel C-5416, File HQS 7236-94-6-40. Intelligence Reports, Camp Farnham, 1943-46.
Reel C-5416, File HQS 7236-94-6-42. Intelligence Reports, Camp Sherbrooke, 1943-46.
Reel C-5416, File HQS 7236-94-6-44. Intelligence Reports, Camp Grande Ligne, 1943-46.
Reel C-5419, File HQS 7236-94-14-40. Reports for the Psychological Warfare Committee, Camp Farnham, 1944-46.

Reel C-5419, File HQS 7236-94-14-42. Reports for Psychological Warfare Committee, Camp Sherbrooke, 1945-46.
Reel C-5419, File HQS 7236-94-14-44. Reports for Psychological Warfare Committee, Camp Grande Ligne, 1944-46.
Reel C-5419, File HQS 7236-94-14-45. Reports for Psychological Warfare Committee, Camp Sorel, 1945-46.
Reel C-5420, File HQS 7236-96-41. Construction and Maintenance, Camp Île-aux-Noix, 1940-44.
Reel C-5420, File HQS 7236-96-42. Construction and Maintenance, Camp Sherbrooke, 1942-45.
Reel C-5420, File HQS 7236-96-44. Construction and Maintenance, Camp Grande Ligne, 1943-46.
Reel C-5421, File HQS 7236-99. Organization and Administration, Camp Sorel, 1945.
Reel C-8436, File HQS 9139-1-40. Re-education, Camp Farnham, 1944-46.
Reel C-8436, File HQS 9139-1-42. Re-education, Camp Sherbrooke, 1944-46.
Reel C-8436, File HQS 9139-1-44. Re-education, Camp Grande Ligne, 1944-46.
Reel C-8436, File HQS 9139-1-45. Re-education, Camp Sorel, 1945-46.
Reel C-8436, File HQS 9139-2-40. Material for Broadcasting to Germany, Camp Farnham, 1944-46.
Reel C-8436, File HQS 9139-2-42. Material for Broadcasting to Germany, Camp Sherbrooke, 1944-46.
Reel C-8436, File HQS 9139-2-44. Material for Broadcasting to Germany, Camp Grande Ligne, 1944-46.
Reel C-8436, File HQS 9139-2-45. Material for Broadcasting to Germany, Camp Sorel, 1945-46.
Vol. 6576, File 1-1-5. Employment and Pay of Internees, 1939-43.
Vol. 6576, File 1-2-4. Policy – U.K. re. Treatment and Rations, 1941.
Vol. 6583, File 3-3-5 (40). YMCA Gifts and Donations, Camp Farnham, 1942-43.
Vol. 11,247, File 9-1-3 (40). Complaints, Camp Farnham, 1942.
Vol. 11,247, File 9-1-3 (42). Complaints, Camp Sherbrooke, 1943.
Vol. 11,249, File 9-5-3-40. IRC Report, Camp Farnham, 1940-41.
Vol. 11,249, File 9-5-3-41. IRC Report, Camp Île-aux-Noix, 1940-41.
Vol. 11,249, File 9-5-3-42. IRC Report, Camp Sherbrooke, 1940-41.
Vol. 11,250, File 10-2-3-40. Intelligence Reports, Camp Farnham, 1941-42.
Vol. 11,253, File 11-2-40. Inspection Reports, Camp Farnham, 1940-41.
Vol. 11,253, File 11-2-41. Inspection Reports, Camp Île-aux-Noix, 1940-41.
Vol. 11,253, File 11-2-42. Inspection Reports, Camp Sherbrooke, 1940-41.
Vol. 11,254, File 13-3-5. Returns, Camp Farnham, 1940-41.
Vol. 11,254, File 13-3-10. Returns, Camp Île-aux-Noix, 1940-41.
Vol. 15,397-15,398. War Diary of Internment Camp Farnham, 1940-46.
Vol. 15,399. War Diary of Internment Camp Île-aux-Noix, 1940-43.
Vol. 15,399-15,401. War Diary of Internment Camp Sherbrooke, 1940-46.
Vol. 15,403-15,404. War Diary of Internment Camp Grande Ligne, 1943-46.
Vol. 15,404. War Diary of Internment Camp Sorel, 1945-46.

Department of National Defence, Directorate of History and Heritage (DHH)

Chiefs of Staff Committee Papers. 193.009 (D29), Vol. 28. Chiefs of Staff Miscellaneous Memoranda, 1944.
Directorate of Prisoners of War Papers. 113.3P4 (D2). Directorate Narrative, 1945.

Eastern Townships Research Centre (ETRC)

Eastern Townships Collection. 98-003. Box no. 121. "Oral History of Eastern Townships' Anglophone Women during the Second World War." Interviews by Carol Gaskell, Judy Green, and Susan Lefebvre, 1991.

Other Sources

Abella, Irving, and Harold Troper. *None Is Too Many: Canada and the Jews of Europe, 1933-1948.* Toronto: Lester and Orpen Dennys, 1982.

Adachi, Ken. *The Enemy That Never Was: A History of Japanese Canadians.* 1976; Toronto: McClelland and Stewart, 1991.

Aly, Gotz. *The Final Solution: Nazi Population Policy and the Murder of the European Jews.* London: Oxford University Press, 2000.

Aly, Gotz, Peter Chroust, and Christian Pross. *Cleansing the Fatherland: Nazi Medicine and Racial Hygiene.* Baltimore, MD: Johns Hopkins University Press, 1994.

Applebaum, Anne. *Gulag: A History.* New York: Doubleday, 2003.

Asada, Teruhiko. *Night of a Thousand Suicides: The Japanese Outbreak at Cowra.* Sydney: Angus and Robertson, 1970.

Auger, Martin F. "The HARIKARI Club: German Prisoners of War and the Mass Escape Scare of 1944-45 at Internment Camp Grande Ligne, Quebec." *Canadian Military History* 13, 3 (2004): 49-67.

–. "Prisoners of the Home Front: A Social Study of the German Internment Camps of Southern Quebec, 1940-1946." MA thesis, University of Ottawa, 2000.

–. "The Problem of Nazism in the German POW Officer Camps of Southern Quebec, 1942-1945." 14th Military History Colloquium, London, 10 May 2003.

–. "L'université barbelée: La rééducation de prisonniers de guerre allemands dans les camps d'internement du sud du Québec, 1943-1946." 54e Congrès de l'Institut d'Histoire de l'Amérique Française (IHAF), Ottawa, October 27, 2001.

Aziz, Philippe. *Doctors of Death.* 4 vols. Geneva: Ferni Publishers, 1976.

Bacque, James. *Other Losses: An Investigation into the Mass Deaths of German Prisoners at the Hands of the French and Americans after World War II.* 2nd ed. Bolton, MA: Little, Brown, 1999. First published 1989.

Barber, Noel. *Prisoner of War: The Story of British Prisoners Held by the Enemy.* London: George G. Harrap, 1944.

Barenblatt, Daniel. *A Plague upon Humanity: The Secret Genocide of Axis Japan's Germ Warfare Operation.* New York: HarperCollins, 2004.

Barker, A.J. *Behind Barbed Wire.* London: B.T. Batsford, 1974.

Bartov, Omer. *The Eastern Front, 1941-45: German Troops and the Barbarization of Warfare.* New York: St. Martin's, 1986.

Bartrop, Paul R., and Gabrielle Eisen, eds. *The Dunera Affaire: A Documentary Resource Book.* Melbourne, Australia: Schwartz and Wilkinson, 1990.

Beede, Benjamin R., ed. *The War of 1898 and U.S. Interventions, 1898-1934: An Encyclopedia.* New York: Garland Publishing, 1994.

Bergen, Doris. *War and Genocide: A Concise History of the Holocaust.* Lanham, MD: Rowman and Littlefield, 2002.

Bernard, Yves, and Caroline Bergeron. *Trop loin de Berlin: Des prisonniers allemands au Canada (1939-1946).* Sillery, QC: Éditions du Septentrion, 1995.

Berner, Brad K. *The Spanish-American War: A Historical Dictionary.* Lanham, MD: Scarecrow Press, 1998.

Berry, William A. *Prisoner of the Rising Sun.* Norman: University of Oklahoma Press, 1993.

Best, Geoffrey. *Humanity in Warfare.* New York: Columbia University Press, 1980.

Betcherman, Lita-Rose. *The Swastika and the Maple Leaf: Fascist Movements in Canada in the Thirties.* Toronto: Fitzhenry and Whiteside, 1975.

Bevege, Margaret. *Behind Barbed Wire: Internment in Australia during World War II.* St. Lucia: University of Queensland Press, 1993.

Bischof, Günter, and Stephen E. Ambrose, eds. *Eisenhower and the German POWs: Facts against Falsehood.* Baton Rouge: Louisiana State University, 1992.

Bley, Helmut. *South-West Africa under German Rule, 1894-1914.* Evanston, IL: Northwestern University Press, 1971.

Boatner, Mark Mayo. *The Civil War Dictionary.* New York: David McKay, 1988.

Boot, Max. *The Savage Wars of Peace: Small Wars and the Rise of American Power.* New York: Basic Books, 2002.

Bosworth, Allan R. *America's Concentration Camps.* New York: Norton, 1967.

Boudreau, Joseph A. "Western Canada's 'Enemy Aliens' in World War One." *Alberta Historical Review* 12 (Winter 1964): 1-9.

Boyanian, D. *Armenia: The Case for a Forgotten Genocide.* Westwood, NJ: Educational Book Crafters, 1972.

Broadfoot, Barry. *Years of Sorrow, Years of Shame: The Story of Japanese Canadians in World War II.* Toronto: Doubleday Canada, 1977.

Buffinga, John O. "The War Prisoners' Aid of the YMCA and Hermann Boeschenstein's Role as an Ethnic Mediator (1943-1947)." *Canadian Ethnic Studies* 20, 2 (1988): 53-70.

Burt, Kendal, and James Leasor. *The One That Got Away.* London: Collins, 1956.

Canada. *Debates of the House of Commons.* Vol. 1. Ottawa: Edmond Cloutier, 1940.

–. *Defence of Canada Regulations (Consolidation).* Ottawa: Edmond Cloutier, 1941.

–. *Orders and Instructions, Internment Camps.* Ottawa: Department of National Defence, 1945.

–. *Red Cross and Prisoners of War Conventions.* Ottawa: Edmond Cloutier, 1942.

–. *Regulations Governing the Maintenance of Discipline among and Treatment of Prisoners of War.* Ottawa: J.O. Patenaude, 1939.

–. *Report of the Department of National Defence for the Fiscal Year Ending 31 March 1944.* Ottawa: Edmond Cloutier, 1944.

–. *Report of the Department of National Defence for the Fiscal Year Ending 31 March 1945.* Ottawa: Edmond Cloutier, 1946.

Caplan, Arthur L. *When Medicine Went Mad: Bioethics and the Holocaust.* Totowa, NJ: Humana Press, 1992.

Carlson, Lewis H. *We Were Each Other's Prisoners: An Oral History of World War II American and German Prisoners of War.* New York: Basic Books, 1997.

Carr-Gregg, Charlotte. *Japanese Prisoners of War in Revolt: The Outbreaks of Featherston and Cowra during World War II.* New York: St. Martin's, 1978.

Carter, David J. *Behind Canadian Barbed Wire: Alien, Refugee and Prisoner of War Camps in Canada, 1914-1946.* Calgary: Tumbleweed, 1980.

–. *P.O.W. behind Canadian Barbed Wire: Alien, Refugee and Prisoner of War Camps in Canada, 1914-1946.* Elkwater, AB: Eagle Butte Press, 1998.

Cazeneuve, Jean. *Essai sur la psychologie du prisonnier de guerre.* Paris: Presses Universitaires de France, 1945.

Cepuch, Stefania H. "'Our Guests Are Busy': The Internment and Labour of German Prisoners of War in Ontario, 1940-1946." MA thesis, Queen's University, 1992.

Cesarani, David, and Tony Kushner, eds. *The Internment of Aliens in Twentieth Century Britain.* London: F. Cass, 1993.

Chang, Iris. *The Rape of Nanking: The Forgotten Holocaust of World War II.* New York: Basic Books, 1997.

Charny, Israel W., ed. *Encyclopedia of Genocide.* Santa Barbara: ABC-CLIO, 2000.

Christgau, John. *"Enemies": World War II Alien Internment.* Ames: Iowa State University Press, 1985.

Ciccocelli, J.A. "The Innocuous Enemy Alien: Italians in Canada during World War II." MA thesis, University of Western Ontario, 1977.

Clarke, Hugh V. *Barbed Wire and Bamboo: Australian POW's in Europe, North Africa, Singapore, Thailand and Japan.* St. Leonard, Australia: Allen and Unwin, 1992.

Costelle, Daniel. *Les prisonniers.* Paris: Flammarion, 1975.

Dallin, David J., and Boris I. Nicolaevsky. *Forced Labor in Soviet Russia.* New Haven, CT: Yale University Press, 1955.

Dancocks, Daniel G. *In Enemy Hands: Canadian Prisoners of War, 1939-45.* Edmonton: Hurtig, 1983.

Daniels, Roger. *Concentration Camps: North American Japanese in the United States and Canada.* Malabar, FL: Krieger, 1989.

Dawidowicz, Lucy. *The War against the Jews, 1933-1945.* New York: Rinehart, 1975.

Daws, Gavan. *Prisoners of the Japanese: POWs in World War II in the Pacific.* New York: Morrow, 1994.

Dear, Ian. *Escape and Evasion: POW Breakouts in World War II.* London: Cassell and Company, 2000.

Draper, Paula Jean. "The Accidental Immigrants: Canada and the Interned Refugees." PhD diss., University of Toronto, 1983.

–. "The Accidental Immigrants: Canada and the Interned Refugees." Pts 1 and 2. *Canadian Jewish Historical Society Journal* 2, 1 (1978): 1-38; 2, 2 (1978): 80-112.

Drechsler, Horst. *Let Us Die Fighting: The Struggle of the Herero and Nama against German Imperialism (1884-1915).* London: Zed Press, 1980.

Dreisziger, N.F. "7 December 1941: A Turning Point in Canadian Wartime Policy toward Enemy Ethnic Groups?" *Journal of Canadian Studies* 32, 1 (1997): 93-111.

Duliani, Mario. *La ville sans femmes.* Montreal: Société des Éditions Pascal, 1945.

Duliani, Mario. *The City without Women: A Chronicle of Internment Life in Canada during the Second World War.* Oakville, ON: Mosaic Press, 1994.

Dwork, Deborah, and Robert Jan van Pelt. *Holocaust: A History.* New York: W.W. Norton, 2002.

Dyal, Donald H. *Historical Dictionary of the Spanish American War.* Westport, CT: Greenwood Press, 1996.

Falk, Stanley L. *Bataan: The March of Death.* New York: Norton, 1962.

Farcy, Jean Claude. *Les camps de concentration français de la Première guerre mondiale, 1914-1920.* Paris: Anthropos, 1995.

Faulk, Henry. *Group Captives: The Re-education of German Prisoners of War in Britain, 1945-1948.* London: Chatto and Windus, 1977.

Feig, Konnilyn G. *Hitler's Death Camps: The Sanity of Madness.* New York: Holmes and Meier, 1981.

Fischel, Jack R. *Historical Dictionary of the Holocaust.* Lanham, MD: Scarecrow Press, 1999.

Fischer, Gerhard. *Enemy Aliens: Internment and the Homefront Experience in Australia, 1914-1920.* St. Lucia, Australia: University of Queensland Press, 1989.

Fitzgerald, Alan. *Italian Farming Soldiers: Prisoners of War in Australia, 1941-1947.* Carlton, Australia: Melbourne University Press, 1981.

Flory, William E.S. *Prisoners of War: A Study in the Development of International Law.* Washington, DC: American Council of Public Affairs, 1942.

Foner, Philip S. *The Spanish-Cuban-American War and the Birth of American Imperialism, 1895-1902.* New York: Monthly Review Press, 1972.

Fooks, Georgia Green. *Prairie Prisoners: POWs in Lethbridge during Two World Conflicts.* Lethbridge, AB: Lethbridge Historical Society, 2003.

Foy, D.A. *For You the War Is Over: American Prisoners of War in Nazi Germany.* New York: Stein and Day, 1984.

Friedlander, Henry. *The Origins of Nazi Genocide: From Euthanasia to the Final Solution.* Chapel Hill: University of North Carolina Press, 1995.

Gansberg, Judith. *Stalag U.S.A.: The Remarkable Story of German POWs in America.* New York: Crowell, 1977.

Gaskell, Carol. *Women's Words: Eastern Township Anglophone Women Remember the Second World War.* Lennoxville, QC: s.n., 1995.

Geiser, Carl. *Prisoners of the Good Fight: The Spanish Civil War, 1936-1939.* Westport, CT: Lawrence Hill and Company, 1986.

Gilbert, Martin. *The Holocaust: A History of the Jews of Europe during the Second World War.* New York: Henry Holt and Company, 1986.

Gillman, Peter, and Lilly Gillman. *"Collar the Lot!": How Britain Interned and Expelled Its Wartime Refugees.* London: Quartet Books, 1980.

Gold, Hal. *Unit 731: Testimony.* Tokyo: Yenbooks, 1996.

Graber, G.S. *Caravans to Oblivion: The Armenian Genocide.* New York: John Wiley and Sons, 1996.

Granatstein, J.L., and J.M. Hitsman. *Broken Promises: A History of Conscription in Canada.* Toronto: Oxford University Press, 1977.

Granatstein, J.L., and Desmond Morton. *A Nation Forged in Fire: Canadians and the Second World War.* Toronto: Lester and Orpen Dennys, 1989.

Gutman, Yisrael, and Michael Berenbaum, eds. *Anatomy of the Auschwitz Death Camp.* Bloomington: Indiana University Press, 1994.

Hadley, Michael L. *U-Boats against Canada: German Submarines in Canadian Waters.* Montreal: McGill-Queen's University Press, 1985.

Halbrook, Stephen P. *Target Switzerland: Swiss Armed Neutrality in World War II.* Rockville Centre, MD: Sarpedon, 1998.

Hall, E.R. *The Burma-Thailand Railway of Death.* Armadale, Australia: Graphic Books, 1981.

Harris, Sheldon. *Factories of Death: Japanese Biological Warfare, 1932-45 and the American Cover-up.* London: Routledge, 1994.

Hartigan, Richard Shelly. *The Forgotten Victim: A History of the Civilian.* Chicago: Precedent, 1982.

Häsler, Alfred A. *The Lifeboat Is Full: Switzerland and the Refugees, 1933-1945.* New York: Funk and Wagnalls, 1969.

Heer, Hannes, Bernd Boll, Walter Manoschek, Christian Reuther, and Hans Safrian. *The German Army and Genocide: Crimes against War Prisoners, Jews and Other Civilians in the East, 1939-1944.* New York: New Press, 1999.

Hicks, George L. *The Comfort Women: Japan's Brutal Regime of Enforced Prostitution in the Second World War.* New York: Norton, 1995.

Hilliker, John F. *Documents on Canadian External Relations.* Vol. 9, *1942-1943.* Ottawa: Canadian Government Publishing Centre, 1980.

–. *Documents on Canadian External Relations.* Vol. 10, *1944-1945.* Ottawa: Canadian Government Publishing Centre, 1987.

Hilmer, Norman, Bohdan Kordan, and Lubomyr Luciuk. *On Guard for Thee: War, Ethnicity, and the Canadian State, 1939-1945.* Ottawa: Minister of Supply and Services Canada, 1988.

Holian, Timothy J. *The German-Americans and World War II: An Ethnic Experience.* New York: Peter Lang, 1996.

Howard, Michael, George J. Andreopoulos, and Mark R. Shulman, eds. *The Laws of War: Constraints on Warfare in the Western World.* New Haven, CT: Yale University Press, 1994.

Hutchinson, John F. *Champions of Charity: War and the Rise of the Red Cross.* Boulder, CO: Westview Press, 1996.

Iacovetta, Franca, Roberto Perin, and Angelo Principe, eds. *Enemies Within: Italian and Other Internees in Canada and Abroad.* Toronto: University of Toronto Press, 2000.

Igersheimer, Walter W., and Ian Darragh. *Blatant Injustice: The Story of a Jewish Refugee from Nazi Germany Imprisoned in Britain and Canada during World War II.* Montreal and Kingston: McGill-Queen's University Press, 2005.

Jackson, Robert. *The Prisoners, 1914-18.* London and New York: Routledge, 1989.

Jakobson, Michael. *Origins of the Gulag: The Soviet Prison Camp System, 1917-1934.* Lexington: University Press of Kentucky, 1993.

Jones, Ted. *Both Sides of the Wire: The Fredericton Internment Camp.* 2 vols. Fredericton, NB: New Ireland Press, 1989.

Keefer, Ralph. *Grounded in Eire: The Story of Two RAF Fliers Interned in Ireland during World War II.* Montreal: McGill-Queen's University Press, 2001.

Keegan, John. *A History of Warfare.* New York: Vintage Books, 1994.

Keegan, John, and Richard Holmes. *Soldiers: A History of Men in Battle.* Toronto: Prospero Books, 1999. First published 1985.

Kelly, John Joseph. "Intelligence and Counter-Intelligence in German Prisoner of War Camps in Canada during World War II." *Dalhousie Review* 58, 2 (1978): 285-94.

–. "The Prisoner of War Camps in Canada, 1939-1947." MA thesis, University of Windsor, 1976.

Kennedy, J. de N. *History of the Department of Munitions and Supply.* 2 vols. Ottawa: Edmond Cloutier, 1950.

Keshen, Jeffrey A. *Propaganda and Censorship during Canada's Great War.* Edmonton: University of Alberta Press, 1996.

–. *Saints, Sinners, and Soldiers: Canada's Second World War.* Vancouver and Toronto: UBC Press, 2004.

Keyserlingk, Robert H. "Agents within the Gates": The Search for Nazi Subversives in Canada during World War II." *Canadian Historical Review* 66, 2 (1985): 211-39.

–. "The Canadian Government's Attitude toward Germans and German Canadians in World War II." *Canadian Ethnic Studies* 16, 1 (1984): 16-28.

Kilford, C.R. "The Re-education of German Prisoners of War in Canada during World War II." Master of Defence Studies Research Project, Canadian Forces College, 2003.

Kinvig, Clifford. *Death Railway.* New York: Ballantine Books, 1973.

–. *River Kwai Railway: The Story of the Burma-Siam Railroad.* Herndon, VA: Brassey's, 1998.

Knox, Donald, ed. *Death March: The Survivors of Bataan.* New York: Harcourt Brace Jovanovich, 1981.

Koch, Eric. *Deemed Suspect: A Wartime Blunder.* Toronto: Methuen, 1980.

Kochan, Miriam. *Britain's Internees in the Second World War.* London: Macmillan, 1983.

–. *Prisoners of England.* London: Macmillan, 1980.

Kogon, Eugen. *The Theory and Practice of Hell: The German Concentration Camps and the System behind Them.* New York: Farrar, Straus and Cudahy, 1950.

Kordan, Bohdan S., *Enemy Aliens, Prisoners of War: Internment in Canada during the Great War.* Montreal and Kingston: McGill-Queen's University Press, 2002.

Kordan, Bohdan S., and Peter Melnycky, eds. *In the Shadow of the Rockies: Diary of the Castle Mountain Internment Camp, 1915-1917.* Edmonton: Canadian Institute of Ukrainian Studies Press, 1991.

Kotek, Joël, and Pierre Rigoulot. *Le siècle des camps: Détention, concentration, extermination – Cent ans de mal radical.* Paris: JC Lattès, 2000.

Krammer, Arnold. *Nazi Prisoners of War in America.* New York: Stein and Day, 1979.
–. *Undue Process: The Untold Story of America's German Alien Internees.* Lanham, MD: Rowman and Littlefield, 1997.
Lafitte, François. *The Internment of Aliens.* New York: Penguin Books, 1940.
Laflamme, Jean. *Les camps de détention au Québec durant la Première guerre mondiale.* Montreal: n.p., 1973.
Laprise, Andrée. "Des civils internés pendant la deuxième guerre mondiale: Le camp des femmes de Kingston (1939-1943)." MA thesis, Université de Montréal, 2000.
Laqueur, Walter. *Guerrilla: A Historical and Critical Study.* Boston: Little, Brown, 1976.
Lasserre, André. *Frontières et camps: Le refuge en Suisse de 1933 à 1945.* Lausanne: Payot, 1995.
Lee-Whiting, Brenda. "Enemy Aliens: German-Canadians on the Home Front." *The Beaver* 69, 5 (1989): 53-58.
Leigh, Maxwell. *Captives Courageous: South African Prisoners of War in World War II.* Johannesburg: Ashanti, 1992.
Le May, G.H.L. *British Supremacy in South Africa, 1899-1907.* Oxford: Clarendon Press, 1965.
Lifton, Robert J. *The Nazi Doctors: Medical Killing and the Psychology of Genocide.* New York: Basic Books, 1986.
Linn, Brian McAllister. *The Philippine War, 1899-1902.* Lawrence: University of Kansas Press, 2000.
–. *The U.S. Army and Counterinsurgency in the Philippine War, 1899-1902.* Chapel Hill: University of North Carolina Press, 1989.
Long, Gavin. *The Final Campaigns: Australia in the War of 1939-1945.* Canberra: Australian War Memorial, 1963.
Luciuk, Lubomyr. *In Fear of the Barbed Wire Fence: Canada's First National Internment Operations and the Ukrainian Canadians, 1914-1920.* Kingston, ON: Kashtan Press, 2001.
–. *Internment Operations: The Role of the Old Fort Henry in World War I.* Kingston, ON: Delta, 1980.
–, ed. *Righting an Injustice: The Debate over Redress for Canada's First National Internment Operations.* Toronto: Justinian Press, 1994.
Lugan, Bernard. *La guerre des Boers, 1899-1902.* Paris: Perrin, 1998.
McBride, Michelle. "From Internment to Indifference: An Examination of RCMP Response to Fascism and Nazism in Canada from 1934 to 1941." MA thesis, Memorial University, 1997.
McCormack, Gavan, and Hank Nelson, eds. *The Burma-Thailand Railway: Memory and History.* Chiang Mai, Thailand: Silkworm Books, 1993.
Macdonald, Jake. "The Beast of War and the Beautiful Lake." *The Beaver* 76, 2 (1996): 29-31.
McIntosh, Dave. *Hell on Earth: Aging Faster, Dying Sooner: Canadian Prisoners of the Japanese during World War II.* Toronto: McGraw Hill Ryerson, 1996.
McKale, Donald M. *Hitler's Shadow War: The Holocaust and World War II.* New York: Cooper Square Press, 2002.
Mackenzie, S.P. "The Shackling Crisis: A Case-Study in the Dynamics of Prisoner-of-War Diplomacy in the Second World War." *International History Review* 17 (1995): 78-98.
–. "The Treatment of Prisoners of War in World War II." *Journal of Modern History* 66 (1994): 487-520.
MacLaren, Roy. *Canadians behind Enemy Lines, 1939-1945.* Vancouver: University of British Columbia Press, 1981.
McLaughlin, K.M. *The Germans in Canada.* Ottawa: Canadian Historical Association, 1985.
Maddocks, Roy R. "A.G.L. McNaughton, R.B. Bennett and the Unemployment Relief Camps,

1932-1935." MA thesis, Carleton University, 1974.
Madsen, Chris M.V., and R.J. Henderson. *German Prisoners of War in Canada and Their Artifacts.* Regina: Hignell Printing, 1993.
Margolian, Howard. *Conduct Unbecoming: The Story of the Murder of Canadian Prisoners of War in Normandy.* Toronto: University of Toronto Press, 1988.
Marie, Jean-Jacques. *Le goulag.* Paris: Presses Universitaires de France, 1999.
Martin, Adrian R. *Brothers from Bataan: POWs, 1942-1945.* Manhattan, KS: Sunflower University Press, 1992.
Marvel, William. *Andersonville: The Last Depot.* Chapel Hill: University of North Carolina Press, 1994.
Mason, W. Wynne. *Prisoners of War: Official History of New Zealand in the Second World War, 1939-1945.* Wellington: War History Branch, Department of Internal Affairs, 1954.
Masson, Philippe, and Alain Melchior-Bonnet, eds. *Dictionnaire de la Seconde guerre mondiale.* Vol. 1. Paris: Librairie Larousse, 1979.
Melady, John. *Escape from Canada! The Untold Story of German POWs in Canada, 1939-1945.* Toronto: Macmillan, 1981.
Miller, Stuart Creighton. *"Benevolent Assimilation": The American Conquest of the Philippines, 1899-1903.* New Haven: Yale University Press, 1982.
Moore, Bob, and Kent Fedorowich. *The British Empire and Its Italian Prisoners of War, 1940-47.* Basingstoke, UK: Palgrave, 2002.
Moore, Bob, and Kent Fedorowich, eds. *Prisoners of War and Their Captors in World War II.* Oxford: Berg, 1996.
Moore, Bob, and Barbara Hately-Broad, eds. *Prisoners of War, Prisoners of Peace: Captivity, Homecoming and Memory in World War II.* Oxford: Berg, 2005.
Moorehead, Caroline. *Dunant's Dream: War, Switzerland and the History of the Red Cross.* London: HarperCollins, 1998.
Morton, Desmond. *The Canadian General: Sir William Otter.* Toronto: Hakkert, 1974.
–. *A Military History of Canada.* Toronto: McClelland and Stewart, 1992.
–. *Silent Battle: Canadian Prisoners of War in Germany, 1914-1919.* Toronto: Lester, 1992.
–. "Sir William Otter and Internment Operations in Canada during the First World War." *Canadian Historical Review* 55, 1 (1974): 32-58.
Moynihan, Michael. *Black Bread and Barbed Wire: Prisoners in the First World War.* London: Leo Cooper, 1978.
Muller-Hill, Benno. *Murderous Science–Elimination by Scientific Selection of Jews, Gypsies, and Others: Germany, 1933-1945.* Oxford: Oxford University Press, 1988.
Nasson, Bill. *The South African War, 1899-1902.* London: Arnold, 1999.
Okazaki, Robert Katsumasa. *The Nisei Mass Evacuation Group and P.O.W. Camp 101, Angler, Ontario.* Scarborough, ON: Markham Litho, 1995.
O'Toole, G.J.A. *The Spanish War: An American Epic, 1898.* New York: W.W. Norton, 1984.
Page, Don. "Tommy Stone and Psychological Warfare in World War Two: Transforming a POW Liability into an Asset." *Journal of Canadian Studies* 16, 3-4 (1981): 110-20.
Pakenham, Thomas. *The Boer War.* New York: Random House, 1979.
Panyani, Panikos. *Minorities in Wartime: National and Racial Groupings in Europe, North America, and Australia during the Two World Wars.* Oxford: Berg, 1993.
Paul, Allen. *Katyn: Stalin's Massacre and the Seeds of Polish Resurrection.* Annapolis, MD: Naval Institute Press, 1991.
Porter, Cecil. *The Gilded Cage: Gravenhurst German Prisoner of War Camp 20, 1940-1946.* Huntsville, ON: Fox Meadow Creations, 1999.
Priebe, Eckehart J. *Thank You, Canada: From Messerschmitt Pilot to Canadian Citizen.* West Vancouver: Condor, 1990.
Proctor, Robert. *Racial Hygiene: Medicine under the Nazis.* Cambridge, MA: Harvard Uni-

versity Press, 1988.

Pronay, Nicholas, and Keith Wilson, eds. *The Political Re-education of Germany and Her Allies.* London: Croom Helm, 1985.

Rachamimov, Alon. *POWs and the Great War: Captivity on the Eastern Front.* Oxford: Berg, 2002.

Rees, Laurence. *Horror in the East: Japan and the Atrocities of World War II.* New York: Da Capo Press, 2002.

Repka, William, and Kathleen Repka. *Dangerous Patriots: Canada's Unknown Prisoners of War.* Vancouver: New Star Books, 1982.

Rettig, Andrew. "A De-programming Curriculum: Allied Reeducation and the Canadian-American Psychological Warfare Program for German POWs, 1943-47." *American Review of Canadian Studies* 29, 4 (1999): 593-619.

Richard, Guy. *L'Histoire inhumaine: massacres et genocides des origins à nos jours.* Paris: Armand Colin, 1992.

Robin, Martin. *Shades of Right: Nativist and Fascist Politics in Canada, 1920-1940.* Toronto: University of Toronto Press, 1992.

Robin, Ron. *The Barbed-Wire College: Reeducating German POWs in the United States during World War II.* Princeton: Princeton University Press, 1995.

Robinson, Daniel. "Planning for the 'Most Serious Contingency': Alien Internment, Arbitrary Detention, and the Canadian State, 1938-1939." *Journal of Canadian Studies* 28, 2 (1993): 5-20.

Roland, Charles G. *Long Night's Journey into Day: Prisoners of War in Hong Kong and Japan, 1941-1945.* Waterloo, ON: Wilfrid Laurier University Press, 2001.

Rolf, David. *Prisoners of the Reich: Germany's Captives, 1939-1945.* London: Leo Cooper, 1988.

Roy, Patricia, J.L. Granatstein, Masako Lino, and Hiroko Takamura. *Mutual Hostages: Canadians and Japanese during the Second World War.* Toronto: University of Toronto Press, 1990.

Russell, Edward F.L. *Knights of Bushido: A Short History of Japanese War Crimes.* Mechanicsburg, PA: Stackpole Books, 2002.

Saunders, Kay, and Roger Daniels, eds. *Alien Justice: Wartime Internment in Australia and North America.* St. Lucia, Australia: University of Queensland Press, 2000.

Schoenberner, Gerhard. *The Yellow Star: The Persecution of the Jews in Europe, 1933-1945.* New York: Fordham University Press, 2005.

Shelley, Lore, ed. *Criminal Experiments on Human Beings in Auschwitz and War Research Laboratories: Twenty Prisoners' Accounts.* San Francisco: Mellen Research University Press, 1991.

Shirer, William L. *The Rise and Fall of the Third Reich: A History of Nazi Germany.* New York: Fawcett Crest, 1992, First published 1960.

Simpson, A.W. Brian. *In the Highest Degree Odious: Detention without Trial in Wartime Britain.* Oxford: Clarendon Press, 1992.

Smith, Arthur L. Jr. *The War for the German Mind: Re-educating Hitler's Soldiers.* Providence, RI: Berghahn Books, 1996.

Smith, David Edward. "Emergency Government in Canada." *Canadian Historical Review* 50, 4 (1969): 429-48.

Smith, Joseph. *The Spanish-American War: Conflict in the Caribbean and the Pacific, 1895-1902.* London: Longman, 1994.

Smith, Page. *Democracy on Trial: The Japanese American Evacuation and Relocation in World War II.* New York: Simon and Schuster, 1995.

Solzhenitsyn, Aleksandr Isaevich. *The Gulag Archipelago, 1918-1956.* New York: Harper and Row, 1985.

Speed, Richard B. *Prisoners, Diplomats and the Great War: A Study in the Diplomacy of Cap-*

tivity. New York: Greenwood Press, 1990.

Spies, S.B. *Methods of Barbarism? Roberts and Kitchener and Civilians in the Boer Republics, January 1900-May 1902.* Cape Town: Barber and Rousseau, 1977.

Stacey, C.P. *Arms, Men and Governments: The War Policies of Canada, 1939-1945.* Ottawa: Department of National Defence, 1970.

–. *Canada and the Age of Conflict.* 2 vols. Toronto: University of Toronto Press, 1981.

–. *Six Years of War: The Army in Canada, Britain and the Pacific.* Ottawa: Roger Duhamel, 1966.

Stanton, John. "Government Internment Policy, 1939-1945." *Labour/Le Travail* 31 (Spring 1993): 203-41.

Stent, Ronald. *A Bespattered Page? The Internment of His Majesty's "Most Loyal Enemy Aliens."* London: Andre Deutsch, 1980.

Stetz, Margaret, and Bonnie Oh, eds. *Legacies of the Comfort Women of World War II.* Amonk, NY: M.E. Sharpe, 2001.

Sunhara, Ann Gomer. *The Politics of Racism: The Uprooting of Japanese Canadians during the Second World War.* Toronto: Lorimer, 1981.

Tanaka, Yuki. *Hidden Horrors: Japanese War Crimes in World War II.* Boulder, CO: Westview Press, 1998.

Tanaka, Yuki. *Japan's Comfort Women: The Military and Involuntary Prostitution during War and Occupation.* London: Routledge, 2001.

Taylor, Mary. *Black Mark: The Japanese-Canadians in World War II.* Toronto: Oberon Press, 2004.

Thompson, John Herd. *Les minorités ethniques pendant les guerres mondiales.* Ottawa: Société historique du Canada, 1991.

Tingley, K.W., ed. *For King and Country: Alberta in the Second World War.* Edmonton: Reidmore Books, 1995.

Ukranian Canadian Civil Liberties Association. *Roll Call: Remembering the Internees.* Kingston, ON: Kashtan Press, 1999.

Vance, Jonathan F. "Canadian Relief Agencies and Prisoners of War, 1939-45." *Journal of Canadian Studies* 31, 2 (1996): 133-47.

–, ed. *Encyclopedia of Prisoners of War and Internment.* Santa Barbara: ABC-CLIO, 2000.

–. "Men in Manacles: The Shackling of Prisoners of War, 1942-1943." *Journal of Military History* 59, 3 (1995): 483-504.

–. *Objects of Concern: Canadian Prisoners of War through the Twentieth Century.* Vancouver: UBC Press, 1994.

Vandervort, Bruce. *Wars of Imperial Conquest in Africa, 1830-1914.* Bloomington and Indianapolis: Indiana University Press, 1998.

Vincent, Carl. *No Reason Why: The Canadian Hong Kong Tragedy: An Examination.* Stittsville, ON: Canada's Wings, 1981.

Vischer, A.L. *Barbed Wire Disease: A Psychological Study of the Prisoners of War.* London: John Bale, Sons, and Danielsson, 1919.

Wagner, Jonathan F. *Brothers beyond the Sea: National Socialism in Canada.* Waterloo, ON: Wilfrid Laurier University Press, 1981.

–. "The Deutscher Bund Canada, 1934-1939." *Canadian Historical Review* 58 (June 1977): 176-200.

Waiser, Bill. *Park Prisoners: The Untold Story of Western Canada's National Parks, 1915-1946.* Saskatoon: Fifth House, 1995.

Ward, W. Peter. "British Columbia and the Japanese Evacuation." *Canadian Historical Review* 57, 3 (1976): 289-309.

Waterford, Van. *Prisoners of the Japanese in World War II.* Jefferson, NC: McFarland, 1994.

Weinberg, Gerhard L. *A World at Arms: A Global History of World War II.* Cambridge: Cam-

bridge University Press, 1994.
Weissenborn, Georg K., ed. *German-Canadian Yearbook.* Vol. 13. Toronto: University of Toronto Press, 1994.
Wentzel, Fritz. *Single or Return: The Story of a German POW in British Camps and the Escape of Lieutnant Franz von Werra.* London: William Kimber, 1954.
Whitaker, Reg. "Official Repression of Communism during World War II." *Labour/Le Travail* 17 (Spring 1986): 135-66.
Williams, Peter, and David Wallace. *Unit 731: The Japanese Army's Secret of Secrets.* London: Hodder and Stoughton, 1989.
Williamson, Samuel R. Jr., and Peter Pastor, eds. *Essays on World War I: Origins and Prisoners of War.* New York: Columbia University Press, 1983.
Winter, Barbara. *Stalag Australia: German Prisoners of War in Australia.* North Ryde, Australia: Angus and Robertson, 1986.
Woodworth, Steven E., ed. *The American Civil War: A Handbook of Literature and Research.* Westport, CT: Greenwood, 1996.
Yahil, Leni. *The Holocaust: The Fate of European Jewry, 1932-1945.* New York: Oxford University Press, 1990.
Yoshiaki, Yoshimi. *Comfort Women: Sexual Slavery in the Japanese Military during World War II (Asia Perspectives).* New York: Columbia University Press, 1995.
Ydewalle, Charles, d'. *An Interlude in Spain.* London: Readers Union and Macmillan, 1946.
Zawodny, J.K. *Death in the Forest: The Story of the Katyn Forest Massacre.* Notre Dame, IN: University of Notre Dame Press, 1962.

Index

Printed and bound in Canada by Friesens
Set in Minion and Helvetica Condensed by Artegraphica Design Co. Ltd.
Copy editor: Anne Holloway
Proofreader: Gail Copeland